LIBRARY OF NEW TESTAMENT STUDIES
307

Editor
Mark Goodacre

RADICAL MARTYRDOM AND COSMIC CONFLICT IN EARLY CHRISTIANITY

PAUL MIDDLETON

t&t clark

Published by T&T Clark
A Continuum imprint
The Tower Building, 11 York Road, London SE1 7NX
80 Maiden Lane, Suite 704, New York, NY 10038

www.tandtclark.com

British Library Cataloguing-in-Publication Data
A catalogue record for this book is available from the British Library

ISBN 0-567-04164-6 (hardback)

Typeset by CA Typesetting, www.sheffieldtypesetting.com
Printed and bound in Great Britain by Biddles Ltd., King's Lynn, Norfolk

Te martyrum candidatus laudat exercitus
(Te Deum)

CONTENTS

PREFACE

These days, martyrdom is a serious business. The interface between the worlds of politics and religion has never been more important, and yet religion perhaps has never been more misunderstood. The academic study of Theology and Religious Studies surely has a crucial, but as yet unrecognized, contribution to make in contemporary political and cultural discourse.

Originally my PhD thesis, this project began in 2000, when the world was a different place. Although my thesis statement remained unchanged, I could not help but be shaped by unfolding events. My direct contribution to the discussion of contemporary 'martyrdom' is brief, and restricted to the Introduction. Nonetheless, this project is concerned with a group of people whose deaths were regarded as bizarre, fringe and not a proper expression of their religion: those early Christians, whom I have called the *Radical Martyrs*.

This book is a milestone on a long educational journey, which has taken me from Glasgow to Edinburgh – via Princeton. At each institution, I have benefited from the teaching and support of a great many academics. However, I would particularly like to thank John Barclay, Joel Marcus and John Riches, who encouraged my first faltering steps on the path of New Testament Studies in Glasgow. At Princeton Theological Seminary, my guides were Brian Blount (with whom some of the ideas in this book took shape), James Charlesworth and Beverly Gaventa. I am grateful to them for contributing to a year of study on which I look back with fondness.

New College, Edinburgh, is as stimulating an environment in which anyone could hope to study, and I am especially grateful to those whose comments and observations had some effect on the course of this book. The comments and insights of an anonymous reader have also been greatly appreciated, as were those of my examiners, Judith Lieu and Paul Foster. Nonetheless, the greatest influence on this work was my supervisor, Larry Hurtado, who demonstrated both patience and impatience in appropriate measure, and whose often vigorous engagement and illumination I will always value.

As I have laboured on the road to the production of this book, I have enjoyed the company of many travelling companions, who have offered advice, friendship and, most importantly, coffee. In particular, George Newlands has been a reliable source of all three, for which I thank him, especially for reading through the manuscript. Above all, David Smith has been an ever present support, considerably lightening my step on the road, and it is to him I dedicate this book.

LIST OF ABBREVIATIONS

A. Cyprian	*Acts of Cyprian*
A. Euplus	*The Acts of Euplus*
A.V.	Tertullian, *Against the Valentinians*
AB	Anchor Bible Commentary Series
ABD	*Anchor Bible Dictionary*
ACM	H. Musurillo, *The Acts of the Christian Martyrs* (Oxford: Clarendon Press, 1972)
A.H.	Irenaeus, *Against Heresies*
ANRW	*Aufstieg und Niedergang der römischen Welt*
Ant.	Josephus, *Antiquities of the Jews*
Apoc. Peter	*The Apocalypse of Peter*
Apoc. Elij.	*Apocalypse of Elijah*
Asc. Isa.	*The Ascension of Isaiah*
BGU	Aegyptische Urkunden aus den Museen zu Berlin: Griechische Urkunden (Berlin, 1863–)
BNTC	Black's New Testament Commentaries
BR	*Biblical Research*
BZHT	Beiträge zur Historischen Theologie
CBQ	*Catholic Biblical Quarterly*
Ep. Barn.	*The Epistle of Barnabas*
Exhortation	Origen, *Exhortation to Martyrdom*
Fuga	Tertullian, *De Fuga in Persecutione*
Gos. Thom.	*The Gospel of Thomas*
H.E.	Eusebius, *Historia Ecclesiastica*
HDR	Harvard Dissertations in Religion
HHS	Harvard Historical Studies
HTR	*Harvard Theological Review*
ICC	International Critical Commentary
Ignatius, *Eph.*	Ignatius, *Letter to the Ephesians*
Ignatius, *Magn.*	Ignatius, *Letter to the Magnesians*
Ignatius, *Pol.*	Ignatius, *Letter to Polycarp*
Ignatius, *Rom.*	Ignatius, *Letter to the Romans*
Ignatius, *Smyrn.*	Ignatius, *Letter to the Smyrnians*
Ignatius, *Trall.*	Ignatius, *Letter to the Trallians*
JBL	*Journal of Biblical Literature*
JECS	*Journal of Early Christian Studies*
JETS	*Journal of the Evangelical Theological Society*
JHS	*Journal of Hellenic Studies*
JJS	*Journal of Jewish Studies*
JQR	*Jewish Quarterly Review*
JR	*Journal of Religion*
JRE	*Journal of Religious Ethics*

JRS	*Journal of Roman Studies*
JSJ	*Journal for the Study of Judaism*
JSNT	*Journal for the Study of the New Testament*
JSNTSup	*Journal for the Study of the New Testament*, Supplement Series
JTS	*Journal of Theological Studies*
Mart. Agapê	*The Martyrdom of Agapê, Irenê, Chionê, and Companions*
Mart. Apoll.	*The Martyrdom of Apollonius*
Mart. Carpus	*The Martyrdom of Carpus, Papylus, and Agathonicê*
Mart. Conon	*The Martyrdom of Conon*
Mart. Fruct.	*The Martyrdom of Fructuosus and Companions*
Mart. Ignatius	*The Martyrdom of Ignatius*
Mart. Isa.	*The Martyrdom of Isaiah*
Mart. Justin	*The Acts of Justin and Companions*
Mart. Lyons	*The Letter of the Churches of Lyons and Vienne (The Martyrs of Lyons)*
Mart. Marian	*The Martyrdom of Marian and James*
Mart. Marinus	*The Martyrdom of Marinus*
Mart. Perpetua	*The Martyrdom of Perpetua and Felicitas*
Mart. Pionius	*The Martyrdom of Pionius*
Mart. Pol.	*The Martyrdom of Polycarp*
Mart. Potamiaena	*The Martyrdom of Potamiaena and Basilides*
Mart. Ptol.	*The Martyrdom of Saints Ptolemaeus and Lucius*
MBT	Münsterische Beiträge zur Theologie
NIGTC	New Interntational Greek Testament Commentary
NHL	J. M. Robinson (ed.), *The Nag Hammadi Library in English* (Leiden: E. J. Brill, 1988)
NICNT	New International Commentary on the New Testament
NovT	*Novum Testamentum*
NovTSup	*Novum Testamentus* Supplement
NRT	*La nouvelle revue théologique*
n.s.	new series
NTR	New Testament Readings
NTS	*New Testament Studies*
Peregrinus	Lucian of Samosata, *The Passing of Peregrinus*
Pss. Sol.	*The Psalms of Solomon*
SBL	Society of Biblical Literature
Scap.	Tertullian, *Ad Scapulam*
Scorp.	Tertullian, *Scorpiace*
SJT	*Scottish Journal of Theology*
SNT	Studien zum Neuen Testament
Spec. Leg.	Philo, *Special Laws*
Strom.	Clement of Alexandria, *Stromata*
Syr. Apoc. Baruch	*Syriac Apocalypse of Baruch*
T. Benj.	*Testament of Benjamin*
T. Job	*Testament of Job*
T. Moses	*Testament of Moses*
Test. Truth	*The Testament of Truth*
TDNT	*Theological Dictionary of the New Testament*
TDOT	*Theological Dictionary of the Old Testament*
THKNT	Theologischer Handkommentar zum Neuen Testament
TLNT	*Theological Lexicon of the New Testament*
Trypho	Justin, *Dialogue with Trypho*

Tranq.	Seneca, *On the Tranquillity of the Mind*
VC	*Vigilae Christianae*
VT	*Vetus Testamentum*
War	Josephus, *The Jewish War*
WBC	Word Biblical Commentary

INTRODUCTION: MAKING MARTYRS

Introduction

This project seeks to re-examine Christian martyrology, focusing on a particular form of early Christian death, a phenomenon that I am terming *radical martyrdom*. Radical martyrs are those Christians who so desired death, that they intentionally sought out arrest and martyrdom. Until now, these Christians have been relegated to the deviant margins of early Christian martyrology, and ignored by scholars considering questions concerning the origins and theology of Christian martyrdom. The omission of the radical martyrs from these scholarly enterprises is quite unjustified, and this project is intended to redress the balance.

Martyrdom and Persecution

From its inception, Christianity was a religion in crisis. It was a movement that began within the synagogues of Judaism at a time of political unrest in Palestine. It endured isolation, the trauma of 'splitting' from Judaism,[1] and attracted mistrust from its pagan neighbours. Moreover, that its adherents worshipped an executed criminal did not endear the new and vulnerable religion to the Roman State, neither did its unprecedented exclusivity.[2]

Persecution forms a potent backdrop to much early Christian reflection. However, it would appear to be the case that the fear of persecution was greater than its actuality. Potter warns that texts that allege orchestrated persecution must be viewed with a high degree of caution when attempting to reconstruct the historical situation of the early Church.[3] In an important article in 1963, Ste Croix reopened the question, 'Why were the early Christians persecuted?'[4] In it, he argued that in the first two centuries of the Church's life, there was really very little in the way of persecution afflicting it. Today, the view that Christians

---

1.   But see J.M. Lieu, '"The parting of the ways": theological construct or historical reality?', in *Neither Jew nor Greek: Constructing Early Christianity* (London/New York: T&T Clark, 2002), 11–30. For discussion and bibliography, see below, 104–6.

2.   Of course, Judaism was also monotheistic, but theirs was a religion of a conquered people and therefore tolerated to a large degree by the Romans. In any case, state-funded sacrifice for the Emperor's health was carried out twice daily in the Temple (see M.P. ben Zeev, 'Did the Jews enjoy a privileged position in the Roman world?', *Revue des études juives* 154 [1995], 23–42). The new religion of Christianity called previously pluralist pagans to monotheism (I use 'pagan' as a non-pejorative term for those who were neither Christian nor Jew in the ancient world).

3.   So D.S. Potter, 'Persecution of the early church', *ABD*, V, 231–5.

4.   G.E.M. de Ste Croix, 'Why were the early Christians persecuted?', *Past and Present* 26 (1963), 5–23.

experienced incessant and orchestrated persecution from the Roman State has been replaced with the opinion that persecution, where it happened at all, was 'local, sporadic and random'.[5]

A few years after Ste Croix's article, Barnes complained that, tainted with hagiography and presupposition, the literature on the subject of the juridical basis of the persecution of Christians before 250 CE, though vast, was 'to a large degree worthless'.[6] Indeed, since Hopkins argues that the Christians did not register on the Roman Imperial radar in the first century, he goes so far as to suggest that the Christians 'manufactured' the persecutions: 'Christians needed Roman persecutions, or at least stories about Roman persecutions, rather more than Romans saw the need to persecute Christians…[the Christians] nurtured a sense of danger and victimisation'.[7] Hopkins, of course, overstates the case. Nevertheless, if those who see a measure of exaggeration in the Christians' presentation of their suffering are in any way correct, we are left with another set of questions, especially in the light of Perkins' conclusion, that the early Church consciously constructed a self-understanding of the Christian as sufferer.[8]

However, as I will argue in Chapter 2, a lack of an official Imperial policy of persecution against the Christians does not mean that Christians did not experience persecution or trouble. Granted, initially, very few Christians were persecuted for *being* Christians. Rather, it was the outworking of their religion that brought them into conflict with local communities. However, these experiences of trouble and hardship were interpreted by the Christian communities as persecution for 'the Name' (e.g. Mk 13.13; διὰ τὸ ὄνομά). This explains the discrepancy between Christian and non-Christian presentations regarding the extent of persecution. Nonetheless, despite a lack of Imperial policy against the Church until late in the third century, Christians certainly were victims of abuse, victimization and persecution from earlier years.

Persecution, in some cases, led to death, and so Christian reflection on death, particularly death *for* the new religion, became one of its most pressing theological tasks. Why were Christians being persecuted? How could they make sense of the violent deaths of fellow-believers? That these questions were answered convincingly ensured the survival and, indeed, facilitated the spread of Christianity.[9] The stories of the Christian martyrs became some of the most poignant and powerful tales in the Roman world, so much so that the narratives of the martyrs' deaths became prized possessions, and were passed widely between Christian communities.[10] These martyrologies are the focus of this book.

5.   T.D. Barnes, 'Legislation against the Christians' (*JRS* 58 [1968], 32–50), 38. See also Ste Croix, 'Why Were the early Christians persecuted?'; T.D. Barnes, *Tertullian* (Oxford: Oxford University Press, 1987); R.L. Fox, *Pagans and Christians* (London: Viking, 1986), 419–92.

6.   Barnes, 'Legislation', 32.

7.   K. Hopkins, 'Christian number and its implications' (*JECS* 6 [1998], 185–226), 198.

8.   See J. Perkins, *The Suffering Self: Pain and Narrative Representation in Early Christianity* (London: Routledge, 1995), for a study of self-representation in early Christianity.

9.   Hopkins ('Christian number'), in an article tracing the growth of Christianity in the first three centuries, pointedly observes that persecution was good for Christianity.

10. Perkins, *Suffering Self*, 24.

For the present task, the historicity of the martyr acts is of secondary importance to the interpretation, theology and narrativization of martyrdom. This is not to say that the acts are of no historical value.[11] However, the primary question of concern in this project is the extent to which martyrological narrative mirrored, developed or even constructed a theological universe, and how, in turn, that universe affected Christian attitudes to martyrdom.

In 249 CE, Decius issued an edict demanding that every citizen of the Roman Empire offer sacrifice to his image, and that they acquire a certificate to prove compliance. Although this edict was not *aimed* directly at Christians, it did lead to the first period of 'Imperial' persecution, though again, the crime was non-compliance rather than *being* Christian.[12] This first Empire-wide persecution will mark the end of the historical scope of this project. With the onset of Imperial persecution, the dynamics of martyrdom change dramatically. The sheer numbers of Christians who lapsed during the Decian and later periods of persecution, and subsequently sought readmission to the Church complicated the attitude to and theologies of martyrdom.[13]

In particular, those like Cyprian, who favoured readmission after penance for the lapsed, had to counter both confessors, who used their authority to grant indulgences to deniers without penance, and also the more rigorous, who held that there could be no readmission at all for deniers. This led to a relative downplaying of the value of martyrdom, and more so radical martyrdom, in 'proto-orthodox' circles.[14] Nonetheless, examples of radical martyrdom can be found throughout the Decian and Great Persecutions.[15] However, even though there was more opportunity for such volitional acts in these periods of persecution, I principally wish to demonstrate that this radical martyrdom mentality occurs much earlier, and is by no means the behaviour of fringe groups or heretics. We will therefore concentrate on the pre-Decian period, tracing the development of Christian martyrology – in terms of theology and presentation – from its beginnings through to the mid-third century.

Martyrdom and Scholarship

The study of Christian martyrdom is an already crowded field. General investigations into the phenomenon are well served especially by the work of Campenhausen and Frend.[16] Further studies have examined the theology of

11. See T.D. Barnes, 'Pre-Decian *Acts Martyrum*', *JTS* (n.s.) 19 (1968), 509–31. Barnes assesses a number of 'pre-Decian' martyrologies to determine which can said to be 'authentic and contemporary'. In contrast G.A. Bisbee, *Pre-Decian Acts of Martyrs and Commentarii* (HDR; Philadelphia: Fortress Press, 1988), attempts to develop a methodology to uncover historical substrata of accounts of Christian trials.

12. See R. Selinger, *The Mid-Third Century Persecutions of Decius and Valerian* (Frankfurt: Peter Lang, 2002); W.H.C. Frend, *Martyrdom and Persecution: A Study of a Conflict from the Maccabees to Donatus* (Oxford: Basil Blackwell, 1965), 389–439.

13. For a general discussion of the problem, see Frend, *Martyrdom and Persecution*, 415–29.

14. See especially Cyprian, *On the Lapsed*.

15. A.J. Droge and J.D. Tabor, *A Noble Death: Suicide and Martyrdom among Christians and Jews in Antiquity* (San Francisco: HarperSanFrancisco, 1992), 152–8.

16. H. von Campenhausen, *Die Idee des Martyriums in der alten Kirche* (Göttingen: Vanden-

martyrdom,[17] its history and origins,[18] Jewish martyrdom and its influence on Christianity,[19] literary presentation of martyrdom[20] and, more recently, Gender Studies and martyrdom.[21] Often, the early Christian martyrs are invoked in contemporary discussion, especially in terms of political resistance. So, for Crossan, martyrdom is an act of what he calls 'ethical eschatology', and as such is

> an unfortunate necessity, an unwanted inevitability of conscious resistance to sys-tematic evil. Otherwise, resistance itself colludes with the violence it opposes. Such collusion may entail, minimally, desiring or provoking martyrdom (but every martyr needs a murderer). It may entail, maximally, the hunger-striker or the suicide attacker... Such collusive actions are not eschatologically ethical.[22]

hoeck & Ruprecht, 1964); Frend, *Martyrdom and Persecution*. Other important general studies include, Droge and Tabor, *A Noble Death*, and pertinent texts have been collected by H. Musurillo, *The Acts of the Christian Martyrs* (Oxford: Clarendon Press, 1972), T. Baumeister, *Genèse et evolution de la théologie du martyre dans l'Eglise ancienne* (trans. R. Tolck; Berne: Peter Lang, 1991), and J.W. van Henten and F. Avemarie, *Martyrdom and Noble Death: Selected Texts from Graeco-Roman, Jewish and Christian Antiquity* (London/New York: Routledge, 2002).

17. T. Baumeister, *Die Anfänge der Theologie des Martyriums* (MBT, 45; Münster: Aschendorff, 1979); B.A.G.M. Dehandschutter, 'Example and discipleship: some comments on the biblical back-ground of the early Christian theology of martyrdom', in J. den Boeff and M.L. van Pollvan de Lisdonk (eds), *The Impact of Scripture in Early Christianity* (Leiden: E.J. Brill, 1999), 20–7.

18. D. Boyarin, *Dying for God: Martyrdom and the Making of Christianity and Judaism* (Stan-ford: Stanford University Press, 1999); G.W. Bowersock, *Martyrdom and Rome* (Cambridge: Cambridge University Press, 1995).

19. J.W. van Henten, *The Maccabean Martyrs as the Saviours of the Jewish People: A Study of 2 and 4 Maccabees* (Leiden: E.J. Brill, 1997); *idem*, 'Zum Einfluβ jüdischer Martyrien auf die Literatur des frühen Christentums II. Die Apostolischen Väter', *ANRW* II.27.1 (1993), 700–23; W. Rordorf, 'Wie steht es um den jüdischen Einfluss auf den christlichen Märtyrerkult', in *Lex Orandi Lex Credendi* (Université de Neuchâtel Publications de la Faculté de Théologie, XI; Freiburg: Universitätsverlag, 1993), 166–76. M. de Jonge, 'Jesus' Death for Others and the Death of the Maccabean Martyrs', in G.P. Luttikhuizen and A.S. van der Woude (eds), *Texts and Testimony: Essays in Honour of A.F.J. Klinj* (Kampen: Uitgeversmaatchappij J.H. Kok, 1988), 142–51; H.W. Surkau, *Martyrien in jüdischer und früchristlicher Zeit* (Göttingen: Vandenhoeck & Ruprecht, 1938); O. Perler, 'Das vierte Makkabäerbuch, Ignatius von Antiochien und die ältesten Martyrerberichte', *Rivista di Archeologia Christiana* 25 (1949), 47–72.

20. C. Butterweck, *'Martyriumssucht' in der alten Kirche?: Studien zur Darstellung und Deutung frühchristlicher Martyrien* (Tübingen: J.C.B. Mohr [Paul Siebeck], 1995); E. Mühlenberg, 'The martyr's death and its literary presentation', in E.A. Livingstone (ed.), *Studia Patristica XXIX* (Oxford: Pergamon Press, 1997), 85–93; T. Rajak, 'Dying for the Law: the martyr's portrait in Jewish-Greek literature', in M.J. Edwards and S. Swain (eds), *Portraits: Biographical Representation in the Greek and Latin Literature of the Roman Empire* (Oxford: Clarendon Press, 1997), 39–67.

21. B.D. Shaw, 'Body/power/identity: passions of the martyrs', *JECS* 4 (1996), 269–312; F.C. Klawiter, 'The role of martyrdom and persecution in developing the priestly authority of women in early Christianity: a case study of Montanism', *Church History* 49 (1980), 251–61; S.D. Moore and J.C. Anderson, 'Taking it like a man: masculinity in 4 Maccabees', *JBL* 117 (1998), 249–73. For a more traditional approach, see W.H.C. Frend, 'Blandina and Perpetua: two early Christian heroines', reprinted in D.M. Scholer (ed.), *Women in Early Christianity* (Studies in Early Christianity, 14; New York/London: Garland Publishing Inc., 1993), 87–97.

22. J.D. Crossan, *The Birth of Christianity: Discovering What Happened in the Years Immediately after the Crucifixion of Jesus* (Edinburgh: T&T Clark, 1999), 285.

He goes so far as to claim that 'martyrdom is … the final act of ethical eschatology'.[23] Similarly, Everett Ferguson[24] explores a comparison between modern concepts of non-violent resistance with early Christian martyrdom, and concludes that, although martyrdom was not a tool to effect a 'political policy', 'the Acts of the Martyrs and related literature belong to the history of civil disobedience, and perhaps few exercises of non-violent resistance for the sake of higher law have accomplished as much'.[25]

Radical Martyrdom

However, there is a category of early Christian death that falls outside Crossan and Ferguson's martyrological radar. Ferguson writes: 'It is true that Christians were sometimes guilty of deliberate provocation. But the model that was commended as normative Christian conduct showed a more submissive demeanor in its resistance.'[26]

Beliefs and practices varied in the early Church in regard to martyrdom, a fact frequently overlooked, and, where it is acknowledged, it is a position to be 'guilty of'. I am particularly interested a group of early Christians who demonstrated a strong desire, not only to embrace death when it came, but to actively seek it, even if that meant provoking their own arrest and death – the *radical martyrs*.

As we will see, martyrdom was at one time a sign, *par excellence*, of one's orthodox credentials. However, by the early third century, a desire for martyrdom, particularly where it was deemed to be over enthusiastic, came to be associated with so-called 'heretical' sects, such as the Montanists.[27] Therefore, radical martyrdom itself came to be regarded as heretical behaviour, and was specifically condemned by 'the orthodox',[28] who denied to them the honorific title of 'martyr'. The tendency to make martyrs, therefore, was equally balanced by the desire to *unmake* them. This point will be illustrated below, in regard to contemporary discussions concerned to show how particular 'martyrological activities' do not qualify as martyrdoms. These same discussions took place in the early Church through the battle for the right to define orthodoxy and heresy; in that war, the 'proto-orthodox' sought to 'unmake' the radical martyrs.

Scholarship has, more or less, bought wholesale into this sidelining of radical martyrdom. In studies of martyrdom, radical martyrdom has been judged to be of marginal interest. It has been dismissed as an aberration, and not part of the 'normal' Christian attitude to martyrdom.[29] In contrast, I will argue that radical

---

23. Crossan, *Birth*, 289.

24. E. Ferguson, 'Early Christian martyrdom and civil disobedience', *JECS* 1 (1993), 73–83.

25. Ferguson, 'Early Christian martyrdom', 82.

26. Ferguson, 'Early Christian martyrdom', 81.

27. This is fully argued in Chapter 1.

28. G.E.M. de Ste Croix, 'Aspects of the Great Persecution', *HTR* 47 (1954), 75–109 (83). For discussion of 'orthodoxy' especially in relation to martyrdom, see below, 16–29.

29. That is, that one should not seek death, but accept it when the opportunity presented itself. Among those who contrast the two types of martyrdom, but do see radical martyrdom as somehow deviant are: G. Buschmann, *Das Martyrium des Polykarp übersetz und erklärt* (Kommentar zu den

martyrdom, at least as an ideal, was a significant, rather than marginal, strand of second-century Christian thinking. A great many early Christians up to, and indeed beyond, the end of the second century were altogether more enthusiastic about death than is generally acknowledged. Within the spectrum of belief that made up early Christianity, many Christians embraced or idealised the significant phenomenon of radical martyrdom, and may even be said to have demonstrated a 'lust for death'.[30]

However, this attitude eventually came to be associated with heresy, and so the pervasiveness of this movement throughout the second century has been largely overlooked. This is a serious omission rendering much scholarly discussion of the theology and origins of Christian martyrdom incomplete; any comprehensive account of the development of Christian martyrdom must surely take account of this movement. It is the aim of this project to make up for the omission of radical martyrdom in recent research.

First, I will demonstrate the prominence of the radical martyrs in pre-Decian martyrology (Chapter 1). It will be shown that radical martyrs make their presence felt even within those texts regarded as 'proto-orthodox'. Accepting radical martyrdom into the mainstream theology of Christian martyrdom, rather than comprising a fringe activity, has consequences for questions of both the theology and origins of martyrdom. Both of these aspects will be addressed in the remainder of the project.

I will argue that Christians believed they were participants in an apocalyptic 'holy war' between God and Satan. However, not only did they believe themselves to be *participants* in this war, they actually saw their deaths as *contributing* to the final outcome. Martyrs were, in effect, God's foot soldiers on the front line of cosmic conflict; death through martyrdom was their most potent weapon in bringing about victory in that war.

Making and Unmaking Martyrs

Martyrdom and Holy War

Martyrdom is, of course, very much part of contemporary discourse. Since the attack on the 'Twin Towers' on 11 September 2001, martyrdom, or death for a religious or political cause, has made a significant impact on contemporary popular consciousness.[31] In the last few years, there has also been an increase in

Apostolischen Vätern, 6; Göttingen: Vandenhoeck & Ruprecht, 1998); F.W. Weidmann, ' "Rushing judgment?" Wilfulness and martyrdom in early Christianity', *Union Seminary Quarterly Review* 53 (1999), 61–9; Campenhausen, *Die Idee des Martyriums*; and Butterweck, *'Martyriumssucht'*.

30. See, also, D.W. Amundsen, 'Did early Christians lust after death?', *Christian Research Journal*, 18 (1996), 11–21. Although Amundsen responds to his own question with an emphatic 'no', the article at least admits there is a question to be discussed. Amundsen does not discuss the case of Pothinus (*Mart. Lyons* 1.29), who despite being over ninety years of age and physically quite infirm, was given divine strength to survive prison that he might die before the crowds, διὰ τὴν ἐγκειμένην τῆς μαρτυρίας ἐπιθυμίαν – because of his lust for martyrdom.

31. A consciousness already scarred by the 'religious' deaths of members of the 'People's Temple',

reportage of Palestinian suicide bombings, actions invariably regarded as martyrdoms by certain Palestinian groups.[32] In such acts, and countless others, there
is a fusion of religious and political themes. However, this fusion is imprecise,
for whereas the aims of such martyrdom operations (so far as we are able to
ascertain aim) appear to be political (whether a protest at American 'globalised
power', or the demand for a Palestinian State), the mode of attack appears to
be framed in an unmistakeably religious cast,[33] especially in the context of
Islamicist[34] notions of Holy War.[35]

Nonetheless, one of the most powerful, if not the dominant response to the
events of 9/11, was to deny that religion had any real part to play in the events.
Politicians, in the face of rising anti-Islamic violence in the West, sought to
disassociate Islamic belief from the hijackers' actions.[36] However, in the discourse of those behind the attack, religious themes are very much at the centre.
Osama bin Laden set the conflict, as he saw it, within the parameters of apocalyptic Holy War:

> The world has been divided into two camps: one under the banner of the cross (as the
> head of the infidels, Bush, has said), and one under the banner of Islam … Adherents
> of Islam, this is your day to make Islam victorious.[37]

Jonestown (1978), the Branch Davidians at Waco (1993), participants of the Solar Temple cult (1994,
1995, 1997), and members of Heaven's Gate at the passing of the Hale-Bopp comet (1997). For a
convenient introduction to all of these movements, see J.R. Hall, P.D. Schuyler and S. Trinh,
Apocalypse Observed: Religious Movements and Violence in North America, Europe and Japan
(London/New York: Routledge, 2000); see also J.D. Tabor, 'Patterns of the end: textual weaving
from Qumran to Waco', in P. Schäfer and M.R. Cohen (eds), *Toward the Millennium: Messianic
Expectations from the Bible to Waco* (Leiden: E.J. Brill, 1998), 409–30.

32. For discussion, see N.S. Ateek, 'What is theologically and morally wrong with suicide bombings? A Palestinian Christian perspective', *Studies in World Christianity* 8 (2002), 5–30.

33. The ambiguous nature of the role of religion in such actions is discussed by S. Goldenberg,
'The men behind the suicide bombers', *Guardian*, 12 June 2002 (http://www.guardian.co.uk/
israel/Story/0,2763,735785,00.html). Goldenberg argues that, although the actions of the suicide
bombers do have religious content, they are primarily political operations.

34. I am using the rather imprecise term 'Islamicist' to avoid two opposite problems. In the first
place, I wish to distance the particular actions under discussion from mainstream Islamic faith; but
secondly, I want also to recognize that a particular understanding of Islam is a major contributory
factor in the self-understanding of 'suicide bombers'.

35. See E. Tyan, 'Djihād', in H.A.R. Gibb (ed.), *Encyclopaedia of Islam* (Leiden: E.J. Brill, 1965),
II, 538–9.

36. So Tony Blair took great care to stress that the 'war on terror' was not a war on Islam
(http://www.cnn.com/2001/WORLD/europe/09/27/gen.blair.meeting/). See also B.B. Lawrence,
Shattering the Myth: Islam beyond Violence (Princeton, NJ: Princeton University Press, 2000).
Lawrence attempts to overturn the stereotype of the Muslim as *necessarily* violent and anti-
Western. His principal argument is that Islam is many things, comprising a wide spectrum of belief
and practice, much of it pluralist and accommodating. Lawrence reacts against the tendency to
homologize all Islamic experience, casting it as the 'Enemy of the West' and, in that regard, the heir
of communism.

37. Reported in *The Scotsman*, Friday 2 November 2001. Apocalyptic elements abound even in
this short soundbite: radical dualism; call to battle; and a belief that the war will be won.

The language of Holy War/*Jihād* sits uncomfortably with Westerners. With no modern Holy War tradition to draw upon – in the sense that religion propels a State to war[38] – Westerners have been quick to disregard religion as a motivating factor for political behaviour; where it does appear, it is simply dismissed as fanaticism. Others have sought to re-examine Islamic tradition, especially of *jihād*, so that the moral aspect of *jihād* (striving), rather than violence or war is stressed. So Partner argues Islamic tradition teaches that although force may be justified in some circumstances, it is the lesser *jihād*.[39]

In contrast, Johnston warns that *jihād* in its violent form is taken seriously as a potentially normative response by many in the Islamic world to a perceived danger to the Islamic community.[40] Certainly, there are Islamicist voices which confirm Johnston's point. Two days after the 'Twin Towers' attack, the headline of *Al Risala*, the weekly newspaper of Hamas, cried, 'Allah has answered our prayer'.[41] Similarly, some in the Arab world do not disapprove of Palestinian suicide operations, with the father of one suicide bomber proclaiming, 'We [the Palestinians] love martyrdom; they [the Israelis] love life'.[42] Importantly, 'martyrdom' and *jihād* are closely linked. Those who lose their lives within the context of a divine Holy War are deemed to be *shahid* (witnesses),[43] martyrs, who, in turn, provide an example of bravery and righteousness to those who will follow in their footsteps.

Defining Martyrdom

How do political and academic communities respond to such beliefs? We could, with Lewis, simply dismiss such talk as heretical.[44] For, while some are busy making and proclaiming martyrs, it has been equally important for others to 'unmake' them, as it were. It has been strenuously argued that those who take the lives of others are simply not martyrs. So, a distinction is drawn between 'martyrdom' and other forms of violent death. For example, George W. Bush, in

38. The possible exception of the Crusades obviously precedes the post-Enlightenment, modern, democratic state. Nevertheless, 'crusading' language was recently employed by George W. Bush in respect of the Iraq conflict of 2004; http://news.bbc.co.uk/1/hi/world/americas/ 1547561.stm.

39. P. Partner, *God of Battles: Holy Wars of Christianity and Islam* (Princeton, NJ: Princeton University Press, 1998). The word itself is a verbal noun meaning striving, associated in the Qu'ran with striving for the religion. The meaning of war or aggression became associated with the term, usually in the sense of striving against others for Islam. There are, of course, peaceful ways of striving. See M. Khaduri, *War and Peace in the Law of Islam* (Baltimore: The Johns Hopkins University Press, 1955), 55–82. However, Tyan, 'Djihād', regards this approach as being 'wholly apologetic'.

40. J.T. Johnston, *The Holy War Idea in Western and Islamic Tradition* (Pennsylvania: Pennsylvania State University Press, 1997); see also M.J. Akbar, *The Shade of Swords: Jihad and the Conflict between Christianity and Islam* (London: Routledge, 2002).

41. http://www.ourjerusalem.com/arabpress/story/arabpress20010921.html.

42. Goldenberg, 'The men behind the suicide bombers'.

43. Arabic links the concept of martyrdom to witness, as in the Greek term μαρτύς.

44. B. Lewis, *The Crisis of Islam: Holy War and Unholy Terror* (London: Weidenfeld and Nicholson, 2003).

a 2002 White House Speech, asserted that those whom some Palestinians regard as martyrs are 'not martyrs, they are murderers'.[45] Similarly, in scholarly discourse, Hurtado urges the same kind of distinction. He points to

> a very different kind of 'martyr' whose victory consists, not in his/her own death, but in killing as many others as possible! It would be a failure of nerve for Christian and Jewish scholars not to complain about the 'high-jacking' of the terms 'martyr' and 'martyrdom' by some violent groups today.[46]

Yet on what basis might this be done? Would it be possible to come up with a definition of martyrdom that would take account of early Christian and Jewish martyrs, like Stephen, James and Ignatius, but at the same time incorporate a whole host of individuals up to our present day, who died in a wide variety of circumstances, yet are generally regarded as martyrs in some sense of the word? Any list of modern martyrs would include Rosa Luxemburg, Dietrich Bonhoeffer, Patrice Lamumba, Ché Guevara, Malcom X and Martin Luther King.[47] The challenge would be to construct a definition that would encompass these modern examples, and probably include those killed in heroic combat on the battlefield, yet simultaneously exclude modern Islamicist types of death for a cause (whilst including Samson! Judg. 16.30).[48] The term 'martyrdom' has become something of a 'wax nose', and, for some, 'sadly democratized'.[49]

> Because of…mass violence, the notion of martyrdom has broadened out and become imprecise: it extends to groups sacrificed to contemporary barbarism. Whole peoples become martyrs: the Armenians, the Jews, the gypsies, the Biafrans, the Cambodians; the list grows longer.[50]

This is not a new problem. Defining just what constitutes even ancient martyrdom is a slippery enterprise.[51] Most scholars who have made attempts at defi-

---

45. George W. Bush, speech delivered on 4 April 2002. http://www.whitehouse.gov/news/releases/2002/04/20020404-1.html.

46. L.W. Hurtado, 'Jesus' death as paradigmatic in the New Testament', *SJT* 57 (2004), 413–33 (emphasis original). I take the opposite view in an unpublished paper delivered to the British New Testament Conference, September 2003, entitled, 'September 11th through the lens of early Christian martyrdom'.

47. This list is from E. Weiner and A. Weiner, *The Martyr's Conviction: A Sociological Analysis* (Brown Judaic Studies, 203; Atlanta: Scholars Press, 1990), 8–9. They make the point how difficult it is to define martyrdom precisely. Interestingly two recent books on twentieth- century martyrdom do not deal with the question of the definition. See S. Bergman (ed.), *A Cloud of Witnesses: 20th Century Martyrs* (London: HarperCollins, 1997); A. Chandler (ed.), *The Terrible Alternative: Christian Martyrdom in the Twentieth Century* (London/New York: Cassell, 1998). Martyrdom has been an important and contested term throughout history, particularly at the Reformation. Gaining the power to make and 'unmake' martyrs has always been crucial. For general discussion, see B.S. Gregory, *Salvation at Stake: Christian Martyrdom in Early Modern Europe* (HHS, 134; Massachusetts: Harvard University Press, 1999).

48. Compare Josephus, *Ant.* 5.317 and Heb. 11.32–3.

49. B. Chenu, C. Prud'homme, F. Quéré and J. Thomas, *The Book of Christian Martyrs* (trans. J. Bowden; London: SCM Press, 1990), 13.

50. Chenu, Prud'homme, Quéré and Thomas, *Christian Martyrs*, 13.

51. Henten and Avemarie, *Martyrdom*, 2–8.

nition take the New Testament usage relating to the idea of *witnessing* as a starting point,[52] for it was only in the second half of the second century that the word μαρτύς took on its present meaning.[53] Thus, for van Henten and Avemarie, 'a martyr is a person who in an extremely hostile situation prefers a violent death to compliance with a demand of the (usually pagan) authorities'.[54] However, even this seemingly obvious definition does not do for some of our earliest martyrs, most notably Agathonicê,[55] whereas the Palestinian suicide martyr could be interpreted as offering resistance to an oppressive State authority (and that will entirely depend on whether one dwells in a Palestinian refugee camp or an Israeli settlement).

Even the *Shorter Oxford English Dictionary* is of little help. It defines a martyr as 'one who undergoes death (or great suffering) on behalf of any belief or cause, or through devotion to some object'. This definition is too broad to make the distinction called for. Furthermore, just how would one persuasively argue that those who die under the auspices of a group called the *Al-Aqsa Martyrs' Brigade* are not in fact martyrs? In this regard, Boyarin's question is pertinent: 'Whose martyrdom is this, anyway?'[56] Perspective appears to be the most significant factor in defining martyrs.[57]

Therefore, when van Henten attempts to be more detailed in what constitutes a 'Martyr Act', an interesting problem arises. He insists that a Martyr Act should follow a basic outline: a pagan edict leads to a clash of loyalty in the Christian or Jew. The potential martyr finds himself in conflict with the State, but refuses to compromise his religious convictions, leading to explicit confession and death.[58] Again, van Henten's description does not encompass every case of martyrdom, but, in describing a Martyr Act in this way, he opens the door to one particularly disturbing modern example, which is worth exploring in some detail.

A Modern 'Martyr Act'?

On 3 September 2003, Paul Hill, a former Presbyterian minister, was executed by the State of Florida for the murder of a doctor who carried out abortions. In

52. See B.A.G.M. Dehandschutter and J.W. van Henten, 'Einleitung' (in B.A.G.M. Dehandschutter, J.W. van Henten and H.J.W. van der Klaauw (eds), *Die Entstehung der jüdischen Martyrologie* [Leiden: E.J. Brill, 1989], 1–19), 5–8.

53. Baumeister, *Anfänge*, 239–45. The first use of the term with new meaning appears in the *Mart. Poly* (τοὺς μαρτυρήσαντας; 1.1). The first occurrence of the Latin term is found in the *Acts of the Scillitan Martyrs* (*hodie martyres in caelis sumus*; 15). There is no settled Hebrew term to cover martyrdom until the third century, when השם קדש (sanctification of [God's] name) became the favoured description (Henten and Avemarie, *Martyrdom*, 3).

54. Henten and Avemarie, *Martyrdom*, 3.

55. See *Mart. Carpus* 42–4, and discussion below, 33–4.

56. Boyarin, *Dying for God*, Chapter 4.

57. I am not saying that there are no criteria for *distinguishing* these types of death from one another, simply that the term martyr is employed by different groups to describe different types of death, usually for political or theological (or both) purposes. This seemingly small point has important implications for scholarly discussion of both ancient and contemporary martyrdom.

58. Henten, *Maccabean Martyrs*, 7.

the press conference on the eve of his execution, Hill stated, 'I believe the State, by executing me, will be making me a martyr.'[59] Similarly, protesters outside the prison held placards affirming their belief that Hill was a martyr. Many websites support his actions, including one drawing parallels between Hill and Dietrich Bonhoeffer:

> Bonhoeffer and Hill were clergymen who were at odds with the passivity and coward-ice of their fellow Christians to resist a holocaust ... Paul Hill witnessed the abortion holocaust as a Presbyterian minister in Pensacola, Florida – and determined to resist it. Both men spoke out for years at a cost to themselves and their careers as clergymen – but were determined to defend the defenseless ... Bonhoeffer joined the plot to assas-sinate Hitler ... Paul Hill took up arms to end the baby killing of abortionist John Britten ... To the very end of their lives, Bonhoeffer and Hill refused to recant their beliefs that their actions were justified. There was no retreating for these men of God. They were not ashamed that their fight against murder had put them in prison. With their lives at stake, they bravely upheld the principle of active resistance to evil and evil governments. The Nazi holocaust and the American murder of 45 million unborn children did not conquer the spirit of these men. They followed Christ in life and in death and challenge us to do the same today.[60]

Both men are deemed to be Christian martyrs, and to all intents and purposes this retelling of Hill's story does constitute a Martyr Act as described by van Henten. From Hill's supporters' point of view, the State issued an edict that allowed the massacre of infants, creating a clash of loyalty in the Christian. This led to crisis, where in 'defending the defenceless' the potential martyr took the action of 'justifiable homicide', just as Bonhoeffer had joined the plot to kill Hitler.[61] The act was subsequently accompanied by confession of faith and a refusal to recant, and as a result he underwent martyrdom.

I am in no way seeking in this discussion to deny any moral distinction between acts such as Bonhoeffer's and Hill's. My point is that the enterprise of seeking a universal definition of martyrdom, as if one can proclaim a *bone fide* martyrdom if a set of criteria is satisfied, is misguided. *Martyrs are not defined; martyrs are made.*[62] Discussion over whether or not Paul Hill, Palestinian sui-cide bombers, or those who hijacked aeroplanes on 11 September 2001 are martyrs is perhaps not the best way in which to assess the morality of their

59. http://news.bbc.co.uk/1/hi/world/americas/3077040.stm.

60. http://www.mttu.com/Articles/Men%20of%20Courage%20%20Paul%20Hill%20and%20 Dietrich%20Bonhoeffer.htm.

61. Although Bonhoeffer was immediately declared to be a martyr by Reinhold Niebuhr, his involvement in the plot to assassinate Hitler led many to question his suitability for the title, regarding his arrest, imprisonment and death to have been on political and secular grounds, rather than reli-gious. For a helpful discussion, see S.R. Haynes, *The Bonhoeffer Phenomenon: Portraits of a Prot-estant Saint* (London: SCM Press, 2004), 99–103.

62. For a particularly insightful exposition of this point, see Weiner and Weiner, *Martyr's Convic-tion*, 87–127, where they explore the way in which Nazi propaganda 'created' martyrs. They explain: 'In the hands of a skilled propagandist, martyrdom and the convictions it represents can be manipu-lated to attain predetermined aims. The capacity of the martyr to infuse meaning and to inspire commitment can be used by astute leaders to manipulate sentiments and actions during times of stress' (87).

actions. For in contemporary political (and religious) discourse it would seem that to call someone a martyr is simply to say that it is a death of which the speaker/writer approves – and very little else.

To illustrate, in the case of Paul Hill, it was not the United States judiciary who created a martyr: they executed a criminal. Rather, those who approved of Hill's actions *made* him a martyr. By retelling his story in a certain way, they created a narrative utilizing unmistakably Christian martyrological language, and reinforced their own (Christian) understanding of how the world works. To reinforce (and perhaps justify) their world-view, the example of ancient Christian martyrs is used as a template. Like Hill, the early Christians did not recant under pressure, and were finally executed by the State. The discrepancy over what the State believed it was doing and the reinterpretation of Hill's supporters is caused by a clash of narratives.

Martyrological Discourse

Some, like Chenu (et al.) may protest, claiming passivity is paramount in a martyr. 'The martyr does not seek punishment and is never taken with arms in hand – the sole exception being Joan of Arc'.[63] It is illuminating that even this group of writers, who understand martyrdom very narrowly, find an exception. In any case, George Bernard Shaw's reflections on this exception bring the whole question of who makes a martyr into focus.

> Joan of Arc, a village girl from Vosges, was born in 1412; burnt for heresy, witchcraft and sorcery in 1431; rehabilitated after a fashion in 1456; designated venerable in 1904; declared Blessed in 1908; and finally canonised in 1920.[64]

The question Shaw invites us to consider with these words is surely this: when did Joan of Arc *become* a martyr? Was it in 1431, 1456, 1904, 1908, or 1920? I am suggesting that Joan of Arc became a martyr only when people began calling her one.

> According to one sociological theory of martyrdom, the 'Theory of Narration', martyrdom is essentially a story; a structured transmission of happenings within a body of oral and written traditions. Ultimately, the text is the most important factor in martyrdom. The historical veracity of the events recorded is a secondary issue. Once they are embodied in a text, the fact that they did not occur does not detract from their persuasive power. To understand martyrdom is essentially to understand a story.[65]

Similarly, for Lieu, stories and narratives produced by a community project their particular understanding of the world, or their 'image of reality'. Therefore, texts make 'presentations' about people, places, and situations: 'Such "presenta-

---

63. Chenu, Prud'homme, Quéré and Thomas, *Christian Martyrs*, 13. On explaining their exception, the remark, 'it would be hypocritical to reproach her, for her country was at war'.

64. G.B. Shaw, Preface to *Saint Joan: A Chronicle Play in Six Scenes and an Epilogue* (London: Chronicle, 1924).

65. Weiner and Weiner, *Martyr's Conviction*, 12. For a fuller treatment of the narration theory, see 87–127.

tion" has to be seen both as belonging to the literary construction of the text and as grounded in the text's social context and function.'[66] These literary presentations, she observes, cannot be relied upon to mirror the external 'reality'. Instead, they will address particular needs that may be internal or external to the literature itself.

What actions that will be affirmed or denied as martyrdom will largely depend on the interpretive community's image of reality. A martyrdom is, therefore, a type of narrative which describes a death which reinforces a group's (whether religious, political or national) view of the world. It is difficult to find objective criteria that distinguish a martyr from a terrorist or a criminal; the answer to that question will entirely depend on the image of reality of the questioner. If one shares the image of reality held by the State of Florida, then Paul Hill was a dangerous, fanatical criminal. If, alternatively, one is a subscriber to *The Abortion Abolitionist*,[67] then Hill is a hero, who carried out God's orders, and very much part of the rank of the martyrs.

Making Christian Martyrs

Just as it is the stories of Paul Hill's death, and not the State of Florida, that made him a martyr, it was the narratives describing particular Christian deaths, rather than the Romans, that made Christian martyrs. Christian reflection on martyrdom had to make sense of the world in which the Christians found themselves, and also the experiences of suffering which they endured. Texts, traditions and stories created a new world with new signs, symbols and values. These texts dialogued with and reinforced the structures of that world, constructing, in Gerd Theissen's phrase, a 'semiotic cathedral'.

> [The early Christians] built a semiotic cathedral out of narrative, ritual and ethical materials, a world of signs *and* a world in which to live. For its inhabitants this world was quite simply 'true' and plausible.[68]

Importantly, that world clashed with the Roman world. The dominant narrative in the first centuries experienced by the Church was the *Imperium*. The Romans had their own 'semiotic temples' of signs and rituals, which the Christians were seen to transgress.[69] This led to conflict, which the Christians interpreted as persecution, and the Romans interpreted as good government. The Romans in regard to the Christians, like the State of Florida in relation to Paul Hill, simply believed themselves to be executing seditious criminals who refused to be good Roman citizens.[70] Boyarin emphasizes this debt to narrative in the making of martyrdom.

---

66. J.M. Lieu, *Image and Reality: The Jews in the World of the Christians in the Second Century* (Edinburgh: T&T Clark, 1996), 2.

67. http://www.theabortionabolitionist.com/. Volume 1: Issue 3 has an extensive discussion about the issues surrounding Paul Hill's execution.

68. G. Theissen, *A Theory of Primitive Christianity* (trans. J. Bowden; London: SCM Press, 1999), 286.

69. P. Zanker, *The Power of Images in the Age of Augustus* (Ann Arbor: University of Michigan Press, 1988).

70. This point is argued in Chapter 2, especially, 61–8.

> I propose we think of martyrdom as a 'discourse', as a practice of dying for God and of talking about it … For the 'Romans', it didn't matter much whether the lions were eating a robber or a bishop, and it probably didn't make much of a difference to the lions, either, but the robber's friends and the bishop's friends told different stories about those leonine meals.[71]

It was the stories told about these deaths that made the difference between an execution, a martyrdom or even dinner! Romans and Christians saw the same events, but interpreted them in different ways because of the larger narratives they employed to describe the events. No amount of definition, checklists or criteria could convince a Roman soldier that the death of a Christian was martyrdom, any more that he could be convinced that he was involved in 'persecution'. Any historical investigation into Christian interaction with the Roman State must simply deal with two contrasting images of reality.

As in modern times, it is the stories told about certain deaths, whether orally, written or more often presented through mass media, that determine what kind of deaths they are. It is the telling of stories that gives martyrdom its power. 'Martyrdom becomes influential through the narratives that celebrate it.'[72] This is important, since the radical martyrs, who are the main focus of this project, have been not only written out of Christian martyrology from the third century onwards but also omitted from scholarly narratives of early Christian martyrdom.

However, at the same time, scholars have struggled to identify a satisfactory set of criteria for defining martyrdom. By allowing discourse to identify martyrdom, we may highlight stories of radical martyrdom contained in early Christian martyrological narratives, demonstrating the pervasiveness of radical martyrdom in the early Church. Radical martyrdom, we will conclude, must be taken into account in any theological map of Christian martyrdom.

In Chapter 2, I examine the conflict between the Christian and Roman 'images of reality', explaining both why the Christians experienced persecution, and how, despite the fact that most of this persecution was local, the Christians could interpret it as coming from the Roman State. For Perkins, it was precisely words rather than actions that constituted Christianity's contribution and challenge to the Roman world.[73] It is the words, stories and ideas, and particularly the theological *world* that nourished them which will be the focus for the remainder of the project. In turning to the theology of martyrdom, early Christian texts will be examined for both the world behind the text and also the world these texts *create*.[74] For if we adopt a narrative approach to martyrology, then even if these

71. Boyarin, *Dying for God*, 94–95.

72. Weiner and Weiner, *Martyr's Conviction*, 12. It must, of course, be acknowledged that the vast majority of people killed for their beliefs and faith, both in the ancient and contemporary world, do not have their stories told. Perhaps they are martyrs in need of an adequate narrative.

73. Perkins, *Suffering Self*, 9. *Pace* R. MacMullen ('What difference did Christianity make?' *Historia* 35 [1986], 322–43) who argues this question must be answered in terms of what Christians actually did.

74. This is what Paul Ricoeur has called the 'world in front of the text'. P. Ricoeur, *Essays on Biblical Interpretation* (ed. L.S. Mudge; London: SPCK, 1981), 98–104.

martyrological discourses 'do not represent "reality", they do have real effects'.[75] One of the real effects of these narratives was to cradle and reflect a theological universe that enabled radical martyrdom to be seen as the most appropriate form of Christian living. Not only would Christians choose martyrdom rather than deny Christ, but they would actively embrace death. Death was valorised, and somehow interpreted as a more attractive state of being than life.

In Chapter 3, I turn to this interpretative universe and examine the Christian theology of radical martyrdom. The question of how the desire for radical martyrdom could be considered to be rational for the early Christians is addressed. I will argue that the Christians conceived themselves as being engaged in cosmic conflict against Satan, in which martyrdom was the most potent weapon possessed by the Christians. Their deaths actually contributed to the coming eschatological victory of God over the forces of evil. Therefore, choosing death was not only an explicable course of action, it became the most appropriate for faithful Christians to take. Supporting this theology was a radically deconstructed Christian cosmology, where spatial and temporal boundaries were dissolved. Most significant, I will argue, was the way in which the radical martyrs interpreted life and death.

Next, the origins of Christian martyrdom and its theological world will be reconsidered (Chapter 4). The new theology of early Christian martyrology which I am proposing clearly requires a fresh look at the origins of its theology and practice. In order to trace the evolution of a movement, especially one whose actions seem to us rather strange, we must ascertain what were the crucial elements that came together to form the world-view making the conviction possible. What were the ingredients that came together to form the social and theological matrix in which Christians could believe that offering themselves to death was the most productive way to serve Christ?

Having identified the individual components of the world-view, their sources are examined. How were they adopted into the developing Christian milieu? Therefore, in investigating the origins of Christian martyrology, Judaism and Graeco-Roman Noble Death traditions will be examined as potential sources. I will conclude that although the origins of Christian martyrdom defy simple clear lines of trajectory, a specific Christianizing of Jewish Holy War tradition deserves more attention as a source for Christian martyrological reflection.

Finally, I will assess the extent to which the components that combined to form the radical martyr's world-view – the bricks and mortar of their 'semiotic cathedral' – are already to be found in the New Testament (Chapter 5), and how the New Testament authors helped shape the developing theology and world-view of radical martyrdom and cosmic conflict. We will discover that although, with one exception, no single New Testament author calls for radical martyrdom, their contribution to the symbolic world in which this radical martyrological movement could emerge and flourish was significant.

---

75. Perkins, *Suffering Self*, 3.

Chapter 1

RADICAL MARTYRDOM IN EARLY CHRISTIANITY

Introduction

As we have seen, discourse plays a pivotal role in defining what is and what is not martyrdom. Similarly, what did or did not constitute 'authentic' martyrdom in the early Church was played out in the arena of orthodoxy and heresy, and it is to this topic we now turn.

Orthodoxy and Heresy

How one conceives 'orthodoxy' and 'heresy' depends entirely on the theological presuppositions held.

> A heresy is a *crime of perception* – an act of seeing something that, according to some custodian of reality, is not truly there. Heresy, therefore, is always relative to an orthodoxy ... From the perspectives of those conventionally labeled heretics, the orthodox themselves are heretics.[1]

No one at any time has thought herself to be a heretic.[2] If one holds to a position that has clearly and consciously deviated from a previously established road, then it is more likely thought to be a development than a departure, a reformation or a (re)discovery of what was always the case. On other occasions, the 'heretics' attempt to demonstrate the priority of their belief-system over their opponents' beliefs, a point famously argued by Bauer, who, in his classic 1934 treatment on the subject, made the claim that what came to be known as 'heresy' developed quite independently of 'orthodoxy', and in many places actually preceded it.[3] The

---

1.   L. George, *The Encyclopedia of Heresies and Heretics* (London: Robson Books, 1995), xii (emphasis original).

2.   Tertullian is aware of the problem (*Against Marcion* 4.4), 'I say that my Gospel is the true one. Marcion says that his is. I assert that Marcion's Gospel is adulterated. Marcion says that mine is.'

3.   W. Bauer, *Orthodoxy and Heresy in Earliest Christianity* (trans. R.A. Kraft and G. Krodel; Philadelphia: Fortress Press, 1971). There has been extensive discussion of the Bauer thesis. General support has come from H.D. Betz, 'Orthodoxy and heresy in primitive Christianity', *Interpretation* 19 (1965), 299–311; H. Koester, 'ΓΝΩΜΑΙ ΔΙΑΦΟΡΟΙ: the origin and nature of diversification in the history of early Christianity', *HTR* 58 (1965), 279–318; and more recently, B.A. Pearson, *Gnosticism, Judaism, and Egyptian Christianity* (Minneapolis: Augsberg Fortress, 1990), especially 194–213. The question of orthodoxy and heresy in relation to the myriad of first- and second-century Christian groups has been reopened by B.D. Ehrman, *Lost Christianities: The Battle for Scripture and the Faiths We Never Knew* (Oxford: Oxford University Press, 2003).

question of what was orthodox and what constituted heresy was fiercely contested in the first few centuries of the Church, itself, regarded by some to be a Jewish heresy.[4]

The detail of Bauer's thesis and his critics need not detain us. Bauer's proposal – that heresy almost always preceded orthodoxy – is difficult to maintain.[5] Nonetheless, his more general attack on a reconstruction of Christian history, where heresy was always seen as a later corruption of earlier orthodoxy, has largely prevailed, a point recognized by Robinson:

> [Bauer' thesis] has not served us well if it has provided for us a *certainty* about the character of primitive Christianity in various areas. If however, it has merely provided us with an *uncertainty* about the character of primitive Christianity in particular areas, we can live with that.[6]

Early Christianity was not homogeneous. We simply cannot divide the early Christians into orthodox and heretics for, as Dunn concludes, there was 'no single normative form of Christianity in the first century'.[7] Nonetheless, it is worth noting that martyrdom was one of the criteria initially employed to separate the orthodox from the heretics. However, as we shall see, by the third century, this begins to change. Therefore, in this chapter, we examine different approaches to martyrdom found within the second- and third-century Church. We will do this without the spectre of orthodoxy and heresy directing our conclusions, but instead, will strive to be guided by Bauer's dictum: 'Must not the historian, like the judge preside over the parties and maintain as a primary principle the dictum *audiatur et altera pars* (let the other side be heard)?'[8]

---

4.   Paul, of course, persecuted the Christian Church as a Jewish heresy; Gal. 1.13, 23; 1 Cor. 15.9; Phil. 3.6; Acts 8.3; 9.1, 21; 22.4, 19; 26.10–11. Similarly Jesus is associated with 'heresy' at Mk 3.22; 14.63–4; Jn 10.33; 19.7; Acts 7.54–60. Mt. 5.17–20 and 7.21–3 appear to Jesus from charges that he operated apart from orthodox Judaism, and his followers are identified as excommunicees from the synagogue in John (9.22; 12.42; 16.2).

5.   The most extensive critique of Bauer's thesis is by T.A. Robinson, *The Bauer Thesis Reexamined: The Geography of Heresy in the Early Christian Church* (New York: The Edwin Mellen Press, 1988); but see also F.W. Norris, 'Ignatius, Polycarp, and I Clement: Walter Bauer reconsidered', *VC* 30 (1976), 23–44. For the earliest criticism, see H.E.W. Turner, *The Pattern of Truth: A Study of the Relations between Orthodoxy and Heresy in the Early Church* (London: A.R. Mowbray & Co., 1954), especially, 39–94.

6.   Robinson, *Bauer Thesis*, 205 (his emphasis). Although Robinson uses the (apparently pejorative) word, 'merely', it is important to remember that conclusion stood against what for centuries had been the accepted historical reconstruction. For a similar assessment of Bauer's achievement, see also, Norris, 'Ignatius', 42.

7.   J.D.G. Dunn, *Unity and Diversity in the New Testament: An Inquiry into the Character of Earliest Christianity* (London: SCM Press, 1977), 373.

8.   Bauer, *Orthodoxy*, xxi–xxii. However, some scholars believe the pendulum has swung too far in the other direction so that 'the Fathers are no longer put on a par with the heretics; they are put on the defensive, and it assumed that the heretics are the true religious geniuses, and even more, the bearers of the authentically radical spiritual breakthrough inaugurated by Jesus ... The historian is not content to assure the heretics a fair hearing; the historian has become an advocate in their cause. We have done an about-face from Tertullian's *de praescriptione haereticorum* to *de praescriptione patrum*'. P. Henry, 'Why is contemporary scholarship so enamoured of ancient

Death in Early Christian Perspective

Within the Christian movement by close of the second century, there was an inexplicable enthusiasm for death. By this, I mean more than an acceptance of death, however enthusiastic, when opportunity for martyrdom presented itself. I will demonstrate a desire on the part of some early Christians to embrace radical martyrdom as the most appropriate form of Christian 'living'. It is my intention in this section, to outline briefly the spectrum of beliefs and attitudes towards death and martyrdom in the second century, particularly in relation to radical martyrdom.

Early Christianity may be described as a diverse constellation of communities holding a variety of beliefs.[9] Though interpretations differed, these communities had in common forms of devotion to Jesus Christ.[10] By the second century, Gnostic, Jewish and Gentile groups all practised what they believed to be authentic Christianity.[11] These communities differed in attitudes to the law, circumcision and Christology,[12] leading to fierce battles for 'orthodoxy'. As one would expect, there was also a range of views as to the significance or effectiveness of martyrdom. Indeed, the view and the practice of martyrdom was a significant signal of one's 'orthodox' credentials. Martyrdom became one of the battle-grounds over which 'orthodoxy' and 'heresy' would be fought.

Martyrdom and Early Christian 'Orthodoxy'

First, we are on fairly safe territory with the claim that, on the whole, the second-century Church Fathers were unanimous in their praise of martyrdom. Death in the *correct circumstance* was essentially positive. For Clement of Alexandria, 'the Gnostic' (by this he means the true Christian), the one with true knowledge,

> can readily give up his life because of his distaste for the body, and so avoids denying his faith and does not fear death because of the hope for earthly rewards. He will approach death with gladness and thankfulness, both to God who had predestined him for martyrdom, and the one who gave the opportunity for death.[13]

heretics?' in E.A. Livingstone (ed.), *Studia Patristica XVII* (Oxford: Pergamon Press [1982], 123–6), 124–5.

9. So Theissen, *Theory*; Bauer, *Orthodoxy*.

10. For a lengthy survey of the development of devotion to Christ in early Christian movements, both 'proto-orthodox' and those groups which represented 'radical diversity', see L.W. Hurtado, *Lord Jesus Christ: Devotion to Jesus in Earliest Christianity* (Grand Rapids: Eerdmans, 2003), 487–648.

11. So Ehrman, *Lost Christianities*; G. Lüdemann, *Heretics: The Other Side of Christianity* (trans. J. Bowden; London: SCM Press, 1996).

12. See, for example, A.F. Segal, 'Jewish Christianity', in H.W. and G. Hala (eds), *Eusebius, Christianity and Judaism* (Leiden: E.J. Brill, 1992), 326–51; R.E. Brown, 'Not Jewish Christianity and Gentile Christianity but types of Jewish/Gentile Christianity', *CBQ* 45 (1983), 74–9; A.F.J. Klinj and G.F. Reinink, *Patristic Evidence for Jewish-Christian Sects* (NovTSup, 36; Leiden: E.J. Brill, 1973); and J. Munck, 'Jewish Christianity in post-apostolic times', *NTS* 6 (1960), 103–16.

13. *Strom.* 4.4.

His death confirms the truth of his preaching that God is powerful. On death he is reckoned to be a 'dear brother' of Christ because of the 'similarity of his life'. Martyrdom, for Clement, is 'perfection', because it exhibits the perfect work of love. The martyrs die without the fear of infirmity and the desire to go on living, and so can offer their full soul and not 'bearing with it their lusts'. They are to be praised in the same way as those fallen in war are praised by the ancients, for the confession of God is martyrdom, and a life lived in knowledge of God, obeying the commandments. Clement is largely enthusiastic about Christian death; a martyr's death is to be striven for.[14]

Ignatius of Antioch is perhaps the most celebrated ancient proponent of martyrdom. While being transferred from Syria to Rome, where he was condemned to be sent to the amphitheatre and killed there by wild beasts, he wrote to the Christians in Rome, pleading with them not to interfere on his behalf:

> I am writing to all the churches, and I give injunction to everyone, that I am dying willingly for God's sake, if you do not prevent it. I plead with you not to be an 'unreasonable kindness' to me. Allow me to be eaten by the beasts, through which I can attain God. I am God's wheat, and I am ground by the teeth of wild beasts, so that I may become pure bread of Christ ... Do me this favour ... Let there come upon me fire, and the cross, and struggle with wild beasts, cutting and tearing apart, racking of bones, mangling of limbs, crushing of my whole body ... may I but attain to Jesus Christ.[15]

It has been suggested that this pleading to be allowed to die should not be taken at face value. What, after all, could the Roman Christians do to prevent his death? Is his insistence on the Church not to intercede a hidden plea that they do try something? However, the language Ignatius uses, though highly emotive, fits very well with other martyr language and concepts, as we shall see.

Secondly, it is possible that Ignatius fears that, through the prayers of the Roman church, God may prevent his death. For Ignatius, death is the way to attain God: 'the one who is near to the sword is near to God, the one who is in the company of wild beasts is in the company of God'.[16]

Therefore, to prevent or hinder his death, or even to intercede on his behalf would, according to Ignatius, literally be aiding the Devil.[17] In his stance, Ignatius sees himself as standing in a long tradition of martyrs, for many others had gone before him; in his own words, 'those who have preceded me from Syria to Rome'.[18]

Another enthusiastic proponent of martyrdom among the early Church Fathers was Tertullian. For him, the 'sole key to unlock Paradise is [one's] own life's blood'.[19] Death was a welcome release from an evil world: 'Nothing matters to

14. *Strom.* 4.4.
15. Ignatius, *Rom.* 4.1–5.3.
16. See Ignatius, *Smyrn.* 4.
17. Ignatius, *Rom.* 7. Similarly, in the *Acts of Andrew*, Andrew is incensed that his followers arranged to have him rescued from the cross.
18. Ignatius, *Rom.* 10.2.
19. Tertullian, *Bapt.* 1.

us in this age but to escape from it with all speed'.[20] For Tertullian, martyrdom was all that prevented some from losing their salvation – it was the 'second supplies of comfort'.[21]

> [God] has chosen to contend with a disease and to do good by imitating the malady: to destroy death by death, to dissipate killing by killing, to dispel tortures by tortures, to disperse in a vapour punishments by punishments, to bestow life by withdrawing it, to aid the flesh by injuring it, to preserve the soul by snatching it away.[22]

In a rather macabre praise of death, Wisdom is portrayed as the slayer of her children. Tertullian wished 'to be slain by her in order to become a son'.[23] Death through martyrdom is better than living an incident-free life.[24]

Not only was martyrdom looked upon positively but it also became a yardstick for measuring commitment to the faith. A sure sign of a 'heretical' sect was their failure to contribute to the host of martyrs.[25] Addressing Emperor Antoninius Pius (138–61), Justin claimed that the followers of Simon, Meander and Marcion were not true Christians on account that 'they are not persecuted or killed' by the Roman officials.[26]

Many of the early Church Fathers reserved their greatest vitriol, not for those who persecuted them, but for the 'heretical' Christians who did not embrace martyrdom.

> Now we are in the midst of an intense heat, the very dogstar of persecution ... the fire and the sword have tried some Christians, and the beasts have tried others; others are in prison, *longing for martyrdom* which they have tasted already, having been beaten by clubs and tortured ... We ourselves, having been appointed for pursuit, are like hares being hemmed in from a distance – and *the heretics go about as usual!*[27]

Therefore, while some Christians waited in prison longing for martyrdom, others believed that there was no need to confess before the earthly archons. Instead, they held that confession need only be given before heaven, and so denial before the courts in order to preserve one's life was an acceptable option.[28] Dubbed the

20. Tertullian, *Apol.* 41.5.
21. Tertullian, *Scorp.* 6.
22. Tertullian, *Scorp.* 5.
23. Tertullian, *Scorp.* 7. A point attacked in disgust by the writer of the Gnostic, *Test. Truth* 32.20–1.
24. It should probably be mentioned that Tertullian did not in fact undergo martyrdom.
25. Justin was the first early Christian to write a treatise against what he called 'heresies' (αἵρεσις; *Apol.* I.26). In Acts, the term is employed neutrally (5.17; 15.5; 26.5; see also Josephus meaning parties within early Judaism). Where it is found with a negative connotation (Acts 24.5, 14; 28.22; 1 Cor. 11.19; Ignatius, *Eph.* 6.2), it is used in the sense of divisiveness rather than wrong belief.
26. Justin, *Apol.* I.26.
27. Tertullian, *Scorp.* 1, 5, 7 (emphasis added).
28. Tertullian, *Scorp.* 10.1, says that Valentinus taught this. I will of course regard the 'Gnostic' Christians as displaying a legitimate expression of Christianity in the course of this project. Elaine Pagels (*The Gnostic Gospels* [New York: Random House, 1979]) has convincingly shown that the attitude a Christian community had to martyrdom was directly linked to its view of the death of Jesus; see also *idem*. 'Gnostic and orthodox views of Christ's passion: paradigms for the Christian's response to persecution?', in B. Layton (ed.), *The Rediscovery of Gnosticism* (2 vols; Leiden: E.J.

'Gnostics', this loose federation of Christians held a radically different view of martyrdom than that expressed by the Fathers.

The Gnostics and Martyrdom

Tertullian could remark that the Gnostics and the Valentinians, in attempting to preserve their lives, preferred a 'wretched life to a blessed one'.[29] Criticism was levelled at both those who did not approve of martyrdom and also those who under pressure denied that they were ever Christians. According to Justin, true Christians would never avoid confession: 'He who denies anything either does so from condemning it; or knowing himself to be unworthy of it and alien to it, avoids the confession of it: none of which applies to the true Christian.'[30]

The sociological effects of both successful martyrdom and denial were not lost on the early Church. Martyrdom was promoted as a means of strengthening fragile communities, invigorating the resolve of future martyrs and helping to define strong community barriers. Successful martyrs brought the new religion to the attention of pagan society[31] and, significantly, won many converts.[32] The blood of the martyrs was indeed seed.[33] The deaths of the Christians were a public testimony to unbelievers,[34] and the reactions of pagan onlookers are often recorded in the *Acts*.

> Who indeed would not admire the martyrs' nobility, their courage, their love of the Master? For even when they were torn by whips until the very structure of their bodies was lain bare down to the inner veins and arteries, they endured it, making even the bystanders weep for pity.[35]

Deniers, in contrast, brought scorn upon the Christian communities, weakening their group cohesion, as loyalty to the group was undermined. It was therefore important to dissuade potential deniers from doing so. The *Martyrs of Lyons* describes how, after a few Christians had denied, doubt began to sweep through the church.[36] However, the community were given renewed hope by those who successfully endured,[37] and the story serves as a stark warning that those who deny may not only face eternal punishment, but temporal consequences too:

Brill, 1980), I, 262–83. As in some 'Gnostic' texts, Jesus escapes crucifixion, so the Christian should avoid death. Naturally, 'Gnostic' Christians had their own fierce polemic against 'foolish Christians' who accepted martyrdom.

29. Tertullian, *Scorp.* 1.
30. Justin, *Apol.* II.2. Pliny also informs Trajan that he has heard Christians will not curse Christ (*Epistles* 10.96).
31. Bowersock, *Martyrdom and Rome*, 66.
32. Justin, *Apol.* II.12.
33. Tertullian, *Apol.* 50.
34. *Mart. Carpus* 40; Eusebius, *H.E.* 5.2.4–5; *Mart. Marinus* 6.1; *Mart. Fruct.* 6.3.
35. *Mart. Pol.* 2.2.
36. *Mart. Lyons* 1.11–12.
37. *Mart. Lyons* 1.24–5. After the martyrdom of Sanctus, renewed hope swept through the community. Dramatically, Biblis, a former denier, 'came to her senses' and confessed. It is as though the witness of Sanctus woke some of the deniers from sleep.

> Those who admitted what they were were detained as Christians, but no other charge was preferred against them. The others, however [those who denied], were held on the charge of being murderers and criminals and were punished twice as much as the rest. For, they [the rest] were comforted by the joy of martyrdom, their hope in the promises, their love for Christ, and the Spirit of the Father; whereas the others were greatly tormented by their conscience, so that as they passed by they were easily distinguished by their looks from all the others. The former advanced joyously, with majesty and great beauty mingled on their countenances ... but the others were dejected, downcast, ill-favoured and devoid of all comeliness. In addition, the pagans taunted them for being ignoble cowards; they were accused of homicide, and had forfeited that glorious, honourable, and life-giving name.[38]

The pitiful state of the deniers strengthened the resolve of the others.

Doubtless, the deaths of many members of a particular group had consequences on how that group saw itself in relation to the outside world. The apocalyptic world-view of the Christians already encouraged a tight view of group definition with high boundaries; deniers threatened those boundaries, explaining the vehemence of the attacks against them. Origen provides a comprehensive account of the way in which deniers were viewed: they were deceivers, an abomination; their souls were corrupt; they were joined to another god; they served Satan and renounced their baptism; they did not love God and were built on weak foundation; and, crucially, hell awaited them.[39]

Of course, the Christians on the end of such criticism had their own responses.

> The foolish – thinking [in] their heart [that] if they confess, 'We are Christians', in word only (but) not with power, while giving themselves over to ignorance, to a human death, not knowing where they are going to nor who Christ is, thinking that they will live, when (really) they are in error – hasten towards the principalities and the authorities. They fall into their clutches because of the ignorance that is in them ... It is in this way that they [drew] error to themselves. [...they do] not [know] that they [will destroy] themselves. If the [Father were to] desire a [human] sacrifice, he would become [vainglorious].[40]

The writer of the *Apocalypse of Peter* was horrified that those who called themselves bishops and deacons were misleading 'little ones', and encouraging them to go to their deaths, erroneously believing that 'through martyrdom salvation comes'.[41] The 'orthodox' were false teachers who hastened towards the authorities, giving themselves over to destruction. Furthermore, according to the 'Gnostics', they were 'empty martyrs' since they only witnessed to themselves.[42] Therefore, those who taught others, 'If we deliver ourselves up for the Name, we shall be saved' were guilty of leading their followers to a meaningless death.[43]

---

38. *Mart. Lyons* 1.33–5.

39. Origen, *Exhortation*, 5, 7, 10, 17, 18, 27, 48; See also Justin, *Apol.* I.8, 12; II.2; and Clement, *Strom.* 4.7.

40. *Test. Truth* 31.21–32.21.

41. *Apoc. Peter* 78.31–80.7. See also Pagels, *Gnostic Gospels*, 93.

42. *Test. Truth* 33.25.

43. *Test. Truth* 34.4–6.

In a climate where Christians were suffering, and the call to martyrdom was terrifyingly real, a significant section of early Christianity openly called into question the value of martyrdom.[44] Each time a Christian recanted, or denied the faith even under torture, the credibility of the new religion was damaged. It was vital to attack those Christians who saw no value in martyrdom with as much vehemence as possible. Therefore, those who saw nothing to be gained in confession and death were regarded as 'false brethren' who had

> reached such a pitch of audacity that they even pour contempt upon the martyrs, and vituperate those who are killed on account of confessing the Lord, and who ... thereby strive to follow in the footsteps of the Lord's passion, themselves bearing witness to the one who suffered.[45]

Tertullian, disgusted by their cowardice, complains, 'when, therefore, the faith is greatly agitated and the church on fire ... then the Gnostics break out; then the Valentinians creep forth; then all the opponents of martyrdom bubble up'.[46]

For Irenaeus,

> The church in every place, because of the love which she cherishes towards God, sends forth throughout all time, a multitude of martyrs to the Father; while all others not only have nothing of this kind to point to among themselves, but even maintain that bearing witness is not at all necessary.[47]

Martyrdom for the earliest Church Fathers was *the* sign of orthodoxy. Those who saw no value in dying for the faith or, worse, those who attacked the martyrs for their actions were regarded as false brothers who were ashamed of the Name, cowardly clinging to a wretched life. Therefore, the number of martyrs a particular group produced easily identified their 'orthodox' credentials. However, by the time Clement of Alexandria came to write on the subject, contributing martyrs was no longer a guarantee of a group's orthodoxy.

Radical Martyrs

Clement of Alexandria is arguably advocate par excellence of what came to be known as the 'orthodox' approach in the second century. In his *Stromata*, Clement identifies three different attitudes to martyrdom held by Christians in the second century. First, there is the so-called 'orthodox' practice, which of course was Clement's position. Secondly, there were those who refused martyrdom – the 'impious' who had a 'cowardly love of life'. This Christian group regarded martyrs as self-murderers, whose deaths were merely suicide. Real martyrdom for them was wholly 'true knowledge of God', a position which, interestingly, would influence developing 'orthodox' thought in the third century.

The other 'heretical' group, identified by Clement, who were not of the true tradition, were markedly different from the 'Gnostics' in their approach to mar-

---

44. Pagels, *Gnostic Gospels*, 83.
45. Irenaeus, *A.H.* 3.18.5.
46. Tertullian, *Scorp.* 1.
47. Irenaeus, *A.H.* 4.33.9.

tyrdom. Unlike Clement's Gnostic opponents, this group was not afraid of death. The problem was their appetite for it.

Criticism of Radical Martyrdom

Those Christians who, in Clement's view, rushed too eagerly toward martyrdom are criticized along with the 'cowards'. Clement complains:

> We too blame those who have rushed on death, for there are some who are really not ours but share only the name, who are eager to hand themselves over in hatred against the creator, athletes of death. We say that these men take themselves off without witness, even if they are officially executed. For they do not preserve the characteristic mark of faithful witness, because they do not know the real God, but give themselves up to a futile death.[48]

Those who rush into death, he claims, hate life by demonstrating 'hatred to the Creator'. They 'share the same name' as Clement's group, but do not 'belong' to them. Their deaths are vain for they do not 'know God' – though Clement does not say in what way they do not know God. It is not clear whether it is their rush towards death alone that causes the negative reaction in Clement, or also some point of doctrine that causes them to be outside Clement's boundary. In any case, for Clement, it is this 'knowing God' that is the characteristic mark of 'believers' martyrdom'.

It was not that Clement disapproved of martyrdom under the right circumstances (though with Clement there does seem to be a lessening of its appeal); rather, this was a group whose appetite for death was too strong. They were eager to be arrested and executed, and often were. While there is in fact some corroborating evidence of distaste for radical martyrdom among what came to be 'orthodox' texts, radical martyrdom, as we shall discover, constituted an important and prominent element in the development of the Church, leading directly from New Testament traditions.[49]

What is noteworthy, however, is the way in which Clement distances himself from these radical martyrs. In the first instance, he does not deny that they look like martyrs. Indeed, they are arrested, undergo trial, and officially executed. Under Justin's definition, they would appear to be authentic believers. Secondly, Clement does not even deny that they share the name 'Christian'. These Christians, who died for the Name, holding fast to their confession under torture, and were officially executed, have been, at a stroke of Clement's pen, written out of the rank of faithful servants.

Radical Martyrdom and Scholarly 'Orthodoxy'

Traditionally, the accepted view of the early Christian 'orthodox' position on martyrdom has been that Christians accepted death when it came, but on no

---

48. Clement, *Strom.* 4.16.3–17.3. Clement judges the deaths of these Christians futile on the basis that they do not know God. Yet Clement characterizes them as those who rush on to death, hating the creator, to the extent that they are athletes of death. It is this characteristic that is evidence that they do not know God.

49. The New Testament traditions of radical martyrdom are fully explored in Chapter 5, below.

account were they to seek martyrdom, nor provoke it. It is therefore, Clement's 'third way' that has influenced the way in which historians have viewed the actions of those Christians who chose death. That enthusiasts for martyrdom existed is not denied, but they have been judged as veering from the orthodox line. The voices that articulated a strong desire for death within early Christianity have been, with some embarrassment, covered up. 'It is true that Christians sometimes were *guilty* of deliberate provocation. But the model which was commended as *normative* Christian conduct showed a more submissive demeanour in its resistance.'[50] For Ferguson, provoking martyrdom is something of which one could be *guilty*.

While provoked martyrdom came to be despised, it is, using Bauer's language, a phenomenon that was simply Christianity for many second-century Christians. Therefore, those Christians who believed that martyrdom was the greatest service they could offer to God have had their actions dismissed as 'aberrations and excesses',[51] and certainly not orthodox: 'It is an established tradition within *the Christianity which became identified as orthodox* that those who intentionally sought martyrdom would not be recognised as martyrs.'[52] Even Ignatius' desire for death has been dismissed as 'a neurotic death-wish',[53] an 'abnormal mentality',[54] or a morbid obsession,[55] and certainly not the 'normal' attitude to martyrdom.[56] Of course, this leaves us with the question of just what the 'normal' attitude to martyrdom was and, more importantly how, or even whether, we today should adjudicate between competing ancient theologies claiming to represent the true voice of the Church.

The Quintus Pericope

Those who defend the traditional reading of early Christian attitudes to martyrdom point to the description of a failed radical death in *The Martyrdom of Polycarp*:

> There was a Phrygian named Quintus who had only recently come from Phrygia, and when he saw the wild animals he turned cowardly. Now he was the one who had given himself up and had forced some others to give themselves up voluntarily. With him the governor used many arguments and persuaded him to swear by the gods and offer sacrifice. *This is the reason, brothers, that we do not approve of those who come forward of themselves: this is not the teaching of the gospel.*[57]

50. Ferguson, 'Early Christian martyrdom', 81 (emphasis added).
51. Amundsen, 'Lust after death', 18.
52. M. Reasoner, 'Persecution', in R.P. Martin and P.H. Davids (eds), *Dictionary of the Later New Testament* (Downers Grove, IL: InterVarsity Press, 1997), 907–14 (913) (emphasis added).
53. K.R. Morris, '"Pure wheat of God" or neurotic deathwish?: a historical and theological analysis of Ignatius of Antioch's zeal for martyrdom', *Fides et Historia* 26 (1994), 24–41.
54. Ste Croix, 'Why were the early Christians persecuted?', 24.
55. G.W. Williams, *The Sanctity of Life and the Criminal Law* (New York: Knopf, 2nd edn, 1970), 254.
56. A.B. Luter, 'Martyrdom', in R.P. Martin and P.H. Davids (eds), *Dictionary of the Later New Testament and Its Development* (Downer Grove, IL: InterVarsity Press 1996), 717–22 (720).
57. *Mart. Pol.* 4 (emphasis added).

In this text, presenting oneself for arrest is criticised; it is not the teaching of the gospel.[58] Here, it seems, is clear evidence that radical martyrdom was disapproved of in the mid-second century.

However, there are several problems with this conclusion. First of all, it is not altogether clear whether Quintus is really criticized for giving himself up, or for the fact that he denied. If it really is the former, then the logic would demand that the author thought that everyone who gave themselves up ended up denying. This is clearly not the case. It is only Quintus' *denial* that enables the conclusion, 'This is the reason, brothers, that we do not approve of those who come forward of themselves'. Had Quintus not denied, this conclusion could not have followed.[59] The pericope represents an unconvincing and rather clumsy reproof of radical martyrdom.

Secondly, it is not clear that the Quintus pericope is quite at home in its present location. We are not prepared for it, neither is it referred to again in the whole work. The unit actually interrupts the flow of the story, and of course, as we have just noted, it does not fulfil its function entirely convincingly. Immediately before the incident, the crowd call out, 'Away with these atheists! Go and get Polycarp' (3.2). There then follows the information about Quintus (4), before a report of Polycarp hearing (ἀκούσας) something, yet not being disturbed and deciding to stay in Smyrna (5.1).[60] If the Quintus paragraph be allowed to stand in its place, then it would seem that Polycarp hears of Quintus' action and, on the basis of not being disturbed by his cowardice, decides to stay in Smyrna. This is just about possible, but when the Quintus paragraph is omitted there is the more pleasing result:

> [The crowd] shouted, 'Away with these atheists! Go and get Polycarp'. Now at first when the most admirable Polycarp heard of this, he was not disturbed and even decided to stay in Smyrna; but most people advised him to slip out quietly, and so he left ...

The sense of the narrative now flows more logically. Polycarp hears that the crowd has called for him to be arrested, yet being untroubled by them decides at first to stay in Smyrna. However, others are more alarmed by the threat of his arrest and persuade him to leave the city.

Granted, there are no extant manuscripts that do not include the Quintus pericope. However, given that the earliest of the six manuscripts of Pseudo-Pionius, which preserve the complete text as we have it, dates from the tenth

---

58. Οὐκ οὕτως διδάσκει τὸ εὐαγγέλιον. Cf. *A. Cyprian* 1.5.

59. This appears to be the position of Peter of Alexander (*Canon* 9). Those who give themselves up are not to be criticized so long as they follow through with their confession.

60. Some writers are at pains to point out that Polycarp is not seeking death. So Luter ('Martyrdom', 721) can say, 'Polycarp does not seek martyrdom, but refusing to take an oath to Caesar, he accepts his execution with steadfast courage'. However, he does not flee when given the opportunity, which is precisely the course of action upon which Clement would come to insist. Ultimately, those who would later follow Polycarp's example would be dismissed as being deviant in their attitude to martyrdom.

century,[61] it is entirely possible that a good deal of redactional activity took place in its transmission. This is made all the more likely since the Pseudo-Pionius tradition diverges from the much earlier Eusebius account to quite a large degree.[62]

A motive for inserting the Quintus story may have been to counter a Montanist movement that encouraged more enthusiastic martyrs.[63] The interpolation hypothesis solves an important dating issue, for although most commentators date the writing of Polycarp in either the sixth or seventh decade of the second century,[64] this is too early for the Montanist controversy. When Frend reaches the end of the second century in his study, he remarks, 'If there are grounds for believing that the Quintus story in the Acts of Polycarp is an insertion, this would be the period for it.'[65] Those grounds are compelling, if not conclusive.

If the Quintus paragraph is later than Clement, then Clement, writing near the close of the second century, becomes the *first* voice tempering that of those who were enthusiastic for death. No Christian voice before Clement condemns those who rush towards death, or those who provocatively give themselves up to arrest. Even if the Quintus story was originally part of a mid-first-century narrative, then there is still a substantive difference from Clement, in that the ground for criticizing Quintus' action is the fact that he turned cowardly (the radical martyrs would certainly also severely criticize Quintus). This fact, together with the need for Clement to address the situation, points in the direction of the conclusion that radical martyrdom, rather than a more circumspect attitude to death, would have been at the very least a popular position of Christians in the second century,[66] in presentation if not in practice.[67]

61. For the manuscript, see Bisbee, *Pre-Decian Acts*, 82 n. 12.

62. The differences between the two traditions are exploited by H. von Campenhausen, 'Bearbeitung und Interpolationen des Polykarpmartyriums', in *Aus der Frühzeit des Christentums: Studien zur Kirchengeschichte des ersten und zweiten Jahrhunderts* (Tübingen: J.C.B. Mohr [Paul Siebeck], 1963), 253–301, while the integrity of the letter and the priority of Ps.-Pionius are defended by Barnes, 'Pre-Decian *Acta Martryum*', 510–14, and Buschmann, *Martyrium des Polykarp*. Bisbee (*Pre-Decian Acts*, 119–32) also offers discussion and comparison of the two texts, concluding that although Eusebius preserves an older form, even his version shows evidence of redaction.

63. See especially Buschmann (*Martyrium des Polykarp*) who regards the whole narrative to be combating Montanists! Droge and Tabor (*Noble Death*, 160 n. 26) meanwhile, though accepting that *Polycarp* has undergone redaction, see no need to reach the conclusion that the paragraph reflects an anti-Montanist position. The conclusion of Droge and Tabor is influenced overmuch by their insistence that no distinction should be drawn between the Montanist and third-century 'orthodox' attitudes to martyrdom.

64. See discussion in B.A.G.M. Dehandschutter, 'The Martyrium Polycarpi: a century of research', *ANRW* II.27.1. (1993), 485–522 (497–502); and Bisbee, *Pre-Decian Acts*, 119–21.

65. Frend, *Martyrdom and Persecution*, 347.

66. This point holds true even if the Quintus pericope is original as it demonstrates that radical martyrdom was important enough to merit discussion.

67. As we will see below, would-be martyrs were often thwarted by governors unwilling to carry through mass execution.

Rediscovering the Radical Martyrs

Many voices contemporary with Clement demonstrate some resistance to the direction he takes. Whereas Clement accuses the radicals of hatred towards the Creator because they did not attempt to avoid persecution and death, Tertullian, in contrast, urges Christians to do nothing to avoid death, including flight in the face of persecution: 'Fight not flight', he sloganizes.[68] The distinction between welcoming martyrdom when it comes and seeking it is a fine distinction in any case. We shall see that approval of martyrdom is not dependent on whether or not the death was voluntary or provoked. Indeed, we shall see that, in many cases, unambiguously provoked deaths, and even self-killing, are praised.

Problems with Clement

Clement accuses the radical martyrs of not knowing God. Therefore, their deaths are, de facto, futile. It is at least interesting that Clement in these criticisms sounds like a Gnostic critic of so-called 'orthodox' martyrdom. The Gnostics accused those who embraced martyrdom of being self-murderers, a charge employed by Clement. As well as being 'athletes of death', he accuses the radical martyrs of 'doing away with themselves'.[69]

The crucial question is now (to take Clement on his own terms) whether Clement is here representing the 'orthodox' tradition of the second century or whether he has broken from the tradition of martyrdom or, less negatively, adapted it for a new century. Clement does not judge this group on their actions. They are killed and look like martyrs, yet Clement constructs a narrative around these deaths to deny them the designation of martyr. Put simply, they do not know God, and therefore, despite any action they take, they could never be martyrs. Clement's discourse 'unmakes' these martyrs.

One significant fact that may account for Clement's view of martyrdom (and it is open to question whether he successfully navigates a convincing position between the two he condemns) is that when persecution broke out in Alexandria at the beginning of the third century, rather than stay, as Tertullian would have urged, Clement discreetly fled the city![70] One further factor, and it would be more charitable to identify this as Clement's main concern, is that too many Christians whom he considered heretical on other grounds were getting themselves martyred. If a Christian group could claim to be 'orthodox' by the number of martyrs they produced, then clearly a heretical group that could produce martyrs would cause some problems.

---

68. Tertullian, *Fuga* 9. Tertullian maintains that it is a Christian's duty to undergo martyrdom (*Scorp.* 2).

69. The phrase ἐξάγειν ἑαυτούς became the standard term in the Hellenistic period onward for suicide. See A.J.L. van Hooff, *From Autothanasia to Suicide: Self-Killing in Classical Antiquity* (London/New York: Routledge, 1990), 140, 188; Bowersock, *Martyrdom and Rome*, 68.

70. Droge and Tabor, *Noble Death*, 143.

If martyrdom was a sign of devotion to Christ, a true mark of discipleship, then Montanists and Marcionites contributed their fair share of martyrs.[71] Therefore, if the church had groups on the one hand whose doctrine and practice could be criticized on the account that they produced no martyrs, here were groups on the opposite side who *did* produce martyrs, yet their doctrine was somehow wayward. The sheer number of martyrs coming from so-called 'heretical' groups goes some way in explaining the waning enthusiasm for martyrdom among the so-called 'orthodox'. Here too was the beginning of the association of heresy with radical martyrdom.

Several factors suggest that Clement was indeed departing from a traditional, enthusiastic view of martyrdom in the second century. First, there is Clement's own internal friction. In his haste to condemn heretical groups who happen to lay great importance on the value of martyrdom, he finds himself using the criticisms used by the Gnostics who despised martyrdom, and using their argument for precisely the same reason. The writer of the *Testimony of Truth*, as zealous in attacking heresy as any of the so-called orthodox,[72] like Clement, claimed that those who gave themselves for martyrdom were destroying themselves.[73]

Clement is left steering a difficult middle course between an enthusiasm for martyrdom discernible in his own writings and criticism of that same enthusiasm when it appears in a different group. In doing so, he employs some of the arguments made by the 'Gnostic' sects, which he himself despises. What is clear, however, is that not only did many of the earliest Christian martyrs not seek to avoid death, they actually welcomed and sought it.

Radical Martyrdom in the Early Church

For the 'Gnostics', a martyr's death was meaningless, yet, for other Christians, to die for Christ was glory. 'The fighter does not complain of feeling pain – he wishes it … excited more by victory than injury'.[74] For those who embraced radical martyrdom, the rallying call, typified by Tertullian, was to take control of one's own death. 'Desire not to die on bridal beds, nor in miscarriages,[75] nor in soft fevers, but to die the martyr's death, that He may be glorified who has suffered for you.'[76]

Even when there was a lack of persecution, some Christians found a way to die. A good example of radical martyrdom, coming from as late as the early

71. Bauer (*Orthodoxy and Heresy*) writes, 'There were … more martyrs from among the Marcionites and Montanists, and other heretical groups than orthodoxy would like to admit, and the church took great pains to divest this fact of its significance and seductive splendour'. See *op. cit.*, 136–7, for more on The Anonymous of Eusebius' attack on Montanism, and 135–45 for a favourable description of Montanism.

72. B.A. Pearson, 'The Testimony of Truth', *NHL*, 449.

73. See above, 24–5.

74. Tertullian, *Scorp.* 6.

75. It is interesting that Tertuallian expects women martyrs too. One of the characteristic marks of Christian martyrdom over pagan 'Noble Death' tradition is the far higher proportion of women who undergo death in the Christian tradition. This theme is explored further in Chapter 4.

76. Tertullian, *Fuga* 9.

fourth century, is that of Euplus.[77] 'Outside the veil in front of the prefect's council chamber, a man named Euplus shouted out to them and said, "I want to die; I am a Christian" '.[78] In the text, Euplus' course of action is never condemned. He is later called 'the blessed (μακάριος) Euplus'. He is tried and tortured in order to force him to sacrifice to the gods, but he resisted, and after a long torture, he finally 'endured the contest of martyrdom (τὸν τοῦ μαρτυρίους ἀγῶνα) and received the crown of orthodox belief (ὀρθοδόξου πίστεως)'.[79] For enduring torture, Euplus, despite his voluntary arrest, is counted among the ranks of the blessed martyrs, and received the unfading crown.[80]

The Latin recension goes even further, insisting that it is a Law of Christ (*lex domini mei*) to seek out death.[81] Clearly, the difference between Euplus' story and the Quintus pericope is that, while both handed themselves over of their own accord, Euplus maintained his testimony whereas Quintus denied.

As late as the beginning of the fourth century, therefore, radical martyrs were honoured in spite of the warnings of Clement a century earlier. Many other examples of such behaviour litter the history of the Church. Sometimes, Euplus' direct approach was taken not merely by individuals, but by whole crowds of Christians. In what may be an exaggerated story, Tertullian recounts an occasion where the 'Euplus phenomenon' affected a whole town, when all the Christians presented themselves to a bemused proconsul of Asia, Arrius Antonius, demanding to be martyred. 'On ordering a few persons to be led forth to execution, he said to the rest, "O miserable men, if you wish to die, you have cliffs and nooses!" '[82]

Tertullian clearly approved of the actions of the Christians of Asia and, from his account of the response of the official, it is clear that the proconsul saw the Christians' death-seeking as being indistinguishable from suicide. Tertullian threatens the proconsul to whom he is writing with the same behaviour.

> Your cruelty is our glory. Only see you to it, that in having such things as these to endure, *we do not feel ourselves constrained to rush forth to the combat*, if only to prove that we have no dread of them, but on the contrary, *even invite their infliction*.[83]

Therefore, a significant body of early Christians held giving themselves up to death as an ideal, even to the point of provoking those in authority who would otherwise have left them alone.

---

77. *A. Euplus*. The date given is 304 (see Musurillo, *ACM, xlv* for discussion). The legal basis of Euplus' condemnation is perhaps his flagrant disobedience of Diocletian's edict banning the Christian scriptures, which were to be handed in or burned (see Ste Croix, 'Why were the Christians persecuted?', 22). In the Latin version, Euplus is led to the place of execution with a copy of the scriptures around his neck (*A. Euplus* [Latin], 3).

78. *A. Euplus* 1.1.
79. *A. Euplus* 2.2.
80. *A. Euplus* 2.4.
81. *A. Euplus* (Latin) 1.6.
82. Tertullian, *Scap.* 5.1.
83. Tertullian, *Scap.* 5.1 (emphasis added).

Secondary Martyrdom

There is another form of martyrdom which falls between the radicalized volitional martyrdom that we have so far investigated and the form favoured by Clement, where flight was an acceptable option to avoid death. This is the act of self-disclosure at the trials of other Christians which causes arrest and execution, a phenomenon that has been dubbed *secondary martyrdom*.[84] This is not precisely the same as radical martyrdom as we have encountered it. On strictly historical grounds, the inclusion of this type of martyrdom may appear questionable. However, the literary presentation of these martyrs does place them quite close to our radical martyrs.

Justin, in his second apology, recounts a story of a Christian woman who divorces her husband on the grounds of immoral behaviour.[85] The husband exacts revenge by filing a complaint against her, a *divortium sine causa*,[86] adding that she was a Christian. He also arranged for a centurion friend to denounce his former wife's teacher, Ptolemaeus. In court when Ptolemaeus admits to being Christian, a certain observer, Lucius, outraged by the unreasonableness of the sentence protested:

> What is the charge? He has not been convicted of adultery, fornication, murder, clothes stealing, robbery, or of any crime whatsoever; yet you have punished this man because he confesses the name of Christian?[87]

Lucius was then simply asked if he too was one of them,[88] 'and when Lucius said, "Indeed I am," he [the governor] ordered him to be executed as well … Next a third man also deserted and was sentenced to be punished.'[89]

A similar sequence of events occurs in the account of the persecution of Christians at Lyons. After an outbreak of mob violence against Christians, they were subjected to cruelty by the court. Vettius Epagathus, a young man who 'walked blamelessly in all the commandments and precepts of the Lord … possessing great devotion to God and fervour in spirit',[90] unable to bear the injustice of the situation, requested a hearing so as to speak in defence of the Christians:

> Although he was a distinguished person, the crowd around the tribunal shouted him down. The prefect dismissed the just request that he had put forward and merely asked him if he too were a Christian. When he confessed (ὁμολογήσαντος) he was in clearest tones, he too was accepted into the ranks of the martyrs (τὸν κλῆπον τῶν μαρτύρων).[91]

Had he said nothing, he would have lived, nor would he be considered to be a denier. Although this is not equivalent to the action of say Euplus, Epagathus

---

84. See Droge and Tabor, *Noble Death*, 132.
85. Recorded as *Mart. Ptol.*
86. Musurillo, *ACM*, 39 n. 1.
87. *Mart. Ptol.* 16.
88. Musurillo (*ACM*, 41 n. 14) notes the allusion to the question put to Peter (Mk 14.70), noting that 'Lucius gives a far more courageous reply'.
89. *Mart. Ptol.* 17–20.
90. *Mart. Lyons* 1.9.
91. *Mart. Lyons* 1.10.

drew attention to himself, presented himself for arrest, and undertook a course of action that inevitably led to certain death. In the praise of Epagathus, the *voluntary* nature of his death is stressed:

> Called the Christians' advocate, he possessed the Advocate within him … which he demonstrated by the fullness of his love, *consenting as he did to lay down his life* in defence of his fellow Christians. He was and is a true disciple of Christ following the Lamb wherever he goes.[92]

Whatever the original motivation of Epagathus may have been – most likely, a protest against such injustice without imagining it would result in martyrdom – the author *interprets* Epagathus' action as an example of voluntary death.

The Acts of Cyprian

Even the more 'orthodox' position where it is found often sits uncomfortably alongside a zeal for death. In the *Acts of Cyprian*, the so-called 'orthodox' position is stated: 'our discipline forbids anyone to surrender voluntarily'.[93] However, after his arrest, when Cyprian is asked where the rest of the Christians are, he informs the governor, rather revealingly, 'They may not give themselves up. But if they are sought out by you they will be found.'[94] This statement could certainly be read as saying that the Christians would not take Clement's course of action and flee the city rather than be arrested. However, the conclusion of the story is more dramatic. There is no need for the governor to search them out, for as Cyprian is led to his death, in a scene similar to that which Tertullian describes, the missing Christians all present themselves voluntarily *en masse* to the authorities, wishing to die:

> Then he read from a tablet, 'Thanscius Cyprian is sentenced to die by the sword'.
>   The bishop Cyprian said, 'Thanks be to God!'
>   After the sentence, the crowd of his fellow Christians said, 'Let us also be beheaded with him!'[95]

This is no mere protest. The crowd are cast as being willing to undergo radicalized death. Martyrdom was infectious!

Saturus

Earlier still, in the *Passion of Perpetua and Felicitas*, we come to an important case of radical martyrdom, that of the church leader Saturus. In Perpetua's vision, he was the first to 'ascend the ladder'.[96] He was a crucial element of Perpetua's

---

92. *Mart. Lyons* 1.10 (emphasis added).
93. *A. Cyprian* 1.5.
94. *A. Cyprian* 1.5.
95. *A. Cyprian* 4.3–5.1. We are not told what happened to this group of Christians. Like Tertullian's crowd, we may assume that their demand was not fulfilled since the author would almost certainly have recorded it. Secondly, Cyprian's body was removed from where it had been laid out to be buried and there were sufficient Christians to form a procession.
96. *Mart. Perpetua* 4.5. The ladder appears to be the arena of confession, and ascending it is to navigate the interrogation successfully. At the foot of the ladder is a dragon (4.4) that attempts

church, no less than the 'builder of our strength'. However, he had not been with the group when they were arrested. We are told that Saturus ended up in prison because *he gave himself up of his own accord.*[97] Despite unambiguously giving himself up in circumstances which Clement would certainly condemn, in the *Passion of Perpetua*, Saturus is held up as a noble example to follow. Unlike Quintus, of course, Saturus followed up his voluntary arrest with confession and death. Explicitly, therefore, handing oneself over to the authorities is not only tolerated but also encouraged.

Agathonicê

Finally, radical death reaches a climax at the conclusion of the *Martyrdom of Carpus, Papylus and Agathonicê*. Here, we witness not only a radical martyrdom, but a self-killing. Agathonicê is a member of the crowd who witnesses the martyrdom of Carpus and Papylus. Carpus, before he dies, sees a vision of the glory of the Lord (τὴν δόξαν κυρίου),[98] a vision in which Agathonicê also shares.

> Realising that this was a call from heaven, she raised her voice at once, 'Here is a meal that has been prepared for me. I must partake and eat of this glorious feast!'
> The mob shouted out, 'Have pity on your son!'
> And the blessed Agathonicê said, 'He has God who can take pity on him; for he has providence over all. Let me do what I have come for!' And taking off her cloak, she threw herself joyfully upon the stake.[99]

What may be regarded as Agathonicê's completely unprovoked 'suicide' is not condemned and, even though there is no evidence in the Greek recension to suggest she was anything other than a pagan bystander,[100] she too is considered part of the rank of martyrs:

> And she thus gave up her spirit and died together with the saints. And the Christians secretly collected their remains and protected them for the glory of Christ and the praise of his martyrs.[101]

To be sure, the description of Agathonicê seeing a vision indicates that the author presents the event as a conversion experience, but her response to that vision is to kill herself without trial, without confession, and, importantly, without condemnation. The claim then that suicide has never been an acceptable activity within Christianity is undermined by the presentation of Agathonicê's death.[102]

---

to scare those who would ascend, representing the torture and the wild beasts designed to make apostates. As the first step Perpetua takes is on the dragon's head, the scene demonstrates that ascending the ladder and winning martyrdom is the method by which the dragon (Satan) is defeated.

97. *Mart. Perpetua* 4.5 (emphasis added).
98. *Cf.* Acts 7.55.
99. *Mart. Carpus* 42–4.
100. See Droge and Tabor, *Noble Death*, 138.
101. *Mart. Carpus* 47 (emphasis added).
102. This is very important for Droge and Tabor's project (*Noble Death*). The historicity of

Interestingly, we see later development towards 'orthodoxy' and away from radical martyrdom in the retelling of Agathonicê's story in the Latin recension. For it is only in the Greek recension of the text that her death is portrayed as a self-killing. In the Latin recension, Agathonicê is given a more orthodox martyrdom. She is provided with a trial, and so is brought before the proconsul after the death of Carpus. When she refuses to offer sacrifice, even for the sake of her children (to which, like the Greek recension, she answers, 'My children have God who watches over them'),[103] she is hung on a stake and burned.

Though Musurillo is certainly correct that the Latin text is an abridgement of the older Greek text,[104] his suggestion that there is a lacuna in the Greek text is unlikely.[105] It is difficult to turn Agathonicê's suicide into a more traditional martyr account merely by the addition of text. It is more plausible that Agathonicê's voluntary suicide was transformed into a more 'orthodox'-looking martyrdom as such acts of suicide/unprovoked death came to be despised, though applauded in the second century. In the Latin recension, Agathonicê's narrative undergoes what may be termed 'orthodox corruption'.[106]

Therefore, in the transformation of Agathonicê's death, we see the rewriting of martyrological discourse in action. Although undoubtedly recognized as a martyr by the author of the Greek recension, those who would later retell her story 'deradicalized' her death. When faced with such martyrs, there were two options open for the 'orthodox' revisionists: condemn them as heretics, or rewrite their stories. Clement chose the former, when he dubbed even those who made confession before the authorities, 'athletes of death'. Agathonicê's Latin biographers chose the latter course of action. Both groups consciously rewrote the history of Christian martyrology; both groups 'unmade' the radical martyrs.

Willing Death

As I have argued, radical martyrdom was, despite the efforts of the 'orthodox' revisionists, a course of action chosen, and even valorized, by Christians in the second- and early third-century Church. In early Christian martyrologies, voluntary death is not condemned; indeed, it is the voluntary nature of the Christian's death that is often stressed.

Even in the arena, the voluntary nature of the martyr's death is emphasized; it is the martyrs who bring about, or at least choose, their moment death. For example, the portrayal of Perpetua's death indicates that she died only because of her active co-operation:

Agathonicê's death is not of central importance. The interesting issue is why an author chose to present this death as a self-killing rather than a more 'orthodox'-looking martyrdom. Again, the conclusion that radical martyrdom was not a fringe concern commends itself.

103. *Mart. Carpus* (Latin) 6.3.
104. Musurillo, *ACM*, xv.
105. *ACM*, xvi.
106. Compare B.D. Ehrman, *The Orthodox Corruption of Scripture: The Effect of Early Christological Controversies on the Text of the New Testament* (Oxford: Oxford University Press, 1993).

> Perpetua ... had yet to taste more pain. She screamed as she was struck on the bone;
> then she took the hand of the young gladiator and guided it to her throat. It was as
> though so great a woman, feared as she was by the unclean spirit, *could not be killed
> unless she was willing.*[107]

The presentation of Perpetua's death is such that she *could* only be killed if she
was willing to die. Obviously, questions of historicity could be raised, but they are
beside the point. On a literary and theological level, the narrator affirms the power
of the martyr over Satan; he is unable to despatch her without her consent.[108]

Similarly, Carpus, Papylus and Agathonicê are said to have 'given up' their
lives,[109] and Germanicus drags the wild beasts upon himself to effect his death.[110]
Added to the examples above, we see not only that the Christian martyrs welcomed death to the point of seeking it out, but also that in many instances, even
at the point of death, the protagonists of the martyr acts are presented as being
very much in control of their deaths. Death is welcomed, and the writers of these
stories suggest that the moment to depart the earthly world is in the martyrs' own
hands. What we find in the earliest martyr acts is the conviction that the Christians should take control of their own deaths.

Interestingly, when Tertullian seeks examples for the Christians to model
themselves on, he enthusiastically recounts incidents of voluntary deaths, including self-killings among pagans such as Lucretia, Empedocles, Heraclitus and
Cleopatra,[111] and then calls on Christians to exceed these actions: 'Are we not
called on, then, most joyfully to lay out as much for the true as others do for the
false?'[112] As with Agathonicê, Tertullian's enthusiastic call for Christians to
surpass the example of pagans who took their own lives, demonstrates the intriguing possibility that what would be called suicide today was, at least theoretically,
an acceptable form of martyrdom in the early Church. Tertullian has no difficulty
in invoking courageous pagan self-killing as positive examples for Christian
martyrdom.

Therefore, we witness within the Church of the first three centuries a very
positive attitude towards death and martyrdom, as well as an unmistakable call
for others to follow suit. From the witness of the texts that the Christians produced, martyrdom was sought after: both active self-killing, and the far more
prevalent 'passive suicide',[113] the more traditional form of martyrdom. Perhaps

107. *Mart. Perpetua* 21.8–10 (emphasis added).
108. The *Passion of Perpetua* is explored in some detail below, 98–101.
109. Παρέδωκεν τὴν ψυχήν (37) /ἀπέδωκεν τὴν ψυχήν (41)/ἀπέδωκεν τὸ πνεῦμα (47) for
Papylus, Carpus and Agathonicê respectively. After their sentence of death, Carpus and Papylus
rushed to the amphitheatre 'that they might all the more quickly depart from the world' (36).
Similarly, Polycarp also rushes 'eagerly and quickly' towards the place of execution (*Mart. Pol.* 8).
110. *Mart. Pol.* 3.
111. Lucretia killed herself when her honour was questioned, Heraclitus smeared himself with
cow dung and set light to himself, Empedocles jumped into Mount Etna, and Cleopatra allowed
herself to be bitten by an asp.
112. Tertullian, *Ad Martyras* 4.
113. Importantly, even the so-called orthodox interpretation of martyrdom falls comfortably
within Durkheim's classical definition of suicide ('Any case of death which results, directly or

the phenomenon with which we are dealing may be accurately termed *Roman-assisted suicide*, or at the very least *Christian-assisted execution*!

Pagan Perceptions of Christianity as a Death Cult

Pagans, unaware of the multiplicity of views of martyrdom amongst groups claiming the name Christian, were nonetheless aware of the zeal for death among adherents to the new religion. In many instances this is precisely what Christians were known for; it was the manner of their deaths that brought them to pagan attention. We now examine the ways in which Christians were perceived by the pagans in regard to their attitude to death.[114] This alternative perspective will provide an external balance to that of Christian self-representation. I have argued that radical martyrdom, that is, an enthusiasm for death, was prevalent among the earliest Christians to the point where the faithful would willingly give themselves up. If their pagan neighbours confirm this impression, then the view of the early Christians' stance concerning martyrdom in the first three centuries will have to be dramatically rethought.

Lucian, writing in the second century, says about the Christians:

> The poor wretches have convinced themselves, first and foremost, that they are going to be immortal and live forever, in consequence of which they despise death *and even willingly give themselves over to arrest*.[115]

Similarly, Marcus Cornelius Fronto (c. 100–166) reflects the observations that Christians have no fear of death: 'They despise torments ... while they fear to die after death, they do not fear to die for the present: so does their deceitful hope soothe their fear with the solace of a revival'.[116] To Epictetus, this lack of fear

---

indirectly, from an act, positive or negative, accomplished by the victim himself and in the knowledge that it would necessarily produce this result'). E. Durkheim, *Suicide: A Study in Sociology* (trans. J.A. Spaulding and G. Simpson; London: Routledge, 2002). He writes (67), '[The martyrs] without killing themselves, voluntarily allowed their own slaughter ... Though they did not kill themselves, they sought death with all their power and behaved so as to make it inevitable.' However, this definition blurs more than it clarifies. Of course, self-killing in the ancient world did not attract anything like the negative moral judgement that it carries today. A fuller treatment of this theme is offered in Chapter 4.

There is a growing concern to equate ancient martyrdom with suicide, offset by an equally vociferous concern to resist the equation. This is because of a growing concern with the moral questions surrounding doctor-assisted suicide; see especially Droge and Tabor, *Noble Death*. This has been one more factor that has inhibited scholars from accepting that the evidence points in the direction of the prevalent enthusiasm for radical martyrdom in the early Church. Although appropriation of the early Christians in the debate on doctor-assisted suicide is questionable, one modern phenomenon that appears to be curiously similar is that of 'suicide by cop'. This alarming occurrence, where young (mainly) men provoke police officers into killing them accounts for some 10 per cent of fatal shootings by the police in America (K.R. Jamison, *Night Falls Fast: Understanding Suicide* [London: Picador, 2000], 134); see also http://www.policepsychconsult.com/suicide.htm.

114. A fuller treatment of the general reception of Christians by pagans is given below, 61–8.

115. Lucian, *Peregrinus* 13 (emphasis added).

116. Municius Felix, *Octavius* 8–9. *Octavius* is a Christian apologetic work, set out as a dialogue

and drive for death was madness.[117] He dismissed the readiness of Christians for death as mere habit,[118] demonstrating that, so far as Epictetus was concerned, Christians were so associated with contempt for death as to be unreflective.[119] These three witnesses corroborate the conclusions we drew from the Christian texts.

What Epictetus knows about the Christians is that they are death-seekers, and Lucian confirms that they do present themselves for condemnation. To be sure, each of these witnesses is hostile, but crucially they confirm what many of the Christian texts point towards. These witnesses, of course, were unaware of the details of Christian theology that caused them to act in such ways, but, from what they observed, the Christians had what appeared to the Romans as an unnatural 'lust for death'. If pagans knew anything about the Christians, it was their preparedness for death, but more so, to the outsider, Christianity appeared to be a death-seeking cult.

However, governors were not always ready to offer the Christians the death they so eagerly sought. Perigrinus, when he sought death was thwarted by his release,[120] and we have already noted Tertullian's story of a governor telling would-be martyrs that there were plenty of cliffs and rope if they really wanted to die. Sometimes despite the best efforts of the Christians, the authorities would not oblige. Indeed, so strong could be the urge for Christian death that Justin was forced to argue why straightforward suicide was not an option for Christians, and, importantly, the reason that Justin gives is not that there is something morally wrong with self-killing, rather, if that course of action was taken then no one would then hear the message.[121]

Marcus Aurelius found the spectacle of Christian martyrdom distasteful when compared to the noble deaths of the Romans.[122] He complained that Christians regarded their deaths as spectacles: 'Death should be without dramatics if it is to convince anyone else'.[123] Therefore, Christians appear to be known, perhaps even defined in pagan eyes as the sect that sought death. This fact, taken together with the significant body of Christian evidence pointing in the same direction, renders as suspicious the long tradition of dismissing radical martyrs as aberrations and

between the Christian, Octavius, and the pagan Caecilius, on a journey from Rome to Ostia. Muncius acts as both narrator and arbitrator. The work shows some similarity with Tertullian's *Apology*, although which one is earlier is debated: see S.F.R. Price, 'Latin Christian apologetics: Minucius Felix, Tertullian, and Cyprian' (in M. Edwards, M. Goodman and S. Price, *Apologetics in the Roman Empire: Pagans, Jews, and Christians* [Oxford: Oxford University Press, 1999], 105–29), 111–12. A date anywhere between 160 and 250 CE is therefore possible. However, Frend (*Martyrdom and Persecution*, 252) suggests that this quotation may record an opinion against the Christians current in the decade 150–60 in Rome.

117. Epictetus, *Discourses*, 4.7.1–6.
118. Epictetus, *Discourses*, 4.7.6.
119. Perkins, *Suffering Self*, 20.
120. Lucian, *Peregrinus* 14.
121. Justin, *Apol.* II.4.
122. For a discussion of Noble Death, see below, 116–23.
123. Marcus Aurelius, *Meditations* 11.3.

heretics, relegated to the footnotes in scholarly discussion of the history, theology and origins of martyrdom.

Clearly, within early Christianity, a significant movement had a strong desire for death. It is an attitude of which Pothinus, Bishop of Lyons, is paradigmatic. Even though the young people, who had just been arrested and had not suffered bodily torture before, could not support the burden of imprisonment and died in prison,[124] Pothinus, who was over ninety years of age and physically quite infirm, was given divine strength to survive prison that he might die before the crowds, because of his lust for martyrdom (διὰ τὴν ἐγκειμένην τῆς μαρτυρίας ἐπιθυμίαν).[125]

Conclusion

In one major strand of early Christian practice, a radical zeal for martyrdom may be witnessed, a zeal that can be traced throughout the second century but broken, to some extent, by Clement and Cyprian. Perhaps the association of radical martyrdom with 'heretical' movements was the most significant factor in the sidelining of radical martyrdom, both in history, and in subsequent dealing with the data. The baby of radical zeal for martyrdom was thrown out with the bath water of heresy. This change paved the way for martyrdom to be spiritualised through the practising of asceticism in the fourth and fifth centuries.[126]

In any case we may observe that attitudes to martyrdom among Christian groups in the second century could be plotted on a sliding scale from outright condemnation of martyrdom to a burning, zealous urge to bring about one's own death. Wherever one judges the 'majority' opinion lies, there is clearly the conviction, held by a substantial number of Christians, that death should not be feared, but welcomed, even to the point of seeking it out, or at the very least doing little or nothing to avoid it. There is little warrant, however, for judging these Christians to be heretical, unorthodox, or denying to them the honorific title of martyr.

Clement, as one who fled when presented with the situation of persecution, urged the same course of action for all Christians, declaring that those who did not avoid capture were accomplices in the 'crime of the persecutor'.[127] As we

---

124. For a particularly illuminating study into the conditions prisoners had to endure in Roman prisons, see C.S. Wansink, *Chained in Christ: The Experience and Rhetoric of Paul's Imprisonments* (JSNTSup, 130; Sheffield: Sheffield Academic Press, 1996), 26–95.

125. *Mart. Lyons* 1.29. Compare with Paul's desire to leave this life to be with Christ (Phil. 1.23), τὴν ἐπιθυμίαν ἔχων εἰς τὸ ἀναλῦσαι.

126. After Christianity became legalized, the opportunity to win martyrdom disappeared. Therefore, martyr language came to be associated with those who practised solitude and asceticism, battling, as it were, principalities and powers rather than Roman soldiers; see E.E. Malone, *The Monk and the Martyr: The Monk as the Successor of the Martyr* (Washington, DC: The Catholic University of America Press, 1950). Compare the popular interpretation of Mk 8.34, which is normally associated with denying oneself pleasures during Lent rather than a reference to martyrdom.

127. Clement, *Strom.* 4.77.1.

have seen, most of the second-century heroes did precisely what Clement denounces. They did not avoid persecution, but instead waited, knowing they would be captured. In many cases, they did give themselves up, either directly, or exposed themselves in defence of their fellow Christians. Moreover, where there was a contest in the arena, the narratives show not only provocation but also direct challenging of the wild beasts, with the martyrs 'choosing' the moment of their deaths. Many Christians are praised where they provoked certain death for themselves or, at the very least, did not avoid persecution.

Nonetheless, it was Clement's position that was finally developed and crystallized in the fourth-century council of Elvira.[128] Those who engaged in radical martyrdom, including those who insulted local cults, were judged not to be true martyrs. Similarly, Mesurius of Carthage refused the title to those who did not try to evade the authorities, and banned the bringing of food to those who were awaiting trial.[129] Under these restrictions of what did or did not constitute martyrdom, any volume of the *Acts of the Christian Martyrs* would be rather thin, for were these criteria – defining who was and was not a martyr – rigorously applied, there would have been practically no 'authentic' Christian martyrs in the first two centuries.

128. Canon 60 of the council held in Spain around 305 CE reads, 'If someone smashes an idol and is then punished by death, he or she may not be placed in the list of martyrs, since such action is not sanctioned by the Scriptures or by the apostles.'
129. D.S. Potter, 'Persecution of the early Church', *ABD*, V, 231–5 (235).

Chapter 2

DRAWING BATTLE LINES: CHRISTIANITY AND ROME

Introduction

In this chapter, we begin the task of constructing the world-view of the early Christian martyrs and, in particular, how it interacted with the Roman view of reality. I will attempt to explain how, despite the consensus that persecution of the Church until the mid-third century was for the most part local, the Christians 'imperialized' their suffering. I will argue that scholars, such as Hopkins,[1] look in the wrong place for evidence of persecution, and ultimately I will advocate the reinstatement of a discredited theory, albeit in modified form.

Caesar Is Lord?

It has been important for some scholars to stress that the Church did nothing to provoke their pagan neighbours, and that the persecutions were unjust, constituting a travesty of Roman law.[2] However, I will argue that, in the main, the Christians, however much they may have wished, *could* not be good citizens of the Roman Empire. The standard for even the most nominal display of good citizenship was set far in excess of what the Christians could meet.

The Christians' problem with Imperial Rome was not simply an inherited antipathy to idolatry, preventing them from taking part in local cultic activity, and prohibiting sacrificing to the Emperor. Christian theology and Roman Imperial ideology were meta-narratives competing for the same ground. Both made claims to universality; both had as their focus a *theios aner*. Christianity and the *Imperium* were totalities seeking to explain the physical (and spiritual) realm in ways that were mutually incompatible.

If the Romans represented the power structures of the Empire through ritual, symbol and language, so too did the Christians. What made Roman religion problematic to the Christians and, consequently, Christians problematic to the Romans was that the Powers of both systems competed for the same language, the same rituals and the same symbols.[3] The universe was not big enough to accommodate the claims of both the Christians and the Romans.

---

1. For reference, see above, 1–2.
2. A.N. Sherwin-White, 'Early persecutions and Roman law again', *JTS* (n.s.) 3 (1952), 199–213.
3. This is what Deissmann calls 'polemical parallelism', where 'words derived by Christianity from the treasury of the Septuagint and the Gospels happens to coincide with solemn concepts of the Imperial cult which sounded the same or similar'. A. Deissmann, *Light from the Ancient East: The*

For the Christians, there was but one Lord and one God, but Romans knew that there were many lords and gods. The Emperor was thought to be a mediator, of sorts, between heaven and earth, representing humans to the gods, and also representing the gods, and their power, to humans. Therefore Caesar was κύριος.[4] And so, Augustus could be θεὸς καὶ κύριος καῖσαρ αὐτοκράτωρ,[5] and Nero, ὁ τοῦ παντὸς κύριος Νέρων.[6] Of the many instances of the Emperor being accorded the title κύριος,[7] perhaps the most significant is the example of the anarthrous construction Νέρονος κυρίου, paralleling the Christian acclamation Κύριος Ἰησοῦς.[8] Deissmann, therefore, with some justification, made the claim that 'at the time when Christianity originated, "Lord" was a divine predicate intelligible to the whole Eastern world'.[9]

Until recently, a consensus has existed in New Testament studies that Christians faced persecution because they refused to offer worship to the Emperors that the pontiffs in Rome demanded. It is said that worship of the Emperor was enforced throughout the Empire, and the Christians, because of their strict monotheism, could not take part, and were therefore persecuted, tried and executed. The Apocalypse has been responsible for some of this impression, though by no means all. For much of the twentieth century, commentators have assumed that the book of Revelation was written towards the end of Domitian's reign,[10] and that the Christian recipients must have experiencing State-wide persecution.[11]

New Testament Illustrated by Recently Discovered Texts of the Graeco-Roman World (trans. L.R.M. Strachan; Massachusetts: Hendrickson Publishers, 1995), 342.

4. Κύριος was used of any master, head of household or as a term of respect in the Graeco-Roman world as in the LXX (e.g. Gen. 24.18; Exod. 21.28–9; Judg. 19.22–3). However, in both cases it was used particularly for divine and mortal power: in the case of the latter, it translates the tetragrammaton. See *TLNT*, 2.341–52.

5. In 12 BCE (*TLNT*, 2.346) *BGU* 1197 col I, 15.

6. D. Cuss, *Imperial Cult and Honorary Terms in the New Testament* (Paradosis, Contributions to the History of Early Christian Literature and Theology, 23; Fribourg: University Press, 1974), 75–7; Deissmann, *Light*, 349–57.

7. See, in particular, the extensive discussion in Deissmann, *Light*, 349–62; R.F. Collins, *The Birth of the New Testament: The Origin and Development of the First Christian Generation* (New York: Crossroad, 1993), 67–9; T.H. Kim, 'The anarthrous υἱὸς θεοῦ in Mk 15:39 and the Roman Imperial Cult', *Biblia* 79 (1998), 221–41 (235). Significant also is Taylor's Appendix cataloguing divine honours paid to Caesar; L.R. Taylor, *The Divinity of the Roman Emperor* (Connecticut: American Philological Association, 1931), 267–83.

8. 1 Cor. 12.3. A collection of some of the instances of κύριος used in connection with Nero are found in the 'Ostraka der Sammlung Deissmann', part of P.M. Meyer, *Griechische Texte aus Ägypten* (Berlin: Weidmannsche Buchhandlung, 1916), 105–205, nos 22, 23, 24, 25, 36a, 37, 76. The anarthrous example is no. 39. For κύριος in connection with Vespasian, nos 17, 18, 47, 59, 86, 87; with Domitian, nos 40, 44, 77; Trajan, nos 5, 28, 30a, 33; Hadrian, nos 6, 26, 41, 43; Antoninus Pius, nos 3, 9, 27, 49, 88. For other references, see M.P. Charlesworth, 'Deus noster Caesar', *The Classical Review* 39 (1925), 113–15.

9. Deissmann, *Light*, 341–2, though Jones (D.L. Jones, 'Christianity and the Roman Imperial cult', *ANRW* II.23.2 [1980], 1023–54 [1030 n. 42]) thinks this an exaggeration. See also R.H. Fuller, *The Foundation of New Testament Christology* (London: Lutterworth Press, 1965), 87–9, 231.

10. Following Irenaeus, the earliest extant witness to the Apocalypse, who wrote *c.* 180 CE that the book was written near the end of Domitian's reign (*A.H.* 5.30.3).

11. For example, M. Kiddle, *The Revelation of St John* (London: Hodder & Stoughton, 1940);

The Apocalypse, unless the product of a perfervid and psychotic imagination,[12] was written out of an intense experience of the Christian suffering at the hands of the imperial authorities, represented by the 'Beast of Babylon'.[13]

Certainly, Rome is the target in Revelation, and is accused of causing suffering to the saints. The enemy is named as 'Babylon' (10.21; 14.8; 16.19; 18.2); a common Jewish ascription for Rome (*4 Ezra* 3.1–2, 28–31, *2 Baruch* 10.1–3, 11.1; *Sibylline Oracles* 5.143, 159) after (and because) the Romans destroyed the Temple.[14] That John perceives that Rome has been responsible for the deaths of Christians is confirmed by the fact that the 'Whore of Babylon' is 'drunk with the blood of the saints and the blood of the martyrs of Jesus' (μεθύουσαν ἐκ τοῦ αἵματος τῶν ἁγίων καὶ ἐκ τοῦ αἵματος τῶν μαρτύρων Ἰησοῦ; 17.6), she is identified as the killer of the Christians, and after she has been destroyed, the blood of the prophets and of the saints is found in her (αἷμα προφητῶν καὶ ἁγίων; 18.24). Furthermore, that John sees the Imperial Cult being involved in this persecution, may be read from the activity of worshipping the Beast (13.4, 8, 12; 14.9, 11; 20.4).[15] Therefore, Keresztes concludes, '[Revelation] demonstrates beyond doubt that Christianity was engaged in a death battle with Imperial Rome under Domitian.'[16]

T.F. Glasson, *The Revelation of St John* (Cambridge: Cambridge University Press, 1965); G.E. Ladd, *A Commentary on the Revelation of John* (Grand Rapids: Eerdmans, 1972); W.G. Kümmel, *Introduction to the New Testament* (London: SCM Press, 1975); R.H. Mounce, *The Book of Revelation* (Grand Rapids: Eerdmans, 1977).

12. The book of Revelation has been branded a 'sick text' by Will Self in his introduction to the Pocket Canon Series. He writes, 'Perhaps it's the occlusion of judgemental types, and the congruent occlusion of psyches, but there's something *not quite right* about *Revelation* ... The text is a guignol of tedium, a portentous horror film.' W. Self, *Revelation* (Edinburgh: Canongate, 1998), xii–xiii (emphasis added).

13. J.A.T. Robinson, *Redating the New Testament* (London: SCM Press, 1976), 230. For persecution as the setting for the Apocalypse, see G.R. Beasley-Murray, *The Book of Revelation* (London: Marshall, Morgan & Scott, 1974); and H.B. Swete, *The Apocalypse of St John* (London: Macmillan, 1922). Swete (xcvii) notes that the crisis of persecution was short lived with the assassination of Domitian in 96 CE.

14. It is unlikely that Christians would have used the term Babylon for Rome before these Jewish texts, almost certainly dating Revelation later than 70 CE. However, some scholars (most notably Robinson, *Redating*, 238, and see below, n. 38) have seen in Rev. 11.1–2 evidence that the Temple still stands, and therefore postulate a date before 70 CE for the composition of the Apocalypse. However, ch. 11 contains highly symbolic language and it is not at all clear that the reference to the Temple is to be taken literally, especially as John is reworking material from Ezekiel (especially chs 40–3). Moreover, if the Great City of 11.8 is taken to be Jerusalem, then by 16.17–21 it is destroyed. For further discussion, see A. Yarbro Collins, 'Dating the Apocalypse of John', *BR* 26 (1981), 33–45; D.E. Aune, *Revelation 1–5* (Waco, TX: Word Books, 1997), lvi–lxx; G.K. Beale, *The Book of Revelation: A Commentary on the Greek Text* (NIGTC; Grand Rapids: Eerdmans/Carlisle: Paternoster Press, 1999), 4–27; and S.J. Friesen, *Imperial Cults and the Apocalypse of John: Reading Revelation in the Ruins* (Oxford: Oxford University Press, 2001), 135–51.

15. On this point, see G. Biguzzi, 'Revelation and the Flavian Temple in Ephesus', *NovT* 40 (1998), 276–90, and especially Friesen, *Imperial Cults*.

16. P. Keresztes, *Imperial Rome and the Christians: From Herod the Great to around 200 A.D.* (London: United Press of America, 1990), 99.

Domitian

Domitian, aside from Nero, is the Emperor who figures most prominently in discussions of Christian persecution in the first century. Often dubbed 'the second Nero',[17] Domitian is accused of presiding over the first official Imperial persecution of Christians since that of 64 CE.[18] Reigning from 81 to 96 CE, Domitian has been judged to have been an evil incompetent ruler, persecuting Christians because they refused to acknowledge his egotistical desire to be addressed as *dominus et deus*.

> Domitian insisted on being addressed, by letter or in person, as 'our Lord and God' and all who refused were punished. That his persecution extended to Christians is clearly reflected in the book of Revelation. Emperor deification, including offerings of incense, prayers, and vows, was now obligatory and used as a means to identify the followers of Christ.[19]

Others have observed that the famous Pliny correspondence identifies a group of ex-Christians who had given up the faith twenty years previously.[20] This, they argue would coincide with the reign of Domitian.[21] However, as Wilken has observed:

> In an age when religious distinctions were often blurred, people changed allegiances often and sometimes belonged to more than one religious group in the course of a lifetime. Consequently there was much movement in and out of religious associations and across organizational lines. When Christianity did not meet some people's expectations, they lost interest.[22]

Though Wilken does not connect Pliny's apostates to the alleged Domitian persecutions, this alternative explanation can be put into the context of the more positive, or at least more sympathetic, portrait of Domitian that has recently emerged.[23]

---

17. Eusebius, *H.E.* 3.17. Jones, 'Christianity', 1033. In this article, Jones surveys persecution of the Christians under various Roman Emperors in the first three centuries, yet curiously does not directly investigate any possible link between the promotion of the cult and the Christian persecutions.

18. Eusebius (*H.E.* 4.26.9) links Nero and Domitian as standing alone among the Roman Emperors for bringing calamity upon the Church. Clearly, this is said for apologetic purposes. The claim is that only those emperors considered to be poor rulers persecuted the Church. Barnes ('Legislation', 35) rightly argues that this is no basis for modern assessment of these emperors.

19. D.L. Jones, 'Roman Imperial Cult', *ABD*, V, 806–9 (807).

20. Pliny, *Epistles.* 10.96.

21. So Keresztes (*Imperial Rome*, 97) concludes, 'There can be little doubt that this unhesitating method of applying the worship of the living emperor to eliminate 'non-Christians' [from suspicion] was inherited by him from the time of Domitian.'

22. R.L. Wilken, *The Christians as the Romans Saw Them* (New Haven/London: Yale University Press, 1984), 25.

23. See, for example, B.W. Jones, *The Emperor Domitian* (London/New York: Routledge, 1992) 114–25; and J.T. Sanders, *Schismatics, Sectarians, Dissidents and Deviants: The First One Hundred Years of Jewish-Christian Relations* (London: SCM Press, 1993), 166–9. For a much more positive assessment of Domitian's rule, see L.L. Thompson, *The Book of Revelation: Apocalypse and Empire* (New York/Oxford: Oxford University Press, 1990), 95–115.

Although classical scholars have for some time questioned the New Testament portrayal of Domitian as a persecutor of the Church,[24] it is only in recent years that biblical scholars have followed the classicists in re-examining the evidence and, in turn, their readings of Revelation. Thompson has led the charge of exegetes in a revisionist reading of Domitian's reign.[25]

The impression that Domitian was an evil incompetent ruler, demanding heavenly honours, from sources other than the New Testament, comes in the main from Pliny the Younger, Tacitus and Suetonius. They in turn had a great influence on later Roman historians. The charges levelled against Domitian were many: he was a cunning and devious ruler;[26] he was insane and tyrannical;[27] and possessed an insatiable sexual appetite.[28] They all portrayed him as an unstable despot who murdered opponents, and brought financial ruin upon the Empire.[29]

Nonetheless, Thompson claims that each of these historians had reason to portray Domitian in this way. In the first instance, each of them had friends or relatives exiled or executed under Domitian and, secondly, they felt that the Emperor inhibited free speech, obstructing their promotion.[30] More importantly, these scribes were writing under Trajan, who began a new dynasty, breaking with the past. Therefore, in order to legitimize this new era, anti-Flavian sentiment was positively encouraged.[31] Thompson points to the fact that writers contemporaneous with Domitian judged him more favourably.[32] Moreover, following Viscusi, Thompson asserts that there are no extant inscriptions corroborating the allegation that Domitian wished to be addressed as *dominus et deus*,[33] a designation that has been important for many readings of the Apocalypse.

Thompson's thoroughgoing revision of Domitian's reign has been criticized on a number of points. Whilst acknowledging his challenge to unproven assumptions about Domitian, Slater points out that those writers who are more favourable to the Emperor were employed in his service, providing a reason for an apparent bias.[34] Moreover, in the writings demonstrating that Domitian supposedly allowed criticism of his reign, which Thomson sees as evidence of the pontiff's enlightened attitude to criticism, Slater notes that the Emperor is not in fact

---

24. See, for example, H.W. Pleket, 'Domitian, the Senate and the provinces', *Mnemosyne* 14 (1961), 296–315; Ste Croix ('Why were the early Christians persecuted?') also puts no weight on Revelation and 1 Peter as evidence for State persecution.

25. Thompson, *Revelation*, especially 95–115.

26. For example, Tacitus, *Agricola* 39, 43; Pliny, *Panegyric* 90.5–7; *Epistles* 1.12.6–8.

27. For example, Suetonius, *Domitian* 1.3; Pliny, *Panegyric* 48.3–5.

28. For example, Suetonius, *Domitian* 1.1; 1.3; 22.1; Tacitus, *Histories* 4.2; 4.68.

29. Tacitus, *Germania* 37; Pliny, *Panegyric* 11.4; 76.5; 82.4; Suetonius, *Domitian*, 4.1; 4.4; 5; 12.1; 14.1.

30. Pliny, *Epistles* 3.11.3–4; 4.24.4–5; 7.27.14; *Panegyric* 95.3–4; Tacitus, *Agricola* 2–3, 44–5.

31. Thompson, *Revelation*, 115.

32. See Quintillian, *Institutio Oratoria* 10.1.91; Martial 2.2; 8.15; 8.78; Statius, *Silvae* 3.3.171; 4.1.34–9; 4.3.159; Silius Italicus, *Punica* 3.607.

33. P. Viscusi, 'Studies on Domitian' (PhD dissertation; Ann Arbor University, 1973), 94.

34. T.B. Slater, 'On the social setting of the Revelation to John', *NTS* 44 (1998), 232–56 (236).

mentioned.[35] Ultimately, the same argument Thomson employs to discredit the negative evidence of Suetonius, Tacitus and Pliny may be used against the writers he cites in Domitian's favour. Obviously, those writing under any Emperor would wish to ingratiate themselves to their ruler.[36] This is as true for those who wrote under Domitian as it was for those employed by Trajan.

If Thompson's conclusion about Domitian is overgenerous, at least he has provided a corrective to the villainous portrayal of the Emperor under whom the Apocalypse is thought to have been written, encouraging us to be more critical of the Roman historians. Thomson has succeeded in demonstrating that the image of Domitian as a homicidal megalomaniac, hell-bent on persecuting Christians who refused to worship his image, is a distortion. Scholars now agree that there is little sign of State persecution under Domitian.[37] Indeed, such is the consensus that a Neronic date for the composition of Revelation is again being reconsidered.[38] Therefore, attention has turned away from the Imperial cult as a factor in persecution. Instead, the spotlight has shifted, and brought the practices of the local cults into the limelight.

Christians and Local Cults
Christians adopted a new, and more significantly exclusive, religion that meant upsetting the religious sensitivities of their communities. Being a Christian demanded total and unconditional rejection of 'idolatry', and this included refusing to take part in what would be regarded by ordinary Roman citizens as normal social and cultic activities.

> If one was baptized into Christ Jesus, he could not also be initiated into the cult of Dionysus or Serapis, nor could he participate in many civic and social ceremonies that were, however innocuous to most, to the Christian, as to the Jew, idolatrous.[39]

35. Slater, 'Social setting', 236. The texts in question are Quintilian, *Inst. Orat.* 12.1.40, and Martial 1.8; 4.54.7.

36. Nonetheless, Wilson is probably correct in judging that less specific charges are unlikely to have been contorted; S.G. Wilson, *Related Strangers: Jews and Christians 70–170 C.E.* (Minneapolis: Fortress Press, 1995), 14.

37. Barnes ('Legislation', 36) concludes that, under the reign of Domitian, 'nowhere is there any evidence of any legal ordinance against the Christians'. See also G. Krodel, 'Persecution and toleration of Christianity until Hadrian', in S. Benko and J.J. O'Rourke (eds), *Early Church History: The Roman Empire as the Setting of Primitive Christianity* (London: Oliphants, 1971), 255–67 (260–2).

38. For a Neronic date, see A.A. Bell, 'The date of John's Apocalypse: the evidence of some Roman historians reconsidered', *NTS* 25 (1979), 93–102; R.B. Moberly, 'When was Revelation conceived?', *Biblica* 73 (1992), 376–93; J.C. Wilson, 'The problem of the Domitian date of Revelation', *NTS* 39 (1993), 587–605. However, see n. 14 above. Furthermore, the terminology for the disciples οἱ δώδεκα ἀπόστολοι (Rev. 21.14) is not found before 70 CE, and knowledge of the Nero *redivivus* myth (chs 13 and 17) would indicate a date after Nero's death, and some time afterwards, to allow for its spread. So, A.J.P. Garrow (*Revelation* [NTR; New York/London: Routledge, 1997], 76–9) sets the date under Titus, while the Nero myth was at its height. Aune (*Revelation 1–5*), nonetheless, postulates that a first edition of the Apocalypse appeared under Nero.

39. W. Meeks, 'Social functions of apocalyptic language in Pauline Christianity' (in D. Hellholm [ed.], *Apocalypticism in the Mediterranean and Near East* [Proceedings of the International Colloquium on Apocalypticism, Uppsala, 1979; Tübingen: J.C.B. Mohr, 1983], 685–705), 691.

In a culture where life revolved around cultic worship, abandoning civic cults would have had profound, and perhaps debilitating, social and economic implications for the Christian converts.[40]

However, more important for the Christians were the perceived implications of their actions for whole cities. Such wholesale rejection of the gods was considered to be dangerous by the residents of the cities, for it was believed that the gods could bring down their wrath upon a community, or part of a community who slighted them;[41] 'civic peace, the success of agriculture and freedom from earthquake or flood' were down to 'the benevolence of the gods'.[42] To alienate a deity would threaten the goodwill of the god, and so Christians could be held responsible for disasters that occurred in the community.[43] The fear that such 'atheism' could bring down on a community is well illustrated by Tertullian:

> [Pagans] suppose that the Christians are the cause of every public disaster, every misfortune that happens to the people. If the Tiber overflows or the Nile does not, if there is a drought or an earthquake, a famine or a pestilence, at once the cry goes up, 'The Christians to the lions'.[44]

Christians, therefore, induced in their fellow townsfolk a fear of the wrath of the gods, opening themselves up to the charge of being considered ἄθεοι.[45] They were seen to be abandoning the tradition of their fathers by their exclusivism, an attitude that surprised many in the Ancient world.[46]

> But you [Christians] meanwhile in anxious doubt abstain from wholesome pleasures; you do not attend the shows; you take no part in the processions; fight shy of public banquets; abhor the sacred games, meats from the sacrificial victims, drinks poured out in libation on the altars.[47]

This refusal by Christians to take part in the normal social and cultic activities attracted the charge of *odium humani generis* – haters of the human race – a

---

40. Economic implications are implied by Rev. 13.7 and 16.15, though R. Bauckham (*The Theology of the Book of Revelation* [Cambridge: Cambridge University Press, 1993], 38) thinks that the restriction on buying and selling is probably exaggerated.

41. It is possible that this had been pointed out to the Christian community at Thessalonica where the church is concerned that more than one of its members have died (1 Thess. 4.13).

42. J.M.G. Barclay, 'Conflict in Thessalonica', *CBQ* 55 (1993), 512–30 (515). 'Sacrifice keeps the tenuous balance between the human world and the divine realm intact, assures that the dramatic vagaries of divine dissatisfaction will be held in check. In the Roman context, where sacrifice serves as a first line of defence in the preservation of political stability the refusal to sacrifice or the perversion of the carefully balanced sacrificial relations produces threatening seismic fissures running underneath the foundations of society'; E.A. Castelli, 'Imperial reimaginings of Christian origins: epic in Prudentius's poem for the martyr Eulalia', in E.A. Castelli and H. Taussig, *Reimagining Christian Origins: A Colloquium Honoring Burton L. Mack* (Valley Forge, PA: Trinity Press International, 1996), 173–84 (179).

43. Ste Croix, 'Why were the early Christians persecuted?', 24.

44. Tertullian, *Apol.* 40.

45. See *Mart. Pol.* 9.2.

46. See, for example 1 Pet. 4.3–4. For sources out with the New Testament, see Tacitus, *Annals* 15.44.

47. Minucius Felix, *Octavius* 12.

charge frequently employed during the Neronic persecution.[48] This has refocused the question as to why the Christians faced hostility and persecution. Thompson concludes that local cults are the key. He writes, 'The greater issue revolves around Christians' relation to adherents of traditional cults rather than their relation to the cult of the emperor'.[49]

However, Biguzzi correctly argues that this conclusion fails to take account of the Apocalypse, in which imagery relating to the Imperial cult positively cascades. 'The idolatry of the Beast is depicted by John with an inexhaustible richness of images, formulated by him or creatively remade by re-elaborating biblical precedents and extra-biblical myths'. [50] Biguzzi contrasts general idolatry,[51] based Old Testament stereotypes, such as the worship of wooden idols, with the specific worship of the εἰκών,[52] an individual, singular entity. This εἰκών is the idolatrous image of τὸ θηρίον that comes from the sea, which itself is treated as masculine on four occasions.[53] Nonetheless, Biguzzi's solution is to repeat the claim that Domitian did in fact promote his own imperial cult, despite the scarcity of the evidence.[54]

We have seen that a whole matrix of factors led to conflict between Christian communities and their neighbours, both pagan and Jewish. There is no evidence that the Roman State instigated any programmatic attempt at persecuting Christians; any experience of suffering by Christians was instigated locally, generally as a result of mob action. It also appears to be the case that local pagan hostility to the Christians was in large measure fuelled by the deliberate slighting of civic gods.

However, the consensus that the Imperial Cult was not vigorously promoted has left a vacuum in the question as to why the early Christians were persecuted, for crucially there remains the conflict between actual Christian testimony that the State was somehow instrumental in their experience of persecution and hardship and the official State position, which seemed to be largely unconcerned about this new movement.

In the following section, I will argue that precisely because scholars have correctly concluded that the Emperor Cult was not enforced throughout the Empire, they have set up a false dichotomy between Imperial Cult and local cults as the backdrop for the Christians' experiences of persecution. In investigating persecution of Christians, they have overlooked the function of the Emperor Cult in

48. Ste Croix, 'Why were the early Christians persecuted?', 8.

49. Thompson, *Revelation*, 164.

50. Biguzzi, 'Revelation', 277.

51. Rev. 9.20.

52. Rev. 13.14, 15; 14.9, 11; 15.2; 16.2; 19.20; 20.4.

53. Rev. 13.8, 14; 17.3, 11. See D.A. DeSilva, 'The "Image of the Beast" and the Christians in Asia Minor: escalation of sectarian tension in Revelation 13', *Trinity Journal* 12 (1991), 185–208 (201). DeSilva similarly observes that John has taken some trouble to develop a fierce polemic against the Emperor Cult.

54. See D. Warden, 'Imperial persecution and the dating of 1 Peter and Revelation', *JETS* 34 (1991), 203–12 (207). Warden notes that fewer Imperial Temples were built during the 15-year reign of Domitian than in both the previous and preceding 15-year periods, and concludes (208), 'There is no indication that Domitian himself affected the practice of ruler worship in Asia to any significant degree.'

providing the cohesion that gelled the Empire together. So although it has been noted that in certain pockets of the Empire the Cult of the Emperor was taken up enthusiastically, especially in Asia Minor, this does not sufficiently account for the offence caused by Christians refusing to take part in the cult.[55]

Similarly, though Christian persecution was not instigated from the centre of Imperial power, in the Christian imagination, experience of local hardship was universalized as coming from the State. Why then, did Christians imperialize their experience? In order to answer this question, we now examine the place of the Cult in the Empire, especially in regard to the benefits it offered to all strata of society.

The Emperor Cult

Despite the clear Roman official position that the Emperor was not *divus* in his lifetime,[56] the Cult of the Emperor spread rapidly throughout the Empire, so that by the fourth decade of the first Christian century, even the Roman elite were recognizing the divinity of the Emperor.[57] The Emperor Cult was the vehicle by which devotion to a powerful ruler was able to function. It grew from its origins in Hellenistic ruler-cults,[58] spreading westward, before finally taking hold in the heart of the Empire, Rome itself.

Greeks associated power with divinity, and therefore adopted worship of the Emperor quite naturally.[59] The Cult became the means by which Rome could assert its power, and protect the worship of both Roma *and* local civic gods. The cult did this through the new type of society it created.

A Stakeholder Society

The city-state was an important feature of the ancient world, generating not a little civic pride. Under Augustus, city cults and prestigious assembly cults blos-

---

55. Similarly, a more satisfactory solution should be sought than simply labelling Roman mistreatment of Christians as an aberration of their own justice system (Sherwin-White). Ste Croix, who dismisses Revelation and 1 Peter as evidence of persecution by the State for refusal to take part in the cult, nonetheless concedes that *some* Christians may have experienced harassment for just this reason. He notes, 'they ought not to have been *compelled* to do anything of the sort, no emperor being officially numbered among the gods of the Roman state until he was dead and had been duly pronounced *divus*' (Ste Croix, 'Why were the early Christians persecuted?' 10).

56. S.F.R. Price, 'Gods and emperors: the Greek language of the Roman Imperial cult', *JHS* 54 (1984), 19–95 (82); *Rituals and Power: The Roman Imperial Cult in Asia Minor* (Cambridge: Cambridge University Press, 1984), 75.

57. K. Hopkins, *Conquerors and Slaves* (Cambridge: Cambridge University Press, 1978), 213. Though the extent to which this represented religious piety or political expediency is debated.

58. For an account of the Eastern ruler cult, see Taylor, *Divinity*, 1–31. For its development in the West, see D. Fishwick, 'The development of provincial ruler worship in the western Empire', *ANRW* II.16.2 (1978), 1201–53.

59. For various understandings of Roman power from the Greek point of view, see G.W. Bowersock, 'Greek intellectuals and the Imperial cult in the second century A.D.', in W. den Boer (ed.), *Le Culte des souverains dans L'Empire Romain* (Vandoeuvres-Genève: Oliver Reverdin, 1972), 177–206.

somed, and represented the cities' interests to Rome.[60] This 'general imperial acceptance of civic cults and the possibility of penalties for non-fulfilment of promised cults combined to create considerable, covert central pressure for the establishment and continuation of cults'.[61] It also led to the standardization of the Imperial Cult which had begun with much novelty between cities, but with the threat of demotion from city status, it was important to make sure the images and practices were the approved version. After all, 'favour would hardly be gained by the display of a deviant image'.[62]

The Emperor Cult gave rival cities an excellent opportunity for competition. The decision as to which city would site an Imperial temple, games or a regular Imperial festival would involve cities putting forward their respective and elaborate claims to be considered more worthy than their neighbours for such honour.[63] Appropriate honours offered to the distant monarch could cast glory upon the city, both in their own eyes and in the eyes of the Emperor far away in Rome, since the Emperor would usually be informed when honours were offered.[64] Therefore, with Zanker, 'it seems clear that mutual competition among cities played a decisive role in the swiftness with which the imperial cult spread'.[65] Civic pride accounts for the fact that the imperial cult was the single largest impetus for building programmes of the second and third centuries.[66] Clearly, the Imperial Cult flourished in a competitive world.[67]

It was not only among cities that rivalry and competition flourished. As a result of the cult, wealthy individuals within each city could gain honour for themselves by outdoing others in the building of altars and statues, drawing attention

60. S.F.R. Price, 'Rituals and power', in R.A. Horsley (ed.), *Paul and Empire: Religion and Power in Roman Imperial Society* (Harrisburg, PA: Trinity Press International, 1997), 45–71 (54).

61. Price, *Rituals*, 66.

62. Price, *Rituals*, 174. P. Zanker, 'The power of images', in R.A. Horsley (ed.), *Paul and Empire: Religion and Power in the Roman Imperial Society* (Pennsylvania: Trinity Press International, 1997), 72–86 (78) observes, 'Competition shows the extent to which cult of the monarchy was accepted. At first there was some attempt at novelty and originality, but that soon gave way to uniformity'. The presence of the power in Rome, therefore, led to competition between the cities. This competition then reinforces the acceptance of that power.

63. Price, 'Rituals', 56. Hence Price can say, 'with the provincial cults the rivalry between cities was almost unbounded'.

64. Hopkins, *Conquerors*, 206. He adds (n. 13), 'This provided towns with an opportunity for self-advertisement and gave ambassadors a legitimate excuse for a trip to court with the prospect of an audience, with enhanced kudos on their return home.'

65. Zanker, 'Power of images', 77. Zanker notes that, in Tarraco, a miracle was associated with the Imperial altar; a palm tree grew up on it.

66. G.W. Bowersock, 'The Imperial Cult: perceptions and persistence', in B.F. Meyer and E.P. Sanders (eds), *Self-Definition in the Greco-Roman World*, vol. 3 of *Jewish and Christian Self-Definition* (Philadelphia: Fortress Press, 1983), 171–82 (173). H. Lietzmann, *Geschichte der Alten Kirche* (Berlin/Leipzig: W. de Gruyter, 1932), 173–4, made the observation, 'daß seit der Kaiserzeit nur noch Kaisertempel gebaut werden'. A.D. Nock, 'The Roman army and the Roman religious year', *HTR* 45 (1952), 187–252, concurs, finding 'not many exceptions' (237–8).

67. Price, *Rituals*, 122, and especially 62–5. For a modern analogy, consider the vast sums of money cities spend in order to win the competition to host the Olympic Games.

to themselves in the process by means of inscription.[68] Prominent citizens were afforded an opportunity to demonstrate their own status by the ostentatious presentation of lavish honours for the Emperor, providing enjoyment at great expense for their fellow citizens.[69] By the second decade of the Common Era, local dignitaries could sponsor games, enhancing the social role of the priests, appointed to perform rituals and inaugurate games.[70]

Through festivities, rituals and statues, altars and other 'hardware' of the cult, 'the imperial cult, like the cults of the traditional gods, created a relationship of power between subject and ruler'.[71] It gave cities the chance to express their dominance over others and emphasized the prominence of local leaders and priests. Priesthoods of the cult were highly prized, being seen as a sign of upward mobility.[72] Through ceremony and procession, nobles, freedmen and slaves could reaffirm their relative position to one another, and their subordination to the Emperor.[73] That is to say, 'the cult was a major part of the web of power that formed the fabric of society'.[74] The Emperor Cult was an important influence for stability and order in society, a role that had traditionally belonged to the Olympian gods.[75] Establishing social and political order had, therefore, an essentially religious context.[76]

The social elite had a stake in the continuance of the cult of the Emperor. Through its rituals and processions and festivals, they could reinforce their positions of influence and prominence. However, the imperial cult's popularity was sustained by the extent to which it encouraged, or at the very least facilitated, the involvement, if not empowerment, of the poor, down to even the most abused slave.

Festivals were a time of celebration, a time when even the poor could participate (since it would be important that the prominent have the populace present in order to demonstrate their prominence over them!).[77] Festivals meant feasts, and feasts meant meat, a rare treat for all but the wealthiest citizens.[78] Importantly, everyone could participate in the cult and feel they had a stake in the Empire – all

---

68. So, for example, the following inscription is found on a statue base: 'Anicia Pudentilla in her will ordered two statues to be erected at a cost of 30,000HS/Manlia Marcina her mother and heir had that done, adding 8000HS of her own/G. Manilius her son-in-law executor'. (*The Inscriptions of Roman Tripolitania* 22; quoted by Hopkins, *Conquerors*, 220).

69. Zanker, 'Power of images', 74.

70. See Zanker, 'Power of images', 80–1.

71. Price, 'Rituals', 71.

72. Bowersock, 'Imperial Cult', 172.

73. Hopkins, *Conquerors*, 210.

74. Price, 'Rituals', 71.

75. See R.A. Horsley, 'Introduction', in R.A. Horsley (ed.), *Paul and Empire: Religion and Power in Roman Imperial Society* (Harrisburg, PA: Trinity Press International, 1997), 1–24 (23).

76. The link between Roman gods and social order is explored in J.H.W.G. Liebeschuetz, *Continuity and Change in Roman Religion* (Oxford: Clarendon Press, 1979).

77. Processions are a particularly good vehicle for both participation and demonstration of hierarchy.

78. Hopkins, *Conquerors*, 210.

this without the need for democracy![79] 'Cults were generally the product of a joint decision of both the council and the people, whatever the significance of individuals in providing the initial impetus',[80] and so it may be that Price is correct in suggesting that the city as a whole would be involved in establishing and running the imperial cult.[81] Cult worship gave people who were not near Rome a direct link to the Emperor and gave them an opportunity to express their allegiance.[82] Imperial festivals were a highlight in the life of the poor, affording opportunity for high spirits and civic pride.[83] This was the cult's great strength. Even whilst reinforcing a social system of centralized power, it still encouraged social participation, and even social benefit.

If the poor had something to be gained from the cult of the Emperor, then even more so, relatively speaking, had the slave, for the cult afforded the maltreated slave a means of justice. Statues of the Emperor that littered the Empire were a place of refuge and sanctuary – the idea being that the refugee sought the protection and justice the Emperor would dispense were he himself present.[84] The practice, like the cult itself, came from the tradition of the Greek temples that had long been places of sanctuary. Asylum too had a 'clear religious background'.[85]

Though debtors and those convicted of crime could claim sanctuary, the statues were used most often by slaves protesting against cruel treatment by their masters,[86] so much so that the right for slaves to do so had been established by the middle of the first century.[87] In considering such appeals, the Emperor had to steer a course between not eroding the power of masters over their slaves, whilst earning a reputation as a merciful and just Emperor.[88]

It is of some significance that the statues represented the presence of the Emperor. The view that the Emperor was embodied in the statue could be demonstrated negatively in the desecration of such images when the Emperor was unpopular.[89] Statues, altars, festivals and processions, as well as offering people

---

79. Horsley, 'Introduction', 17.

80. Price, 'Rituals', 57.

81. Price, 'Rituals', 57.

82. Zanker, 'Power of images', 76.

83. Zanker, 'Power of images', 74.

84. Hopkins, *Conquerors*, 221.

85. Price, *Rituals*, 192. Greek temples had been places of sanctuary. Payment of fines or petitions could also be brought to the statues.

86. Seneca, *On Mercy* 1.18, as found in Hopkins, *Conquerors*, 222. Though the possibility or the dream of clemency may have been more prevalent than actualized, there must have been some success for slaves. Sellers of slaves in Rome could reassure buyers by claiming that the slave was 'neither a gambler, nor a thief, nor had ever fled to [Caesar's] statue' (quoted by Hopkins, *Conquerors*, 223).

87. Hopkins, *Conquerors*, 222.

88. Hopkins, *Conquerors*, 222. However, this is not to say that the statues were worshipped as objects, rather they were symbols of the Emperor's power, his presence and his mercy.

89. So, Galba's standard was torn down and dashed on the ground (Tacitus, *Histories* 1.41), and Domitian's statues were toppled and attacked by mobs after his assassination. The scene is graphically described by Pliny (*Panegyric* 52): 'It was our delight to dash those proud faces to the ground, to smite them with the sword and savage them with the axe, as if blood and agony could follow from every blow. Our transports of joy, so long deferred were unrestrained; all sought a form of vengeance

of all strata a place in the running of the Cult, emphasizing the relative position of one to another, and to the Emperor, did something more. They created a sense of the Emperor's omnipresence. He was present through the rituals of the cult, and seen to uphold justice through his statues. 'Cults, acts, sacrifice, ritual, public games, feasts all underwrote the conception of the emperor's supremacy and the benefits derived from the existing order.'[90] Ritual is a way of conceptualizing the world, and this is how the Imperial Cult functioned.[91] It defined not only the position of the Emperor but also the place of the State, the cities and individuals in relation to him: with the cult, everyone knew where they were.

Symbols of the Empire were all around, and so, consequently, was the Emperor. There were daily reminders of the Emperor's association with gods: coins signifying victory and personified virtues of the Empire, such as, 'liberty restored, concord, joy, loyalty, etc. … '.[92] There were statues: 'public places were filled with or dominated by representations of royalty, most of them put there by private citizens'.[93] Imperial temples were placed at the most prominent positions in a city, integrating the Cult with the centre of public, social, economic and religious life.[94] Oaths were even sworn by the Emperor in the same way as was the custom to swear by a god, such as Jupiter – the Emperor's name invoked as though it were an appeal to the 'religious and moral order'.[95]

It was through all these pervasive symbols that the Emperor could be familiar to all people throughout the Empire, even though most people would never have seen him.

> The king of a large empire, never seen by most of his subjects, legitimates his power by associating himself and his regime with the mystic powers of the universe. Reciprocally, subjects who rarely see an emperor come to terms with his grandeur and power by associating him with the divine.[96]

It was through his presence that the Empire was bound together. There was little other than Roman popular piety promoted by the Cult of the Emperor, with its

---

in beholding those mutilated bodies, limbs hacked in pieces … '. The intensity of the feeling of Pliny's description (written, of course, under a new Imperial dynasty) chimes with the scenes at the toppling of the statue of Saddam Hussein in Baghdad (9 April 2003), also marking the end of a regime (for pictures of the event, see http://news.bbc.co.uk/1/hi/in_depth/photo_gallery/2933629.stm). The concern of the coalition forces to destroy the many images of Saddam Hussein around Iraq also illustrates the perceived power of images. See Hopkins, *Conquerors*, 225–6, for other acts of aggression towards statues and symbols of the Emperor. Perhaps John has these statues in mind in his 'the Image of the Beast' language (Rev. 13.13–14).

90. Hopkins, *Conquerors*, 218.

91. Price, 'Rituals', 49.

92. Hopkins, *Conquerors*, 219–20.

93. Hopkins, *Conquerors*, 221.

94. See Price, 'Rituals', 61–4, for examples. See also Zanker ('Power of images', 73), who notes King Herod's choosing of an imposing place for the Temple of Roma and Augustus in Caesarea, which 'dominated the harbour and shaped the whole outline of the city' (Josephus, *Ant.* 15.339).

95. Hopkins, *Conquerors*, 225.

96. Hopkins, *Conquerors*, 197. In an era before mass media, statues and coins denoted presence and power.

symbols of power and success and presence that could add the cohesive gel to a disparate Empire. Zanker argues that it was this visual unity of the Empire that bound it together and that the common visual language was almost entirely based on the ways in which homage was paid to the ruler.[97]

The Emperor represented the social, political, and moral order, within a religious framework, just like the gods.[98]

> The cult served a religious purpose in its veneration of palpable uncontested power, a political purpose in focussing allegiance to the empire and its ruler, and a social purpose in the way it involved wealthy freedmen in the responsibilities of the cult administration.[99]

As Hopkins rightly argues, 'the fusion of god and emperor reflected the coalescence of the moral and political order'.[100] The central place of the Emperor, therefore, played a crucial role in holding the Empire together. It provided a framework in which social strata could be maintained. It allowed the poor to participate in festivals, and held out the aspiration of justice and clemency even to the lowliest slave.

Importantly, set in a religious context, the Cult of the Emperor allowed State, city, provincial, and familial gods to flourish. When a nation was conquered, they could maintain worship of their own deities. They were also obliged to worship the gods of Rome, and this synthesis of Emperor and Roman gods, combined with the integration of local deities of conquered peoples into the Roman pantheon, was an effective means of assimilation and control.[101] Crucially then, the Imperial Cult was intrinsically bound up with local cults, especially outside Rome; the *Imperium* upheld and protected the traditional cults of the populace. Assimilation meant belonging to the Empire, belonging to the empire meant loyalty to the Emperor.

> Loyalty to the emperor, seen as divine or favoured by the gods was probably the only universal symbol of belonging available to the Romans and valid for all social groups in all provinces of the empire.[102]

---

97. Zanker, 'Power of images', 86. Cf. R. Gordon, 'The veil of power', in R.A. Horsley (ed.), *Paul and Empire: Religion and Power in Roman Imperial Society* (Harrisburg, PA: Trinity Press International, 1997), 126–37 (129–30). He argues that the metaphor of the body was a symbol of unity for the diverse Empire. The Emperor, the head, provided the example, particularly of piety that served to unite the Empire. Horsley ('Introduction', 20) concludes, 'In the most civilized areas of the empire, the imperial cult provided the principal means by which disparate cities and provinces were held together and social order produced.'

98. Hopkins, *Conquerors*, 198.

99. J.E. Stambaugh and D.L. Balch, *The New Testament in Its Social Environment* (Philadelphia: Westminster Press, 1986), 130.

100. Hopkins, *Conquerors*, 200.

101. Price ('Gods and emperors', 86) gives statistics for the frequency of gods attached to Emperors. Emperors are most often associated with Zeus as head of the pantheon; next he would be associated with the particular local deity of the city honouring him; and thirdly there may be a link with a god, remembering a particular exploit which that god was associated with.

102. Hopkins, *Conquerors*, 227.

Herein lies the critical dynamic in comprehending how despite a lack of State-wide persecution or, more importantly, the lack of a central promotion of the Emperor Cult, Christian discourse could vigorously and credibly present it as such. The issue is not so much that local people wished enthusiastically to promote the cult; rather local communities felt horror that a group from within should eschew it publicly and vociferously, when the cult was its primary means of representing itself to Rome. The Cult bound the Empire together and protected the worship of traditional gods. This is also why Christians could see their own experience of suffering as coming from the State. Everyone had something to lose if this crucial means of devotion to the Emperor was disrupted, and therefore the Christians threatened not just the carefully cultivated reputation of a city, but the social and perhaps even the cosmic order – the very symbols of reality.

Clash of Realities

In many ways, the Roman State was a multicultural achievement. The Graeco-Roman conception of the universe (the way things were) operated beneath a flexible pantheon. Gods existed, and were therefore worthy of honour, or, at the very least, it was thought best not to upset them. Conquered peoples contributed their own gods to the Roman pantheon, and the Romans encouraged continued devotion to ancestral and civic deities.

> Rome respected its traditional principle that every nation had the right to observe the religion established by its ancestors, but on the other hand, it applied its other principle that Rome had the right to rule the world and to subordinate to its institutions the religions of subject nations.[103]

The only condition was that Roman gods, and particularly Roma, were also to be worshipped. Since power was associated with the gods, conquered nations had little reason to resist this view of reality; if the Romans had superior military might, their gods must also be the more powerful. Political hierarchy on earth reflected the power relations of the divinities.[104] This was not religious faith; it was just how things were.

Jews, Christians and Romans

However, if there was no problem assimilating diverse peoples and gods within the Roman State and heavenly pantheon, the same was not true of the monotheis-

---

103. Keresztes, *Imperial Rome*, 90. On the Jews being granted a privileged position see also Bowersock, 'Imperial cult', 174; and E. Schürer, *The History of the Jews in the Age of Jesus Christ* (3 vols; Edinburgh: T&T Clark, 1973), I, 378–81.

104. This is not a foreign concept to Hebrew theology, where Yahweh is the mightier national god than the gods of the nations who are destroyed in the Canaanite conquest. Military defeat was interpreted as their god's punishment for wrongdoing. Only after the total collapse of Judah was Yahweh transformed from a national deity to a transnational God. After the Roman destruction of the Temple, Jewish theology once again had to contend with the defeat of Yahweh by the Roman gods. From the beginning, Christians, who worshipped a crucified god, inverted this cosmic system. Persecution and suffering, rather than being a sign that their god was weaker than the pagans', in fact signalled the imminent victory of God. See below, especially Chapter 5.

tic Jews and Christians. Monotheism was an odd concept for the popular ancient mind.[105] Only Jews and Christians practised it.[106] In a world of many strange nations, and life with many facets, it would seem natural to assume that many gods operated systems as diverse as the weather and the safety of emperors. Monotheism was to all extents and purposes atheism – and that was dangerous. Omission of a rite could bring divine punishment.[107] Gods were quick to take offence, and as in ancient Hebrew theology, disaster and misfortune were read as divine displeasure:[108] the *Pax Romana* depended on the *Pax Deorum*. Those who spurned the gods, therefore, were seen to be wilfully and deliberately wishing misfortune upon local communities and the Empire. The Graeco-Roman ancients had only encountered this sort of behaviour stemming from monotheism from the Jews, but Judaism was a national religion that had a long and distinguished past, unlike this new, strange Christian religion.[109]

As a Jewish sect, early Christianity was somewhat camouflaged from wider Graeco-Roman society. In many places, pagans could not distinguish between Jews and Christians,[110] and so Christians, in some senses, were shielded for a while against the hostility that new religions faced in the ancient world. However, this is not to say that Christians were invisible. Whereas Jewish practice was tolerated, Jews were by no means popular. At best, they were 'licensed atheists'.[111] Pagan contempt for Jews

> was bolstered by a feeling that Jews were strange and inferior. It was a protest against religious customs which seemed strange and superstitious. It was a reaction against the apparent snobbery of a race which insisted on maintaining exclusiveness, especially in regard to the one God. It was also a reaction against Jewish success in converting others to their strange religion.[112]

Therefore, some pagan hostility towards Jews could also be directed at Christians. In addition, and more seriously at first, the Christians faced some measure of persecution from their parent body, and the pagans occasionally noticed the tension between the two groups.

105. Though there had existed a philosophical monotheism; see L.W. Hurtado, *One God, One Lord: Early Christian Devotion and Ancient Jewish Monotheism* (Edinburgh: T&T Clark, 1998), 129–30.

106. For discussion, see L.W. Hurtado, 'First-century Jewish monotheism', *JSNT* 71 (1998), 3–26.

107. Cicero, *In Verrem* ii.72 (184); *de Legibus* ii. 9 (22).

108. For a survey of natural phenomena, such as lightning strikes, eclipses and comets, and occurrences of unexplained fires and strange deaths being interpreted by the Romans as signs of divine pleasure, see Liebeschuetz, *Continuity*, 155–64.

109. Ste Croix, 'Why were the early Christians persecuted?', 27.

110. See Wilson (*Related Strangers*) and Boyarin (*Dying for God*), both of whom argue for a much-later and less-clear-cut separation of Jews and Christians. It would seem that this distinction would only hold true for Christians who were ethnically Jewish. From an early period, at least in Rome in the sixties, pagans did seem to be able to distinguish between the two (see below, 106 n.19).

111. Ste Croix, 'Why were the early Christians persecuted?' Although Judaism was never a *religio licita*. J.L. Daniel surveys pagan attitudes to Jews in an anachronistically titled article, 'Anti-Semitism in the Hellenistic-Roman period', *JBL* 98 (1979), 45–65.

112. Daniel, 'Anti-Semitism', 65.

In 49 CE, the Jews were expelled from Rome because they were continually making disturbances on account of Chrestus.[113] Most commentators assume that Suetonius meant Christ,[114] and this would simply have been one of a number of controversies that occurred between Jews and Christians.[115] However, the pagan authorities, even in Luke's schematized treatment of Jewish-Christian conflict, are interested only where there is a financial implication for citizens of the Empire.[116] The Jews, for their part, may have been worried that the actions of Christians would have an impact on their religious freedom for, though there was a considerable amount of prejudice levelled against the Jews, they had been granted some 'privileges' throughout the Empire.[117] Despite clashes between the Jews and various Emperors, Jews were allowed to carry out their own practices, without the need to place images of the Emperor in the temple. Instead, a State-funded sacrifice on behalf of the Emperor took place daily.[118]

> Rome recognised the right of the Jews to live according to their ancient customs and as a special privilege granted them exemptions from all functions which were in opposition to or interfered with their religious laws.[119]

Clearly this Jewish exemption from some State ritual had to be an exception since it went against the larger view of reality. Jewish practice had to be a one-off aberration. When former pagans called other pagans to a strange new monotheistic, and therefore atheistic, sect, something had to be done.

The Romans in the 'World' of the Christians

Despite the animosity the Christians believed was being aimed at them, the early church's response to Rome appears, at first sight, reasonably positive. In the Gospels, Romans are often portrayed in a positive light,[120] and attempts are made to exonerate the Romans from responsibility for the death of Jesus.[121] Walaskay

---

113. Suetonius *Claudius* 25.4; Acts 18.2.

114. So Tertullian, *Apology* 3.5. The issue is discussed by S. Benko, 'Pagan criticism of Christianity during the first two centuries A.D', *ANRW*, II.23.2 (1980), 1055–1118 (1056–61); and Jones 'Christianity', 1028. The main arguments against the association of Chrestus with Christ are that it is considered unlikely that Suetonius would be so ignorant, and the possibility that Chrestus may have been a Jewish rebel which was common enough. It is at least interesting that Paul urges the church in Rome to be subject to the State (13.1–7) and to avoid Jewish practices (2.17–29).

115. R.F. Collins (*Birth*, 33; 229 n. 193) observes that there are 11 mob scenes which follow a similar sequence of events: Acts 6.12+7.56–8; 14.4–5; 14.19–20; 16.19–23; 17.1–7; 17.13; 18.12–17; 19.21–40; 21.26–22.24; 23.7–10; 25.24. See also Gerd Lüdemann, *Early Christianity according to the Tradition of Acts: A Commentary* (Minneapolis: Fortress Press, 1989), 185, for more on Luke's pattern for Jewish behaviour.

116. So, for example, the authorities intervene in Acts 16.16–24 after Paul casts a spirit of divination out of a slave girl, ruining her owner's financial product.

117. Keresztes, *Imperial Rome*, 90. However, ben Zeev ('Privileged position?') denies that the Jews were in any sense 'privileged', arguing that other groups in the Empire were accorded the same religious freedoms.

118. Schürer, *History*, I.486; II.360–2.

119. Keresztes, *Imperial Rome*, 90.

120. See, for example Lk. 7.1–10; 20.19–26; Acts 10.1–11.8.

121. See, among others, J.D. Crossan, *Who Killed Jesus?: Exposing the Roots of Anti-Semitism in the Gospel Story of the Death of Jesus* (New York: HarperSanFrancisco, 1996).

goes as far as describing Luke's Gospel as an *apologia pro imperio*, opposing anti-Roman feeling in order to ensure the Church's survival under the Roman political regime,[122] while Wengst argues that in the third Gospel there are 'virtually no negative statements against Rome and its representatives; rather, they are depicted in an explicitly favourable light'.[123] Similarly, we find injunctions to live at peace with pagan neighbours throughout the epistles.

There was, however, pressure to conform to Roman rituals, the symbols that validated Roman rule. In a world which was to be interpreted through authorized Imperial lenses, some Christians were acutely aware of the dangers that lay in needlessly antagonizing local authorities. The author of 1 Peter exhorts his readers to 'be subject for the Lord's sake to every human institution, whether it be to the Emperor as supreme or to governors ... Honour the Emperor',[124] while the author of 1 Timothy urges 'supplications, prayers, intercessions, and thanksgivings ... for kings and all who are in high position, *that we may lead a quiet and peaceable life*, godly and respectful in every way'.[125] Nonetheless, in these later writings, we are far from Paul's affirmation that the State is the servant of God (Rom. 13.1–7) – a theological position that could not withstand the Neronic persecution – but then, neither is the State the Beast of the Apocalypse.[126] Yet, despite these apparent protests of loyalty, Christians were still viewed with suspicion.

In the ultimate reality of the Christians, Roman power, especially the claims made on behalf of the Emperor, were illusory. The power of Rome came into direct conflict with the power of God; the claim of Caesar to be 'Lord' clashed with the same claim of Christ. It is this clash of Lordships that so often dominates the critical standoff in the martyr acts. For example, in the *Martyrdom of Polycarp*, Polycarp is urged to make the confession, κύριος καῖσαρ, in order to save his life,[127] but refuses; it is Christ, and not Caesar, who is his King and Saviour.[128]

Interestingly, Paul acknowledges this religious, cultural and political backdrop before which the Corinthian church's decision about eating food sacrificed to idols should be made. And so, Paul says that although the general population believed there were many θεοί and κύριοι, the (Christian) *reality* was, as the Christians knew, there was only one θεός, the Father, and one κύριος, Jesus.[129] All other claims to the titles θεός and κύριος were to be judged false. Therefore, deliberate or not, Paul negates any pretension of the Emperor and of the cultic

---

122. P.W. Walaskay, *'And so we came to Rome': The Political Perspective of St Luke* (Cambridge: Cambridge University Press, 1983), 64–7.

123. K. Wengst, *Pax Romana and the Peace of Jesus Christ* (London: SCM Press, 1987), 89–90.

124. 1 Pet. 2.13–17.

125. 1 Tim. 2.1–2 (emphasis added). See also Rom. 13.1–7; and Tit. 3.1 for the way in which a more benign view of the State is reflected in the New Testament.

126. J.H. Elliot, *A Home for the Homeless: A Sociological Exegesis of 1 Peter, Its Situation and Strategy* (London: SCM Press, 1982), 86.

127. *Mart. Pol.* 8.2.

128. *Mart. Pol.* 9.3.

129. 1 Cor. 8.5–6.

deities to be θεοί or κύριοι. For the Christians, 'Κύριος Ἰησοῦς',[130] there could be no other. The acclamation, 'Jesus is Lord' confronted the world of Rome where, by contrast, Caesar was Lord. Christian belief, therefore, not only confronted but also nullified the claims of Rome.

The juxtaposition of the power of Rome and the power of Christ is found par excellence in the Apocalypse, the document that perhaps most inhabits the mythological world-view of the Imperial Cult. In Revelation, God has no equal, and all who would attempt to usurp the power of God will fail; the kings of the earth will be utterly destroyed, and Babylon the Great humiliated. For in the Revelation of St John, God is the παντοκράτωρ,[131] a word that has all but one of its occurrences in the New Testament in the Apocalypse,[132] and lays the direct challenge of God to the universal claims of the Emperor to be the ruler of the world. God is the one who sits on the throne, and so the Kingdom of God comes into direct conflict with Caesar's Kingdom, for both claimed eternal rule and kingship over the whole earth.[133] Christ, for John, is the King of kings and Lord of lords (κύριος κυρίων ... βασιλεὺς βασιλέων).[134] More powerful than any king or lord on earth, at the final battle, he will destroy any world power that aligns itself with the Beast.

Elsewhere in the New Testament, Christ is affirmed to be King. However, the competing kingly claims of the cults of Caesar and Christ are explicitly brought together in the Acts of the Apostles and in John, demonstrating clear Christian consciousness of the direct competition between the two cults. Curiously, the connection is found in both cases in the mouths of Jews. In the dispute at Thessalonica (Acts 17.1–7), the Jews accuse the Christians of saying that there is another king other than Caesar, namely, Jesus.[135] Similarly, the competing claims of Jesus and Caesar are brought into focus in the trial of Jesus before Pilate.[136]

---

130. 1 Cor. 12.3. Naturally, there are a huge number of occurrences of Κύριος Ἰσοῦς in the New Testament, notably dense in 1 and 2 Thessalonians which has led some commentators to see the Imperial Cult as the background to those letters; J.R. Harrison, 'Paul and the Imperial gospel at Thessaloniki', *JSNT* 25 (2002), 71–96; Y. Khiok-Khng, 'A political reading of Paul's eschatology in I & II Thessalonians', *Asia Journal of Theology* 12 (1998), 77–88.

131. Though an uncommon designation for the gods, it is a very common, though exclusive, description for the God of Israel in the LXX, rendering both צבאות and שדי (*TDNT*, III.914–15; *TDOT*, XII.217–18).

132. Κύριος ὁ θεὸς ὁ παντοκράτωρ occurs at Rev. 1.8; 4.8; 11.17; 15.3; 16.7; 19.6; 21.22, while the phrase ὁ θεὸς ὁ παντοκράτωρ is found at Rev. 16.14; 19.15.

133. A. Yarbro Collins, *Crisis and Catharsis: The Power of the Apocalypse* (Philadelphia: Westminster Press, 1984), 141.

134. Rev. 17.14. Cf. 19.16. Aune (*Revelation 1–5*, 126–30) also sees a direct challenge to the Emperor by Christ through the introductory formula τάδε λέγει (2.1, 8, 12, 18; 3.1, 7, 14) in the letters to the seven churches which mirror that of the Imperial edict. For example, M. Benner, *The Emperor Says: Studies in the Rhetorical Style in Edicts of the Early Empire* (Gothenburg: Acta Universitatis Gothoburgensis, 1975), 130, describes the following as a '*praescriptio* of the usual type': Τιβέριος Ἰούλιος Ἀλέξανδρος λέγει.

135. Acts 17.7.

136. The Kingship of Jesus is of course a prominent theme in the passion narratives of the evangelists, but in John the claim of Jesus' Kingship is brought into direct competition with the kingship of Caesar.

Ironically, Pilate invites the Jews to acknowledge the(ir) king, but their response sets up the decision that all people throughout the Empire must make: Is Caesar king or is Jesus king? The chief priests side with the Imperium, 'We have no king but Caesar!'[137] Though βασιλεύς was naturally used for Emperors as rulers, it also had the currency of the Divine ruler cult of the ancient east.[138] It was this claim to divinity that directly challenged the Christian belief that there was but one Lord and God.[139]

Other language in the currency of the Imperial Cult was also claimed by Christian theology. A prominent feature of New Testament theology was the emphasis on the *parousia* of Christ at the end of the age,[140] where Jesus would come in glory with trumpets, angels and shouts. Παρουσία in non-Christian usage had the sense of a divine manifestation,[141] or a state visitation of a city by its ruler.[142] Germanicus speaks of his *parousia*,[143] as does an inscription refer- ring to Hadrian: 'The sixty-ninth year of the first *parousia* of the god Hadrian in Greece'.[144]

These occasions too would be marked with processions, celebrations and noise, suggested by an interesting example of the cognate verb, πάρειμι, found in Nero's speech from Corinth, announcing the liberation of Greece. An order is made that as many men as possible from the province should be present for Nero's παρῖναι 'ις Κόρινθον.[145] The entry of Nero into the city proclaiming liberation with the gathering of the faithful strikes a chord with the gathering of the faithful found in 2 Thessalonians to welcome the παρουσίας τοῦ κυρίου … 'Ιησοῦ Χριστοῦ.[146] The arrival of Jesus Christ accompanied by angels and trumpets,[147] with crowds of the faithful to meet him, shades the processions that accompanied the arrival of Emperors into cities in the Empire.[148] What is

137. John 19.15. Neither of these narratives is likely to be historical. In Luke–Acts, the Jews' behaviour is highly schematized, as is the structure of Paul's visits to the towns in which he preaches. Similarly, John has carefully constructed his narrative to show that the Jews are outsiders. Their pro- fession of loyalty to Caesar contrasts with the words of the Passover Seder that they would utter later on that day, 'We have no king but God.' For John, as for most early Christians, the choice is between loyalty to God and loyalty to Caesar (the World/Satan). In this scene, John has the Jews reject God as they reject Jesus and embrace the Imperial Power.

138. *TDNT*, I.564–93.

139. Interestingly see also divine honours directed at Herod in Acts 12.21–3 and within the setting of persecution of the Church.

140. So Mt. 24.3, 27, 37, 39; 1 Cor. 15.23; 1 Thess. 2.19; 3.13; 4.15; 5.23; 2 Thess. 2.1, 8; Jas 5.7– 8; 2 Pet. 1.16; 3.4, 12 (of the coming of the Day of the Lord); 1 Jn 2.28. Other eschatological New Testament documents prefer ἔρχομαι.

141. So Asclepius and Dionysus each have a *parousia*, as do souls as new gods entering the divine sphere (*Corpus Hermetica* 1.22, 26). See further, *TLNT*, III.54 n.4.

142. See *TLNT*, III.53–5.

143. *TDNT*, V.859.

144. *TDNT*, V.860.

145. G.H.R. Horsley (ed.), *New Documents Illustrating Early Christianity: A Review of Greek Inscriptions and Papyri Published in 1979*, IV (New South Wales: Macquarie University, 1987), §78.

146. 2 Thess. 2:1. See also the meeting of the Lord in 1 Thess. 4.17.

147. 1 Thess. 3.13; 4.16.

148. Jesus' triumphal (royal?) entry into Jerusalem (Mk 11: 1–11 and parallels) also seems to

intriguing is that Paul contrasts the παρουσία of Christ [from God] with the παρουσία of the man of lawlessness (ὁ ἄνομος) by the activity of Satan.[149] It is tempting to see an imperial reference in the one who, like Christ, has a παρουσία, but is really from Satan, and will be slain by the breath of Jesus' mouth, particularly since the Thessalonian correspondence is especially rich in language associated with the Imperial Cult.[150]

There is also, in Paul, an unmistakable attack on the chief achievement and benefit of the Roman colonial programme, the *pax et securitas*.[151] When people cry εἰρήνη καὶ ἀσφάλεια, sudden destruction will come upon them.[152] The peace and security afforded by the Roman power is nothing compared to the power that will be revealed by the Day of the Lord. Once again Imperial power is found lacking by the challenge of the power that lies behind the Christians' reality. Here in Paul, we find implicit what is explicit in the Apocalypse; the ceremony, the power, the peace of the Roman *Imperium* will be swept away by the coming of the Emperor's nemesis. 'Paul's message of imminent *parousia*, the Lordship of Christ, the grace and benefaction of Jesus posed an obvious challenge and threat to the *Pax Romana* and the Benefactor Roma.'[153] On the Day of the Lord, Christ will come with trumpets and processions of angels, and utterly destroy the power and the pretensions of Rome in the final battle. Ultimately, Rome cannot offer peace, and it cannot offer security; those who put their trust in the *pax et securitas* of Rome, like all enemies of Christ, will face destruction.

When this Day of the Lord comes with force and destruction, there can be but one Saviour.[154] Here again, Jesus as σωτήρ is contrasted with Caesar's claim. It was through the *pax et securitas* ensured by Rome that Caesar could be known as Saviour, and indeed σωτήρ was an official designation for the Emperor.[155] In the tradition of the gods, who brought safety, order and benefits to cities,[156] the Emperor was seen as the upholder of order, the protector of borders, and the supreme benefactor of the Empire. Of Augustus it was written:

subvert the power of an Imperial visitation to a city, especially as the Messianic cries of the crowds speak of the coming kingdom of David. The royal entry is more explicit in Matthew's interpretation of the scene through the quotation of Zech. 9.9, Ἰδοὺ ὁ βασιλεύς σου ἔρχεταί σοι (21.5).

149. 2 Thess. 2.8–9.

150. J.R. Harrison, 'Imperial gospel', 84. A.L. Moore, *Parousia in the New Testament* (Leiden: E.J. Brill, 1966), 110–14.

151. Wengst, *Pax Romana*, 19–21, 77–9; K.P. Donfried, 'The cults of Thessalonica and the Thessalonian correspondence', *NTS* 31 (1985), 336–56; H. Koester, 'From Paul's eschatology to the apocalyptic schemata in 2 Thessalonians', in R.F. Collins (ed.), *The Thessalonian Correspondence* (Louvain: Louvain University Press, 1990), 441–58 (449–50), among others.

152. 1 Thess. 5.2–3.

153. Khiok-Khng, 'Political reading', 79.

154. See Acts 2.21.

155. *TLNT*, III.344–57. Similarly, σωτήρ was applied to future Emperors including Vespasian (see Josephus, *War* 3.459 and 8.71); see Deissmann, *Light*, 346.

156. Zeus is the Saviour of the Universe because he 'has arranged everything for the preservation and protection of the whole' (Plato, *Laws* 10.903*b*).

> Providence, which governs the course of our lives, has shown attention and goodness and has provided for us the most perfect good for life by producing the emperor, whom it has filled with virtue in order to make him a benefactor of humanity. So it has sent to us and to others a saviour who has put an end to war and will restore order everywhere: Caesar, by his appearing, has realised the hopes of our ancestors; not only has he surpassed earlier benefactors of humanity, but he leaves no hope to those of the future that they might surpass him. The god's birthday was for the world the beginning of the good news (εὐαγγελίου) that he brought.[157]

It is striking just how much of this acclamation to Augustus mirrors Christian praise to Christ: uniquely virtuous; a saviour and benefactor of humanity, who in bringing an end to war ushers in an era of peace; the fulfilment of ancestral hopes, whose greatness will never be surpassed; and proclaimed a god whose birthday marked a new beginning of the world.

Nonetheless, come the Day of the Lord, military might and the Roman 'gift of peace' would be useless. No Emperor could really be the Saviour of the World. No Emperor could prevent the appearing of the Day of the Lord; no Emperor could rescue even one soul from God's judgement.[158] Despite great military might, the Imperial power would stand helpless on the Day of Judgement. Rome and her armies, victorious in many a battle, would be utterly crushed in the final battle.[159] What Harrison says of Paul is surely true of practically the whole Christian corpus: it 'strips the imperial cult of a prize claim; there is only one *epiphany* and *parousia* worth waiting for – Christ's'.[160] Although many of the writings of the New Testament are far from hostile to the Empire, imperial power was a mere shadow beside that of Christ's. Despite the pretensions of the pontiffs of the Empire, their offer of peace and security was illusory; Christ alone was ὁ σωτὴρ τοῦ κόσμου.[161]

The Christians in the 'World' of the Romans

Christian language and symbols competed for the same ground as Roman Imperial ideology. This is not to say that the Romans were aware of this. Indeed, the Romans seemed to know very little of the Christians and their theology, as we will explore below. Christians were viewed with suspicion simply because they appeared to be un-Roman. And they were – on every front. In the Christian mind, all points of Roman ideology were challenged, their gods were scorned, and the Emperor 'dethroned'. Christians, in their theology, subverted Roman ideology and replaced it with their own. Crucially, this had consequences for the way in which they behaved within the Empire and towards its rituals and symbols.

---

157. Priene inscription (9 BCE) quoted and translated by C. Spicq, *TLNT*, III.353.

158. Cf. Mt. 10.28//Lk. 12.4–5.

159. I will argue that the early Christians saw themselves as being engaged in a form of Holy War in the following chapter.

160. Harrison, 'Imperial gospel', 84.

161. Jn 4.24; 1 Jn 4.14. See also Lk. 2.11; Phil. 3.20; 2 Tim. 1.10 (compare with 1 Timothy where the Saviour is always God); Tit. 1.4; 2.13; 3.6; 2 Pet 1.1, 11, 20; 3.3, 18.

Ultimately, though some Christians tried to take what they supposed to be a relatively accommodating stance towards Rome, one could not be a good Christian and do everything the Romans expected good citizens to do. Christians could not participate in the symbols of Rome because there was no room in their conception of reality for those symbols. So, whereas the Romans could accommodate the Christian god on the same terms as other deities, the Christian God could not accommodate Roman deities.[162]

This competition for symbols and language was asymmetric. The Romans had power. Their gods had brought them good fortune, military conquest and, of course, an Empire. The Emperor sat at the centre of this power. Their way of seeing the world was the way the world was, and binding together the whole Empire was the Emperor Cult. Social cohesion, civic order, right religion, the protection of the gods' honour, the promotion of sport and arts and the safety of each person in the Empire depended on the Emperor. Celsus expresses incredulity that the Christians did not participate in state affairs, including offering due honours and sacrifices. Reflecting the Imperial dogma which the Christians challenged, he retorts: 'Whatever you receive in this life you receive from him'.[163] This remarkable claim demonstrates the way in which the Imperial Cult functioned at the heart of civic life. The narrative promoted by the Roman Empire was simple: all life revolved around the Emperor.

However, the Christians knew differently. Their God was the locus of true power. All honour, glory, power, riches and strength belonged to the Lamb (Rev. 5.12). The Romans, not understanding the complexity of Christian theology, saw only an absurd attack from a new seditious movement whose beliefs, or rather their practices, flew in the face of all that was real. We have seen how the ground looked from the Christian point of view, but how did the Romans see the Christians? Where did the followers of this new faith fit into the Roman view of the world?[164]

Why were Christians persecuted? For Christians, the answer was blindingly obvious, it was διὰ τὸ ὄνομα. As they had been warned,[165] adherence to the name of Jesus caused them to appear before governors and kings, and suffer and die. Suffering for 'the name' was what it meant to be a Christian. Suffering was therefore incorporated into the world-view of the Christians.[166] To be devoted to

---

162. However, see Benko, 'Pagan criticism'. His conclusion (1110) that, 'by and large the Roman State and its citizens showed tolerance toward Christianity which the church failed to reciprocate' does not take seriously the fact of the asymmetric power struggle. That Christians made claims for Christ that belonged to the Emperor went largely unnoticed, which explains the relative 'tolerance' of the State. In contrast, for the Christians, that honours due to God alone were being given to a man, particularly when great military power resided with that man, was an unacceptable blasphemy that demanded a response. The Christians could not accommodate the claims of God and the claims of Caesar in the name of what Benko terms 'tolerance'.

163. Origen, *Contra Celsum* 8.65.

164. Pagan references to Christians are helpfully collected by Benko, 'Pagan criticism', 1055–118. See also Wilken, *The Christians*.

165. Mt. 10.17–23; 24.9; Lk. 21.12; Jn 15.21; Acts 5.41; 1 Pet. 4.14.

166. So, for example, Phil. 1.12–14; Jas 1.2–3; Heb. 12.3; 1 Pet. 1.6–7; 4.12; Rev. 7.14.

Christ was inevitably to attract the hatred of the world.[167] It is no exaggeration to claim that in the general Christian imagination, the more one suffered, the more faithful a Christian one could be judged. This was the lens through which Christians interpreted their situation. What, however, did the Romans think the Christians were doing?

The first bout of notable persecution came under Nero in 64 CE for the suspicion of arson. Tacitus, writing 50 years after the event, reflects the suspicion that Nero was himself responsible for the fire, and also his successful attempt to deflect blame onto the Christians. If this is true, and there is good reason to suspect that no such charge was made,[168] what is generally overlooked is how easy it was for Nero to make the populous believe that the Christians were responsible. If the fire was not the historical cause of the outbreak of persecution against the Christians, then from where did the popular hatred come required to sustain such an attack? Moreover, how was such popular hatred sustained, so that by the time of Tacitus he could still reflect it?

> But all human efforts, all the lavish gifts of the emperor and propitiations of the gods, did not banish the sinister belief that the conflagration was the result of an order. Consequently, to get rid of the report, Nero fastened the guilt and inflicted the most exquisite tortures on a class hated for their abominations, called Christians by the populace. Christus, from whom the name had its origin, suffered the extreme penalty during the reign of Tiberius at the hands of one of our procurators, Pontius Pilate, and a deadly superstition, thus checked for the moment, again broke out not only in Judea, the first source of the evil, but also in the City, where all things hideous and shameful from every part of the world meet and become popular. Accordingly, an arrest was first made of all who confessed, then, upon their information, an immense multitude was convicted, not so much for the crime of arson as of their hatred of the human race. Mockery of every sort was added to their deaths. Covered with the skins of beasts, they were torn by dogs and perished, or were nailed to crosses, or were doomed to the flames and burnt, to serve as a nightly illumination when daylight had expired. Nero had offered his gardens for the spectacle, and put on a show in the circus, mingling with the people in the dress of a charioteer or standing up in a chariot. *Hence, even for criminals who deserved extreme and exemplary punishment*, there arose a feeling of compassion, for it was not, as it seemed, for the public good, but to glut one man's cruelty, that they were being destroyed.[169]

There are several points of interest in Tacitus' version of events. First is the attitude towards the Christians that Tacitus displays and attributes to the masses. Christians are a class hated for their abominations, with their 'deadly superstition';

167. So, for example, Jn 15.18–20.

168. Although Tacitus (and Sulpicius Severus, following Tacitus, *Chronicles* II.29) links the Christians with the fire, he nonetheless believes they are innocent. Pliny the Elder (*Natural History* 17.1, 5), Suetonius (*Nero* 38) and Dio Cassius (76.6) blame Nero without any doubt. However, interestingly none of these writers mention the Christians in connection with the fire. Moreover, no anti-Christian writer mentions a charge or suspicion of arson, nor does any early Christian writer make a defence against any charge of incendiarism. See Keresztes, *Imperial Rome*, 69–73. In contrast, J. Bishop (*Nero, the Man and the Legend*, London: R. Hale, 1964) claims that the charge has foundation, in that an apocalyptic Christian or Jewish group began the fire to hasten the Day of the Lord.

169. Tacitus, *Annals* 15.44 (emphasis added).

it is 'an evil', having at its centre the worship of an executed criminal. Tacitus openly suggests that arson was not the primary reason for which they were punished; rather, it was because they were haters of the human race.[170] Further-more, Tacitus affirms his belief that they are indeed criminals, and though feelings of compassion arose for them because of the suspicion that they suffered to satisfy Nero's cruelty, he also insists that they were deserving of extreme punishment. For Tacitus, the charge of misanthropy, coupled with that of following a strange superstition, practising unspecified abominations, justified punishment, even death, especially when it was found spreading into Rome.

Whether or not Tacitus accurately records the historical situation of 64 CE, it is likely that he is here reflecting at least his own, and probably the popular, conception of Christians in his own time. They may not have been guilty of fire-raising, but they were guilty of something that, in Tacitus' view, merited the death penalty.

Pliny too, in his famous letter to Trajan, assumed that Christians deserved the death penalty.

> Meanwhile, in the case of those who were denounced to me as Christians, I have observed the following procedure: I interrogated these as to whether they were Christians; those who confessed I interrogated a second and a third time, threatening them with punishment; *those who persisted I ordered executed. For I had no doubt that, whatever the nature of their creed, stubbornness and inflexible obstinacy surely deserve to be punished* ... Those who denied that they were or had been Christians, when they invoked the gods in words dictated by me, offered prayer with incense and wine to your image, which I had ordered to be brought for this purpose together with statues of the gods, and moreover cursed Christ – none of which those who are really Christians, it is said, can be forced to do – these I thought should be discharged. Others named by the informer declared that they were Christians, but then denied it, asserting that they had been but had ceased to be, some three years before, others many years, some as much as twenty-five years. They all worshipped your image and the statues of the gods, and cursed Christ.[171]

In this famous letter, Pliny saw death as a fitting penalty for stubborn unshake-able obstinacy, in what he later calls a 'depraved, excessive superstition', though his preferred solution was rehabilitation.[172] Pliny was not exactly sure what the charges against Christians were, or whether being a Christian was sufficient for a guilty verdict. 'And I have been not a little hesitant as to ... whether the name itself, even without offences, or only the offences associated with the name is to be punished'. What really concerns Pliny is what to do about those who recant or used to be Christians. It is primarily on this matter that he wrote to Trajan. He wonders 'whether pardon is to be granted for repentance, or, if a man has once been a Christian, it does him no good to have ceased to be one'. Trajan's reply confirmed Pliny's approach. While Christians were not to be hunted down, they were nonetheless to be punished if the charge, that is, of being a Christian, was proven. If, however, the accused was no longer a Christian, they were to be freed.

---

170. *Odium humani generis.*
171. Pliny, *Epistles* 10.96 (emphasis added).
172. Marcus Aurelius (*Mediations* 11.3) also states that Christians died for their obstinacy.

Too much has been read into this important correspondence. We do not find evidence that Christianity was illegal, in the sense that an edict had been passed to that effect,[173] otherwise the Emperor could hardly have responded so cautiously. Indeed, this is exactly the complaint of Tertullian when he protests against the way in which Christians were treated in this episode.[174] Nor can it be claimed that Christians were persecuted simply for the *nomen* alone,[175] if that is understood to mean that nothing other than the name Christian was offensive to the Romans. Pliny simply assumed that behind the name 'Christian' there were excesses and a general anti-social attitude worth punishing.[176]

At the end of the day, Pliny was not really interested in investigating the belief system of the sect he encountered. His question was purely operational. Nonetheless, as Barnes has observed, Pliny's treatment made Christianity a unique 'crime' in the Empire in one respect: whereas *being* a Christian was worthy of punishment, *having been* one was not.[177] Now that the markets were busy again, Pliny saw no need for excessive bloodshed, and so his wish was to pardon those who had recanted.

Aside from inflexible obstinacy and the possible negative economic affect on the temple trade,[178] the name Christian carried with it a whole bank of other crimes and misdemeanours. Christianity was a new cult, a suspicious association, and in the popular imagination such novelty led to debauchery and crime.

> Greco-Roman society in general had little respect for new movements. The Roman State in particular was suspicious of any new assembly or association, lest it might develop into a political organisation in conflict with the Roman State.[179]

Antiquity was taken to be proof of the authenticity of a rite in the Roman mind,[180] a quality Christianity lacked, and a weakness Celsus exploited. He claimed that the Christians lacked the approval of antiquity for their doctrine.[181] Christianity strongly resembled a secret *collegium* or *hetaeria*, of the sort already forbidden by Trajan.[182] Meeting at night or daybreak, sharing common meals where both

173. Contra Keresztes, *Imperial Rome*.

174. Tertullian, *Apol.* 2.7–8. See R.M. Grant, *Augustus to Constantine: The Thrust of the Christian Movement into the Roman World* (London: Collins, 1971), 100–2 for discussion.

175. Benko, 'Pagan criticism', 1072.

176. A.N. Sherwin-White, *The Letters of Pliny: A Social and Historical Commentary* (Oxford: Clarendon Press, 1966), 780–1. However, there is precedent for banned association; Pliny the Elder (*Naturalis Historia* 29.54) reveals that being a member of the Druidic cult was illegal in itself.

177. Barnes, 'Legislation', 48.

178. Christians may have abstained from the Temple trade on the basis of an interpretation of 1 Cor. 8–10. The Christians were certainly known for regarding the Temples as 'dead houses' (Municius Felix, *Octavius* 8).

179. Slater, 'Social setting', 252. See also R. Stark, 'The class basis of early Christians from a sociological model', *Sociological Analysis* 47 (1986), 216–25 (225); and Wilken, *Christians*, 32–5, for the identification of the Christians as a *hetaeria*, or political club.

180. Benko, 'Pagan criticism', 1106 n. 184. Josephus' defence of Judaism in the *Antiquities* is based on the long traditions of the Jewish religion.

181. Origen, *Contra Celsum* 3.14; 5.33; 5.65.

182. Benko, 'Pagan criticism', 1076. See also Sherwin-White, 'Early persecution', 205. J. Gagé

sexes took part, with an origin outside Italy (*prava et externa religio*),[183] the early practitioners of Christianity were bound to attract suspicion. Christianity was regarded as a *superstitio*[184] *nova ac malefica*,[185] thought by Plutarch to lead to atheism, magic, rites, depravity and barbarism.[186] Looking like the Bacchanalia, which, consisting of nocturnal activities, including overindulgence in feasting and drinking and ecstatic dancing in the forest,[187] shocked Roman sensibilities, so that it was outlawed in the second century BCE, the Christians were regarded as another *sacra nocturna* that took part in immoral sexualized rites. Indeed, it may be, as Wilken suggests, that the Roman experience of the Bacchanalia influenced their attitudes to new religious movements such as Christianity.[188]

Morton Smith's reconstruction of Pliny's interrogation of the Christians is instructive, as it highlights many of the possible 'crimes' lurking behind the name 'Christian' in the Roman mind.

> What's this I hear of nocturnal meetings?
> We're working people, so we have to meet before dawn. Like all working people, we've got to be at work by sunrise.
> What are the spells you sing?
> They aren't magical spells, they're hymns.
> Do you evoke, as a demon, that crucified criminal?
> No, we worship him as a god.
> What is the oath you take at your meetings?
> We only swear not to commit any crime.
> Do your secret meals take place at your nocturnal meetings?
> No, we come back later – at the end of the day, like everybody else.
> What's the menu?
> Mostly just bread and a little wine; we're poor.
> What about eating a body and drinking blood?
> That's a lie! That's what our enemies say. We never do anything like that.
> Very well, have her racked and see if she sticks to her story. Where's the other one?[189]

(*Les Classes sociales dans l'Empire romain*, Paris: Payot, 1971, 308) argues that Christianity resembled a funerary or burial society, while Celsus charges Christians with forming associations contrary to the laws (*Contra Celsum* 1.1).

183. Livy 39.14.3.

184. The term *superstitio* was 'regularly used at this time for private and foreign cults' (Sherwin-White, *Letters of Pliny*, 708).

185. Suetonius, *Claudius* 5.25; *Nero* 16.2. M. Smith (*Jesus the Magician: Charlatan or Son of God?* [California: Seastone, 1998], 66–70) translates this term as 'practitioners of magic' and notes that the term *odium humani* was a common charge made of magicians. Christians are also linked with astrologers and soothsayers in the Pseudo-Hadrian (*c.* 140) as a class that the populous despise (Benko, 'Pagan Criticism', 1080–1). Magicians were also often charged with *contumacia* (obstinacy), an offence listed by Pliny against the Christians. For a discussion of the Christians' defence against accusations of magic, see N. Janowitz, *Magic in the Roman World: Pagans, Jews and Christians* (Religion in the First Christian Centuries; London/New York: Routledge, 2001), 16–20.

186. Plutarch, *De Superstitione* 2.

187. Livy 39.8–19. See Wilken, *The Christians*, 16–17; Frend, *Martyrdom and Persecution*, 84–6.

188. Wilken, *The Christians*, 17.

189. Smith, *Jesus the Magician*, 69–70.

Smith's reconstruction draws out the Christians' insistence that they did nothing wrong, and that, to their minds, they were like other members of the Empire in many respects, trying to be good citizens. The Romans, however, suspected them of participating in illegal and suspicious nocturnal activities, invoking demons and taking part in immoral rites.

More than anything else, it was these crimes of immorality (*flagitia*) associated with Christianity that fuelled prejudice against them. This prejudice was reinforced by the Christians' unfathomable refusal to offer sacrifice to the Emperor and to honour the gods, especially at times of crisis. Crucially, crimes of immorality and spurning of the gods went hand in hand according to the Roman mind: 'the baker's wife full of vices, an enemy to faith and chastity, she also despises the gods'.[190] Extravagant claims made by those who observed the behaviour of the Christians make it clear that we are obviously dealing with prejudice, rather than any objection to belief or doctrine.[191] It is the impression that the new cult members were incestuous, debauched, seditious cannibals, who fed on the flesh of children that caused most concern. A novel found on a second-century papyrus tells of an alleged Christian initiation that involves child-murder, cannibalism and orgies.

> At that moment another naked man arrived ... He threw the boy's body on its back, struck it, opened it, removed the heart and placed it over the fire ... When it was sufficiently prepared, he distributed portions of it to the initiates ...[192]

Another charge of cannibalism and child sacrifice is recounted by Minucius Felix, who claims Cornelius Fronto (100–166 CE) as his source:[193]

> A young baby is covered in flour ... [and it] is killed ... It is the blood of this infant (I shudder to mention it) it is this blood that they lick with thirsty lips; these are the limbs they distribute eagerly; this is the victim by which they seal their covenant.[194]

It is not difficult to see these charges as a misunderstanding of the Eucharist, where the body of the παῖς θεοῦ is broken and distributed, and where the new covenant is sealed in the blood of the same child which all drink. Similarly,

---

190. Lucius Apuleius, *Metamorphoses* 9.14. M.Y. MacDonald (*Early Christian Women and Pagan Opinion: The Power of the Hysterical Woman* [Cambridge: Cambridge University Press, 1996], 51–9) observes that this is the first pagan reference to Christian women. She notes that his assessment of their character is that they are immoral. The author of 1 Peter appears to be aware of the popular link between refusing to take part in cultic activities and immorality as he addresses both at 1 Pet. 2.13–17.

191. Barnes observes ('Legislation', 49), 'rulers united with the ruled in a common prejudice'.

192. Quoted in Wilken, *The Christians*, 18.

193. E. Champlin (*Fronto and Antonine Rome* [Cambridge: Harvard University Press, 1980], 65–6) suggests that it may have been Fronto who brought the charges of Oedipean unions and 'Thyestean' banquets to prominence. Wilken (*The Christians*, 17) notes that by the late second century 'such charges had become widespread'.

194. Minucius Felix, *Octavius* 9.5–6. He goes on to recount a lurid orgy involving incest among other things. For other charges against the Christians of cannibalism, see Athenagoras, *Plea on behalf of the Christians*, 31–6; Justin, *Apol.* I.7; *Mart. Lyons* 1.52; Tertullian, *Apol.* 9.8; and Origen, *Contra Celsum* 6.27.

charges of immorality could naturally emerged with a little knowledge of Christian practices, such as the holy kiss shared between brothers and sisters, inviting the charge of incest, a vile crime that particularly offended the gods.[195] Though these charges were clearly untrue, and Minucius Felix composes them in the mouth of a Christian enemy, it demonstrates that such charges were current. It is also worth noting that, because so-called 'orthodox' and 'heretical' groups made such accusations against one another,[196] we should not be too surprised if pagan onlookers saw such vehement attacks as confessions of mutual guilt.[197]

Christians were seen, therefore, as a destabilizing influence on society. They slighted the gods, inviting divine disaster. Something may also have been known about the Christians' apocalyptic beliefs, which probably lie behind Fronto's assertion that 'they threaten the universe will be destroyed by fire'.[198] The Christians would have unsettled the pagans by their behaviour, leading, not surprisingly, to lynch mobs demanding that the Christians be punished. Though Hadrian instructed proconsul Minucius Fundanus, in response to a question posed by his predecessor, Silvanus Granianus, that public hysteria was no grounds for persecution, it reveals that Christians attracted such hysteria, and it is worth bearing in mind how easily it was for Nero, a century earlier, to fasten the blame for the fire onto the Christians.[199]

Conclusion

Christians, in the eyes of the populous of the Empire, were deeply unpopular. Public opinion clearly constituted a crucial factor in the persecution of Christians.[200] The Christians were aware of their unpopularity, so that Luke could write that in every place Christianity was spoken against (Acts 28.22).[201] I have sought to put content to the hatred from Roman sources, most of which were confirmed by the writer of 1 Peter. He was aware of the suspicion of wrongdoing (2.12; 4.15), immorality and civic disloyalty (2.13–17), he knew that they were regarded as a curiosity (3.15), and that the pagans were largely ignorant of the faith (2.15).

195. Tacitus, *Annals* 12.5.5, 8.
196. So, for example, Clement accuses the Carpocratians of 'love feasts' (*Strom.* 3.2.10), and Justin hints that fellow Christians may be guilty of cannibalism (*Apol.* I.26), though he himself does not know if the charge is true. Though Benko takes these charges seriously ('Pagan criticism', 1092), there is no reason to see these charges as having any more basis than the pagan accusations against the proto-orthodox Christians.
197. S. Benko, *Pagan Rome and the Early Christians* (Bloomington: Indiana University Press, 1984), 68; E. Gibbon, *The Decline and Fall of the Roman Empire* (6 vols; London: J.M. Dent, 1910), III.80–1.
198. Minucius Felix, *Octavius* 8.
199. Slater, 'Social setting', 247–8.
200. That much of the persecution came from local quarters is reflected in Acts 14.4–7; 16.19–22; and especially Mk 13.9–13//Lk. 21.12–17; Mt. 21.12–17.
201. For other references to the Christians' awareness that they are held in low esteem, see Acts 5. 17–31; 8.1–3; 1 Thess. 2.14–16; Gal. 1.13–14; Heb. 10.32–9.

The fact that the *Haustafeln* are reinforced may be a defence against the charge that the cult promoted social disorder (2.18–3.7; 5.1–5), but ultimately, Peter knew that it was the refusal to be seen to pay homage to the Emperor (2.17) and participate in honouring the gods (4.4) that was at the heart of the Romans' complaint against them. Though he could not advocate honouring the civic gods, he could advocate honouring the Emperor. However, though the Christians could believe themselves to be paying the Emperor appropriate respect, so far as the Romans could see, they were not performing the appropriate rituals, without which loyalty could not be demonstrated. The same exclusiveness that made the Jews unpopular applied equally, indeed more so, to the early Christians. Without the protection of ancient tradition,[202] and without Jewish ethnicity, Christians were perceived to decadently flout Roman traditions.[203]

Rejection of gods was an absurd rejection of the obvious power structures of the Empire. As we have seen, the Imperial Cult was one way in which people in the Empire could represent themselves to the Imperial power. The cult protected the worship of the gods and maintained the social and moral order. To attack the *Imperium* was to slight the gods; to attack the gods was to launch an attack on Rome. The *Pax Romana* was dependant on the *Pax Deorum*. Those who brought dishonour to the gods endangered the safety of Rome and her Empire. The gods brought Rome into being, and those who attack them were regarded as

> men ... of a reprobate, unlawful, and desperate faction ... who, having gathered together from the lowest dregs the more unskilled, and women, credulous and, by the facility of their sex, yielding, establish a herd of a profane conspiracy, which is leagued together by nightly meetings, and solemn fasts and inhuman meats – not by any sacred rite, but by that which requires expiation – a people skulking and shunning the light, silent in public, but garrulous in corners.[204]

That kind of attitude fuelled the prejudice against the Christians. Christians upset the social order. 'The *Christiani* deviated from those norms which the Romans set up for the preservation of their State and society.'[205] It caused the mobs to demand that local governors take action against them, and that is why a group Christians appeared before Pliny, apparently because they had caused some kind of negative effect on the temple trade. Pliny, therefore, ordered them to sacrifice to the gods and curse Christ.

---

202. Tacitus, for example, though he had a low regard for Judaism, thought it 'vindicated by its antiquity' (*Histories* 5.5).

203. Although Elliot's (*Home for the Homeless*, 82) point that we are witnessing 'social alienation rather than hatred' is valid, the negative feelings expressed towards the Christians could be legitimately experienced as hatred. E. Colwell's assertion ('Popular reactions against Christianity in the Roman Empire', in J.T. McNeill, M. Spinka and H.R. Willoughby [eds], *Environmental Factors in Christian History* [Chicago: University of Chicago Press, 1939], 53–71], 53, 57–8) that the persecutions were *caused* by the 'sectarian exclusiveness of Christianity' is correct so far as it goes. However, it was the world-view of the Christians that prevented them from being more 'ecumenical'. The Caesar cult and the Christ cult could not coexist.

204. Minucius Felix, *Octavius* 8.

205. Benko, 'Pagan criticisms', 1065.

And here lay the problem. No one was forced to make sacrifices to the gods, yet Pliny makes those suspected of being Christians do it. There is a threefold pattern: worship the Roman gods, offer sacrifice to the Emperor and curse Christ. It was not that these things were required by law, but that Pliny had learned that Christians would not do them. Inviting the first two tests would not seem an unreasonable demand to a Roman official. Indeed, the converse is true; *it would take someone actively opposed to the peace of the Empire to refuse to follow those instructions.* If, in Roman eyes, it was devotion to Christ that caused someone to attack irrationally the peace of the Empire, then it became reasonable to persuade someone to curse this new god in order to demonstrate true loyalty to Rome.

And so, there could be no compromise, no middle ground between the Christians and the *Imperium*. Romans expected recognition of the Imperial power and respect towards the gods. This was the base line of belonging to the Empire and wishing its well-being. Sacrifices to the gods and to the Emperor were seen as rituals affirming good citizenship. Those who refused to take part were seen to be committing wilful acts of sedition and treason, destabilizing the Empire, and risking its safety by offending the gods. In addition, Christians were seen to belong to a new, superstitious organization that practised immorality. They were dangerous atheists, who were growing in number, and spreading across the Empire. They had to be tried and encouraged to recant their madness, thereby becoming good citizens. If, however, they continued to hold to their superstition, then they had to be eliminated; the social and moral order of the Empire depended upon it, and the gods demanded it.

Celsus neatly captures the Romans' sheer inability to see the Christians' point of view, their incredulity that Christians would refuse to take part in the cultic foundation of the Empire, and the reason that the new faith had to be stamped out. He writes: 'If everyone followed the Christians' example and opposed the emperor, the result would be anarchy and everything would be destroyed *including Christian worship*!'[206]

Crucially, in the trial of Christians, both the Christian and the 'authorized' Roman realities were reinforced. The confession, 'ἐγὼ χριστιανός εἰμι', which the Christian longed to make was heard by Roman ears as a confession of being a member of a seditious, obstinate, stubborn and superstitious cult that threatened the very fabric of reality – in other words, an enemy of the State. The Christians, in contrast, saw an opportunity to assert their own loyalty to God through the means by which one was ultimately called: to suffer for the Name. In their respective behaviours, Roman authorities and Christians alike reinforced the respective views held about the other, and, more importantly, reinforced their respective image of reality. It is the Christian construction of reality to which we turn in more detail.

---

206. Origen, *Contra Celsum* 8.68 (emphasis added).

Chapter 3

TOWARDS A THEOLOGY OF RADICAL MARTYRDOM

Introduction

So far, we have examined the way in which Christian texts reported the incidence of martyrdom, and established that, for a significant number of early Christians, the phenomenon of radical martyrdom was promoted as a model of service or devotion to Christ. We concluded that those who sought (and found) death at the hands of the authorities should not be written off as heretics deviating from an established martyrological tradition, for they represented a no-less authentic early view of Christian death.

Furthermore, we have studied how Christians could, despite the lack of an Imperial policy of persecution, legitimately believe the State was their enemy, even though virtually all experiences of persecution came from local quarters. Even if, as some claim, the Christians did everything possible to be good citizens of the Empire, so far as the Romans were concerned, the Christians brazenly and provocatively flouted the religious sensitivities and practices of the Empire. This slight was seen as a direct attack on the gods, the Emperor and the State, since the gods were the guardians of the State, and the Emperor was the guardian of religion in the State.

We have seen that the two cults collided on the same ideological ground. Both the Emperor and Christ laid claim to the cosmos, demanding loyalty from all people. In the coming eschatological War, Christ would be victorious over the forces of Rome/Satan. How did this battle for the cosmos affect the lives and stories of the Christians? In particular, how did martyrdom fit into this conflict? If I am correct in concluding that early Christians (at least ideally) sought death, then how was this position maintained theologically? Or, to frame the question differently, can we discover an early Christian theological world-view that would make radical martyrdom a coherent option for the early Christians to take?

Later, in Chapters 4 and 5, we will ask how that world-view came together, first examining possible influences from Jewish and Graeco-Roman beliefs about death, and then, specifically, how the New Testament authors contributed both to the world-view and the theologies that enabled radical martyrdom to flourish. In this chapter, we turn now to the way in which early Christian martyrdom was presented. In doing so, I will highlight key theological elements common to most martyrologies, and begin to piece together the symbolic world that the radical martyrs inhabited that gave birth to and nurtured their theologies of martyrdom.

The Early Christian Presentation of Martyrdom

Martyrdom as Contest

Language used to describe the struggles of the martyrs is varied. Yet, imagery associated with the Graeco-Roman Games is frequently employed. In texts produced by the Christians, martyrs are often described as athletes or gladiators locked in combat as they head towards their deaths, which are, of course, interpreted as victory.

Virtually every one of the early Christian martyr acts recording the death of the protagonists reaches its climax in the public arena of the games. Indeed, many Christians did in fact meet their deaths at the ἀγών,[1] which were regularly put on in order for a town to bring glory to itself, and to be seen to offer praise to the honour of the Emperor. On occasions such as the birthday of the Emperor, governors were required to hold games, or some other form of public entertainment for the city.[2] The games not only entertained but also held together a complex mix of political, religious and social elements of the Empire. In the stadium, the power, justice and glory of the Empire were celebrated amid the spectacle of gladiatorial duels, wild beasts and, importantly for our purposes, the execution of criminals.[3]

The *Martyrs of Lyon* (177 CE) reflects the practice where condemned criminals – in this case, Christians – were used as entertainment in the arena in place of

---

1.   Ἀγών and its related words usually refer to activity in the Greek stadium. At first, in ordinary Greek usage, it related to an assembly of Greeks in a stadium, but later represented any kind of struggle or contest, whether physical or verbal, such as debate. Specifically, it came to be used of the virtuous struggle of the pious. G.W.H. Lampe (*A Patristic Greek Lexicon* [Oxford: Clarendon Press, 1961], 25–6) lists the primary usage of ἀγών, ἀγωνίζομαι and ἀγώνισμα, as well as the secondary usage of ἀγωνιστής and ἀγωνοθέτης among the Christian Fathers to be related to martyrdom.

2.   The martyrdom of Perpetua and her colleagues takes place at military games to mark the birthday of the Emperor Geta (*Mart. Perpetua* 7.9). See Apuleius, *Metamorphoses* 10.18, where a governor of Corinth shows himself to be praiseworthy by funding a three-day gladiatorial display. The costs of putting on games could be immense and began to spiral out of control as patrons attempted to outdo one another (T. Wiedemann, *Emperors and Gladiators* [London: Routledge, 1998], 134–5). See also R. Duncan-Jones, *The Economy of the Roman Empire* (Cambridge: Cambridge University Press, 1982), 153–4; and K. Hopkins, *Death and Renewal* (Cambridge: Cambridge University Press, 1983), 6–8, who terms such patronage as a 'status tax'.

3.   L.L. Thomson, 'The martyrdom of Polycarp: death in the Roman games', *JR* 82 (2002), 27–52 (27). The games were particularly popular in the first two centuries of the Common Era, a fact which, rather ironically, may be attributed to Augustus' *pax Romana*. With no real battles to fight, the amphitheatre became an 'artificial battlefield' where 'war had been transformed into a game, a drama to be repeatedly replayed' for public amusement (Hopkins, *Death and Renewal*, 2, 29). Even in the games' earlier period, previous battles were staged and re-enacted in the arena. The first-known gladiatorial games held by the Campanians in 310 BCE celebrated their victory, with Roman help, over the Samnites. These games celebrated and recreated the battle (Livy 9.40.17). For a brief survey of sociological analyses of the judicial element of the games, see K.M. Coleman, 'Fatal charades: Roman executions staged as mythological enactments', *JRS* 80 (1990), 44–73 (45–9).

more expensive professional gladiators, boxers or swordsmen.[4] Even where the Christians did not fight with wild animals or gladiators, the arena was often the setting where they came up against fierce interrogation, and the authorities tried to make potential martyrs recant.[5] Nonetheless, in many of the martyr acts, the Christians do meet their deaths fighting wild animals.

Christian reflection on these deaths appropriated the image of combatant, not only literally, but also symbolically.[6] The trials, the fight with beasts and the tortures inflicted upon the followers of Christ were almost always portrayed as a contest;[7] Christians could be 'athletes' or 'combatants', whether or not they ended up facing wild animals.[8] Tertullian explicitly employs athletic or military metaphors in his writing on martyrdom. He saw the Christians as soldiers serving under God's oath not to commit idolatry.[9] Trials or interrogations of Christians, with the pressure placed on the believer to recant, marked the fulcrum of battle.

> I am challenged by the enemy. If I surrender to them, I am as they are. In maintaining this oath, I fight furiously in battle, am wounded, hewn in pieces, slain. Who wished this fatal issue to his soldier, but he who sealed him by such an oath.[10]

Importantly, Barton[11] notes the similarity of this oath (*sacramentum*) taken by Tertullian, which he also commends to other Christians, with the oath taken by gladiators (*sacramentum gladiorum*): 'I will endure to be burned, to be bound, to

4. See Pagels, *Gnostic Gospels*, 85; Chenu, Prud'homme, Quéré and Thomas, *Christian Martyrs*, 4; Frend (*Martyrdom and Persecution*, 5) notes that the substitution of criminals for gladiators had been made legal by the Emperor and Senate the year before the events described in *the Martyrs of Lyons*.
5. So although the time of the animal games were past, with animal hunts only taking place in the morning (Wiedemann, *Emperors and Gladiators*, 55), Polycarp is still interrogated and executed in the amphitheatre, a setting which Bisbee (*Pre-Decian Acts of Martyrs and Commentarii*, 122) considers 'an improbable place for a trial'. However, since mob rule appears to have played a significant role in the arrest and execution of Christians, often overturning the normal course of law (Hopkins, *Death and Renewal*, 16; Ste Croix, 'Why were the early Christians persecuted?', 15), Thomson ('Martyrdom of Polycarp', 35–7) considers the context of the trial to be at least historically plausible. A. van den Hoek ('Clement of Alexandria on martyrdom', in E.A. Livingstone [ed.], *Studia Patristica XXVI* [Oxford: Pergamon Press, 1993], 324–41 [325]) demonstrates that unofficial action by crowds accentuated the Christians' vulnerability more so than actual State persecution.
6. For the suggestion that athletic imagery becomes more prominent as Christian deaths at actual games increase, see S. Mitchell, 'Festivals, games and civic life in Roman Asia Minor', *JRS* 80 (1990), 183–93.
7. For example, Tertullian, *Scorp.* 6; Origen, *Exhortation* 17–20; *Mart. Lyons* 1.42; 2.6–8; *Mart. Fruct.* 6.1. In later Christian reflection, the ἀγών became representative of the struggle to live the Christian life rather than the specific struggle against the interrogator as one (potentially) approached death (see Dehandschutter, 'Example and discipleship', 25–6).
8. For example, *Mart. Carpus* 35; *Mart. Lyons* 1.1; 1.17; *Mart. Perpetua* 10; Origen, *Exhortation* 1, 17–20, 34, 42, 49; *Mart. Ignatius* 5.
9. So for example, Tertullian, *Ad Martyras* 3.
10. Tertullian, *Scorp.* 4.4.
11. C.A. Barton, 'Savage miracles: the redemption of lost honor in Roman society and the sacrament of the gladiator and the martyr', *Representations* 45 (1994), 47–71 (56 n. 8). See also Hopkins, *Death and Renewal*, 24.

be beaten, and to be killed by the sword.'[12] Similarly, Tertullian also compares himself to those amateurs who cry out advice to the already skilled gladiators.[13]

> You are about to pass through a noble struggle in which the living God acts the part of superintendent, in which the Holy Ghost is your trainer, in which the prize is an eternal crown of angelic essence, citizenship in the heavens, glory everlasting. Therefore your master, Jesus Christ, who anointed you with his spirit, and led you forth into the arena, has seen it good, before the day of conflict, to take you from a condition more pleasant in itself, and imposed on you a harder treatment, that your strength may be the greater.[14]

A wealth of contest imagery was available to those who reflected upon Christian martyrdom – no doubt influencing the way death for the religion was narrated. Within the acts themselves, athletic imagery is liberally used. Blandina, considered doubly weak, being both a slave and a girl,[15] defeats the torturers through her power (δυνάμεως).[16] She is, therefore, cast in the role of a noble athlete (γενναῖος ἀθλεητής).[17] Similarly, the new catechumen, Martus, also displayed the characteristics of a noble contestant (γενναῖον ἀγωνιστήν) in his struggle.[18] In contrast, within the Christian community at Lyons, there were those who were not yet ready to undergo martyrdom. They are described as untrained, unprepared and weak, being unable to bear the strain of an ἀγῶνος μεγάλου.[19] They had not undergone the training and self-discipline required to produce endurance (ὑπομονή), the necessary quality to become a successful athlete and martyr. Nonetheless, note that even their unreadiness to face death was still cast in athletic language.

Endurance (ὑπομονή)[20] is identified as the key element in Ignatius' strategy to confront suffering.[21] It is the same quality that an athlete develops in self-training for the contest,[22] and is applied to those who faced torture in order to force apostasy, yet managed to resist. Those who desire to follow the martyrs' example must also undergo training and preparation for the contest.

---

12. Petronius, *Satyricon* 117.

13. Tertullian, *Ad Martyras* 1.

14. Tertullian, *Ad Martyras* 3. See also *Apology* 50.10, where the golden crown is compared to that which the gladiators win. It should be pointed out that Tertullian was actually against gladiatorial games (*de Spectaculis* especially 15.2, 6).

15. Shaw, 'Body/power/identity', 308. Even within the text, Blandina is considered by men to be 'cheap, ugly, and contemptuous' (*Mart. Lyons* 1.17).

16. *Mart. Lyons* 1.17, 18.

17. *Mart. Lyons* 1.19.

18. *Mart. Lyons* 1.17.

19. *Mart. Lyons* 1.11.

20. For a discussion of the transformation of a passive 'feminized' term into one of honour, see Shaw, 'Body/power/identity', 278–91.

21. Ignatius, *Magn.* 1.1; *Trall.* 4.1. Compare *T. Job* 17.7 where endurance is considered better than anything.

22. Ignatius, *Eph.* 3.1; see also *Mart. Pol.* 2; *Mart. Lyons* 1. 6, 7; *Mart. Potamioena* 4–5. For the training of gladiators to produce endurance, see L. Robert, *Les Gladiateurs dans l'Orient grec* (Paris: E. Champion, 1940), 16–23.

> Gathering here ... we celebrate the anniversary of his [Polycarp's] martyrdom, both as memorial for those who have already fought the contest and for the training and preparation of those who will do so one day.[23]

Athletic imagery is linked quite explicitly with the quality of endurance in the *Martyrdom of Carpus, Papylus, and Agathonicê*. During his torture, Papylus endured three pairs of torturers as he is scraped, and by not uttering a sound is said, like Blandina and Maturus, to have 'received the angry onslaught of the adversary like a noble athlete'.[24] Papylus' silence under torture points to another element borrowed from the games that is crucial in the description of martyrdom: the importance of public witness.

Martyrdom as Public Witness

Martyrdom was a public spectacle for both Romans and Christians.[25] For the Romans, it was important that law-breakers be punished as publicly as possible to act as a deterrent for would-be deviants. The games were public entertainment that reinforced the social, moral and religious order.[26] The Christians, as a threat to that order, had to be publicly executed in the arena. For the Romans, this did not constitute *persecution* of Christians; it was *prosecution* of individuals deemed to be a threat to the State.[27] However, the Christians did not play the part of the criminal:

> You find that criminals are eager to conceal themselves, avoid appearing in public, are in trepidation when they are caught, deny their guilt, when they are accused; even when they are put to the rack, they do not easily or always confess; when there is no doubt about their condemnation, they grieve for what they have done. In their self-communings they admit their being impelled by sinful dispositions, but they lay the blame either on fate or on the stars. They are unwilling to acknowledge that the thing is theirs, because they own that it is wicked. But what is there like this in the Christian's case? The only shame or regret he feels is at not having been a Christian earlier. If he is pointed out, he glories in it; if he is accused, he offers no defence; interrogated, he makes voluntary confession; condemned he renders thanks. What sort of evil thing is this, which wants all the ordinary peculiarities of evil-fear, shame, subterfuge, penitence, lamenting? What! Is that a crime in which the criminal rejoices; to be accused of which is his ardent wish, to be punished for which is his felicity?[28]

Whereas it was usual for guilty condemned parties to lower their eyes, Polycarp looks straight at the crowd and, shaking his fist at it, denounces the atheists.[29] It

23. *Mart. Pol.* 18.3.
24. *Mart. Carpus* 35.
25. D.S. Potter, 'Martyrdom as spectacle', in R. Scodel (ed.), *Theatre and Society in the Classical World* (Ann Arbor: University of Michigan Press, 1993), 53–88.
26. The clash of gods has already been noted in Chapter 3. Explicitly, Polycarp's subversive use of 'atheists' (9.2) may be noted, as well as the crowd's belief, in Lyons, that the Christians are receiving just punishment from the gods (*Mart. Lyons* 1.60).
27. A.J. Droge, 'The crown of immortality: towards a redescription of Christian martyrdom', in J.J. Collins and M. Fishbane (eds), *Death, Ecstasy, and Other Wordly Journeys* (New York: State of New York Press, 1995), 155–69 (156).
28. Tertullian, *Apol.* 1.10–13.
29. *Mart. Pol.* 9.2.

is also stressed that Perpetua stares at the crowd as she enters the arena.[30] By refusing to play the part of the criminal, Tertullian demonstrates that the Christian does not fit the role of law-breaker. In these simple acts of defiance, some scholars have seen subtle acts of resistance to Roman power.[31] However, while this is certainly exploited on a literary level,[32] one wonders whether any Roman would have noticed.[33]

In any case, for the Romans, as for the Christians, the drama took place in public. There were no private martyrdoms.[34] 'Be exposed to the public; it is for your own good. For he who is not publicly exposed by humans is publicly exposed by God.'[35]

One consequence of the acts taking place in public is that the crowd take on an important role in the martyrological drama. Sometimes they are recorded as being extremely hostile:[36] they demand the martyrs' arrest or appearance;[37] they call for certain punishments;[38] even, on occasion, they take part in the execution or mob violence;[39] or they desecrate the remains of the martyr.[40]

---

30. *Mart. Perpetua* 18.2. It is difficult to overstate the perceived importance of directly gazing at one's accusers. Pliny the Elder (*Historia Naturalis* 11.54.144) recounts that of Caligula's twenty thousand gladiators, only two were able to stand unflinching when threatened, and were therefore considered to be invincible.

31. So especially J.C. Scott, *Domination and the Arts of Resistance* (New Haven: Yale University Press 1990), 203–6; Thomson, 'Martyrdom of Polycarp', 38–41; Hopkins, *Death and Renewal*, 11; Potter, 'Martyrdom as spectacle', 53. For Shaw ('Body/power/identity', *passim*) the martyrs' bodies became the locus for the struggle.

32. What Thomson ('Martyrdom of Polycarp', 39) says of Polycarp ('Both church and empire could claim that its power and justice were inscribed on Polycarp's burnt skin') could be said of all of the martyrs. These acts of resistance, and certainly the steadfastness in holding to the confession, rendered the victory of Roman justice ambiguous at best. In the Christian literary presentation of these deaths, no such ambiguity exists; the Christians are the true victors. See also Perkins, *Suffering Self*, 33.

33. Although Seneca (*Epistles* 78.15–19) does suggest that torturers are beaten by their victim smiling at them.

34. Bowersock (*Martyrdom*, 42) correctly notes, 'it was hardly in the interests of advancing the case for Christianity to suffer martyrdom in a place where few could witness it'. In times of peace, attitudes to martyrdom changed, so that Gregory the Great (*Dialogues* 3.26.7–8) can distinguish between two types of martyrdom: public, that is the type we are concerned with in this project, and hidden martyrdom, available to all Christians, without the need to shed blood. See C. Straw, 'Martyrdom and Christian identity: Gregory the Great, Augustine, and tradition', in W.E. Klingshirn and M. Vessey, *The Limits of Ancient Christianity: Essays on Late Antique Thought and Culture in Honor of R.A. Markus* (Ann Arbor: University of Michigan Press, 1999), 250–66.

35. Tertullian, *Fuga* 9.4.

36. *Mart. Pol.* 12.2; *Mart. Lyons* 1.3, 15, 17, 30, 39, 50, 53, 57; *Mart. Potamiaena* 3. Though the games were regarded as somehow noble, the execution of criminals was regarded as a somewhat savage activity, during which the upper classes went for lunch. Such was the reputation for barbarity of the crowd, Seneca (*Epistles* 7.2) pointedly notes, 'In the morning, men are thrown to the lions and bears. At midday, they are thrown to the spectators themselves.'

37. *Mart. Pol.* 3.2; *Mart. Lyons* 1.43.

38. *Mart. Pol.* 12.2, 3; *Mart. Perpetua* 18.9.

39. *Mart. Pol.* 8.3; 31.1; *Mart. Lyons* 1.7, 31, 44.

40. *Mart. Lyons* 1.57, 60. Polycarp's remains are cremated at the instigation of 'the Jews'

On other occasions, amazement is expressed at the courage of the martyrs. The soldiers who come to arrest Polycarp are amazed at his piety, and are sorry to have to arrest such an old man.[41] Similarly, the governor is amazed at Polycarp's joyful courage and gracious countenance as he is questioned,[42] and, as Polycarp dies, 'even the crowd marvelled that there should be such a difference between the unbelievers and the elect'.[43]

The impact of their deaths on the pagan crowds was not lost on the Christians, and they urged one another to die well. Putting on a good show, not reacting to the pain, and keeping the soul tranquil were all important and explicit elements in the making of a good death for the sake of the unbelievers.[44] On many occasions, the fact that the martyr was able to undergo the tortures without cries of pain is especially noted:

> After being tossed a good deal by the animal, she no longer perceived what was happening because of the hope and possession of all she believed in and because of her intimacy with Christ. Thus she too was offered in sacrifice, while the pagans themselves admitted that no woman had ever suffered so much in their experience.[45]

From the description of Blandina's experience, we see that intimacy with Christ acts as an anaesthetic to the pain of tortures. In her earlier tortures, her confession Χριστιανή εἰμι was also said to bring relief from her suffering. 'This blessed woman like a noble athlete got renewed strength from her confession of faith; her admission, Χριστιανή εἰμι ... brought her refreshment, rest, and insensibility to her present pain'.[46]

On other occasions, the Christians are said to have been able to keep miraculous tranquillity *for the purpose of* impressing the crowd.[47] 'We do not find it hard to die for God ... we make every effort not to die a coward's death'.[48] Consequently, a recurring theme on the potency of martyrdom is how the resolve of the Christians in the face of death brought admiration from onlookers, and also strengthened the resolve of those about to undergo martyrdom.[49] It has been

---

(*Mart. Pol.* 17.1–18.1). The remains of the martyrs were believed to have power. So, Polycarp's remains are more precious than gold, and, in the *Acts of Thomas*, the dust from the martyred apostle's tomb cures a child.

41. *Mart. Pol.* 7.3.

42. *Mart. Pol.* 12.1. See also *Mart. Carpus* 38–9, where the crowd are amazed at the smiling martyrs.

43. *Mart. Pol.* 16. See also *Mart. Carpus* 38–9.

44. Origen, *Exhortation* 2, 36. Given the importance of gladiatorial imagery, it is interesting to note that the importance of putting on a good show was also important to the gladiators. See especially Seneca, *Tranq.* 11.4.

45. *Mart. Lyons* 1.56. See also the examples of the martyrs who made light of their burden (*Mart. Lyons* 1.6); Blandina (1.19); Alexander (1.52); Papylus (*Mart. Carpus* 35); a crowd who endured the sword without a word (*Mart. Perpetua* 21.8); and Polycarp, who is given strength to endure the flames without being nailed to the post (13.3–14.1).

46. *Mart. Lyons* 1.19.

47. *Mart. Pol.* 2.2; 13.3; *Mart. Carpus* 35; *Mart. Lyons* 1.19, 51, 56. See also *Mart. Isa.* 5.8–14.

48. *Mart. Apoll.* 27.

49. *Mart. Lyons* 1.11; *Mart. Apoll.* 47.

suggested that it was in fact through martyrdom that pagans became aware of the existence of Christianity in the second and third centuries.[50] The deaths of the Christians were a public testimony to unbelievers.[51]

> Who indeed would not admire the martyrs' nobility, their courage, their love of the Master? For even when they were torn by whips until the very structure of their bodies was lain bare down to the inner veins and arteries, they endured it, making even the bystanders weep for pity.[52]

The endurance of pain was a notable virtue in antiquity.[53] Seneca holds as examples of courage not only athletes[54] but also those tortured in the arena as examples of courage to be emulated.

> What blows do athletes receive on their faces and all over their bodies! Nevertheless, through their desire for fame, they endure every torture, and they undergo these things not only because they are fighting but in order to be able to fight. Their very training means torture ... Think of all the brave men who have conquered pain ... of him who did not cease to smile, though that very smile so enraged his torturers that they tried upon him every instrument of their cruelty. If pain can be conquered by a smile, will it not be conquered by reason? You may tell me now of whatever you like – of colds, hard coughing-spells ... yet worse than these are the stake, the rack, the red-hot plates, the instrument that reopens wounds while the wounds themselves are still swollen and that drives their imprint still deeper. Nevertheless, there have been men who have not uttered a moan amid these tortures. 'More yet!' says the torturer; but the victim has not begged for release. 'More yet!' he says again; but no answer has come. 'More yet!' the victim has smiled, and heartily, too. Can you not bring yourself, after an example like this, to make a mock at pain?[55]

Endurance in the games brought a victor's crown (ἀγών στεφανηφόρος). Similarly, for the martyrs, there was an imperishable crown for those who endured to the end.[56] Therefore, a whole range of athletic, military and gladiatorial imagery was employed to describe and interpret Christian martyrdom. Martyrs were combatants, who struggled for God. They trained in endurance that they

---

50. Bowersock, *Martyrdom and Rome*, 66.

51. *Mart. Carpus* 40; Eusebius, *H.E.* 5.2.4–5; *Mart. Marian* 6.1; *Mart. Fruct.* 6.3. Despite the representations of some of the crowds being sympathetic to the martyrs in at least some Christian texts, the fact that there are no instances where the crowd called for Christian prisoners to be freed leads Coleman ('Fatal charades', 58) to doubt whether Christians in the arena ever received public sympathy. However, whether this option was open to the crowd in such cases is debatable, and in any case since the point of recounting these particular stories is the martyrdom, there would be little point in recording any account where the potential martyr is thwarted by being set free.

52. *Mart. Pol.* 2.2.

53. See Shaw, 'Body/power/identity', 291–300.

54. For the training an athlete or gladiator underwent in order to build up endurance, see D.S. Potter, 'Entertainers in the Roman Empire', in D.S. Potter and D.J. Mattingly (eds), *Life, Death, and Entertainment in the Roman Empire* (Ann Arbor: University of Michigan Press, 1999), 256–325 (306).

55. Seneca, *Epistle* 78.15–19.

56. For Germanicus, the messier the death, the more glorious the crown (*Mart. Perpetua* 19.3). See also *Mart. Lyons* 1.36, 38; *Mart. Pol.* 17.1; 19.2; *Mart. Potamiaena* 6; *Mart. Fruct.* 1.4; 4.1; *Mart. Ignatius* 5; Tertullian, *A.V.* 56; *On Patience* 15; Pontus, *Life of Cyprian* 19.

might make successful confession, and secure victory before governors and crowds. Most of all, for the Christians, the goal of public martyrdom was to effect conversion, with Tertullian and Justin among those converted by martyrs;[57] the blood of Christians was indeed seed.[58]

Martyrdom as Cosmic Conflict

The early Christians depicted their arrests, trials and, in particular, the moment where they were faced by their interrogator and urged to recant, as an ἀγών. In both a literal, and metaphorical sense, they were athletes or gladiators at the games engaged in battle or a contest. But why choose this discourse? Bowersock is surely correct that the historical games themselves provided the Christians with the setting to develop the language of contest in their martyrological discourse,[59] although, as we have seen, this language was applied even where there was no such contest.[60] Nonetheless, Bowersock overlooks a crucial aspect of the metaphor: the apocalyptic dimension. Martyrdom was a *cosmic contest*. More importantly, the martyrs affected the cosmos.[61]

If the Christians' struggle was often played out in the arena (ἀγών) before the crowds of onlookers, and if the battle was against the forces of the Roman Empire, on a more fundamental level, their struggle was cosmic in scale. Standing in the centre of the arena, the beasts before them and the crowds around them, the Christians were depicted as standing beneath the heavens – where the angels waited to receive those who walked through the gate of life – and above the fires of hell – where the Devil waited to devour those he successfully snared. Ultimately, the contest fought by the Christians was against the Devil, and it was primarily because of his activity that they had to endure persecution, trial and danger. The Christians were not only athletes in the games, they were also soldiers in a cosmic war.[62]

---

57. Justin, *Apol.* II.12. There is a hint that the Roman soldier Basilides is converted through the martyrdom of Potamiaena (*Mart. Potamiaena* 3–5). The most dramatic conversion of all is surely that of Agathonicê (*Mart. Carpus* 42–7).

58. Tertullian, *Apol.* 50.13.

59. Bowersock, *Martyrdom and Rome*, especially 18–28.

60. Christian cosmology and the model of Jesus' death would provide the means for interpreting experience of persecution and martyrdom, which would in turn lead to a particular development of that world-view in a complex hermeneutical spiral.

61. Although the apocalyptic dimension of some of the martyr acts has been noted, particularly in the *Passion of Perpetua*, such as: the ladder to heaven; the monster; a heavenly garden; divine old man; white-clad multitude (see C. Rowland, *The Open Heaven: A Study of Apocalyptic in Judaism and Early Christianity* [London: SPCK, 1982], 397–9; J. Balling, 'Martyrdom as apocalypse', in K. Jeppesen, K. Neilsen and B. Rosendal [eds], *In the Last Days: On Jewish and Christian Apocalyptic and Its Period* [Aarhus: Aarhus University Press, 1994], 41–8), the apocalyptic aspects of the act and interpretation of martyrdom have been seriously underplayed, probably because apocalypticism is generally thought to be well on the wane by the second and third centuries.

62. The *Martyrs of Lyons* has an apocalyptic opening (1.3–6), where the scene is set with Satan about to manifest his final appearance. The combatants are God's servants, armed with God's grace, and the slaves of Satan, prepared to charge into battle (1.5). See also, Tertullian, *Scorp.* 4; *On Modesty* 22; Clement, *Strom.* 4.7; Origen, *Exhortation* 34, 51.

Everything that happened to the young church communities was played out on the cosmic stage. Torture, persecution, arrest and death all fitted within the world-view with which the Christians operated. Their enemies were not so much wild beasts and governors, the adversary was Satan. After one of her prison visions, Perpetua realizes 'that it was not with the wild animals that I would fight but with the Devil, but I knew that I would win the victory'.[63] Satan planned his skirmishes with Christians according to his battle strategy.[64] The human players in the trials of the Christians were merely Satan's agents, as Carpus informs his assailant:

> For it was in the beginning that the Devil fell from his rank of glory because of his own wickedness, and hence makes war upon God's love for mankind; hard pressed by the Christians he struggles with them and prepares his skirmishes beforehand ... God permits him to tempt man and try to move him away from piety. And so believe me, my good consul, you are subject to no small folly.[65]

The consul, by his questioning and torture, played the role of Satan in attempting to move Carpus away from his piety. Ostensibly, in the *Martyr Acts*, Satan does not desire the physical death of the martyrs; his purpose is to cause denial.[66] Clearly, the Romans were not primarily interested in killing the Christians, but to dissuade them from their defiance.[67] Ironically, the authorities, considering themselves to be benevolent in seeking to persuade the malefactors to choose life, acted out the Satanic role though this perceived act of kindness and generosity.[68]

It was Satan's goal to move the Christians away from their confession by changing their allegiance from the God who made heaven and earth,[69] and offer sacrifice to the State or local gods. But sacrifice to gods was, to the Christians, the worship of demons, for 'the Christian God relativised all other gods into evil spirits and demons'.[70] The persecution of Christians was part of the war raged

63. *Mart. Perpetua* 10.14.
64. Satan tries out different tactics against the Christians (*Mart. Lyons* 1.27).
65. *Mart. Carpus* 17. The idea that the Romans, both officials and crowds, are incited, or even possessed or directed by Satan is alluded to on a number of occasions: *Mart. Pol.* 17.1; *Mart. Lyons* 1.5, 27; *Mart. Perpetua* 3.4; 20.1; and *Mart. Justin* (recension C), where the enemies of the Christians are described as the 'underlings of Satan' (τοῖς ὑπηρέταις τοῦ σατανᾶ), 1.1.
66. For example, *Mart. Pol.* 2.4–3.1; *Mart. Lyons* throughout. This stands in sharp contrast in later Christian medieval depictions of the *artes moriendi* where the devil tempts the dying person to end their own life. Here, to will one's own death is not to win salvation, but damnation (see further, Hooff, *Autothanasia*, 177–8).
67. Ferguson, 'Early Christian martyrdom', 80. A similar point is made by Ste Croix, 'Why were the early Christians perseucted?', 20. See *Mart. Pol.* 9–12; *Mart. Carpus passim*; *Mart. Perpetua* 6; *Mart. Pionius* 4–5, 12, 20; *Mart. Conon* 3–4; *Mart. Agapē* 5.2. Even during the years of official persecution, some governors boasted of never having executed a Christian.
68. However, it may be argued equally persuasively that had the Roman governors managed to dissuade a Christian from her confession, then the victory would be Rome's in bringing a deviant into line with the power of Rome.
69. This designation is often used of God in the martyrological texts, in contrast to those gods who have either created nothing, or have no existence.
70. Morris, 'Pure wheat of God'.

against God by Satan and his demons. The Christians were God's foot soldiers on the front line and they experienced the skirmishes of war through persecution. Satan and his legions were, therefore, directly responsible for the persecutions of Christians.[71]

On the other side, pagans believed that the Christians slighted the gods of the ancient world. In some way, the persecution and punishment meted out to the Christians was interpreted as the revenge of the gods.[72] The pagans themselves felt they had to restore the honour of their traditional gods against the ἄθεοι Christians.[73] The charge made against Polycarp was that he was 'the father of the Christians and the destroyer of our gods – the one that teaches the multitude not to sacrifice and do reverence'.[74]

In this context, to offer sacrifice to the Emperor was to become a denier,[75] and align oneself with demons, with all the attendant consequences. The call to martyrdom, therefore, takes place within the context of lining up with God or Satan; it is a battle between God's soldiers and Satan's servants (*ministri diaboli*).[76] Therefore, just as the Christians were combatants and athletes training in endurance for God, so, too, Satan trained his legions in preparation for the final apocalyptic battle.[77] The opening of the *Martyrs of Lyons* is loaded with apocalyptic overtones, including mention of the eschatological θλίψις[78] that God's saints must endure.

> The intensity of our afflictions here, the deep hatred of the pagans for the saints, and the magnitude of the blessed martyrs' sufferings, we are incapable of describing in detail … The Adversary swooped down in full force, in this way anticipating his final coming which is sure to come. He went to all lengths to train and prepare his minions against God's servants: the result was that we were not only shut out of our houses, the baths and the public square, but they forbade any of us to be seen in any place whatsoever.[79]

71. *Mart. Pol.* 3.1; 17.1; *Mart. Carpus* 5, 17; *Mart. Lyons* 1.3–6, 16, 23, 25, 27, 35; *Mart. Apoll.* 47; *Mart. Perpetua* 4.6–7; 10.11, 14; 20.1; 21:10; *Mart. Fruct.* 1.4; 7.2.

72. *Mart. Lyons* 1.60.

73. *Mart. Lyons* 1.31. For the charge of atheism against the Christians, see Frend, *Martyrdom and Persecution*, 259–60; P. Lampe, *Die Stadrömischen Christen in der ersten beiden Jahrhunderten: untersuchen zur Sozialgeschichte* (Tübingen: Mohr Siebeck, 1987), 166–72.

74. *Mart. Pol.* 12.2. Interestingly, this charge is made by the entire mob, both pagans and Jews from Smyrna. Compare Trajan's complaint about the markets being empty. The mob, in an uncontrollable rage, is sparked off by Polycarp's three-fold confession of being Christian.

75. See E. Ferguson, *Demonology of the Early Christian World* (New York: Edwin Mellen Press, 1984), 121–2. See also *Mart. Carpus* 17; Eusebius, *H.E.* 5.1.5, 25; *Mart. Marian* 2.2, 5; Justin, *Apol.* I.57; II.1; Tertullian, *Fuga* 2; Origen, *Contra Celsum* 8.43.

76. *Mart. Carpus* (Latin) 4.2.

77. The contrast is clearly demonstrated in *Mart. Lyons* 1.27, where the jailers are filled with the devil, while the Christians are filled with the Holy Spirit.

78. Θλίψις often has eschatological connotations, and is associated with the suffering of the faithful at the end of the age: See Mk 4.17//Mt. 13.21; Mk 13.9//Mt. 24.9; Mk 13.24//Mt. 24.29; Mt. 24.21; Jn 16.33; Acts 11.19; 14.22; 20.23; Rom. 5.3; 8.35; 12.12; 2 Cor. 1.4, 8; 2.4; 4.17; 6.4; 7.4; 8.2; Col. 1.24; 1 Thess. 1.6; 3.3, 7; 2 Thess. 1.4; Heb. 10.33; Jas 1.27; Rev. 1.9; 2.9, 10; 7.14.

79. *Mart. Lyons* 1.4–5.

Ultimately, Satan was the great enemy; it was he and his legions that attacked the Christians. Persecution had a demonic origin.[80] The *Martyrdom of Perpetua* is also given an eschatological setting, consciously set in the end time period, where young men and even women receive dreams and visions, 'those extraordinary graces promised for the last stage of time'.[81]

The witness and deaths of Christians affected the cosmic order; they were God's foot soldiers in the final eschatological battle. It is a battle which they won, and we now turn to the mechanism by which the Christians could interpret the deaths of those executed by the State as nothing less than cosmic victory.

Martyrdom as Participation in Christ
Central to early Christian communities was devotion to a martyr crucified by the Roman State;[82] behind every martyrdom was the death of Jesus.[83] Early martyrological reflection portrayed the martyrs as imitators of Christ. Indeed, at times, such reflection appears to create a world in which in order to *become* a disciple of Christ one would have to imitate his death:

> We love the martyrs as the disciples and imitators of the Lord, and rightly so because of their unsurpassed loyalty towards their king and master. May we too share with them as fellow disciples![84]

The authors or redactors of the martyr texts often made the connection between the protagonist and Christ explicit. Of Pothinus, bishop of Lyons, it is written:

> he was brought to the tribunal by the soldiers, accompanied by some of the civil magistrates and the entire mob, who raised all kinds of shouts at him as though he were Christ himself.[85]

The same parallelism is drawn quite consciously between Christ and Polycarp.[86] 'Just as the Lord did', Polycarp waits that he might be delivered (παραδοθῇ) for arrest.[87] The writer employs prominent biblical names from Jesus' pas-

---

80. *Mart. Pol.* 17; *Mart. Carpus* 6–7 (Latin recension 4.2); *Mart. Justin* (recension C) 1.2; *Mart. Lyons* 1.5, 14, 16, 25, 27, 35; *Mart. Perpetua* 10.14; 20.1.

81. *Mart. Perpetua* 1.3, after which follows a quotation from Acts 2.17–18/Joel 2.28.

82. See Pagels (*Gnostic Gospels*) who convincingly argues that the differences between Gnostic and 'orthodox' views of martyrdom are directly affected by their view of the historicity of Jesus' death. Those Gnostics who denied that Jesus was actually crucified were most scornful for the need or desirability of Christian martyrdom.

83. Fox, *Pagans and Christians*, 441. See also, J.C. O'Neill, 'Did Jesus teach that his death would be vicarious as well as typical?', in W. Horbury and B. McNeil (eds), *Suffering and Martyrdom in the New Testament: Studies Presented to G.M. Styler* (London: Cambridge University Press, 1981), 9–27.

84. *Mart. Pol.* 17.3.

85. *Mart. Lyons* 1.30.

86. Some of the following are also listed by Thomson, 'Martyrdom of Polycarp', 48. See also B. Dehandschutter, 'Le Martyre de Polycarp et le development de la conception du martyre au deuxième siècle' (in E.A. Livingstone [ed.], *Studia Patristica XVII* [Oxford: Pergamon Press, 1982], 659–68 [660–1]), who notes that, unlike Jesus, Polycarp refuses to be nailed to the post.

87. *Mart. Pol.* 1.2.

sion,[88] and the police come out to him 'as though against a brigand'.[89] Other explicit comparisons with Christ include his riding into the city on a donkey,[90] and that he is to drink the cup of Christ.[91] There are other possible allusions to the Passion of Christ: Polycarp predicts his own death and its manner;[92] he offers a long prayer for the Church before his arrest;[93] and affirms that the will of God be done,[94] echoing Jesus' Gethsemane affirmation. In the arena, he hears a voice from heaven, which bystanders also hear,[95] and he is killed by a dagger plunged into his side, alluding to the spear that pierced Jesus at the crucifixion.[96] Two other minor points stress the passions of Jesus and Polycarp: the Jews make trouble over his remains;[97] and a centurion stands by witnessing the death.[98]

Whether or not all of these allusions were deliberate, the composite picture stresses, above all, that Polycarp was a 'sharer of Christ' (Χριστοῦ κοινωνός).[99] Polycarp and all the martyrs do not simply imitate Christ,[100] their bodies are completely given over to their master. Christ, it is said, is the 'pilot', or the 'helmsman of the bodies' (κυβερνήτην τῶν σωμάτων) of the faithful.[101] Therefore, identification with Christ forms a crucial element in the self-understanding of the martyrs, and dramatically influenced the way their stories were told.

The martyrs were portrayed as being eager to mimic deliberately the suffering of Jesus. For example, in another incident, martyrs demand to be scourged before a line of gladiators that they may 'obtain a share in the Lord's suffering'.[102] Blandina, the heroine of *Lyons*, is said to be insensitive to the pain because of her 'intimacy with Christ'.[103] Hung on a post as bait for the wild animals, she seemed as though she were hanging on a cross. Therefore, those who were facing torture in the arena 'saw in their sister him who was crucified for them, that he might convince all who believe in him that all who suffer for Christ's glory will have eternal fellowship in the living God'.[104] Her performance causes the pagans to

88. Herod is the name of the chief of police and Polycarp is said to have 'betrayers in his own household who will receive the punishment of Judas' (*Mart. Pol.* 6.2).

89. *Mart. Pol.* 7.1; cf. Mk 14.38.

90. *Mart. Pol.* 8.2; cf. Mk 11.7–11.

91. *Mart. Pol.* 14.2; Mk 14.36.

92. *Mart. Pol.* 4.2; cf. e.g. Mk 8.31; Jn 12.32–3.

93. *Mart. Pol.* 7.3–8.1; cf. Jn 17.

94. *Mart. Pol.* 7.1; cf. Mt. 26.42.

95. *Mart. Pol.* 9.1; cf. Jn 12.28–30.

96. *Mart. Pol.* 16.1; cf. Jn 19.34. In John blood and water comes out of Jesus' side. The blood flows with such force from Polycarp's side that it is like water, and quenches the flames.

97. *Mart. Pol.* 17.1–2; cf. Mt. 27.62–4. Interestingly, the action of the Jews in preventing the Christians from taking the body is at the behest of Satan, following the theme in Revelation (2.11) of the Jews comprising a 'synagogue of Satan'. For the presentation of the Jews in the *Martyrdom of Polycarp*, see Lieu, *Image and Reality*, 57–102.

98. *Mart. Pol.* 18.1; cf. Mk 15.39.

99. *Mart. Pol.* 6.2.

100. So, e.g., *Mart. Pol.* 17.3.

101. *Mart. Pol.* 19.2.

102. *Mart. Perpetua* 18.9, cf. Col. 1.24 and discussion below, 139–40.

103. See also *Mart. Pol.* 2.2–3, where the martyrs are not present in the flesh during torture.

104. *Mart. Lyons* 1.41.

marvel at her suffering so that they 'admitted that no woman had ever suffered so much in their experience'.[105]

This theme of sharing intimacy with Christ through mimetic suffering develops into the idea that Christ actually suffers within the martyrs. Felicitas, in the pains of childbirth, is mocked when it is observed how much more she will suffer in the arena. She replies, 'What I suffer now, I suffer by myself. But then another will be inside me who will suffer for me, just as I will be suffering for him.'[106] Felicitas suffers in childbirth *for* the one inside her. At the day of her death, Christ will be inside her, suffering *for her*, just as she will suffer for Christ. For the martyr, there is a mutuality of suffering of, with and for Christ, and the suffering of Christ with the martyr brings comfort, strength and release.

Martyrdom as Confession of Christ

This theme of identification with Christ is presented most obviously, and most powerfully, in the words of confession on the lips of the martyrs themselves. Therefore, Carpus and Papylus repeatedly claim the name 'Christian' during their tortures. They are Christ's champions. On being asked his name by the proconsul, Carpus replies, 'My first and most distinctive name is that of Christian (Χριστιανός)'.[107] He and Papylus from the outset have been identified as 'witnesses of Christ' (μάρτυρες τοῦ Χριστοῦ).[108] Both persistently make the response, 'I am a Christian' (ἐγω Χριστιανός ἐίμι)[109] when questioned, tortured or asked to make sacrifice to the Emperor.

This confessional formula is of great importance in many of the martyrological texts.[110] For whereas having the name Christian is enough to warrant arrest, torture and death, confessing the name during torture and trial is an important aspect for many of the recorders of the acts; the martyrs suffer for the Name. Indeed, some narratives are shaped to allow maximum prominence to confession, no more so than the *Martyrdom of Saints Justin, Chariton, Charito, Euelpistus, Hierax, Paeon, Liberian*, and their community. In this act, the trial scene is constructed in such a way that each of the accused can make their confession, 'Χριστιανός ἐίμι',[111] so that these confessions are clearly the central element of the story, and the frame on which the narrative hangs.

---

105. *Mart. Lyons* 1.53–6.
106. *Mart. Perpetua* 15.6.
107. *Mart. Carpus* 3.
108. *Mart. Carpus* 1.
109. *Mart. Carpus* 5, 23, 34. Cf. *Mart. Lyons* 1.20, where Sanctus keeps repeating over and over again Χριστιανός ἐίμι to every question instead of giving his name, birthplace, nationality or anything else; 'and the pagan crowd heard not another word from him'.
110. Bisbee (*Pre-Decian Acts*, 45–7) notes that establishing the identity of the accused was an important element in every Roman trial.
111. So in the *Mart. Justin* 3.4; 4.1, 3, 4, 6, 9. Recension B of the text adds the communal confession Χριστιανοί ἐσμεν (5.7). Recension C is even more emphatic, Χριστιανός γεγένημαι καὶ Χριστιανός ἐίμι καὶ Χριστιανός ἔσομαι (3.5). See also the *Acts of the Scillitan Martyrs*, a trial narrative where the confession, *Christianus/a sum* is prominent (9, 10, 13) and *Mart. Perpetua* 3.2;

Of course, on a literary level, it is this confession that forms the climax of each one of the *Acts*, since the action revolves around the challenge to either utter or recant these words. The moment of confession or denial is the fulcrum on which everything else depends. It is the moment where the Christian openly affirms his or her relationship with Christ, making oneself a sacrifice to God.[112]

Polycarp, in his famous confession before the governor and the crowds, explains that it is his intimacy, his relationship with Christ, which prevents him from renouncing his faith. 'For eighty-six years I have been his servant and he has done me no wrong. How can I blaspheme my king and saviour?'[113] Similarly, Perpetua in her 'audacious act of self-assertion'[114] against her father is prepared to renounce every mark of her identity, as a daughter, a mother, perhaps a wife, that is every Graeco-Roman identity marker, except her Christian identity.[115]

Confessing the name of Jesus and publicly identifying with his suffering had several effects. First, it bound the suffering communities to their master, providing additional rationale, not only for their experience of suffering but also for their choosing death in the face of it. It also connected one Christian community to another, creating a language for uniting themselves with a much larger group, which would have been important to otherwise struggling, fragile and isolated communities. Furthermore, remembering the martyrs' stories gave each community a connection with their own past, and provided a model to help when they too would face the ultimate trial. In the *Acts*, a desire is often expressed to follow the example of past martyrs, and give as good a witness as they had done:

> We love the martyrs as the disciples and imitators of the Lord, and rightly so because of their unsurpassed loyalty towards their king and master. May we too share with them as fellow disciples.[116]

6.4. Similarly, the confessions of Polycarp are given prominence by the proconsul sending a herald to announce three times, 'Polycarp has confessed himself to be a Christian' (*Mart. Pol.* 12: ἑαυτὸν Χριστιανὸν ἐῖναι).

112. *Mart. Pol.* 14, 15; *Mart. Lyons* 1.40, 51–2; *Mart. Conon* 6–7; *Mart. Justin* 2.2; Origen, *Exhortation* 3; Ignatius, *Romans* 5; Irenaeus, *A.H.* 4.33.9; Tertullian, *Scorpiace* 6, 7; *Fuga* 9.

113. *Mart. Pol.* 9.3. Polycarp's refusal to blaspheme his master stands in sharp contrast with the readiness of his own slaves (children?) who under torture betray their master (6.1–2), perhaps recalling the 'disciples' passion' of Mk 13.9–13.

114. J. Davies, *Death, Burial and Rebirth in the Religions of Antiquity* (Religion in the First Christian Centuries; London: Routledge, 1999), 208.

115. See J.M. Lieu, '"I am a Christian": martyrdom and the beginning of "Christian Identity"', in *Neither Jew nor Greek* (London/New York: T&T Clark, 2002), 211–31 (214). For discussion on the rejection of family, see Frend, *Martyrdom and Persecution*, 321–2; Shaw, 'Body/power/identity', 20–6; Perkins, *Suffering Self*, 104–13; J.E. Salisbury, *Perpetua's Passion: The Death and Memory of a Young Roman Woman* (New York/London: Routledge, 1997), 5–11. Perpetua's dialogue with her father, where she is urged to recant forms a *leitmotif* in the passion (Henten and Avemarie, *Martyrdom*, 101).

116. *Mart. Pol.* 17. See also *Mart. Pol.* 1, 19, 22; and *Mart. Perpetua* 1.6 for the call to share in fellowship with the martyrs.

'Following in the footsteps' of the martyrs is a recurrent theme in the *Acts*,[117] and this appears to be one of the primary reasons why the stories were told: to strengthen and to provide an example. This obviously affected the way in which the suffering of the martyrs was handled. Clearly, for the stories to work in this way, submitting to, or even rushing to martyrdom must be portrayed as a more attractive option than abandoning or denying the faith. This is achieved through a number of ways.

On a literary level, confessing the name brought comfort in distress, as was the case with the 'noble athlete' slave girl Blandina in the persecution at Lyons. Despite the worries of the Lyons Christians that this weak girl would not be able to withstand the torture, she endured and left her torturers exhausted:

> They testified that even one kind of torture was enough to release her soul, let alone the many they applied with such intensity. Instead, this blessed woman like a noble athlete got renewed strength with her confession of faith: her admission, 'I am a Christian (Χριστιανή εἰμι); we do nothing to be ashamed of', brought her refreshment, rest, and insensibility to her present pain.[118]

Continuing in her confession is what brought relief. Similarly, in a dramatic tableau, not only did Sanctus, one of the martyrs of Lyons, withstand tortures but also his confession of faith was said to be like a 'heavenly fountain of the water of life that flows from the side of Christ' which cooled and strengthened him.[119] Despite being tortured, so that his body was disfigured and bruised out of any recognizable human shape,

> Christ suffering in him achieved a great glory, overwhelming the adversary, and showing as an example to all the others that nothing is to be feared where the Father's love is, nothing painful where we find Christ's glory.[120]

Days later, when the martyr could not even bear the touch of a hand upon his body, he was again tortured, but miraculously, the application of the instruments of torture restored his twisted body. The trial was a cure rather than torture.

The model offered to prospective martyrs was not miraculous deliverance, such as is found in the book of Daniel, which similarly called Jews to stand fast to their religion. *Christians were offered ideal literary types who were tortured and killed.* The hope of miraculous deliverance would be the strength to die well, and the grace to withstand the pain of torture. Most of all, the martyrs knew that they were following the example of Jesus, and therefore sharing in the 'life' of Christ.

However, there was also a disincentive to deny. By the time a Christian came to trial, that trial would take place before the cosmic archons. Whereas a good

---

117. *Mart. Pol.* 1; *Mart. Carpus* (Latin Recension) 6.1, part of Agathonicê's trial; *Mart. Apoll.* 47.

118. *Mart. Lyons* 1.19. So too with Sanctus, who answered all their questions with the same confession (20). Compare *T. Job* 27.3–5, where Satan as an athlete engaged in combat with Job is worn down and left exhausted by Job's endurance.

119. *Mart. Lyons* 1.22.

120. *Mart. Lyons* 1.23.

confession and death led to life, to deny was to fall prey to the Devil. In the midst of the battle in which the Christians were engaged, there could be no neutrality. In a dualistic cosmos, one could align oneself with God or Satan; there was no middle road. Origen warns that those who deny are deceivers[121] and an abomination;[122] their souls are corrupt and, since they are joined to other gods,[123] they are servants of Satan;[124] they are built on weak foundations[125] and do not love God;[126] and, as a consequence of renouncing their baptism,[127] hell waits for them.[128] In sparing themselves further torture and escaping the temporal fire of death, the deniers would face eternal torment in the fire that burns forever.[129]

Therefore, Christians were to take upon themselves the suffering of Jesus. Identifying with Jesus through confession, suffering and death resulted in successful martyrdom and faithful struggle. The alternative was to deny, either through torture or even through refusal to take part in the contest, as other groups of Christians advocated.[130] Within the apocalyptic framework with which the advocates of martyrdom operated, this was disaster, both for the denier and also for the cosmos. Persecution was set by the Christians in an apocalyptic perspective, as can be seen in the case of *Lyons*.[131] The suffering of the Christians signalled that the end was near; their deaths were strikes against Satan:

> Arrayed against him [Satan] was God's grace, which protected the weak, and raised up sturdy pillars that could by their endurance take on themselves all the attacks of the Evil One. These then charged into battle, holding up under every sort of abuse and torment; indeed they made light of their great burden as they sped on to Christ, proving without question that the sufferings of this present time are not to be compared with the glory that shall be revealed in us.[132]

Therefore, the martyrs were the foot soldiers of God. They were involved not just in an earthly battle against their persecutors but in a cosmic one against Satan and his legions. Persecution, trials, and fighting with the beasts in the arena constituted the battlefield on which this war was to be fought. Faithfulness and endurance were the weapons with which the Christians were armed. 'Charging

121. Origen, *Exhortation* 5.
122. Origen, *Exhortation* 7.
123. Origen, *Exhortation* 10.
124. Origen, *Exhortation* 17.
125. Origen, *Exhortation* 48.
126. Origen, *Exhortation* 27.
127. Origen, *Exhortation* 17.
128. Origen, *Exhortation* 18.
129. For other warnings against denying, see *Mart. Pol.* 6, where the betrayers receive the punishment of Judas; *Mart. Lyons*, especially 1.32–5, where even the earthly fate of the deniers is no better than those who suffer for Christ; Clement, *Strom.* 4.7; Justin, *Apology* I.8, 12; II.2. See also Origen, *Exhortation* 10; Tertullian, *Scorp.* 5, 8, 9, 10, 13; Justin, *Trypho* 14, 46; *Mart. Carpus* (Latin) 4.4; *Mart. Justin* 4. 3–4; and *Mart. Apoll.* 27–30, where death is preferred to the alternative.
130. For the 'Gnostic' approaches, see above, 21–5. This of course includes those who fled persecution. According to Tertullian (*Fuga* 10), the Spirit brands a runaway.
131. For the development of the antagonism towards Christians in Lyons, see Frend, *Martyrdom and Persecution*, 5–13.
132. *Mart. Lyons* 1.6.

into battle'[133] was giving themselves over to torture. 'Making light of their burden'[134] was the way in which victory was to be achieved. Accepting pain and torture with grace was to deny the gods of the world victory over the Christians' god. The Christians could advance the war in Christ's favour by holding fast to their confession and swelling the ranks of martyrs.[135] For Justin, the opportunity for martyrdom testified to the truth of Christianity and that the 'new covenant has come'.[136]

The contest motif with its elements of struggle, combat and war set an impressive backdrop to the experiences of the Christians. In order to compete successfully in this contest, the Christian had to participate in Christ, and become a sharer in his suffering. Ultimately, sharing in Christ's suffering resulted in participating in his victory.

Martyrdom as Participation in Christ's Victory

If the martyrs were contestants at the games and soldiers in a battle, the ultimate result was victory. In death, they are described as victors and conquerors.[137] Participation in Christ meant not only sharing in his suffering; through suffering and death, the faithful martyrs participated in Christ's victory over death and Satan. Through the weapon of confession and sharing in Christ's suffering, the martyrs were victors and conquerors.

> The Christian is snatched by faith from the jaws of the devil, but by martyrdom he fells to the ground the enemy of his salvation. By faith the Christian is delivered from the devil, by martyrdom he merits the crown of perfect glory over him.[138]

They win life and the crown; they gain the wreath of immortality.[139] Over them Satan has not prevailed.

> Those who were condemned to the beasts endure[d] terrifying torments ... the purpose was that, if possible, the tyrant might persuade them to deny the faith by constant torment. For many were the stratagems the Devil used against them. But thanks be to God, he did not prevail over them.[140]

Christ also is said to triumph through Pothinus, bishop of Lyons. Despite his great age and the weakness of his body, he held on to his life, so that through it

---

133. Compare *Apoc. Elij.* 4.30–3 where the righteous rush into battle against the Lawless One.

134. Justin, *Trypho* 11.

135. *Mart. Lyons* 1.10, 12, 13; *Mart. Pol.* 14.

136. Justin, *Trypho* 11.

137. Origen, *Exhortation* 42; Tertullian, *Scorp.* 6, 11; *Mart. Pol.* 19; *Mart. Lyons* 1.36, 42; 2.6–8; *Mart. Apoll.* 47.

138. Tertullian, *Scorp.* 6. Compare, in the fourth century, John Chrysostom (*de Droside martyre*, 2), who describes martyrdom as the disgrace of devils and the denunciation of Satan.

139. *Mart. Lyons* 1.36; *Mart. Pol.* 17.1; 19.2; *Mart. Pionius.* 22.2; *Mart. Fruct.* 4.1. On the adaptation of the crown of honour, see Z. Stewart, 'Greek crowns and Christian martyrs', in E. Lucchesi and H.D. Saffrey (eds), *Antiquité païenne et chrétienne: mémorial André-Jean Festugière* (Geneva: Cramer, 1984), 119–24.

140. *Mart. Pol.* 2.4–3.1.

Christ might triumph (δι' αὐτῆς Χριστὸς θριαμβεύσῃ).[141] Similarly, a 'weak woman' is transformed by 'putting on Christ, that mighty and invincible athlete, and had overcome the Adversary in many contests and through her conflict had won the crown of immortality'.[142] She also is a source of inspiration for those to follow in the battle.[143]

The tortures and deaths of the martyrs are set against the backdrop of Christ's suffering and death, but also his resurrection, and promise of the Second Coming[144] signalling Satan's total defeat. Their experiences were signs of end-time suffering,[145] reinforcing the apocalyptic dimension to their struggle. In the meantime, holding fast to their confession, the martyrs won their skirmishes with the Devil before his final overthrow. Sanctus, by withstanding torture and sticking to his confession, Χριστιανός εἰμι, brought glory to Christ, 'overwhelming the Adversary',[146] and gave example to the Christians.[147] Sanctus' victory over Satan is achieved because, through his suffering, 'Christ suffered in him',[148] so completing an important triad of themes in the death of martyrs: confession; participating in the suffering of Christ; and winning the victory over Satan.

Furthermore, Satan could also be overcome through the rescuing of souls he believed he had already triumphed over. Sanctus, through his successful witness, causes one of those who had previously denied to 'awake from sleep'. His torture was the catalyst that brought Biblis to her senses:

141. *Mart. Lyons* 1.29.
142. *Mart. Lyons* 1.42.
143. The story of Blandina highlights a quite extraordinary feature of early Christian martryology; a relatively high proportion of the martyr acts involve women. Whereas Judaism produced women martyrs, and the Graeco-Roman world does furnish us with examples of Noble Death involving women, women feature more prominently in early Christianity. See further, A. Jensen, *God's Self-confident Daughters: Early Christianity and the Liberation of Women* (trans. O.C. Dean; Louisville, KY: John Knox Press, 1996), 81–124; P. Dronke, *Women Writers of the Middle Ages: A Critical Study of Texts from Perpetua to Marguerite Porete* (Cambridge: Cambridge University Press, 1984).

Furthermore, the presentation of women as warriors-martyrs is an interesting issue, for some feminist scholars have detected an obliteration of the sexual dimension of women's experience; women must overcome their femaleness in order to become martyr heroes; so E. Castelli, ' "I will make Mary male": pieties of the body and gender transformation of Christian women in late antiquity', in J. Epstein and K. Straub (eds), *Body Guards: The Cultural Politics of Gender Ambiguity* (New York/London: Routledge, 1991), 24–49; S. Maitland, 'Passionate prayer: masochistic images in women's experience', in L. Hurcombe (ed.), *Sex and God: Some Varieties of Women's Religious Experience* (New York/London: Routledge and Kegan Paul, 1987), 125–40; and G.C. Streete, 'Women as sources of redemption and knowledge in early Christian traditions', in R. Shepard Kraemer and R. D'Angelo (eds), *Women and Christian Origins* (New York/Oxford: Oxford University Press, 1999), 330–54.

144. Justin, *Trypho*, 110.
145. Justin, *Trypho*, 110. Justin draws heavily on the apocalyptic words of Jesus in order to contextualize the experiences of the suffering Christians. He claims (*Trypho* 35) that Jesus foretold that all who confess his name would have to bear suffering when even 'those of our own household put us to death'. He concludes, 'Consequently, we find no fault with either his words or his actions'.

146. Καταργῶν τὸν ἀντικείμενον.
147. *Mart. Lyons* 1.23.
148. Ἐν ᾧ πάσχων Χριστός.

> There was a woman named Biblis among those who had denied Christ, and the Devil thought that he had already devoured her; hoping further to convict her as a slanderer, he brought her to the rack and tried to force her to say impious things about us, thinking she was a coward and easily broken. But once on the rack she came to her senses and awoke as it were from a deep sleep, reminded by that temporal torment of the eternal punishment in Gehenna. Instead she contradicted the blasphemers, saying, 'How could such people devour children when they are not even allowed to drink the blood of brute beasts?'[149] And from then on she insisted she was a Christian, and so was counted among the number of the martyrs.[150]

Satan is so utterly defeated that he cannot hold even those he had devoured. The Devil is humiliated as he is forced to disgorge his prey. The martyr redeemed those who were lost, and strengthened the resolve of others who will wield the sword of confession at Satan, and triumphantly stamp on the Dragon's head.

Christ had already defeated Satan, and the martyrs not only participated in but also contributed to that victory. On account of their treatment of the martyrs, the persecutors stored up wrath for themselves. Though they seemed weak, vulnerable and helpless in the throws of torture, the early Christians were able to transform that apparent earthly defeat into cosmic victory, so that the very cosmos turned on the potential martyrs' decisions to remain faithful or deny. Holding fast to their confession through tortures and trials was a great victory, through which they would attain a martyr's reward and defeat the enemy.[151] 'The noble athletes after sustaining a brilliant contest and a noble victory … [won] the great crown of immortality'.[152] Satan's kingdom crumbled with each martyr's death. Perpetua was already conquering – treading on the head of the Egyptian – as she entered the arena.[153] In the cosmic war in which they were engaged, the Christians claimed victory by their deaths; they were wounded soldiers.[154]

Martyrs participated and contributed to Christ's victory over Satan, but they also won for themselves a glorious reward. As victors at the games, the martyrs were rewarded by Christ. To those who had pursued the contest to death, there was an immortal treasure.[155] Like successful athletes, they win a crown, but theirs is eternal.[156]

Martyrs also play a curious role in salvation.[157] Tertullian claims that the martyrs, by their actions, purge their own sin,[158] buying an exemption from the

---

149. A statement that indicates some food laws were still being observed.

150. *Mart. Lyons* 1.25–26.

151. In the *Acts of Andrew*, martyrdom itself is a reward for all who love, confess and trust the Lord.

152. *Mart. Lyons* 1.36.

153. *Mart. Perpetua* 18.7.

154. Clement, *Strom.* 4.7; Tertullian, *On Modesty* 22.

155. *Sibylline Oracles* 2.45–7.

156. *Mart. Pol.* 17.1; 19.2; *Mart. Lyons* 1.36, 38; *Mart. Perpetua* 19.2; *Mart. Potamiaena* 6; *Mart. Fruct.* 1.4; 4.1; *Mart. Ignatius* 5; Tertullian, *A.V.* 56; *On Patience* 15; Pontus, *Life of Cyprian* 19.

157. The idea that the martyrs imitated the suffering of Christ, which developed into Christ suffering within the martyr, eventually led to the idea that the martyr was, as it were, *alter Christus* (E.L. Hummel, *The Concept of Martyrdom according to St Cyprian of Carthage* [Washington: Catholic University of America Press, 1946], 104–7). This concept appears to have had an effect on their role in salvation, not only for themselves but also for the idea that they could forgive the sins of others.

158. Tertullian, *On Modesty* 22. This idea is also taken up by Origen, *Exhortation* 30, 39; *Homilies*

eternal fire.[159] Significantly, martyrs claim a special place in heaven[160] attaining a higher status,[161] and assisting at the altar in heaven.[162] Therefore, martyrs did not have to wait until the end of time before being resurrected; they were already raised.[163] Martyrdom was considered to be a second baptism,[164] and baptism was the washing away of sins. Therefore, at the point of death, martyrs were sinless, and at death 'attained God'.[165]

It is also hinted that martyrs took on a salvific role on behalf of others.[166] We have already seen the redemptive role in the *Martyrs of Lyons*, where those who had denied were caused to spring to life again through the faithfulness of the martyrs.[167] However, there was also a popular belief that martyrs could forgive the sins of others,[168] and visiting martyrs in prison to benefit from their power was common.[169] In prison, martyrs could intercede for those who had already died,[170] and in the popular imagination this power seemed to follow them into

on *Leviticus* 2. So Droge and Tabor, *Noble Death*, 129, conclude, 'each Christian must become his own savior'.

159. *Mart. Pol.* 2.3.

160. Origen, *Exhortation*; *Mart. Pol.* 47; Tertullian, *A.V.* 43. See also *4 Ezra* 4.33–43; 7.32, 80, 95.

161. Origen, *Exhortation* 14, 15, 49, 50; Clement, *Strom.* 4.4; *1 Clement* 5; Pontus, *Life of Cyprian* 1; compare *4 Ezra* 7.88; *Apoc. Elij.* 4.28.

162. Origen, *Exhortation* 30; *Mart. Fruct.* (alternative ending).

163. A privilege martyrs shared with the apostles and prophets, although the former's status may have been owing to their own martyrdoms.

164. Baptismal imagery is illustrated by the amount of blood. Felicitas' blood is like the blood of childbirth, explicit since she herself has just given birth. Death is therefore clearly associated with birth and baptism (*Mart. Perpetua* 18.3). The crowd cry '*Saluum lotum*' when Saturus is covered in blood; again, it is associated with another baptism (*Mart. Perpetua* 21.1–2). In *Mart. Pol.* 16.1, there is such a quantity of blood that it extinguishes the flames, therefore demonstrating the quality of the water of baptism. It may also symbolize the extinguishing of the fires of judgement, which Polycarp has escaped by his confession and death.

165. Ignatius, *Eph.* 14.1; *Trall.* 12.2; 13.3; *Rom.* 1.2; 2.1; 4.1; 5.3 (attain Christ); 9.2; *Smyrn.* 11.1; *Pol.* 2.3; 7.1; *Ep. Barn.* 7; cf. *4 Ezra* 7.79–80. R.A. Bower demonstrates that, for Ignatius, attaining God and attaining martyrdom are synonymous; 'The meaning of ἐπὶ τυγχάνω in the epistles of St Ignatius of Antioch', *VC* 28 (1974), 1–7; see also Frend, *Martyrdom and Persecution*, 198.

166. Origen, *Exhortation* 30, 50.

167. See above, 87; and *Mart. Lyons* 2.6–8, where it is restated that, by freeing those lost, the martyrs went to God completely victorious.

168. Origen, *Exhortation* 30.

169. By the end of the second century, a confessor who was released from prison automatically attained the status of presbyter in the Roman church (Hippolytus, *Apostolic Tradition* 10.1). On the developing status of a confessor (ὁμολογητής) as distinct from a martyr, see J.A. Jungmann, *The Early Liturgy to the Time of Gregory the Great* (trans. F.A. Brunner; London: Darton, Longman & Todd, 1959), 176. Naturally, the power attributed to martyrs was problematic for the developing Church hierarchy; the gift of forgiving sins was reserved only for bishops, and the power of the martyrs constituted a threat to the bishops' authority. See Klawiter, 'Role of martyrdom'. Klawiter suggests this challenge to the authority of the office of bishop may have been one of the principal reasons why the Montanist movement, which produced more martyrs than most, found itself out of favour.

170. See the remarkable power possessed by Perpetua in 'saving' her brother who had died unbaptized, and the discussion in J.A. Trumbower, '*Apocalypse of Peter* 14, 1–4 in relation to confessors'

death. Commemorating the death of martyrs at their shrines was the beginning of what became a thriving cult of the martyrs.[171] Burial near the martyr's grave was desired, so that the martyrs could guide them on the day of resurrection,[172] or to remind relatives to invoke the spirit of the martyr to pray for their deceased friends.[173] Graffiti on the shrines of martyrs record pleas for the martyrs to intercede for the dead.[174]

The martyrs are also involved in the judgement of their persecutors.[175] Saturnus, on the night before the Christians' deaths, speaks to the crowd who had gathered for the last meal, encouraging them to remember the faces of the Christians, so that they will recognize them when they see them again come the Judgement.[176] Satan will be defeated totally and his legions will suffer with him. The blood of the martyr contributes to their judgement,[177] for just as the Christians belong to their god, so too, the persecutors are following their master, Satan. The Christians share in Christ[178] and not in the sins and judgement of the world.[179] For the others, the reverse is true; those who are not in Christ belong to Satan and share in his destruction.

> The fire you threaten me with burns merely for a time and is soon extinguished. It is clear you are ignorant of the fire of everlasting punishment and of the judgement that is to come, which awaits the impious.[180]

Carpus claims that those who worship demons will share in their folly, and not only in their folly but also in the demons' eschatological punishment. Just as the Christians who participate in Christ's suffering will share in his triumph, so too will the worshippers of demons share in their gods' fate; they will perish in Gehenna.[181] Martyrs are not passive in this drama, they are active combatants.

intercession for the non-Christian dead', in M.F. Wiles, E.J. Yarnold and P.M. Parvis (eds), *Studia Patristica XXXVI* (Leuven: Peeters, 2001), 307–12.

171. Some believed that martyrs remained in shrines; S. Wilson 'Introduction', in S. Wilson (ed.), *Saints and Their Cults: Studies in Religious Sociology, Folklore and History* (Cambridge: Cambridge University Press, 1983), 1–53 (11). On the development of the martyr cult, see H. Delehaye, *Les Origines du culte des martyrs* (Brussels: Société des Bollandistes, 1933); M. Perham, *The Communion of Saints: An Examination of the Place of the Christian Dead in the Belief, Worship, and Calendars of the Church* (London: SPCK, 1980), 1–24; and P. Brown, *The Cult of the Saints: Its Rise and Function in Latin Christianity* (London: SCM Press, 1981).

172. Delehaye, *Origines*; Jungmann, *Early Liturgy*, 182–3.

173. Perham, *Communion of Saints*, 12. Perham believes that this practice was the origin of prayers for the dead found in later formal liturgies. However, the practice of baptism for the dead (1 Cor. 15) may indicate an earlier origin.

174. A sample can be found in Delehaye, *Origines*, 102–7.

175. Origen, *Exhortation* 28; Tertullian, *On Prayer* 4; Irenaeus, *A.H.* 3.18.5, where an inquisition is made of the martyrs' blood.

176. *Mart. Perpetua* 17.

177. Irenaeus, *A.H.* 3.18.5.

178. *Mart. Carpus* 41.

179. *Mart. Carpus* 39.

180. *Mart. Pol.* 11.2.

181. *Mart. Carpus* 7–8.

Seeking death brings judgement upon their persecutors, and this judgement is not an unimportant component of the martyrological schema. Martyrdom was a potent weapon in the eschatological war that inexorably led to ultimate victory.[182]

The Martyrs' Cosmos

The martyrs' deaths were interpreted through the life, death, resurrection and ultimate eschatological victory of Jesus. The martyrs followed his footsteps and, in so doing, laid a path that other Christians desired to follow. The struggle of the Christians was set in the midst of a cosmic arena, where they engaged in combat against Satan and his legions, and won the victor's crown by holding to their confession and dying well. It is to this moment of victory we now turn and examine more closely.

Life and Death
The Christians created a symbolic world where the normal categories of life and death lost their meaning. To live was to die, and to die was to live.

> 'You who are called eloquent, and who believe you understand the true doctrines, listen: if you are scourged and beheaded, do you suppose that you will really ascend into heaven as you think, and that you will receive the reward of good things, as you teach?' 'I do not merely suppose it,' said the saint, 'but I know it certainly and am fully assured of it.'
> '... sacrifice to the gods, lest you be miserably destroyed. For what person with intelligence would choose to relinquish this sweetest light and prefer death to it?' 'And what person of sound mind,' answered Justin, 'would choose to turn from piety to impiety, from light to darkness, and from the living God to soul-destroying demons?'[183]

When the magistrate threatens tortures, the saints all reply:

> This we long for, this we desire, and this will grant us great freedom at the terrible tribunal of Christ, when each one of us shall receive according to his deeds. And so, do as you will. We are Christians, as we have repeatedly said, and we do not sacrifice to idols.[184]

---

182. This conclusion, of course, runs contrary to the more prevalent portrayal of martyrdom within a context of non-violent resistance. For example, Crossan (*Birth*) sees the non-violent death of a Christian as the 'ultimate act of ethical eschatology'. Ferguson ('Early Christian martyrdom') has explored the relationship between modern non-violence movements, such as those led by Martin Luther King and Ghandi. See also the discussion in the Introduction above, 3–5.

However, as we have seen, the martyrs did not die primarily for their own reward, but to participate in a cosmic war and inflict casualties on Satan's side. Therefore, by their deaths, the martyrs do in fact threaten violence. Though the martyrs' threats of punishment are violence eschatologically postponed, the Christian communities believed spacial and temporal boundaries to be blurred. In the symbolic world created by the Christians, eschatologically delayed punishment was still imminent. Ferguson, therefore, may claim too much that 'few exercises of non-violent resistance for the sake of higher law have accomplished as much' (82). And whereas he is undoubtedly right that the *Acts of Martyrs* can take their place in the history of civil disobedience, it is questionable whether the early Christians would have seen themselves in that mould. See also D. Daube, *Civil Disobedience in Antiquity* (Edinburgh: Edinburgh University Press, 1972).

183. *Mart. Justin* (Recension C) 4.1–4.

184. *Mart. Justin* (Recension C) 4.6.

Consistently, dying and facing torture is portrayed as the better choice. Crucially, it is not better because embracing suffering was more noble, rather, if one inhabited the symbolic world of the Christians, it was to any rational person the better, even the obvious, choice.

Similarly, Perpetua brings out the contrast between the ways in which pagans and Christians see suffering, when she notes that her father alone out of all her family would be sad to see her suffer. The rest, presumably Christian, saw her suffering and death as her day of triumph.[185] Perpetua's death as entry through the gate of life is anticipated in the meal shared the day before the contest. This was a rather grizzly occasion where those condemned shared a meal to which others were invited; it was therefore 'a unique meal mediating between the living and the dead'.[186] This is, of course, how the Christians could understand the meal as well. The living – those about to make confession and die – shared a meal with those who would watch them die in the arena – the dead. It turns into a meal of celebration, a love feast.

One of the most striking and consistent interpretative manoeuvres used by the Christians was to reinterpret or, perhaps more accurately, to redefine the categories of life and death. Through the breaking down of temporal and spatial boundaries, taken together with a radical conviction of the part they were playing in the cosmic scheme of things, the early Christians were able to sustain a belief not only that those who died were alive, but that those who were currently alive were dead.

The temporal movement for human beings was not life leading to inevitable death, for life in the world was death, and death in the world was life. Paradoxically, the martyrs believed that the state of death (that is, being alive in the world) could potentially lead to life for the faithful, or continued death for the unfaithful (depending on the choice whether to live or die in the arena). The commands of God brought life, whereas to follow the commands of the Emperor was to court death, even though one's earthly life might be spared.

> One must fulfil the commandments of our Lord Jesus Christ, which lead men to an indestructible life. But the commands of your emperor should not even be entertained by the hearing, leading as they do to destruction and death.[187]

In creating new social symbols, the Christians could challenge and reinterpret the situation of persecution and death positively.[188] Therefore, Christians could have contempt for their earthly bodies,[189] for it was through death that they lived and

---

185. *Mart. Perpetua* 5.5.

186. P. Plass, *The Game of Death in Ancient Rome* (Madison: University of Michigan Press, 1995), 52. Criminals were regarded as being dead from the moment of their sentence.

187. *Mart. Justin* (Recension C) 2.1. Though this recension probably dates to the fifth century (see Musurillo, *ACM*, 57 n. 16), the sentiment expressed is early.

188. See A. Yarbro Collins, *Cosmology and Eschatology in Jewish and Christian Apocalypticism* (Leiden: E.J. Brill, 1996).

189. Death brings liberty at: *Mart. Pol.* 3; *Mart. Carpus* (A) 39; *Mart. Justin* (C) 4.6; *Mart. Perpetua* 11.4; *Mart. Ignatius* 4; Justin, *Trypho* 46; *Apol.* I.57; Origen, *Exhortation* 22.

reached perfection.[190] Death was not to be feared, but welcomed; charging towards death was in reality 'rushing towards life',[191] so much so that the martyr could even be found to express thanks to his persecutor, who sped him on to life.[192]

So well did this imagery of life and death work, that martyrs could be said to be born at the point of death. Conversely, those who succumbed to torture and denied their faith at the moment of trial were said to be stillborn. They had begun the process of birth, only to be snatched dead from the womb by Satan.[193] In the *Martyrs of Lyons*, deniers are stillborn, but are restored or even saved or redeemed, through the deaths of others.

> Through their perseverance the infinite mercy of Christ was revealed. The dead were restored to life through the living; the martyrs brought to favour those who bore no witness, and the Virgin Mother experienced much joy in recovering alive those whom she had cast forth stillborn. For through the martyrs those who had denied the faith for the most part went through the same process and were conceived and quickened again in the womb and learned to confess Christ. Alive now and strengthened they came before the tribunal that they might again be questioned by the governor: for God, who does not desire the death of the sinner but shows him the favour of repentance, made it sweet for them.[194]

When the writer observes, 'the dead were restored to life through the living'[195] a remarkable transformation has occurred. Each category used to understand life has been reversed. Death equals life; life equals death. Death equals victory; life constitutes defeat and failure. Death means reward; life means judgement.[196]

Language reversal is found in the death of Blandina, who rejoices and glories in her death, and is said to be partaking of a bridal banquet while being food for the wild beasts.[197] Similarly, comparisons were often made contrasting the temporal fire with which the martyrs were threatened with the far more impressive eternal fire from which they are escaping, and with which they threatened their persecutors.[198] Saturnus warns those sharing in his final meal to note what the martyrs look like, as they will recognize them again come the day of judgement.[199]

The world of the Christians was highly dualistic, offering each potential martyr a series of profound and stark choices. Life and death; confession and denial; heaven and hell; reward and punishment; Christ and Satan; these were all binary oppositions with no middle way. In the Christians' cosmos, normal spatial and temporal barriers were dismantled, and the fundamental categories of life and death were deconstructed. Crucially, martyrdom affected that cosmos.

190. *Mart. Lyons* 1.9; Tertullian, *Scorp.* 8; *Mart. Ignatius* 1, 7; Origen, *Exhortation* 11.
191. *Mart. Pionius* 20.5; 21.4.
192. *Acts of Scillitan Martyrs* 15, 17; *Mart. Ptol.* 17–18; *Mart. Ignatius* 2.
193. *Mart. Lyons* 1.11.
194. *Mart. Lyons* 1.45–6.
195. *Mart. Lyons* 1.45.
196. So in the *Acts of Thomas* (160), execution is not death but deliverance.
197. *Mart. Lyons* 1.55.
198. *Mart. Pol.* 1.3; 11.2; *Mart. Carpus* 8; *Mart. Carpus* (Latin) 4.4–5; *Mart. Perpetua* 18.1; *Mart. Justin* 2.1; *A.Cyprian* 5.7; *Mart. Conon* 5.7.
199. *Mart. Perpetua* 17.2. The day (*die illo*) of judgement will see the reversal of the present situation, where those who will be martyred will be involved in judging the onlookers and scoffers.

A Cosmos without Barriers

The early Christians created a cosmos without barriers. By dismantling the boundaries between earth and heaven, and present and future, earthly life and struggle took on added significance. The distinction between earthly life and future life, though present, was somewhat blurred. The Christian life was a struggle played out in a cosmic arena, watched by crowds in heaven, crowds on earth, and crowds in hell.

Central to the Christian's reflection on martyrdom was the example of Jesus. The truest form of discipleship for many Christians was to identity themselves as belonging to him, and follow his path to execution. To achieve death for Jesus was to bring reward and victory. The martyrs were athletes or combatants, engaged in nothing less than holy war against the forces of Satan. Fighting with and dying for Christ was their most potent weapon, indeed, the only weapon required for the cosmic conflict in which they were engaged.

Coleman has highlighted how through mythical re-enactments in the arena, the gods could be honoured, and the myths and stories of the glory of Rome reinforced,[200] an activity he describes as 'fatal charades' and which Barton terms 'snuff-plays'.[201] 'A condemned criminal would be dressed and drilled – to be dismembered as Orpheus, gored as Prometheus, penetrated as Pasiphae, castrated as Attis, crucified as Laureolus, or burned as [Mucius] Scaevola'.[202] This practice is reflected in the *Martyrdom of Perpetua*, where the men are dressed as priests of Saturn and the women as priestesses of Ceres.[203] Perpetua, on behalf of the other martyrs, refuses to take part in this pagan charade, stressing that, since they had come to the arena of their own free will, their Christian dignity should remain intact. The military tribune agreed, and the martyrs stand as they are – as Christians. Standing in the arena, having refused to take part in the mythical snuff play of the Romans, and stripped of the robes of the pagan deities, Perpetua sings a psalm, and is said to be 'already standing on the head of the Egyptian'.[204]

However, the Christians participated in their own 'charade'; not only did each martyrdom re-enact the death of Jesus, but also, in the retelling of their stories, the mythical battle between God and Satan was re-enacted in the martyrs' bodies. As the bodies of the martyrs were lacerated and speared; hanged, scraped and whipped; beaten, eaten, strangled and burned, the cosmic battle advanced, as the martyrs struck decisively against Satan.

The life and, most importantly, death of each individual Christian was therefore cast as having cosmic significance. Christians may have comprised a small sect in the Roman world, but before governors and proconsuls the course of the cosmos depended on their confession. Through their deaths, the Christians filled up the necessary number of martyrs required which would trigger Christ's final victory. This is most explicitly seen in the response given to the souls under

---

200. Coleman, 'Fatal charades', 60–76.
201. Barton, 'Savage miracles', 45.
202. Barton, 'Savage miracles', 45.
203. *Mart. Perpetua* 18.4.
204. *Mart. Perpetua* 18.7 (*Perpetua psallebat caput iam Aegyptii calcans*).

the altar in Rev. 6.9, where the souls are told to wait a only little while longer until the full compliment of martyrs is complete.[205] However, this idea of somehow filling up a set number of deaths is found in the *Acts of the Martyrs*. Polycarp gives thanks that he will have 'a share among the number (ἐν ἀριθμῷ) of the martyrs',[206] while in *The Martyrs of Lyons*, we are told that 'every day the worthy were arrested to fill up the number of the martyrs' (ἀναπληροῦντες ἀριθμόν).[207] Furthermore, on two further occasions, the Lyons martyrs are counted among τῳ κλήρῳ τῶν μαρτύρων.[208]

Given the apocalyptic orientation of *The Martyrs of Lyons*, both ἀναπληροῦντες ἀριθμόν and ὁ κλῆρος τῶν μαρτύρων should be given their full eschatological significance, since it is set immediately prior to Satan's final assault (1.5). In this context, it should be taken to mean that those in Lyons saw themselves contributing to this particular eschatological number, rather than to a simple count of local martyrs. Significantly, when Rev. 14.4 is cited (1.10), the author crucially equates 'following the Lamb' with death.

Moreover, the concept of a complement of martyrs being required before the End has parallels in other contemporary apocalypses. In *1 En.* 47; *4 Ezra* 4; and *2 Bar.* 23, there is clear evidence of the *numerus iustorum*, 'the number of the righteous', predetermined by God to face death. This number reaches completion in *1 En.* 47.4, so the hearts of the holy ones rejoice that their blood *had been required*.[209] The concept of the 'number of the martyrs' is linked, therefore, to a decisive eschatological moment.

Therefore, in the eschatological battle – the cosmic conflict – Christians were called to struggle and to overcome. They could win victory only through good confession, leading to death. In doing so, they filled up the number of martyrs required to trigger the end, and with it final victory.

A Cosmos in Action: The Visions of Perpetua [210]
The first prison vision of Perpetua is paradigmatic of this struggle:[211]

> I saw a ladder of tremendous height made of bronze, reaching all the way to the heavens, but it was so narrow that only one person could climb up at a time. To the sides of the ladder were attached all sorts of metal weapons: there were swords, spears, hooks, daggers, and spikes; so that if anyone tried to climb up carelessly or without paying attention, he would be mangled and his flesh would adhere to the weapons.

205. This is fully argued in Chapter 5 below, especially 152–3.

206. *Mart. Pol.* 14.

207. *Mart. Lyons* 1.13.

208. *Mart. Lyons* 1.26, 48.

209. Emphasis added. Significantly, the notion of a set number before the end has parallels in the New Testament and beyond, though not necessarily signifying martyrdom, so that, in Paul, the number of the Gentiles must first come in (Rom. 11.25). The number of the elect is also found in *1 Clement* 2.4; 59.2, as is the number of the saved (58.2).

210. Wansink (*Chained in Christ*, 62–3) notes that intense dreams were a common feature of prison life.

211. In what follows, I will offer an exegesis of this vision demonstrating how it neatly fits the general theology of martyrdom that I have outlined. For a Jungian analysis of this dream, see

At the foot of the ladder lay a dragon of enormous size, and it would attack those who tried to climb up and try to terrify them from doing so. And Saturnus was the first to go up, he who was later to give himself up of his own accord. He had been the builder of our strength, although he was not present when we were arrested. And he arrived at the top of the staircase and he looked back and said to me: 'Perpetua, I am waiting for you. But take care; do not let the dragon bite you'.

'He will not harm me,' I said, 'in the name of Christ Jesus'.

Slowly, as though he were afraid of me, the dragon stuck his head out from underneath he ladder. Then, using it as my first step, I trod on his head and went up.

Then I saw an immense garden, and in it a grey-haired man sat in shepherd's garb; tall he was, and milking sheep. And standing around him were many thousands of people clad in white garments. He raised his head, looked at me, and said: 'I am glad you have come, my child'.

He called me over to him and gave me, as it were, a mouthful of the milk he was drawing; and I took it in my cupped hands, and consumed it. And all those who stood around said: 'Amen!' At the sound of this word I came to, with the taste of something sweet still in my mouth. I at once told this to my brother, and we realised that we would have to suffer, and that from now on we would no longer have any hope in this life.[212]

In this, the first of Perpetua's prison visions, many of the theological themes we have been discussing are evident.

The first element in the dream is the ladder, most obviously reminiscent of Jacob's ladder (Gen. 28),[213] though others have point to the similarities with Jewish ascent myths.[214] The ladder, the first component of Perpetua's vision, is a dramatic symbol of the trial and struggle of the Christians before their accusers.[215]

F. Oberholzer, 'Interpreting the dreams of Perpetua: psychology in the service of theology', in M.H. Barnes (ed.), *Theology and the Social Sciences* (Maryknoll, NY: Orbis Books, 2001), 293–312; and also Salisbury, *Perpetua's Passion*, 99–104. The visions of Perpetua have also received attention from Rowland, *Open Heaven*, 396–402; P.C. Miller, 'The Devil's gateway: an eros of difference in the dreams of Perpetua', *Dreaming* 2 (1992), 45–53; A.L. Petterson, 'Perpetua – prisoner of conscience', *VC* 41 (1987), 139–53; Munoa, 'Jesus', 317–23; and C.M. Robeck, *Prophecy in Carthage: Perpetua, Tertullian, and Cyprian* (Ohio: The Pilgrim Press, 1992), 19–86. Though the prison diaries are written in the first person, T.J. Heffernan, 'Philology and authorship in the *Passio Sanctarum Perpetuae et Felicitatis*', *Traditio* 50 (1995), 315–25, is surely correct in his conclusion that this section of the Passion has undergone substantial editing.

212. *Mart. Perpetua* 4.3–9.

213. Musurillo, *ACM*, 111 n. 5; Frend, 'Blandina and Perpetua', 92; Petterson, 'Prisoner of conscience', 147. See also the later *Acts of Montanus and Lucius* 7.6, where the sign of Jacob (*signum Iacobi*) is to be given in response to a request for a sign of where heaven was. Oberholzer ('Interpreting the dreams', 299) rejects this identification, considering it unlikely that a recently converted pagan would use dream imagery from Genesis; see also Robeck, *Prophecy in Carthage*, 27.

214. Dronke, *Women Writers*, 7–8. Rowland (*Open Heaven*, 22, 398, 510 n. 175) points to the Jewish mystical *Hekaloth* literature, where pious Jews could be said to have a 'ladder in one's house' in order to ascend to the world above (*Hekaloth Rabbati* 13.2; see also the discussion of heavenly ascent in Philo, *De Somniis*), while Salisbury (*Perpetua's Passion*, 100–1) advances ancient Assyrian dream tradition as a possible source. For discussion on heavenly ascent as a goal of the pious, see M. Smith, 'Ascent to heaven and the beginning of Christianity', *Eranus–Jahrbuch* 50 (1981) 403–29; *idem*, *Jesus the Magician*; and also M. Himmelfarb, 'The practice of ascent in the ancient Mediterranean world', in J.J. Collins and M. Fischbane (eds), *Death, Ecstasy, and Other Worldly Journeys* (New York: State of New York Press, 1995), 123–37.

215. Robeck (*Prophecy*, 27–9) associates the ladder with Christian life in general, drawing on the

Suspended between heaven and 'hell', the ladder represents both the challenge and the final destination of the combatants who pass or fail the impending test. The ladder is itself a place of danger, with spikes, hooks and other instruments of torture, surely representing the instruments of torture that the potential martyr will face in the effort to persuade her to recant.[216] In the vision, the important reversal of the cosmos, typical of Christian martyrological discourse, is at play: to navigate the ladder safely is to die in life, whereas to be mangled on the hooks, impaled by the spears or devoured by the dragon, though death in the vision, would represent survival in the arena, through offering worship to the Emperor. The dragon is of enormous size and has a two-fold role. First, it attacks those who attempt to climb the ladder, but it also tries to frighten away would-be combatants from even approaching the ladder.[217]

That the dragon represents the devil is clear from the method by which it is despatched. After Perpetua's fourth vision,[218] in which she fights the Egyptian, she realizes that her struggle is to be against the Devil.[219] The manner of her victory over the Egyptian is by treading on his head.[220]

> I put my two hands together linking the fingers of one hand with those of the other and thus I got hold of his head. He fell flat on his face and I stepped on his head (*calcaui illi caput*).[221]

Similarly, she defeats the dragon in her first vision by standing on its head (*calcaui illi caput*), indeed, using its head as the first step of her ascent up the ladder. Within Jewish and Christian tradition, a serpent or dragon represented supernatural agency in opposition to God, particularly explicit in the Apocalypse (especially ch. 12).[222]

'two-ways' biblical tradition found in, for example, Deut. 30.19, where the choice is between blessing and cursing, and similarly Ps. 1.6; Jer. 21.8, as well as Qumranic and pseudepigraphal traditions. Robeck also points to parallels with Christian tradition, particularly Mt. 7.14. Although nothing in Robeck's analysis is implausible, it is a somewhat trite interpretation of a major symbol of the vision, especially one which leads to the conclusion that there was no hope left in this life.

216. Rowland (*Open Heaven*, 398) notes that in Jewish mystical tradition there is often an obstacle or difficulty in ascending to heaven (so *Asc. Isa.* 9.1; *3 En.* 1.3, 7).

217. The dragon is therefore successful if it succeeds in causing injury to a climber, which would represent causing a denial of being Christian under torture, or if he manages to turn Christians cowardly before they get to the arena. As we have seen, both of these occurrences represent a victory for Satan. Though both these diabolical victories occur in other *Acts*, everyone in the *Martyrdom of Perpetua* defeats Satan/the dragon.

218. *Mart. Perpetua* 10.1–14.

219. How the identification is made is not clear. Robeck (*Prophecy*, 62–3) makes several, though rather unlikely, suggestions. It could be on account of the colour of his skin (in the *Ep. Barnabas*, the devil is referred to as 'the black one'). Or since the Egyptian prepares for the fight by rolling in the dust, there may be a connection with the *Shepherd of Hermas* (vision 4.1.5–6; cf. Gen. 3.14), or that Egypt was the place of slavery and bondage. Whether any of the above would adequately explain the connection in the mind of Perpetua is rather unlikely.

220. Probably an allusion to Gen. 3.15, though Munoa ('Jesus', 318–20) believes the principle influence on the whole of Perpetua's vision to be Daniel 7.

221. *Mart. Perpetua* 10.11.

222. For a survey, see Robeck, *Prophecy*, 23–4; D.S. Russell, *The Method and Message of Jewish*

The conflict is, therefore, confirmed to be against Satan. Since ascending the ladder represents death in the earthly arena, martyrdom is again confirmed to be the method by which Christians defeated Satan and his forces. Perpetua concludes at the end of the vision where she has trodden on the dragon's head that 'we would no longer have any hope in this life'.[223] Similarly, in the fourth vision, where paradoxically defeating the Egyptian means death in the arena, Perpetua not only knows that she will be fighting with the Devil, she knows that her death will constitute victory.[224]

Crucially, the victory is achieved through Jesus Christ. When Perpetua is warned about the dragon, she responds that it will not harm her *in nomine Iesu Christi*. The martyrs participate in the victory of Jesus Christ over the powers of the dragon. This underscores that the Christians believed that Satan's intentions were not to cause the deaths of the believers. The consequences of not being harmed by the dragon meant dying a martyr's death. In contrast, for the dragon to do any harm, somehow death would be avoided.

For those who navigated the dragon and the weapons, paradise awaited. In Perpetua's vision, at the ladder's summit was an immense garden.[225] A grey haired shepherd,[226] milking sheep, greets Perpetua and, expressing pleasure that she has come, addresses her as child.[227] Sitting as he was, amid thousands of people

---

Apocalyptic (Philadelphia: Westminster Press, 1964), 123–4, 276–7. Oberholzer ('Interpreting the dreams', 299) takes the dragon to represent the arguments used by her father to dissuade her from martyrdom. Artemidorus, the second-century author of the first book on dreams interprets venomous animals as powerful men, and the head of such creatures as parents (Salisbury, *Perpetua's Passion*, 100). Since all efforts to dissuade Christians from undergoing martyrdom were seen as diabolical, there is no contradiction between these interpretations.

223. *Mart. Perpetua* 4.10.

224. *Mart. Perpetua* 10.14.

225. On the particular picture of heaven in Perpetua's vision, see C. McDannell and B. Lang, *Heaven: A History* (New Haven/London: Yale University Press, 1988); E. Gardner (ed.), *Visions of Heaven and Hell before Dante* (New York: Italica Press, 1989); and J.N. Bremmer, 'The Passion of Perpetua and the development of early Christian afterlife', *Nederlands Theologisch Tijdschrift* 54 (2000), 97–111.

226. For the image of God as shepherd, see Isa. 40.10–11; Jer. 31.10; Ezek. 34.6–31; Ps. 23.1; Sir. 18.13.

227. The designation 'child' is in Greek in an otherwise Latin document, in some way highlighting its importance. Oberholzer ('Interpreting the dreams', *passim*) interprets the dreams of Perpetua as stemming from the trauma of her impending martyrdom and the tension caused by the relationship she has with her father. The figure here, who affirms her as child, as well as the trainer in the fourth vision who calls her daughter, by virtue of her Christian identity, stand in contrast with the broken relationship with her father over the same religious identity. Oberholzer is, quite rightly, suspicious of commentators who project their own religious associations with the imagery of Perpetua's dream, rather than first examining what they may have meant to a young, recently converted Roman. Robeck (*Prophecy*, 45–56) in particular, looks for 'scriptural themes' in each of Perpetua's visions, and is particularly vexed by Perpetua's belief that she has the ability to intercede for her dead non-Christian brother. Nonetheless, the *Passion* has been through several hands, and associations with Jewish and Christian tradition would have been made at a very early stage. Therefore, even if the imagery of shepherds, ladders or dragons came from something other than Jewish-Christian imagery, it is legitimate to make these connections, not least because the original editors would have believed that such visions were inspired by God.

clothed in white, who later cry 'Amen', surely calls to mind the image in the Apocalypse, where God is surrounded by the throngs of worshippers, and those whose garments have been made white by the blood of the lamb.

Perpetua is then given cheese to eat,[228] and as she consumes it the crowd say 'Amen'. At that moment, Perpetua wakes and realizes that she will count herself among the martyrs in heaven, and in turn put on a white robe.[229] The reward for faithfulness to death is to journey to paradise, attaining God, and a place in heaven.[230]

Conclusion

The early Christian reinterpretation of the world in which they lived served a dual function. First it enabled a positive reassessment of the distressing circumstances in which they found themselves, making sense of their experiences of persecution and suffering. Secondly, however, it became a potent lens that put such a positive spin on hardship, that Christians sought persecution in order to demonstrate their own faithfulness, and to reinforce their position as God's chosen agents of eschatological salvation.

The second-century Christians reset their experiences of suffering in the context of an apocalyptic contest. They participated in Christ's battle with Satan. They claimed their place as Christ's warriors by holding fast to the Name, refusing to choose physical life and deny. By holding to their confession, they bought life through death. Their deaths were inspirational models for other Christians to follow.

The cosmos was divided as two armies: Christ's and Satan's. By denouncing the gods of the pagans, Christians brought themselves into conflict with the authorities. Since death was such a potent weapon in the fight against evil, and since it brought a martyr's reward, enthusiastic and faithful Christians sought it out, deliberately seeking arrest, or wilfully bringing themselves to the authorities'

---

228. Musurillo (*ACM*, 113) renders *caseo* as milk, smoothing over the difficulty of the shepherd appearing to draw cheese from the sheep. Some form of Eucharistic practice may also be imagined here, with the cupping of the hands to receive the cheese. The Montanists, with whom Perpetua is closely associated (Barnes, *Tertullian*, 77) used bread and cheese at their celebration of the Eucharist according to Epiphanius (*Panarion* 49.2) and Augustine (*Liber de haeresibus* 1.28), though Augustine believed they used goat's cheese. On Augustine's use of *The Passion*, particularly his use of its Montanist elements, see K.B. Steinhauser, 'Augustine's reading of the *Passio sanctarum Perpetuae et Felicitatis*', in E.A. Livingstone (ed.), *Sudia Patristica XXXIII* (Leuven: Peeters, 1997), 244–9.

229. That those clad in white represent former martyrs is strengthened by Saturus' dream, where he and Perpetua actually recognize some of the martyrs known to them among the inhabitants of heaven. Rowland (*Open Heaven*, 398) sees this vision of paradise as the 'place of the righteous dead'. However, as we noted above, the common belief at the time was that only martyrs attained heaven immediately after death, so Tertullian (*On the Soul* 55.4) in a commentary on the visions of Perpetua. However, see Bremmer, 'Passion of Perpetua', 101–2, for a discussion of contrary views.

230. So later, 'The day of their victory dawned, and they marched from the prison to the amphitheatre joyfully as though they were going to heaven' (*Mart. Perpetua* 18.1).

attention. Though these radical martyrs came to be despised by the later 'ortho-dox' Christians, it was their Christian world-view, their zeal for Christ and their desire to participate fully in Christ's victory over Satan that drove these foot-soldiers to their deaths. The lust for martyrdom was, therefore, an explicable consequence of the socio-theological response to the world in which these early Christians faithfully sought to live.

Chapter 4

THE ORIGINS OF CHRISTIAN MARTYRDOM

Introduction

In the course of the last two chapters, I have argued that many early Christians embraced radical martyrdom. This phenomenon was not an aberration or deviation from an established normative behaviour. As I have demonstrated, it was central to a significant number of early Christians' self-understanding of their identity as Christians, and to the living out of that identity.

I argued that theologies of martyrdom must be extended to take full account of these second- and third-century Christians, too often regarded as being outside the 'normal attitude to martyrdom', and therefore, up until now, ignored in constructions of early Christian theologies of martyrdom. Similarly, any investigations into the origins of Christian martyrdom must include this group of martyrs, who, though marginalized by scholars, were somewhat more central to the life of the early Church.

These early Christians, I have argued, saw themselves as participating in a cosmic war between God and the forces of Satan. Moreover, their deaths contributed to the war effort to the point of affecting its outcome. We now turn to the question of the origins of Christian martyrdom. How did it develop in the way it did? From where did the system of thought come? If, to use Gerd Theissen's phrase, the 'semiotic cathedral' in which the early Christians inhabited enabled this type of martyrdom, from which quarries were the bricks fashioned, and who aided its construction?

The question is complex. Not only are we speaking of a particular action, death, or even willing death, but also a whole thought system in which that death was interpreted. What came first, the desire/opportunity for death or the rationale? Therefore, we have at least three elements of Christian martyrdom seeking an origin: the action; the theologizing; and the thought world, that is, the conceptual system that interpreted, sustained and even encouraged Christian martyrdom.

Here we are also in danger of confusing historical and literary questions. Our evidence is primarily literary, even if it describes historical events. The distance between event and record may have been relatively short in terms of time, but lengthened considerably by a whole series of factors: the decision process that inspired the production of the material in the first place; the use to which it was put; evidence of redaction; and so on. Treading carefully, we proceed to an examination of the possible sources of Christian martyrdom.

The State of the Question

Daniel Boyarin[1] in his assessment of the state of the question distinguishes two clear camps. The first of these is represented by Frend,[2] who judges the roots of Christian martyrdom to be planted firmly in the soil of Judaism:[3] 'without Maccabees and without Daniel, a Christian theology of martyrdom would scarcely have been possible'.[4] Lining up in opposition to Frend is Bowersock,[5] who rejects this Jewish background for martyrdom, judging the Christian understanding to be 'something entirely new', and in turn borrowed by Judaism. 'Without the glorification of suicide in the Roman tradition, the development of martyrdom in the second and third centuries would have been unthinkable.'[6]

Boyarin's own interest in Jewish and Christian martyrdom is the extent to which martyrological discourse illuminates his thesis concerning Christian origins and, in particular, how it helped Jews and Christians to invent themselves as two discrete entities. Boyarin argues that Christian and Jewish identities were less clear cut than theories of Christian origins generally allow for. Therefore, on the Frend versus Bowersock debate, he observes that

> both of these seemingly opposite arguments are founded on the same assumption, namely, that Judaism and Christianity are two separate entities, so that it is intelligible to speak of one (and not the other – either – one) as the point of origin of a given practice.[7]

Instead, Boyarin argues that it is this assumption that needs questioning. Rather than comprising two discrete entities – Judaism and Christianity – he argues, 'all Judaisms and all Christianities' up to the fourth century shared 'features that make them a single semantic family in the Wittgensteinian sense'.[8] Therefore,

> the 'invention' of martyrdom, far from being evidence for Christian influence on Judaism or the opposite, is most plausibly read as evidence for the close contact and the impossibility of drawing sharp and absolute distinctions between these communities or their discourses throughout this period.[9]

However, although Boyarin's thesis warns us of the danger against creating artificial divisions in the first century between all Jews and all Christians where

---

1. Boyarin, *Dying for God*; see also his article, 'Martyrdom and the Making of Christianity and Judaism', *JECS* 6 (1998), 577–627.

2. Frend, *Martyrdom and Persecution*.

3. H.A. Fischel, 'Prophet and martyr', *JQR* 37 (1946–7), 265–80, 363–86, Surkau (*Martyrien*), Perler ('Das vierte Makkabäerbuch'), and Baumeister (*Anfänge*) all trace the origins of Christian martyrdom as coming, either exclusively, or principally, from Judaism.

4. Frend, *Martyrdom and Persecution*, 65. Bauermeister (*Genèse et evolution*) includes Dan. 11.29–12.4; 2 Macc. 6.12–17, 30–1; 7.7–9, 30–42; *4 Macc.* 1.1, 7–12; 17.11–22 in his inventory of texts displaying the theology of early Christian martyrdom. See also *idem, Anfänge*.

5. Bowersock, *Martrydom and Rome*.

6. Bowersock, *Martyrdom and Rome*, 72–3.

7. Boyarin, *Dying for God*, 93.

8. Boyarin, *Dying for God*, 8. Compare the work of R.A. Markus (*The End of Christianity*, Cambridge: Cambridge University Press, 1990), who argues that the borders between even paganism and Christianity were less pronounced than generally accepted until the fourth century when Christianity finally declared its borders.

9. Boyarin, *Dying for God*, 117.

they may not have existed,[10] Boyarin himself does not deny there was any distinction between Christians and Jews by the second century. His point is simply that the 'border between them was so fuzzy that one could hardly say precisely at what point one stopped and the other began'.[11] So, Boyarin asks us to imagine Judaisms and Christianities as a spectrum, with Marcionite Christianity, having no regard for Judaism, at one end, and, at the other, Jews for whom Jesus meant nothing.[12] But along the continuum it becomes difficult to separate Christians from Jews.

Without denying the value of Boyarin's approach, there are a number of problems with it. In earliest Christian literature, 'the Jews' appear to comprise a body that can be distinguished from the Christians; they do appear to constitute an 'other'.[13] Furthermore, while accepting that anti-Jewish polemic, where sharp distinctions are drawn, may disguise actual closeness, such as in Matthew or John,[14] this is hardly the case with Gentile Christians. Furthermore, if 1 Thess. 2.14–16 is authentic,[15] then even Paul, himself 'a radical Jew',[16] is capable of making a distinction between those whom he considers Jews and Christians.[17]

10. The politics of this approach are exposed well by Alexander (P.S. Alexander, '"The parting of the ways" from the perspective of rabbinic Judaism', in J.D.G. Dunn [ed.], *Jews and Christians: The Parting of the Ways A.D. 70 to 135* [The Second Durham-Tübingen Research Symposium on Earliest Christianity and Judaism, Durham, September 1989; Tübingen: J.C.B. Mohr (Paul Siebeck) 1991], 1–25), who notes that the attempt to see in the first century two discrete groups, 'barely conceals apologetic motives – in the case of Christianity a desire to prove that Christianity transcended or transformed Judaism, in the case of Jews a desire to suggest that Christianity was an alien form of Judaism which deviated from the true path'.

11. Boyarin, *Dying for God*, 11.

12. Boyarin, *Dying for God*, 8.

13. Most notably in John, where they are opposed to those who confess Jesus is the Christ (9.22; 12.42; 16.2), though also Mt. 28.15 (cf. 12.9; 13.54 for 'their' synagogues); Acts 9.23; 12.3; 13.45; 17.5; 22.30; 26.2 where the 'Jews' plot against the Christians. Cf. Rev. 3.9.

14. The literature on the relationship between Judaism and Christianity is almost endless. See especially, W.D. Davies, *Christian Engagements with Judaism* (Pennsylvania: Trinity Press International, 1999); W. Horbury, *Jews and Christians: In Contact and Controversy* (Edinburgh: T&T Clark, 1998); P. Borgen, *Early Christianity and Hellenistic Judaism* (Edinburgh: T&T Clark, 1996); J.M.G. Barclay and J. Sweet (eds), *Early Christian Thought in Its Jewish Context* (Cambridge: Cambridge University Press, 1996); Wilson., *Related Strangers*; Dunn (ed), *Jews and Christians*; idem, *The Partings of the Ways: Between Christianity and Judaism and Their Significance for the Character of Christianity* (London: SCM Press, 1991); J. Lieu, J. North and T. Rajak (eds), *The Jews among Pagans and Christian in the Roman Empire* (London: Routledge, 1992); Sanders, *Schismatics*; C. Rowland, *Christian Origins: An Account of the Setting and Character of the Most Important Messianic Sect of Judaism* (London: SPCK, 1985).

15. Among those who argue for the integrity of the letter are: K.P. Donfried, 'Paul and Judaism: 1 Thessalonians 2: 13–16 as a test case', *Interpretation* 38 (1994), 242–53; and R.F. Collins, 'Apropos the integrity of 1 Thess', in R.F. Collins, *Studies on the First Letter to the Thessalonians* (Leuven: Leuven University Press, 1984), 96–135. The opposite view is advanced by B.A. Pearson, '1 Thessalonians 2:13–16: a deutero-Pauline interpolation', *HTR* 64 (1971), 79–91; and D. Schmidt, '1 Thess. 2:13–16: linguistic evidence for an interpolation', *JBL* 102 (1983), 269–79.

16. D. Boyarin, *A Radical Jew: Paul and the Politics of Identity* (Berkeley: University of California Press, 1994).

17. Although, where Paul would place himself probably depends on what situation he was addressing (cf. 1 Cor. 9.19–23)!

Boyarin must therefore insist that Christian literature that distinguishes itself from Judaism does not reflect the actual thinking of Christians on the ground, which of course may be the case, but the evidence is too thin on which to build his case.

Secondly, Boyarin makes much of the celebrated case of Rabbi Akiba being confused as a Christian by the authorities.[18] Granted, there are some cases of mistaken identity – hardly surprising given Christianity was a Jewish sect – nonetheless, pagans were generally good at distinguishing between the two.[19] Therefore, although Boyarin has highlighted several dangers in making too simplistic a division between ancient Judaism and Christianity, the question of the origin of Christian martyrology may still be posed in its traditional form.

Furthermore, there is a third possibility for the origins of Christian martyrdom not mentioned by Boyarin, possibly because it does not affect his primary concern with Christian and Jewish identity. Some scholars have sought to locate Christian martyrological reflection in the Graeco-Roman Noble Death tradition,[20] where Christians re-enacted their own form of this tradition, employing its virtues and making it their own.

Therefore, we will investigate each of these possibilities in turn, beginning with Judaism, moving on to the Noble Death tradition, before turning to examine the Bowersock thesis. In doing so, we will discover to what extent each has a claim to explain the origins of the Christian understanding of dying for God.

Judaism as a Source of Christian Martyrology

Judaism is an obvious starting point when investigating the origins of any Christian system of thought. Whether one sees the relationship between the two religions in terms of kinship or continuum, Judaism clearly played a massive role in shaping Christian theology. For many scholars, the Christian martyrological system was born in the crisis afflicting Judaism in the mid-second century BCE. 'As in so much of the doctrine and practice of the primitive church, the Christian view of the martyr's role prolongs but also succeeds Judaism.'[21]

Decades before Frend's work, Judaism had already been described as 'eine Religion des Martyriums'.[22] Greater attention was given to reflection on death

18. For Boyarin (*Dying for God*, 105), 'Rabbi Akiva is the Polycarp of Judaism'.
19. Tacitus, although describing Christians as coming from Judea and that they are loathed for their 'hatred of the human race', is nonetheless able to distinguish between the two. Despite holding Judaism in low regard, he concedes that it is vindicated by its antiquity (*Histories* 5.5). Christians, in contrast, are deserving of torture and death. Pliny makes no mention of the Christians relationship with Judaism, rather, they are guilty of unspecified crimes. For a survey of pagan attitudes to Christians, see Lieu, '"The Parting of the Ways"'. Lieu concludes that pagans could generally tell the difference, but in some regions it was more difficult.
20. So Coleman, 'Fatal charades'; D. Seeley, *The Noble Death: Graeco-Roman Martyrology and Paul's Concept of Salvation* (JSNTSup, 28; Sheffield: JSOT Press, 1990; and Droge and Tabor, *Noble Death*.
21. Frend, *Martyrdom and Persecution*, 80.
22. W. Bousset and H. Gressman, *Die Religion des Judentums im späthellenistischen Zeitalter* (Tübingen, 1926), 374, cited in Dehandschutter and Henten, 'Einleitung', 2. However, compare

within and, in particular, for the religion in response to the heightened experiences of persecution, especially from the period of the reign of Antiochus Epiphanes, reflected in Daniel, the books of Maccabees, and other Apocryphal and Pseudepigraphal writings.[23] From this period onward, stories began to circulate about Jews who preferred death rather than transgress the Law.[24] Paradigmatic is the story of Daniel and the three friends (Dan. 3; 6). Of course, unlike the characters in this story of miraculous delivery, the readers of this text were suffering torture and death, a fact perhaps acknowledged in the story itself. For, as the three youths are threatened with the fiery furnace, should they refuse to worship the golden image, they reply:

> If it be so, our God whom we serve is able to deliver us from the burning fiery furnace; and he will deliver us out of your hand, O king. *But even if he does not*, be it known to you, O king, that we will not serve your gods or worship your idols.[25]

Although this miraculous deliverance did not materialize for those under the reign of Antiochus who chose to follow the youths' example, deliverance was simply postponed to an eschatological future time (Dan. 12.1–3).[26] Therefore, the theology of the second and fourth books of Maccabees, as well as much Intertestamental literature, anticipates future vindication of those who die for the Law.

The Maccabees

Frend points to the period of the Maccabean martyr tradition as the starting point for his thesis, claiming that it furnished Christianity with material it readily utilised.[27] Central to both 2 and *4 Maccabees* are the deaths of Eleazar and the family of seven brothers and their mother.[28] King Antiochus, having taken the Jerusalem Temple after an unsuccessful Jewish uprising led by Jason (2 Macc. 5.5–16), decreed that the Jews were to abandon their ancestral traditions (6.1). All those who refused to comply were executed (6.9), so that women who had their sons circumcised were thrown off the ramparts with their babies around their necks (6.10), and a group of Sabbath observers were burnt alive in caves

---

J. Davies (*Death*, 203), who concludes that Rabbinic Judaism was not at all enthusiastic about martyrdom. For a survey of Rabbinic attitudes and further discussion, see A.M. Gray, 'A contribution to the study of martyrdom and identity in the Palestinian Talmud', *JJS* 54 (2003), 242–72.

23. For a survey, see Droge and Tabor, *Noble Death*, 69–112; and J.J. Collins, 'Apocalyptic eschatology and the transcendence of death', *CBQ* 36 (1974), 21–43.

24. For this theme in the Maccabees, see below, 127–9. Consider Taxo in the *Testament of Moses* (9.6) who proclaims, 'Let us die rather than transgress the commandments of the Lord of Lords.'

25. Dan. 3.17–18 (emphasis added).

26. These verses are the only passage speaking of a general resurrection in the Old Testament. For a survey of the development of the doctrine of the resurrection in this period, see W.E. Nickelsburg, *Resurrection, Immortality, and Eternal Life in Intertestamental Judaism* (Harvard Theological Studies, 26; Cambridge: Harvard University Press, 1972); J.J. Collins, 'Apocalyptic eschatology'; and *idem*, 'The root of immortality: death in the context of Jewish wisdom', *HTR* 71 (1978), 177–92.

27. For a very full discussion of the Maccabean martyr tradition, see Henten, *Maccabean Martyrs*, and also Rajak, 'Dying for the Law'.

28. 2 Maccabees 6–7; *4 Maccabees passim*.

(6.11). The heart of 2 Maccabees is, however, the more detailed accounts of Eleazar, a ninety-year-old teacher of the law who chooses to die rather than eat pork (6.18–31; also *4 Macc*. 5–7), and the torture and execution of seven brothers (7.1–42; also *4 Macc*. 8–18), who similarly refused to eat the banned meat.

Undoubtedly, there are many similarities between the presentations of the Jewish martyrs and their Christian counterparts. Apart from the obvious setting of the stories as a struggle between an earthly ruler and those faithful to God,[29] and the effective ultimatum to recant or die, there are also apparent similarities in the language employed to describe the Jewish standoffs. In particular, there is the presence of contest imagery as the backdrop to the accounts, particularly in *4 Maccabees*,[30] with repeated calls to endurance,[31] and, eventually, to overcome.[32] The martyrs insist that apostasy is not an option, despite torture,[33] and, ultimately, the conviction that punishment awaits the persecutors.[34]

Even the phenomenon of radical death finds some resonance within Jewish tradition. There are examples of those who rush towards death (Razi in 1 Maccabees 6), or take their own lives rather than transgress the law (Taxo in *T. Moses* 9–10) or endure the shame of capture by an enemy (so the Masada tradition, see Josephus, *War* 1.148, 150).[35] Therefore, given the strength of the tradition of Eleazar – which Frend dubs 'the first Act of the Martyrs'[36] – and the stories of

29. In fact, the image of the Jew up against a powerful king is a common enough feature of Jewish storytelling, found as early as Exod. 5.1–5, but especially in wisdom literature and court tales. See J.J. Collins, 'The court tales of Daniel and the development of apocalyptic', *JBL* 94 (1975), 218–34; J.C.H. Lebram, 'Jüdische Martyrologie und Weisheitsüberlieferung', in J.W. van Henten, B.A.G.M. Dehandschutter, and H.J.W. van der Klaauw (eds), *Die Entstehung der jüdischen Martyrologie* (Leiden: E.J. Brill, 1989), 88–126.

30. *4 Macc*. 9.24; 11.20; 16.16; 17.11 (ἀγὼν θεῖος).

31. *4 Macc*. 1.11; 6.9, 11–13; 15.30; 17.12, 23.

32. More than half of the occurrences of νικάω in the LXX are found in *4 Maccabees*: 1.11; 3.17; 6.10, 33; 7.4, 11; 8.2; 9.6, 30; 11.20; 13.2, 7; 16.14; 17.15, 24.

33. 2 Macc. 12.40; *3 Macc* 2.32–3; 7.10–16 (where three thousand apostates are butchered as punishment for their sin); *4 Macc*. 13.15.

34. 1 Maccabees 6; 2 Macc. 7.14, 17, 19; *4 Macc*. 9.9, 24, 32; 10.11, 15, 21, 23; 11.26, 34; 12.12, 18; *Mart. Isa*. 2.14; *T. Mos*. 9.7.

35. For traditions of suicide in Judaism, see D. Goodblatt, 'Suicide in the sanctuary: traditions on priestly martyrdom', *JJS* 46 (1995), 10–29; Droge and Tabor, *Noble Death*, 97–106; and D.J. Ladouceur, 'Josephus and Masada', in L.H. Feldman and G. Hata (eds), *Josephus, Judaism and Christianity* (Leiden: E.J. Brill, 1987), 95–113.

36. Frend, *Martyrdom and Persecution*, 45. However, because there is hardly any information about the arrest, interrogation and execution of Eleazar, Henten (*Maccabean Martyrs*, 101), concludes, '2 Macc. 6:18–31 can hardly be called an act of a martyr'. Nonetheless, the narrative, along with 2 Maccabees 7 comprises 'the oldest Jewish martyr texts' (Henten and Avemarie, *Martyrdom and Noble Death*, 4 n. 10). Second Maccabees spends more time on the martyrs than 1 Maccabees, which gives their sufferings only a few verses (1.57, 60–3; 2.29–38), yet even here there is brevity (6.10–7.42) with only a few of their words recorded. J.A. Goldstein (*II Maccabees* [AB, 41A; New York: Doubleday, 1983], 6) notes that in the original work of which 2 Maccabees is an abridgement, it is likely that there would have been something more akin to the long speeches and graphic descriptions of the martyrs' tortures found in *4 Maccabees*. Significantly, it is only the account of the martyrdoms, where Josephus chooses to take 2 Maccabees over 1 Maccabees as his source. For a discussion of Josephus' sources, see J.A. Goldstein, *I Maccabees* (AB, 41; New York: Doubleday,

the seven brothers and their mother, coupled with several suicide traditions within Judaism,[37] the Jewish matrix, of which death was an important part, is justifiably deemed to be a fertile starting point to uncover the origins of Christian martyrdom. Indeed, in those centres where zealous martyrs existed in the Church, particularly in North Africa, Frend argues that it was owing to a strong influence of contemporary Judaism.[38]

   This influence of Jewish martyrological tradition, it is claimed, can be seen directly in Christian martyrologies. Perler argues for *4 Maccabees* being the primary source for Christian reflection on their martyrs, noting vocabulary in common, particularly connected with the games,[39] and observing that Eleazar and Bishop Pothinus were both 90 years of age.[40] Perler even offers *4 Maccabees* as the source of a Christian enthusiasm for martyrdom.[41] However, although Frend believes documents such as the *Martyrs of Lyons* imitate the style of *4 Maccabees*, he sees 2 Maccabees as a more likely source.[42] Frend draws parallels between the mother of the seven brothers and Blandina, the slave girl in Lyons.

> The most obvious point of contact between the two is the identification of the heroic mother of the Maccabean youths and the slave Blandina. She is also a 'noble mother' who 'encouraged her children' and 'sent them forth triumphant to their living'. Having 'completed her task and endured all the tortures of the children hastened after them'.[43]

If, as Frend implies, the texts in quotations were verbal parallels between the two documents, then the case for 2 Maccabees being a source for the *Martyrs of Lyons* would be irresistible. However, this is not the case. The primary identification marker, that is Blandina being identified as a noble mother encouraging her children[44] (καθάπερ μήτηρ εὐγενὴς παρορμήσασα τὰ τέκνα),[45] differs substantially from the supposed Maccabean source, where the mother (ἡ μήτηρ),[46] filled

1976), 56 n. 10, and *II Maccabees*, 26–7 nn. 79, 80. Since 2 Maccabees was in Greek, it was less likely to be regarded as holy by the Jews; instead, it was preserved by the Christian Church.

   37. On suicide and martyrdom among the zealots, see M. Hengel, *The Zealots: Investigations into the Jewish Freedom Movement in the Period from Herod I until 70 A.D.* (trans. D. Smith; Edinburgh: T&T Clark, 1989), 256–71, especially 262–5.

   38. Frend, *Martyrdom and Persecution*, 362. However, Frend scarcely hides his contempt of radical martyrs when, on the same page, he describes those Jews who shared this ideal as constituting the most 'desperate and vindictive elements'.

   39. Perler, 'Vierte Makkabäerbuch', 49–51.

   40. Perler, 'Vierte Makkabäerbuch', 68. For a rebuttal of Perler's conclusions, see Bowersock, *Martyrdom and Rome*, 77–81. Bowersock demonstrates that many of Perler's link words are common in the Imperial age.

   41. Perler, 'Vierte Makkabäerbuch', 64. Of course much depends on the dating of *4 Maccabees*, which may in fact be later than Ignatius' time (see below, 110–11, and nn. 58 and 56).

   42. Frend, *Martyrdom and Persecution*, 29 n. 159. Boyarin also identifies 2 Maccabees as the source for both later Jewish and Christian martyrological reflection.

   43. Frend, *Martyrdom and Persecution*, 19.

   44. Musurillo (*ACM*, 79 n. 27) draws attention to the Maccabean mother on the strength of this phrase.

   45. *Mart. Lyons* 1.55.

   46. 2 Macc. 7.20.

with a noble spirit (γενναίῳ πεπληρωμένη φρονήματι),[47] encourages each of her sons (ἕκαστον δὲ τῶν ἀνθρώπον παρεκάλει).[48]

Furthermore, the manner of the deaths of the two women is radically divergent. Blandina is one of the accused, and is tortured in the same way as those who go before her. The mother's death, though not its manner, is only briefly mentioned in 2 Macc. 7.41, and is only rumoured to be through self-inflicted immolation in *4 Macc.* 17.1. Therefore, Frend's conclusion, 'looking at the evidence as it is, it would be difficult to deny that the writer of the Lyons letter was saturated in Maccabean literature',[49] appears somewhat exaggerated. The matching ages of Eleazar, Pothinus (and Polycarp)[50] is too trivial a point on which to base dependence, and it can hardly be maintained that the Maccabean brothers are enthusiastic martyrs as Perler insists; their determination is to uphold the law, not to die. This is certainly not to say that the authors of the *Lyons* letter and other Christian martyr acts did not know the Maccabean tradition. However, the evidence for this tradition constituting the primary source for the theology of those Christian martyrs is less impressive than Perler and Frend maintain.[51]

Comparing Jewish and Christian Martyrology

In direct conflict with Frend's thesis, Glen Bowersock claims that the influence flowed *from* Christianity *to* Judaism rather than the reverse. The reports of the deaths of the inhabitants of Masada, and the martyr records of the second and fourth books of Maccabees are reckoned by Bowersock to be later than the written accounts of the first Christian martyrdoms. Bowersock judges the stories of the deaths of Eleazar and the seven brothers to be later than the first edition of 2 Maccabees, noting that the martyrdom stories do not occur in 1 Maccabees, and that at least the second story is reckoned by many to be an insertion.[52] *Fourth Maccabees* clearly came from a period under the Roman Empire, and Bowersock suggests that the second book could also come from that period.[53] The Jewish martyrologies, he states, are mere 'retrospective constructions of a posterior

---

47. 2 Macc. 7.21b.

48. 2 Macc. 7.21a.

49. Frend, *Martyrdom and Persecution*, 20.

50. For evidence that the writer of the *Martyrdom of Polycarp* had 'probable' acquaintance with *4 Maccabees*, see S.K. Williams, *Jesus' Death as Saving Event: The Background and Origin of a Concept* (Missoula, MT: Scholars Press, 1975), 235. This may be so, but many of the parallels such as 'endurance in suffering', the attempt to dissuade the martyr on the grounds of age, and 'horrible tortures' do not in themselves require such knowledge.

51. Campenhausen (*Idee des Martyriums*, 49–50) instead believes that the Johannine literature forms the bedrock of the *Lyons* narrative.

52. Bowersock, *Martrydom and Rome*, 10. However, it is ch. 7's dissimilarity from ch. 6 that is the reason for scholars judging it to be a later insertion. Therefore, Bowersock is quite unjustified in taking the two stories as a unit.

53. Bowersock does not offer very much in the way of argument for this position, but does note that the first allusions to the books of the Maccabees does not occur until Clement of Alexandria in the late second century (*Strom.* 5.14.97).

age'.[54] Any similarities between Jewish and Christian martyrdom, he concludes, are a result of the latter influence on the former rather than the other way round.[55] Though Bowersock pushes the dating of 2 Maccabees too far,[56] he is on surer ground that *4 Maccabees* is probably not early enough to be an influence on the gospel of Mark's presentation of Jesus, as Frend suggests,[57] or the foundation of the whole Christian martyrological tradition, as Perler claims.[58]

Nonetheless, Henten also sees a close relationship between Jewish and Christian martyrologies. This is in large part because of his definition of a martyr text.

> A martyr text tells us about a specific kind of violent death, death by torture. In a martyr text it is described how a certain person, in an extreme hostile situation, has preferred a violent death to compliance with a decree or demand of the (usually) pagan authorities. The death of this person is a structural element in such a text, and the execution should at least be mentioned.[59]

According to this definition, both Jewish and Christian martyrdom can be seen as essentially identical phenomena. However, van Henten's definition of a martyr text is problematic. It is simply too broad to register important differences. Any number of deaths from antiquity to the present would qualify as martyrdom under Henten's definition, though many examples of Christian and Jewish martyrdom would not.[60] This in itself is not a problem. However, for purposes of comparison, such a wide acceptance of varied phenomena encourages drawing parallels where none really exist. Therefore, with Bowersock:

---

54. Bowersock, *Martyrdom and Rome*, 9–10. For the suggestion that 2 Maccabees 7 constitutes 'haggadic midrash' on Jer. 15.9, a lament over a mother and her seven sons, see M. Hengel, *Judaism and Hellenism: Studies in Their Encounter in Palestine during the Early Hellenistic Period* (2 vols; trans. J. Bowden; London: SCM Press, 1974), II, 65 n. 299. See also F.M. Abel, *Les Livres des Maccabees* (Paris: Editions du Cerf, 1961); and the analysis offered by F. Loftus, 'The martyrdom of the Galilean troglodytes' (B.J. i.312–3; A. xiv.429–30): a suggested Traditions-geschichte', *JQR* 66 (1976), 213–33 (214–17), suggesting that if the story itself is not a literary creation then, at the very least, it has undergone substantial redactional activity.

55. Bowersock, *Martyrdom and Rome*, 10–11.

56. So, for example, Heb. 11.35–8 appears to build upon Jewish martyr stories (cf. 2 Maccabees. 6–7 and *Mart. Isa.* 5, where the prophet is sawn in half).

57. Frend, *Martyrdom and Perseuction*, 81.

58. Perler, 'Vierte Makkabäerbuch'. A date around 100 CE is favoured by Henten ('Datierung und Herkunft des vierten Makkabäerbuches' in J.W. van Henten, H.J. de Jonge, P.T. van Rooden and J.W. Wesselius [eds], *Tradition and Reinterpretation in Jewish and Early Christian Literature: Essays in Honour of Jürgen C.H. Lebram* [Leiden: E.J. Brill, 1986], 136–49) and J.M.G. Barclay (*Jews in the Mediterranean Diaspora: From Alexander to Trajan (323 BCE–117 CE)* [Edinburgh, T&T Clark, 1996], 369–70, 448–9), while a much earlier date (around 40 CE) is argued by M. Hadas (*The Third and Fourth Book of Maccabees*, New York: Ktav, 1976), and accepted by Perler ('Vierte Makkabäerbuch', 47–8). A date before Caligula is favoured by J. Downing, 'Jesus and martyrdom', *JTS* (n.s.) 14 (1963), 279–93, whereas A. Dupont-Summer (*Le Quatrième Livre des Macchabés*, Paris: H. Champion, 1939) opts for a later second-century setting.

59. Henten, *Maccabean Martyrs*, 7.

60. See the discussion of this problem above, 6–15.

> [Many scholars] have practiced a kind of crude and antiquated literary criticism to
> emphasise banal coincidences in various narratives of resistance to authority and
> heroic self-sacrifice as if every such episode constituted martyrdom.[61]

Similarly, Doran insists that even those deaths that may be termed Jewish martyrdoms should not be confused as being of one single type.[62] He divides Jewish 'death stories' into three different categories – the martyr confrontation, suicides[63] and unjust death in conflict or war[64] – and concludes: 'to define a form one must find not only motifs shared by several works, but also an ordering, a specific patterns of motifs which is shared by several works'.[65] Therefore, the linking of all three kinds of Jewish death stories as if they constitute one 'type' or form is, for Doran, unconvincing.[66] By extension, great care must be taken in simply superimposing a Jewish martyrological template onto Christian stories.

While the point both Bowersock and Doran make is well taken, and bland comparisons are to be resisted, the insistence that comparison be made solely on the basis of literary form may mask important similarities in theological outlook. Clearly, the deaths of Ignatius, Polycarp and Agathonicê differ in terms of literary form, yet they were all recognized as martyrs who imitated their master. Similarly, in many of the varied Jewish 'death stories', defence of the Law is the theological motivation for resisting to death, offering oneself to death or even causing one's own death.

Bowersock, in attempting to separate completely Christian martyrology from its earlier Jewish counterpart, almost divorces Christianity from its Jewish roots. Important elements, such as developing eschatology, resurrection from the dead, and the reinterpretation of the early world in cosmic terms, all of which we will consider further, come from Judaism.[67] Similarly, Doran runs the risk of underestimating shared features of the symbolic worlds inhabited by Jews and Christians which enabled them to interpret suffering and death positively, even if we ultimately conclude that they did so in different ways.

Contrasting Jewish and Christian Martyrology
There are, however, crucial differences that distinguish the phenomenon of Christian martyrdom significantly from its Jewish counterpart. First, the heroes of the

61. Bowersock, *Martyrdom and Rome*, 27–8.
62. R. Doran, 'The martyr: a synoptic view of the mother and her seven sons', in G.W.E. Nickelsburg and J.J. Collins (eds), *Ideal Figures in Ancient Judaism: Profiles and Paradigms* (Septuagint and Cognate Studies, 12; Chicago: Scholars' Press, 1980), 189–221.
63. For example, Razi (2 Macc. 14.37–46).
64. 1 Macc. 2.29–38; 2 Macc. 5.23–6; 6.11.
65. S. Niditch and R. Doran, 'The success story of the wise courtier: a formal approach', *JBL* 96 (1979), 179–93.
66. Against, for example, Loftus, 'Galilean troglodyes', and Nickelsburg, *Resurrection*, 97–102. H. Delehaye (*The Legends of the Saints* [North Bend: University of Notre Dame, 1961], 111–15) divides Christian stories into eye witness accounts and court records.
67. So nowhere does Bowersock consider the apocalyptic element of martyrology.

Maccabean traditions are defenders of the Law.[68] So, Eleazer dies in order to leave a noble example to the young, teaching them 'how to die a good death, gladly and nobly, for our revered and holy laws' (ὑπερ τῶν σεμνῶν καὶ ἁγίων νόμων; 2 Macc. 6.28). Similarly, the seven brothers 'give up body and life for the laws of our fathers (περὶ τῶν πατρίων νόμων; 2 Macc. 7.37)'.[69] In *4 Maccabees*, the Law is again the motivation for death. They die 'for the Law' (διὰ τὸν νόμον; 6.27; 13.9), 'for God' (διὰ τὸν θεόν; 16.25), and even 'for their religion' (διὰ τὴν εὐσέβειαν; 9.6; 18.3).

In contrast, the Law plays no real significance in Christian martyrdom. The Christian does not die for, or in defence of, the Law. Although in both types of death, there exists a conflict between the martyr and the Authority, the cause of that conflict is materially different. In Jewish death, the protagonist dies rather than abandon part of the Law. The Christian narrative focuses on the refusal to take part in a practice expected of all inhabitants of the Empire (Jews excepted), that is, to sacrifice to the gods.

Secondly, although Jewish martyrdoms may, like their Christian counterparts, take place in the midst of a battle or contest,[70] in the Jewish form, the contest has a more temporal locus. The first and second books of the Maccabees locate their stories in the midst of conflict between the Jewish people and King Antiochus. After the king had prohibited Jewish ordinances, many faithful Jews lost their lives, until Judas Macabeaus led a successful revolt. In 2 Maccabees, in contrast to the first book, those who die for the Law take on a pivotal role in the success of that revolt. To be sure, 1 Maccabees has its martyrs:

> But many in Israel stood firm and were resolved in their hearts not to eat unclean food. They chose to die rather than to be defiled or to profane the holy covenant; *and die they did* (καὶ ἀπέθανον).[71]

However, in the second and fourth books of the Maccabees, the narratives of those who died are expanded from the scant description in 1 Maccabees, as they take on far greater prominence for the authors.

In the midst of military disaster, including the ransacking and defilement of the Temple (2 Macc. 5.15–16), the writer turns our attention to the martyrs. The theological interpretation of this military defeat, the general suffering of the people and, in particular, the sacking of the Temple, is put down to God's anger on the people, by the author.[72] Similarly, in the introduction to the martyrdoms, the author assures his readers that, although God is disciplining the people, he has not abandoned them.

---

68. In the Maccabean tradition, some Jews defend the Law through militarily means, others defend it by their death. Here is an example where radically different actions are united by a common overall aim, that is, defence of the Law.

69. See also 2 Macc. 7.9. In 6.30, the martyrs die for 'fear of God'.

70. The actions of the martyrs in *4 Maccabees* are set within a divine context.

71. 1 Macc. 1.62–3 (emphasis added).

72. See the relatively long apology for God's inactivity in saving the Temple (2 Macc. 5.17–20). For the suggestion that 2 Maccabees was written to counter those who believed that Antiochus' persecution demonstrated that God had rejected the Second Temple, see Goldstein, *II Maccabees*, 17.

> Now I beg my readers not to be disheartened by those tragic events, but to reflect that such penalties were inflicted for the discipline, not the destruction of our race. It is a sign of great benevolence that the acts of impiety should not be overlooked for long but rather should meet their recompense at once. The Lord has not seen fit to deal with us as he does with other nations: with them he patiently holds his hand until they have reached the full extent of their sins, but on us he inflicts retribution before our sins reach their limit. So he never withdraws his mercy from us; although he may discipline his people by disaster, he does not desert them.[73]

This is the context of the narration of the martyrdoms of Eleazar and the seven brothers. During their tortures, the brothers affirm that they are suffering as part of God's disciplining of the people (7.18, 32). However, their suffering is not merely an expression of God's wrath, it is its fulfilment. The youngest brother answers the king: 'It is for our own sins that we are suffering, and, though to correct and discipline us our living Lord is angry for a brief time, yet he will be reconciled with his servants' (7.31–2).

With the death of the seventh brother, the anger of God is satisfied, and the time of wrath is ended:

> I, like my brothers surrender my body and my life for our ancestral laws. I appeal to God to show favour speedily to his people and by whips and scourges to bring you to admit that he alone is God. May the Almighty's anger, which has justly fallen on our race, end with me and my brothers (7.37–8)!

The martyrs' obedience to the Law brings about a turn in fortune for the people of Israel. The author immediately narrates Judas Maccabaeus assembling an army of six thousand men who had been faithful. As they begin their successful campaign, 'the Gentiles found Maccabaeus invincible, *now that the Lord's anger had turned to mercy*'.[74] In dying for the Law, the martyrs had died for the Jewish people.[75]

The results of the deaths do not effect or contribute to a cosmic victory; rather, they have the effect of contributing to the earthly struggle of the Jews against those who would attack the Law. If there is a cosmic dimension, it is that God turns back to Israel, having either abandoned, or caused the chastisement of the people, because of their sins. The deaths of the faithful Jewish martyrs mark the fulcrum of the conflict between the Jews and the King.[76]

The context in which these Jewish deaths are set is wholly absent from any early theology of Christian martyrdom. Christian martyrs do not die for the Law, nor for the people. Christian martyrs do not, in the main, die *for* others;[77] the

---

73. 2 Macc. 6.12–16.

74. 2 Macc. 8.5 (emphasis added).

75. See M. de Jonge, 'Jesus' death', 147–8, and especially, Henten, *Maccabean Martyrs*.

76. Some debate surrounds the question of whether the deaths are not only vicarious but also expiatory in 2 Maccabees, as in *4 Maccabees*. So K. Wengst (*Christologische Formeln und Lieder des Urchristentums* [Gütersloh: Mohn, 1972], 69) and Surkau (*Martyrien*, 56) argue that 2 Maccabees does display expiatory atonement, whereas Williams (*Jesus' death*, 82–90) and Seeley (*Noble Death*, 87–91) argue against this position.

77. Though see *Mart. Lyons*, and the cases where sins are covered.

greatest human benefit is to themselves. Therefore, those who attempt to show a smooth adopting of Maccabean martyr theology into Christianity do so without asking the central question: what was martyrdom for? In Maccabean theology, martyrdom is the trigger that satisfies God's righteous anger on the people for transgressing the Law. The dramatic obedience to the Law, even through torture to the point of death, demonstrated by Eleazar and the seven brothers, cancels out the sins of the people, enabling the mercy of God to fall once again on his people through military success.[78]

In this regard, there is a third crucial difference between the world-view of Christians and Jews that both Frend and Bowersock overlook: the Christian and Jewish interpretation of the cause of suffering. For Jews, suffering is caused by God to punish, correct or discipline the Jews for past wrongs;[79] punishment comes directly or indirectly from God. In *2 Maccabees*, it is suggested that the persecution carried out by Antiochus is a sign of God's intolerance of apostasy.[80] 'God responds to the nation's apostasy by withdrawing his protecting arm from his people. This human sin and divine wrath are the theological "reasons" for the martyr's suffering and death.'[81] What the Jewish martyr does is to avert God's wrath from the nation,[82] enabling the Jewish army to defeat their enemies. Crucially, and decisively ruling out any suggestion of a simple borrowing of Jewish martyr theology as advocated by Frend's thesis, there is no suggestion that suffering is visited on the Christian martyrs by God. Suffering in Christian discourse comes from Satan. Resisting torture and suffering is to resist the Devil. For the Christian, to die is to conquer Satan.

Therefore, although there are elements in common between Jewish and Christian martyrologies, and we will return to them later, the theologies of Jewish and Christian martyrdom are so different at the fundamental level – achievement, cause of suffering and purpose – as to demand a more adequate explanation for the development of Christian martyrology. Granted, Judaism was an important source for all early Christian thought. However, the divergence in martyrological thought is so profound as to render any thesis that sees Jewish martyrology as being the sole explanation for the Christian theology of martyrdom as seriously lacking.

---

78. Goldstein (*II Maccabees*, 56) notes that a theology of the efficacy of the martyrs occurs in a set form in 2 Maccabees:

Grave Crisis	ch. 6	14.26–32
Theatrical Martyrdom	ch. 7	14.37–46
Great victory	ch. 8; 10.1–8	ch. 15.

79. Deut. 8.5; Prov. 15.32; Mal. 3.3; Wis. 3.5–6; 11.9; Sir. 2.1–6; 4.17; 18.13; 2 Macc. 6.12–17; 7.33; 10.4; *Pss. Sol.*, 13.7–10; 18.4–5; *2 Bar.* 13.10.

80. 2 Macc 4.16–17; 7.18, 32; see also *2 Bar.* 13.9–10; 78.6.

81. Williams, *Jesus' Death*, 79. The deaths of the martyrs do not cause God to act. In order to press this thesis, Williams makes the unlikely suggestion that the martyrs die for their own sins. See also Seeley, *Noble Death*, 88–9.

82. Henten, *Maccabean Martyrs*.

Noble Death

We turn now to the tradition of a Noble Death as a possible source for Christian theologies of martyrdom. We have already noted that the ancients did not distinguish overmuch between what we today would call suicide and martyrdom. Indeed the ancient world had no word equivalent to suicide with its negative connotations.[83] In fact, self-killing in the right circumstances was an honourable practice in the Graeco-Roman world.[84] Dodds may be exaggerating when he states, 'in these centuries a good many persons were consciously or unconsciously in love with death',[85] but death was a fashionable topic in the Roman world.

Types of Noble Death

Noble Death took many forms: the choosing of death rather than facing capture or humiliation by an enemy;[86] death for the fatherland; or as a means of devotion, for example, to the Emperor.[87] The death of Socrates brought Noble Death into the philosophical realm:[88] 'those who pursue philosophy study nothing but dying and being dead'.[89] For Socrates, suicide 'welcomes the greatest blessing in that other land',[90] and he urged others to come after him as quickly as they could.[91] Socrates' death became the reference point for discussions of suicide in the ancient world.

Although the Stoics were most known for their enthusiastic adoption of suicide, with Seneca calling it the act par excellence of the free man,[92] nearly all the philosophical schools of the Graeco-Roman period had worked out their own position on the theory and practice of suicide.[93] This discussion, in the main, hinged around when it was appropriate to take one's life, and when it was not. Socrates, himself, laid one important qualification on self-killing; one must not

83. For language used in Greek and Latin for self-killing, see the discussion in Hooff, *Autothanasia to Suicide*, 136–7. Hooff counts approximately 167 different Greek words and 173 Latin terms to cover what we would deem to be suicide.

84. In the list of suicides compiled by Y. Grisé, *Le Suicide dans la Rome antique* (Montreal: Bellamin, 1982), 34–52, the greatest number are found between 100 BCE and 100 CE.

85. E.R. Dodds, *Pagans and Christians in an Age of Anxiety: Some Aspects of Religious Experience from Marcus Aurelius to Constantine* (Cambridge: Cambridge University Press, 1965), 135.

86. As with Hannibal, Demosthenes, Cassius, Brutus, Cato and many others.

87. See especially, Hooff, *Autothanasia to Suicide*, 56.

88. A. Yarbro Collins, 'From Noble Death to Crucified Messiah', *NTS* 40 (1994), 481–503 (482).

89. Plato, *Phaedo*, 64A.

90. Plato, *Phaedo*, 64A.

91. Plato, *Phaedo*, 61BC.

92. On Seneca and suicide, see J.M. Rist, *Stoic Philosophy* (Cambridge: Cambridge University Press, 1969), 246–50.

93. A.J. Droge, '*MORI LUCRUM*: Paul and ancient theories of suicide', *NovT* 30 (1998), 263–86 (263). For one survey of the various philosophical schools, see Droge, and Tabor, *Noble Death*, 17–51.

take his own life unless the gods laid a necessity (ἀνάγκη) upon him.[94] Plato fleshes out this necessity, identifying three situations where it would be appropriate to take one's own life: when ordered to do so by the State; in the face of devastating misfortune; or if faced with intolerable shame.[95] Diogenes Laertius (7.130) adds for the sake of country or friends and incurable disease to this list. Therefore, so long as it was rational, and there was good reason, the ancients had no problem with suicide. It constituted the Noble Death.

Noble Death was probably most potently expressed through heroism in battle,[96] so that for Lysias, 'those who die in battle die the most glorious death of all'.[97] So much so, that the thought of a Noble Death was a motivating factor for the warrior's participation in battle.[98] Noble Death in battle was also beneficial to others; warriors died for the fatherland, and for those in it. For example, it is said of the Trojans that 'in the first place [they] died for their fatherland – the noblest glory of all'.[99] Those who died in such battles also left behind an example to be followed by those who survived them. Therefore, Noble Death was a death which was chosen rather than forced;[100] it was deemed to be necessary by the State or by the gods, brought or restored honour, was deemed beneficial for others, was particularly potent in the context of battle, led to immortality and served as an example to be imitated by others.

Jewish Noble Death?

Since, in effect, they died for the Jewish people in the context of battle, Williams argues that the Maccabean martyrs were influenced by the Graeco-Roman tradition of 'beneficial death' for others.[101] Indeed, there are Socratean themes in the presentation of the Maccabean deaths.[102] Socrates approached his death serenely,

94. Plato, *Phaedo* 62C. Aristotle (*Nicomachean Ethics* 1138a9–13), for example, considers someone who kills himself in anger to have committed a crime. Similarly, suicide on the grounds of poverty, passion or pain is considered cowardly (*Nicomachean Ethics* 1116a12–14).

95. Rist (*Stoic Philosophy*, 236), observes that these are the normal reasons given to justify self-killing and are found in both historical accounts and fictional stories as motivation for suicide.

96. On this, see Williams, *Jesus' Death*, 144–6.

97. Lysias, *Epitaphios* 79.

98. Williams, *Jesus' Death*, 144.

99. Euripides, *Troades* 386–7.

100. Barton concludes ('Savage miracles', 47 n. 33) that for the Romans, 'chosen death sacralized, electrified, empowered the person or thing or value, on which it was spent'.

101. Williams, *Jesus' Death*, 169. Williams believes (89, 176) that it is not so much the martyrs' deaths that cause God to turn back to Israel, but the prayers for revenge they make as righteous sufferers enduring torture. However, in both 2 and *4 Maccabees*, the deaths of the martyrs are the turning point in the story that enable military victory. Clearly, the deaths have brought about some cosmic activity. See also M. Hengel, *The Atonement: The Origins of the Doctrine in the New Testament* (Philadelphia: Fortress Press, 1981), 4–32. M. Himmelfarb ('Judaism and Hellenism in 2 Maccabees', *Poetics Today* 10 [1998], 19–40) sees the tradition of Greek hero behind the Maccabean deaths.

102. Williams, *Jesus' Death*, 143. See also the discussion of philosophical death and Jewish tradition in I. Gruenwald, 'Intolerance and martyrdom: from Socrates to Rabbi 'Aquiva', in G.N. Stanton and G.G. Stroumsa (eds), *Tolerance and Intolerance in Early Judaism and Christianity* (Cambridge: Cambridge University Press, 1998), 7–29 (20–6); and Droge and Tabor, *Noble Death*, 17–51.

and promised retribution for those who had condemned him. Others, he claimed, would come after him with the same stance,[103] and crucially, according to Seneca, he asserts, 'Leap upon me, make your assault; I shall conquer you by enduring.'[104] We have already seen the importance of this concept in the Maccabean literature.

The way Josephus recounts the Jewish people's willingness to die, either through being killed by their enemies or by their own hands, places them firmly within the tradition of Noble Death, especially death for the homeland. His descriptions of their deaths are much closer to patterns of Noble Death, which may be explained by the fact that at least half of his audience was Roman. Josephus' purpose was apologetic, demonstrating that the Jews had produced great men worthy of universal admiration.[105] Josephus essentially offers examples of patriotic *exampla*,[106] a category into which the death of Eleazar in 2 Maccabees fits, since he is the forerunner and example to the seven brothers. Furthermore, Josephus, in both his extended reflections on suicide – in favour of the practice, in the case of Masada (*War* 7.320–88), and against it, in the case of Jotapata, when his own life was at risk (*War* 3.362–82) – draws heavily on the Graeco-Roman philosophers, especially the *Phaedo*.[107]

The deaths of the Maccabean martyrs are a call to obedience, furnishing the people with a model of how to die with honour.[108] Death, in the ancient world, including that of the Maccabean martyrs, was vicarious in so far as there was mimetic potential. One was called to re-enact these 'Noble Deaths'[109] literally, or more often imaginatively, in order to overcome death. In philosophical tradition, to overcome death was equated with overcoming the fear of death. Seeley convincingly shows that the concept of Noble Death was current at the time of the composition of Jewish and martyr texts, citing a wide variety of sources.[110]

If Jewish martyrology could be seen to be influenced by Graeco-Roman traditions of Noble death, then could the same be true of its Christian counterpart? For Seeley, Christian reflection on death, and the theology of martyrdom found in *4 Maccabees*, came not from a Jewish context, but from the Graeco-Roman concept of 'Noble Death', that is, death in obedience to a philosophy. At

103. Plato, *Apology* 40; *Phaedo* 63.

104. Seneca, *De vita beata* 27.3.

105. L.H. Feldman, *Jew and Gentile in the Ancient World: Attitudes and Interactions from Alexander to Justinian* (Princeton, NJ: Princeton University Press, 1993).

106. J.W. van Henten, 'Martyrion and martyrdom: some remarks about noble death in Josephus', in J.U. Kalms and F. Siegert (eds), *Internationales Josephus-Kolloquium Brüssels 1998* (Münster: Lit, 1999), 124–41 (136). See especially Henten's *Maccabean Martyrs*, 210–22.

107. For a discussion, see Ladoucer, 'Josephus and Masada', 97–101. This includes a near *verbatim* quotation in *War* 3.372. For a discussion of the presentation of Jewish martyrdom and suicide in this period, see Goodblatt, 'Suicide', *passim*.

108. Seeley, *Noble Death*, 89.

109. A Noble Death has five elements: (1) obedience; (2) the overcoming of physical vulnerability; (3) it is set in a military context; (4) it is vicarious, in that it has mimetic potential; (5) it may have sacrificial elements (though Seeley plays this part down).

110. Seeley, *Noble Death*, 114–41.

first sight, there is some mileage in this. Much Noble Death imagery is present: obedience, overcoming physical vulnerability, military setting, vicariousness and sacrificial metaphor.[111]

Seeley goes so far as to claim that the philosophers could, with Paul ask, 'Death, where is your victory?' even if they could not share in his theology.[112] This assertion demonstrates clearly the gulf between the philosophers and the Christians, though of course Seeley means it to show the opposite. For the Christians, death is not simply denied its victory, death is conquered. Death brings victory and, most importantly, life. For the philosophers, what came after was not really the point of their deaths. 'Now the hour to part has come. I go to die, you go to live. Which of us goes to the better lot is known to no-one except God.'[113] However, no Christian martyr would have been as equivocal. A philosopher will chose death when, on balance, it is judged to be better than living. The Noble Death is more like a noble life confirmed or rescued by a good death. There is no influence on Christian martyrology on this point.

Furthermore, although the Maccabean books were clearly composed in a Hellenistic milieu, as Hengel among others has observed, demonstrating possible influences from Greek philosophy, especially the *Phaedo*,[114] much of what Seeley and Williams see as dependent on the Noble Death tradition can in fact be found within earlier Jewish sources.[115] Forms of non-cultic atonement, such as are evidenced in 2 Maccabees, are found throughout the Old Testament, so Moses (Exod. 32.30–4; Ps. 106.16–23) and Phinehas (Num. 25; Sir. 45.23; 1 Macc. 5.24; Ps. 106: 28–31).[116] Moses' desire to die in solidarity with his people is similar to the role the Maccabean martyrs take upon themselves. Furthermore, that the martyrs die for the Law is thoroughly Jewish, and one of the mechanisms by which God's wrath is averted through these effective deaths is the ancient Jewish tradition of the blood of the righteous calling out for vengeance.[117] Similarly, even in the more Hellenistic *4 Maccabees*, the mother exhorts her sons to die well by recalling their father's teaching of the Law and the Prophets (*4 Macc.* 18.6–19), invoking the example of Old Testament figures who were killed or suffered; namely, Abel, Isaac, Joseph, Phineas, Azariah, Mishael and Daniel.[118]

111. Seeley presents these criteria at the outset and his book seeks to demonstrate the presence of each of them in Paul's interpretation of Jesus' death and in *4 Maccabees*.

112. Seeley, *Noble Death*, 121.

113. Plato, *Phaedo* 42A.

114. Hengel, *Judaism and Hellenism*, 1.98; 2.67.

115. This is of course not to say that we must decide upon one source to the exclusion of the other. Simply, the evidence suggests that the source for Jewish reflection on martyrdom, even though it may look similar, was not primarily Noble Death tradition. This is not to deny that there may have been some influence in the shaping of the stories.

116. For discussion, see Jonge, 'Jesus' death', 148–9, and especially, Henten, *Maccabean Martyrs*, 156–63.

117. Downing, 'Jesus and martyrdom', 282. So, for example Gen. 4.10; Job 16.8; Ezek. 24.7. Cf. *1 En.* 47.1; *T. Mos.* 9.7.

118. Similarly, Isa. 43.2; Ps. 34.19; Prov. 3.18; Ezek. 37.3; and Deut. 32.39 are cited to demonstrate God's faithfulness to those who suffer. By suffering martyrdom, the sons will become Ἀβραμίοι

Devotio

Another possible parallel from the Noble Death tradition may be found in the concept of *devotio*, a voluntary death where life was deliberately surrendered to ensure victory, usually through some form of contract with the gods. The first example is found in the Samnite Wars (340 BCE). The Roman general Publius Decius Mus, devoted himself to the gods of the underworld, and then rushed towards a violent death at the hands of his enemy in order to secure victory for his depleted army.[119] In the seemingly expiatory nature of the sacrifice,[120] *devotio* can look very similar to the deaths of the Maccabees, except that the death takes place on the battlefield.[121]

Nonetheless, this motif of rushing into battle to provoke one's death does appear somewhat similar to radical martyrdom. It is a form of suicide where the 'martyr' forces someone else to deal the fatal blow, and the voluntary nature is stressed.[122] The tradition also came to be associated with dying for the Emperor,[123] perhaps inviting parallels with dying for Jesus or God.[124] However, whereas *devotio* accounts for the majority of provoked self-killings (where motive can be established), provocation is the least frequent form of self-killing in this period,[125] and unlike the Christian counterparts there are no cases of *devotio* among women.[126]

Christian Noble Death?

To be sure, Christian texts dealing with martyrdom do invoke elements of the Noble Death tradition. Justin sees the charge against Christians as the same one

---

παῖδες (*4 Macc.* 9.21; 18.23). See Jonge, 'Jesus' death', 149–50. In *4 Maccabees*, the martyrdom of the seven takes on a cultic form with the language of sacrifice (especially 17.21–2).

119. See Livy 8.9.6–10; 10.28.12–13. H.S. Versnel, 'Two types of Roman *devotio*', *Mnemosyne* 29 (1976), 365–410; W. Burkert, *Structure and History in Greek Mythology and Ritual* (Berkeley: University of California Press, 1979), 64–72; C.A., Barton, 'The scandal of the arena', *Representations* 27 (1989), 1–36, especially 19–24. Cf. Jn 11.50.

120. See J. Bremmer, 'Scapegoat rituals in ancient Greece', *Harvard Studies in Classical Philology* 87 (1983), 299–320 (304–5).

121. Cicero finds the notion that the gods require the deaths of good men offensive; *De natura deorum* 3.15.

122. L.F. Janssen, 'Some unexplored aspects of the *Devotio Deciana*', *Mnemosyne* 4 (1981), 357–81.

123. Hooff, *Authothanasia*, 56; Barton, 'Scandal of the arena', 22. Most infamously, perhaps, for Gaius, to whom when ill, one man promised his life in *devotio* for the Emperor should he recover, and another who promised he would become a gladiator. When Gaius recovered, he held both to their pledge (Suetonius, *Caligula* 27.2; Dio 59.8.3). The reverse is also found where someone might kill himself in protest against the State, so Petronius against Nero, and Arruntius against Tiberius (Hooff, *Autothanasia*, 52).

124. For martyrdom as a form of devotion to Jesus, see Hurtado, *Lord Jesus Christ*, 619–25.

125. See the appendix in Hooff, *Autothanasia*, 235. Provoked death accounts for only 3 per cent of Greek and 5 per cent of Roman suicides.

126. Again women martyrs within Christianity make Christian martyrology somewhat distinctive in the ancient world.

as was made against Socrates, that of introducing new gods.[127] John Chrysostom, in the fourth century, also invokes the death of Socrates, but suggests that Christian martyrdom is superior to that of the philosopher's death.

> But among them [the philosophers] also, it will be said, many have been found contemners of death. Tell me who? was it he who drank the hemlock? But if thou wilt, I can bring forward ten thousand such from within the Church ... And besides, he drank when he was not at liberty to drink or not to drink ... But with us it is all quite the contrary. For not against their will did the martyrs endure, but of their will, and being at liberty not to suffer ... This then you see is no great wonder, that he whom I was mentioning drank hemlock; it being no longer in his power not to drink, and also when he had arrived at a very great age. For when he despised life he stated himself to be seventy years old; if this can be called despising. For I for my part could not affirm it: nor, what is more, can anyone else. But show me some one enduring firm in torments for godliness' sake, as I shew thee ten thousand everywhere in the world. Who, while his nails were tearing out, nobly endured? Who, while his body joints were wrenching asunder? Who, while his body was cut in pieces, member by member? or his head? Who, while his bones were forced out by levers? Who, while placed without intermission upon frying-pans? Who, when thrown into a caldron? Show me these instances. For to die by hemlock is all as one with a man's continuing in a state of sleep. Nay even sweeter than sleep is this sort of death, if report say true.[128]

In the first instance, Chrysostom points out that Socrates had no choice but to drink the hemlock, whereas the Christians go to their deaths of their own free will.[129] Secondly, the violent manner of the deaths of the Christians requires more bravery since drinking hemlock is like falling asleep. Thirdly, Chrysostom claimed to be able to name ten thousand Christian martyrs for every Socrates. And fourthly, Socrates despised his life at a great age, whereas, by contrast, many Christians were being executed in the prime of their lives. It is therefore a much greater thing for Christians to despise their lives. For Chrysostom, the paradigm of pagan death compares rather unfavourably with its Christian counterpart. Similarly, Tertullian holds up famous examples of pagan suicide as models not only to follow but also to surpass, apparently casting Christian martyrdom in the role of a more superior form of Noble Death.[130]

However, there exists a serious question mark over whether or not the citation of Noble Death tradition forms an influence on Christianity, rather than simply reflecting an awareness of it. As we have seen, pagans believed that Christians belonged to a cult in love with death.[131] Therefore, in defence of their actions, Christians pointed to examples of pagan Noble Deaths, celebrated and valorised, as a means of attempting to persuade their pagan critics of the nobility of martyrdom. Citation and allusion to Noble Death tradition does not imply influence, but, rather, Noble Death imagery is employed for apologetic purposes. Furthermore, if Noble Death were the source for Christian martyrology, then it is likely

---

127. Justin, *Apol.* II.10.
128. John Chrysostom, *Homily IV on I Cor. 1.18–20.*
129. Droge and Tabor (*Noble Death*, 162 n. 50) note that this is the first time Socrates' drinking of the hemlock is portrayed as being forced, rather than a voluntary act.
130. See above, 35.
131. See above, 36–8.

to have been more successful in this apologetic purpose than it clearly was. Pagans simply did not register the martyrdom of Christians as constituting examples of Noble Death; it did not fulfil their criteria.

In the first instance, the pagans considered Christian martyrdom to be vulgar and dramatic, with both Epictetus and Marcus Aurelius despising the unreflective nature of Christian death.[132]

> Evidently these Stoics consider the way the Christians die too emotional, too uncontrolled ... A Stoic does not die like that. But then he is a perfectly self-controlled person, who knows how to leave this life with dignity, as a perfectly mature personality, guided by reason and hence without any ostentation.[133]

Secondly, pagan critics attacked Jesus' lack of courage in the Garden of Gethsemane, compared to Socrates' acceptance of his fate.[134] In his *True Doctrine*, Celsus puts into the mouth of a fictitious Jewish character the claim that belief in the divinity of Jesus was impossible since 'after being considered worthy of punishment, [he] concealed himself in a most disgraceful manner'. Similarly, he takes Jesus' Gethsemane prayer as evidence that he could not have possibly foreknown his own death.[135] Therefore, Jesus could hardly provide an example for the despising of torment.[136] Celsus' criticisms are based

> on the widespread ancient notion that a human being worthy of the epithet 'divine' faces death with unwavering resolve, dignity and courage. In other words, he used the standard of the heroic or noble death to judge the passion account.[137]

He was clearly unimpressed. Jesus' death, as presented in the Gospels (perhaps with the exception of John) is not an example of Noble Death.

Thirdly, if there is any underlying unifying theme that characterises the Graeco-Roman understanding of what constitutes Noble Death, it is honour – either to gain or restore it. 'If there is a doctrine of self-killing in the ancient world, it is preferably understood as the deed of someone who hopes to preserve his honour.'[138] In stark contrast, the Christian mode of dying, spectacularly and in public, was anathema to the concept of Noble Death.[139] Moreover, there could be no honour in following and dying for a man executed by the State. The word of

---

132. 'It [the willingness to die] should be deliberate, reasoned, and dignified, and if it is to convince anyone, should be free from theatre' (Marcus Aurelius, *Meditations* 11.3); see also Epictetus, *Discourse* 4.7.

133. J.N. Sevenster, 'Education or conversion: Epictetus and the gospels', *NovT* 8 (1966), 247–62 (255).

134. Origen, *Contra Celsum* 2.42.

135. Origen, *Contra Celsum* 2.9.

136. Origen, *Contra Celsum* 2.38.

137. Yarbro Collins, 'Noble death', 482.

138. Hooff, *Autothanasia*, 131.

139. Consider 1 Cor. 4.9: 'God has exhibited us apostles as last of all, like men sentenced to death; because we have become a spectacle to the world, to angels and men.' What Paul glories in (being exhibited as condemned prisoners) would have been considered to be horrific humiliation, as far from Noble Death as could be imagined. We will pursue the martyrological significance of this verse in the final chapter.

the cross was folly, rather than noble in the eyes of the Romans. So for Justin, the critics of the Christians 'say that our madness consists in the fact that we put a crucified man in second place after the unchangeable and eternal God, the Creator of the world'.[140] As Hengel has shown, crucifixion was a death with no possible honourable spin in the Roman or Greek world.[141] Dying for a crucified man, therefore, could bring no honour.[142]

Aside from the spectacle and humiliation of crucifixion, part of the reason for this form of death being excluded from the realm of Noble Death is that it compromises the body. Generally, any means of death that violated the integrity of the body was considered base.[143] Burning, the mode of death for several Christian martyrs, was considered especially exotic and looked upon with horror; for anything that mutilated the body was revulsion.[144] So, Seneca kills himself with a single cut,[145] a far cry from Ignatius' desire to be ground and mangled by the wild beasts.

Noble Death tradition, therefore, provides some interesting parallels with Christian martyrology. Nonetheless, as with Jewish martyrdom, there are simply too many fundamental differences between the two for the influence of Noble Death tradition to explain developing Christian martyrology adequately, even if that influence is conceived in wholly negative terms.[146] Unlike Noble Death, Christian martyrdom does not confirm or restore the honour of a good life. In Christian martyrdom, the death, as a death, is absolutely crucial. It is the death that contributes to the cosmic battle against Satan. So, whereas there are certainly elements in common (voluntary nature, language of enduring and example to others), the whole point and purpose are different. We must therefore look elsewhere in our quest for the origins of Christian martyrology.

Christian Martyrdom as 'Something Entirely New'

So far I have argued that the origins of the theology of Christian martyrdom cannot be explained by simple trajectories from either the Jewish phenomenon or of Noble Death tradition. The Christians did not simply borrow and develop the Jewish practice (contra Frend), since the crucial element of what martyrdom achieves is so radically divergent in both movements. Moreover, it is seriously doubtful whether many examples of Christian martyrdom even constitute the pattern of Graeco-Roman Noble Death (contra Droge and Tabor, and Seely),

---

140. Justin, *Apol.* I.13.

141. M. Hengel, *Crucifixion in the Ancient World and the Folly of the Message of the Cross* (London: SCM Press, 1977). He notes that there is very little in the way of description of crucifixion in ancient writings and that the Gospels themselves are among the most detailed (25).

142. A criticism made by Celsus (Origen, *Contra Celsum* 6.10).

143. Hooff, *Autothanasia*, 51.

144. Coleman, 'Savage miracles', 48. On the horror of breaching the integrity of the body, see C.P. Jones, 'Stigma: tattooing and branding in Graeco-Roman antiquity', *JRS* 77 (1987), 139–55.

145. Tacitus, *Annals* 15.60–3.

146. Dehandschutter ('Examples and discipleship', 20 n. 3) suggests that Christian theology may have consciously developed in opposition to Roman philosophical movements.

since it was not recognized as such by those most familiar with the tradition. Does this mean, as Bowersock argues, that the Christian version of death for God has no antecedents? 'Martyrdom was not something that the ancient world had seen from the beginning. What we can observe in the second, third, and fourth centuries of our era is something entirely new'.[147]

The Bowersock Thesis

Bowersock insists that Christian martyrdom 'was alien both to the Greeks and the Jews'.[148] Not every heroic death was martyrdom, and so while the deaths of courageous people like Socrates, and the threatened deaths of the three Jews in the fiery furnace of Daniel show glorious examples of resistance to tyrannical authority and suffering before unjust judges, 'never before had such courage been absorbed into a conceptual system of posthumous recognition and antici-pated reward, nor had the very word martyrdom existed as the name for this system'.[149] For Bowersock, it is of particular significance that the word was not employed in its martyrological sense before the mid-second century.

Instead, Bowersock argues that Christian martyr theology was *created* in response to the Graeco-Roman urban centres in which the Christian communities were located. And so, he claims that martyrdom 'had nothing to do with Judaism or Palestine and everything to do with the Greco-Roman world, its tradition, its language, and its cultural tastes'.[150] It was Roman life with spectacle and games, entertainment and legal proceedings that provided the necessary frame on which to develop martyr theology, and so, for Bowersock, 'it depended on the urban rituals of the imperial cult and the interrogation protocols of local and provincial magistrates'.[151] It was the games and other such grand spectacles and, in particu-lar, the Roman trial, which *created* the martyrological genre:

> From the point at which martyrdom emerges in the historical record as a recognizable Christian institution, it has both sophistic and agonistic components, solidly placed in the Graeco-Roman urban space. It may be suggested that without these components, martyrdom as Christians understood it in the history of the early church simply could not have existed.[152]

Whereas Bowersock may indeed be correct that legal trials shaped the genre of martyrology, the components of spectacle, such as contests and athleticism, can be found in literature before the second century. In any case, martyrological texts do much more than employ legal imagery; they are cosmic in their scope. Apocalyptic and eschatological motifs were just as crucial (and probably more so) in the construction of the symbolic worlds in which a positive interpretation of suffering and death was not only possible, but plausible. If Frend's reconstruc-

---

147. Bowersock, *Martyrdom and Rome*, 5.
148. Bowersock, *Martyrdom and Rome*, 8.
149. Bowersock, *Martyrdom and Rome*, 5.
150. Bowersock, *Martyrdom and Rome*, 28.
151. Bowersock, *Martyrdom and Rome*, 54.
152. Bowersock, *Martyrdom and Rome*, 54–5.

tion simplifies the Christian motivation for death as a peculiarly Jewish inheritance, then Bowersock also fails to appreciate the complex factors that were employed in the Christian understanding of the universe, especially in regard to the Jewish heritage of the early Church. Nowhere does Bowersock discuss the Apocalypticism that indelibly marked early Christian understanding of life and death.

Daniel Boyarin, in agreement with Bowersock, argues that the net has been cast too widely in searching for examples of martyrdom. The crucial element in authentic martyrdom, for Boyarin, is the discourse that follows death, that is, the telling of the story and the theologizing of it.[153] Where Boyarin takes issue with Bowersock is in regard to the social-historical model that he presupposes, and with which he operates, namely, a world with discrete communities of Jews and Christians with well-defined boundaries, as well as a clear distinction between Jewish, Christian, Graeco-Roman and Palestinian thought.[154] Boyarin claims that Bowersock has simply replaced the 'naïve and positivistic' model of Jewish martyrdom as having been the source and influence upon Christians[155] with the exact reverse, which is 'equally naïve and positivistic'.[156]

Therefore, although Bowersock is correct that the word 'martyr' was not applied to anyone with the meaning of dying for a witness until Polycarp, and that Ignatius, even despite his intense desire for death, makes no use of martyr terminology,[157] the discourse of martyrdom is present even in the New Testament, where there is already a strong link, which Bowersock down plays, between witnessing and death.[158] So, Bowersock is left arguing that Antipas was not a 'martyr' because he was slain, but rather a 'martyr' who happened also to be slain.

Furthermore, this theme of death as a result of bearing witness is developed in the Apocalypse. It is the faithful witness of those under the altar that has led to their deaths (6.9).[159] Moreover, the μαρτυρία of the two witnesses, who themselves offer a paradigm for all other faithful martyrs, leads directly to their death (11.17). Perhaps it may even be said that their deaths are the climax of their witness. Therefore, though the word 'martyr' may not have been applied to the phenomenon of dying for one's faith before the middle of the second century, clearly the concept of death as a result of faithful witness was in place before the close of the second century.

Moreover, though the *Martyrdom of Polycarp* may be a new kind of genre,[160] it does not employ a radically new way of interpreting suffering and death. The

---

153. Boyarin, *Dying for God*, 94. Compare Bowersock's (*Martyrdom and Rome*, 24) claim that 'martyrology and hagiography constitute a twin literary offspring of early Christianity'.

154. See also Henten, *Maccabean Martyrs*, 157. This is a model on which Williams and Seeley also rely.

155. Cf. Frend, *Martyrdom and Persecution*, 22.

156. See Boyarin, 'Martyrdom', 611–12.

157. Bowersock, *Martyrdom and Rome*, 6.

158. For example, Acts 22.20 of Stephen, and Rev. 2.13 of Antipas.

159. Τὰς ψυχὰς τῶν ἐσφαγμένων διὰ ... τὴν μαρτυρίαν ἣν εἶχον.

160. Bisbee, *Pre-Decian Acts*, 85.

Polycarp narrative does not spring upon us any surprises in its presentation of the martyrs' deaths, nor in its theology of death for God. In Chapter 5, I will show that the component pieces of the symbolic world of the early Christians, which enabled them to present and interpret martyrdom (outlined in Chapter 3), are well under construction in the New Testament. If then, it can be demonstrated that the theology of death, the conceptual world and the function of martyrdom that we find in the *Martyrdom of Polycarp*, with its innovative use of the martyr word, already exists in the first century, then Bowersock's fundamental concern that 'Ignatius betrays no knowledge of the language or the concept of martyrdom'[161] will prove to be rather insignificant. For, as Davies perceptively notes: martyrdom 'was a reality looking for a vocabulary; but the reality as activity came first. There are millions of words in the world. They achieve meaning only when ordered by experience.'[162]

Furthermore, Bowersock's definition of martyrdom, as 'the conceptual system of posthumous recognition and reward', which he takes to be unique to Christianity, is clearly found, contrary to his assertion, in Jewish sources.[163] Williams,[164] for example, traces a four-stage development of the reward for those who suffer for God from earthly recompense[165] to posthumous eschatological reward.[166] Similarly, both Jewish and Christian reflections on death were influenced by the stories and examples of the prophets.[167]

On many current definitions of martyrdom, Bowersock's claim that Christian martyrdom is something entirely new seems absurd. However, one significant contribution he makes is to resist identifying banal comparisons and judge them to constitute an influence. We have seen that, although Christian martyrdom has aspects in common with Noble Death, at a fundamental level the two are different. Similarly, its debt to Jewish martyrology is not as straightforward as is commonly advanced. Nonetheless, Bowersock overplays his hand and dismisses connections and debts that ought to be recognized. He is precisely correct in his statement, 'martyrdom, as we understand it, was conceived and devised in

---

161. Bowersock, *Martyrdom and Rome*, 6.

162. Davies, *Death*, 209.

163. Boyarin ('Martyrdom', 593) suggests that this aspect of martyrdom is 'perhaps the oldest, most clearly pre-Christian element of martyrology', while Henten (*Maccabean Martyrs*, 298 n. 1) states, 'The combination of the conceptions about the effective death and posthumous vindication of the [Jewish] martyrs forms the matrix for the earliest statements about the effective death and resurrection of Jesus of Nazareth'. On the theme of post-mortem vindication, see Rajak, 'Dying for the Law', 40; and Shaw, 'Body/power/identity', 280.

164. Williams, *Jesus' Death*, 94.

165. For example, Psalm 37; Sir. 11.21.

166. So, for example, Dan. 12.2; *1 En.* 22.9–13; 103.3–4; *T. Benj.* 10.8; Wis. 3.4; 5.15, 16; 15.3; 2 Macc. 7.9, 14, 23, 36. The other two stages are: increase in the reputation of descendents (e.g. Sir. 11.28, Wis. 3.16–17; 4.3–6); and gaining an immortal name (e.g. Sir. 41.11–13; 44.8–15; Wis. 4.1, 19; 8.13b; *Pss. Sol.* 13.10–11).

167. So see, for example, 1 Macc. 2: 59–60; *3 Macc.* 6.6–7; *4 Macc.* 16.3, 21; 18.12–13; Mt. 23.35; Acts 7.52; Jas 5.10; *1 Clement* 45.6–7. On the 'christianization' of Old Testament figures, see Dehandschutter, 'Example and discipleship'.

response to complex social, religious, and political pressures'.[168] In stripping away possible influences on early Christian martyrology, perhaps Bowersock makes his own account less complex than it ought to be.

Resetting the Question

Even if the Maccabean martyrologies played less of a role in developing Christian martyr theology than some maintain, the Christian Church inherited much, not least the Old Testament with the example of the prophets' sufferings, from its close relationship to Judaism.[169] It also inherited a Jewish allergy to idolatry and an apocalyptic cosmology, which enabled Christians to divide the world into the two forces so crucial for the conception of their struggle as cosmic conflict. Similarly, the young Church could not help but be influenced by Graeco-Roman conceptions of death, even if it developed its theology in opposition to them. Furthermore, the importance of the Roman games, as identified by Bowersock, must have helped to reinforce and develop the combatant language which the Christians had already adopted.[170] Therefore, the original question posed, from where did Christian martyrology come, will be answered by, in many respects, 'all of the above'. Martyrology, as with all Christian theology, developed within a constellation of cross-cultural ideas. Some it adopted or absorbed, whilst other ideas were actively opposed.

> As latecomers on the religious scene of Mediterranean antiquity, the early Christians interacted with older societies in which the questions of the structure of the universe and of suffering had been answered in varying ways. The early Christians used the language of previous societies to describe their own particular vision of the universe.[171]

Reflecting on their own experiences of suffering and death, together with the example of the crucified Jesus, the Christians developed their own strategy for interpreting these experiences within a Graeco-Roman world, and also with the benefit of a strong Jewish heritage. If we remain with Theissen's semiotic cathedral model, then the Graeco-Roman and Jewish milieu in which the Church developed influenced the plans and even provided some of the raw material used for its construction. In Chapter 3, we saw how the finished structure looked. But how did the early Christians end up with that particular structure? What were the major design influences? In this regard, one important element, previously neglected, will prove to be particularly important, and that is Jewish Holy War.

168. Bowersock, *Martyrdom and Rome*, 5.

169. 'Christianity takes themes of (1) death, (2) resurrection, (3) martyrology, (4) vicarious atonement, (5) messiahship from Judaism, but does not find any of them ready made or united in one place. Instead it hints for what it needs and applies it to the events which it is seeking to explain. A.F. Segal, *The Other Judaisms of Late Antiquity* (Atlanta: Scholars Press, 1987), 123.

170. We have seen already the way in which Christians were cast in the role of gladiators (see above, 72–5).

171. R. Doran, *Birth of a Worldview: Early Christianity in Its Jewish and Pagan Content* (Lanham: Rowman & Littlefield Publishers, Inc., 1999), 3.

Holy War and Cosmic Conflict in Judaism and Early Christianity

I have already shown that an important factor in early Christian martyr theology was the conviction that the martyr was participating in a cosmic contest, a Holy War against Satan and his legions. The Christians were thus able to transform their experience of hardship into positive victory, to the point that some even desired to suffer hardship and death as a means of defeating Satan, and help bring about God's eschatological Kingdom. This victory involved total deconstruction of normal temporal and spatial categories, even those of life and death itself. The means of making this interpretation still need explaining, and we turn now to Holy War tradition in Judaism to find its roots.

Holy War and Ancient Israel

For Gerhard von Rad, a Holy War is a conflict fought with the aid of a miraculous God.[172] In Jewish tradition, God fought exclusively on behalf of Israel and, through battle, led his people into Canaan, the divinely appointed land. Their enemies, the occupants of the land, were defeated and cleared.[173] Aside from this, there is little scholarly agreement. Indeed, Holy War tradition in the Old Testament is often treated with some embarrassment. For many, the bloody conquest of Canaan is at best problematic.[174] Otherwise, the whole idea is discounted: 'The religious doctrine of holy war does not seem to have any intrinsic connection to Israel's covenantal faith'.[175] The difficulty of reaching consensus on the question of Holy War in Israel is caused by the divergence of views regarding textual traditions and dating. Firestone summarizes: 'Real consensus may be found only in the certainty that the concept of holy war developed and changed as the history of the people of Israel evolved from patriarchal to tribal and then to national organization.'[176] Though there is no consensus on the development of Holy War, scholars agree that the book of Deuteronomy holds the 'most theologically canonised expression of Holy War in ancient Israel'.[177]

---

172. G. von Rad, *Holy War in Ancient Israel* (trans. M.J. Dawn; Michigan: Eerdmans, 1991). For a discussion of von Rad's thesis as well as an overview of the subject, see B.C. Ollenburger, 'Introduction: Gerhard von Rad's theory of holy war', in *Holy War in Ancient Israel*, 1991 (*op. cit.*). See Exod. 14.4, 14; 15.3; Ps. 24.9; Isa. 42.13.

173. R. Firestone includes in this category those wars where the people lost since the outcome of these battles were still divinely ordained: 'Conceptions on holy war in biblical and Qur'ānic tradition', *JRE* 24 (1996), 99–123 (103).

174. So, for example, M. Walzer, 'The idea of holy war in ancient Israel', *JRE* 22 (1992), 215–27 (215).

175. Walzer, 'Holy war', 216. However, it is by these Holy Wars that Israel claimed the land, the object of the covenant. Therefore, despite Walzer's protestations, Holy War is a crucial element in Israel's developing sense of nationhood. M. Weinfeld dismisses the wars and doctrine of *herem* as 'the radicalism of the writing desk' (*Deuteronomy and the Deuteronomic School*, Oxford: Clarendon Press, 1972), 167.

176. Firestone, 'Conceptions of holy war', 102.

177. Firestone ('Conceptions of holy war', 104), Rad (*Holy War*) and P.D. Miller (*The Divine*

In the book of Deuteronomy, aside from taking the land appointed to the Hebrews,[178] the main justification for Holy War was to keep the people free from idolatry.[179] The threat from idolatry was dangerous as even Israel would lose their status as God's people should they allow themselves to become infected by their idolatrous neighbours.[180] Therefore, war or violence was justified/demanded in order to keep the people free from contaminating influences. Possessing the land was dependent on obeying God's will (11.22–8), and so all traces of idolatry, including idolaters themselves, were to be completely destroyed. Crucially, the people of Israel were included in this threat.[181] The Deuteronomist, therefore, stresses that if Israel shuns potential contamination from foreign cultic practices, God will continue to bless them in the land. If not, then military disaster would befall them.

However, if suffering was to be interpreted as the punishment for sin, then instances where the righteous seemed to suffer without vindication put pressure on this system.[182] A revised eschatology emerged to cope with the problem of undeserved suffering, and with it the seeds of the doctrine of afterlife and personal reward developed, found first in the book of Daniel.[183] In the absence of earthly vindication for those who remained faithful, final vindication was required, since many of the author's contemporaries had lost their lives remaining faithful to God.[184] So, whereas miraculous deliverance was the reward for faithfulness (chs 3 and 6), the righteous of the later chapters had to wait for post-mortem reward (12.1–3); their 'miraculous delivery' would be resurrection to life.[185]

Warrior in Early Israel, Cambridge: Harvard University Press, 1973) think that Deuteronomy holds a reinterpretation of earlier events, while R.S. Smend (*Yahweh War and Tribal Confederation* [trans. M.G. Rogers; Nashville: Abingdon Press, 1970]); G.H. Jones ("Holy war' or Yahweh war', *VT* 25 [1975], 642–58); and M.C. Lind (*Yahweh Is a Warrior: The Theology of Warfare in Ancient Israel* [Scottsdale: Herald Press, 1980]) believe the book contains a record of evolving theology. The War Scroll at Qumran is based on the presentation of Holy War in Deuteronomy. On Holy War at Qumran, see Hengel, *The Zealots*, 273–81.

178. Deut. 1.6–8; 2.25–37; 3.1–22; 6.10–12; 7.1; 9.1–3; 11.23–5; 20.1–18; 29.6–8; 31.3–6.

179. Deut. 7.1–5, 16–26; 12.1–3; 12.29–13.1; 13.2–19; 16.21–2; 17.2–7; 18. 9–14.

180. Deut. 7.1–4, 9–11; 8.19–20; 11.16–17, 26–8; 28.1–68; 29.15–27; 30.17–18.

181. This included Israelites (13.2–9). Firestone ('Conceptions of holy war', 105) notes, however, that this wholesale destruction of idolatry was limited only to the promised land; there was no question of indiscriminate conquest. Certain lands were off limits as God had already 'given' them to other peoples (24.4–5, 18–23). He also observes (107), 'idolatry within the sacred land was worse than the act of killing – even the mass killing of idolaters'.

182. K. Grayston, 'Atonement and martyrdom', in J.M.G. Barclay and J. Sweet (eds), *Early Christian Thought in its Jewish Context* (Cambridge: Cambridge University Press, 1996), 250–63 (252–3).

183. N. Gillman, 'Death and the afterlife', in J. Neusner, A.J. Avery-Peck and W.S. Green (eds), *The Encyclopaedia of Judaism* (Leiden: E.J. Brill, 2000), 196–212 (199).

184. Collins, 'Apocalyptic eschatology', 34.

185. Nickelsburg, *Resurrection*, 94. Cf. *1 En.* 102–4; *Syr. Apoc. Baruch* 48.48–50; 52.6–7.

Holy War in the Books of the Maccabees

In the first book of Maccabees, the nation was saved by military might, which tolerated even the setting aside of the Sabbath Law (2.40).[186] Though it is affirmed that God fights for the people, human agency in the battle is particularly stressed. It is Mattathias, with his zeal for the Law, who leads the warriors of Israel – 'all who offered themselves willingly for the Law' – into battle (2.42–3), tearing down false altars (2.44–5), and slaying the renegade Jews who had abandoned the Law. Later on, Mattathias' son, Judas, who led the successful revolt, explicitly affirms that it is in God's strength that the battle can be won. So when faced by the Syrians, who vastly outnumber Judas' army, his men ask:

> 'How can we, few as we are, fight so great and so strong a multitude? And we are faint, for we have eaten nothing today'.
>
> Judas replied, 'It is easy for many to be hemmed in by few, for in the sight of Heaven there is no difference between saving by many or by few. It is not on the size of the army that victory in battle depends, but strength that comes from Heaven. They come against us in great insolence and lawlessness to destroy us and our wives and children, and to despoil us; but we fight for our lives and our laws. He himself will crush them before us; as for you, do not be afraid of them.[187]

The battle, like those in the Old Testament, belongs to God.[188] Like those ancient stories, after his victory, 'Judas and his brothers began to be feared, and terror fell on the Gentiles all around them' (3.25).[189] Divine help comes in the form of military victory, through the zealousness of the warriors fighting against an alien enemy, which brought the danger of contamination and idolatry to the Jews.

Second Maccabees develops this concept of classical Deuteronomistic Holy War tradition. The pattern of sin and disaster is emphasized in a way in which it is not in 1 Maccabees. Military disaster has befallen the Jews because of their sin of disobedience to God. The locus of the action is still battle and, as in 1 Maccabees, a battle which Judas will win. However, in contrast, holy warriors zealous for the Law do not achieve victory. In 2 Maccabees, God's favour is turned towards his people because of the faithfulness of a handful of individuals, whose shed blood causes God 'to hearken to the blood that cries out to him' (8.3). God then enables Judas to win the military conflict, for 'his wrath had turned to mercy' (8.5). Therefore, in 2 Maccabees, the context of the battle was still primarily conventional. Uprisings had failed whilst God's anger burned against his people because of idolatry, but the martyrs, in some way, caused God

---

186. See the particularly illuminating excursus on 'The observance of the Sabbath and the holy war', in Hengel, *The Zealots*, 287–90.

187. 1 Macc. 3.17–22. There is a link with Jonathan's speech at 1 Sam. 14.6, and also unmistakeable resonance with Gideon's speech (Judg. 7.2). For other occasions where the leader exhorts his troops, see Deut. 20.2–3; Josh. 8.1; Judg. 3.28; 7.5; 1 Sam. 7.8–9.

188. See also 1 Macc. 3.50–3, 60; 4.8–11, 24–5, 30–3, etc., where God is called to fight on behalf of Israel.

189. Cf. 1 Chron. 14.17. Judas' victories are cast in the mould of the Old Testament warrior figures, especially David (see Himmelfarb, 'Judaism and Hellenism', 21; Goldstein, *I Maccabees*, 248). For the theme of terror falling on Israel's enemies, see Exod. 15.15–16 (cf. 1 Macc. 4.30–3); Exod. 23.27–8; Deut. 2.25; 11.25; Josh. 2.9.

to turn again to the people. Therefore, the next military campaign was successful. Just as the sin of individuals brought collective punishment, so the faithfulness of individuals led to salvation.[190]

However, like the persecuted righteous of Daniel 12, there is also personal eschatological reward for the martyrs. The traditional Holy War ideology has been combined in 2 Maccabees with developing eschatological promise, creating a potent apocalyptic matrix within which to interpret the deaths of the faithful. They have affected the cosmos by turning God's anger away from the people, and in 2 Maccabees, for the first time, a military struggle is placed in an apocalyptic framework.[191]

The apocalypticism of 2 Maccabees has its source in Daniel 7–12, just as the template for the martyrdom stories may be found in Daniel 3 and 6. In addition, Daniel shapes a conflict between the Jews and their captors within the context of apocalyptic struggle. In Daniel, 'one finds for the first time militant apocalypticism accompanying the struggle of adherents of a revolutionary creed opposed to a world Empire'.[192] Elaine Pagels demonstrates how some Jewish apocalyptic groups between 165 BCE and 100 CE produced apocalypses in which battles took place between heaven and hell. In these apocalypses is found radical dualism, with true believers decisively marked out against the enemy.[193] Both Christians and Jews, in due course, reinterpreted this apocalyptic struggle in opposition to Roman Imperial power.[194]

Yet, we have also noted important distinctions between the martyrs of the Maccabees and those of Daniel. Daniel has miraculous deliverance stories, whereas in 2 Maccabees the heroes die. Nonetheless, God's miraculous deliverance is still present in Maccabees in two ways. In the first instance, military victory is granted for the whole people, so that with God's help the land is purged of the oppressive and idolatrous Gentiles. Secondly, the martyrs are miraculously delivered through resurrection. Furthermore, the martyrs contribute in some way

190. D.A. DeSilva, *Introducing the Apocrypha* (Grand Rapids: Baker Academic, 2002), 275.

191. There are heavenly armies (10.29; 11.6–10; 12.17–25), the fight is aided by God (8.23) and God wins the victory (13.15). This is somewhat prepared for in Daniel 7–8, where, according to Collins's reading ('Apocalyptic eschatology', 31–2) conflict on earth is mirrored by conflict in heaven, with war simultaneously declared against the saints of the Most High, the heavenly host (7.21 and 8.10–11), and the people of the saints of the Most High (7.27 and 8.24), perhaps in the tradition of each nation having its own angelic patron (so see 10.21, where Michael is 'your prince').

192. Frend, *Martyrdom and Persecution*, 48.

193. E. Pagels, 'The social history of Satan, the "intimate enemy": a preliminary sketch', *HTR* 84 (1991), 105–28. See especially the War Scroll of Qumran (1QM), where the themes of Holy War, such radical dualism and military apocalypticism are found most fully expressed. A future and final apocalyptic battle will be fought between the sons of light and the sons of darkness, each side led by cosmic forces. In the end, God will intervene on the side of the sons of light and will overcome '[the army of Belial, and all] the angels of his kingdom' (1QM 1.14–15, trans. G. Vermes, *The Complete Dead Sea Scrolls in English* [London: Penguin, 1997], 164).

194. C. Rowland ('The book of Daniel and the radical critique of empire: an essay in apocalyptic hermeneutics', in J.J. Collins and P.W. Flint [eds], *The Book of Daniel: Composition and Reception* [2 vols; Leiden: E.J. Brill, 2001], II.447–67) shows how interpreters of Daniel, beginning with the Christians, used the text in order to critique the dominant power of their own day.

to that victory. Their deaths are cosmic in scope. So whereas their deaths do not directly bring about victory (although *4 Maccabees* comes close), they do create the cosmic conditions for God once again to intervene on the side of the Israelites in the Deuteronomistic Holy War tradition.[195]

Cosmic Conflict in Early Christianity

Therefore, from Daniel to 2 Maccabees, three theological developments, vitally important for the understanding of martyrdom within Christianity, took place. First, the language of war was combined with the concepts of apocalypticism and the dualism of Holy War; the conflict between Jew and Gentile was transposed into combat between God and his cosmic enemies. Secondly, miraculous deliverance of the righteous sufferer was shifted from the earthly realm to the cosmic, through resurrection. Vindication was conceived in terms of personal eschatology, but also deliverance of the people. Third and crucially, Holy War, for the first time, incorporated the contribution of those who died a martyr's death to the final outcome of the battle. In Daniel, the righteous would eventually see the final victory of God, but those who die for the Law in 2 Maccabees actually affect the balance of the cosmos through removing from the people the sin that had prevented God from fighting with them. Their deaths enabled the successful Maccabean revolt against the Seleucids, but ultimately the final hope of victory still lay in God fighting through the might of Israel's conventional military forces as in classical Holy War tradition.

Therefore, nearly all the elements of the conceptual world in which Christian Holy War was fought are found here. Many of the differences between the two can be explained as simple developments or differences in circumstance. There was the language of cosmic conflict and radical apocalyptic dualism, so important in early Christian thought. The martyr's reward was contrasted with the persecutor's punishment. Christians adapted the notion of personal eschatological reward for the martyr within the developing doctrine of general resurrection. Just as the Jewish martyrs overcame by their deaths and contributed to the Holy war, so too Christian martyrs overcame through death, and made a crucial contribution to Holy War. In the cosmic conflict, Satan was the enemy of the Christians, and by their deaths they overcame him, contributing to the final victory.[196] Herein lies the crucial difference that must be accounted for. The deaths of the Jewish

---

195. Similarly, 1QM represents a highly apocalypticized version of Deuteronomic Holy War tradition where God dramatically and decisively intervenes in the *final* Holy War. However, in this tradition there is no stress on the importance of martyrs.

196. In Christianity, Satan becomes the identified cosmic enemy of God, whereas in Judaism, though the battles take on a cosmic nature, Satan is never used in this way, perhaps because of this theology's flirtation with dualism. On the absence of Satan in Jewish thought, see N. Forsyth, *The Old Enemy: Satan and the Combat Myth* (Princeton, NJ: Princeton University Press, 1987). For a survey of Jewish demonology, which comes close to the idea of spirits hostile to God in some apocalyptic writing, see Pagels, 'Social history'. Pagels considers these groups to be 'dissident', for, as Alan Segal notes (Segal, *Other Judaisms*, 57), 'Rabbinic Judaism was especially intolerant of angelologies when the unity of God was in question.'

martyrs do not themselves win the battle, whereas the Christian martyrs' deaths lead directly to eschatological victory.

In Christian discourse, persecution was in no way a punishment for sin. Persecution came from Satan, not from God. There were no human armies to be fought; those who killed the faithful were soldiers of Satan. There was no earthly battle to be won, no earthy outcome to be desired, other than the Christian's escape from the world.[197] In contrast, earthly deliverance was the goal in Macca- bees, with the aim of restoring an independent national State under God. Even after the Roman invasion in 63 BCE, this aim remained an ambition for the Jews for most of the following two centuries. Therefore, martyrdom stories described by Josephus were always against the backdrop of the hope for a restored homeland. The Jewish revolts against the Romans, in both the first and second centuries, demonstrate that hope of military deliverance remained part of the apocalyptic belief in God's protection.[198] There was the enduring hope that God would intervene in human this-worldly affairs.[199]

Therefore, although there stands an apparent gulf between Jewish and Chris- tian war expectations, there is one simple explanation that took Christian marty- rology in a different direction. They never had an army or a homeland, and so no possibility for revolt ever existed. It was the same apocalyptic war tradition of the Jews, but for the Christian it was immediately spiritualized, universalized and transferred to the cosmic realm.[200] Whereas the Jews could and would revolt, for the Christian, 'the fight was not against flesh and blood' – it was primarily cosmic. Consequently, the contribution of the Christian martyr to the cosmos could never be to turn God's wrath into mercy, because suffering was never interpreted as God's wrath. Suffering could never bring God's favour upon an army, because there was no military. Nonetheless, influenced by Jewish Holy War tradition, it was the martyrs themselves who constituted their army.

Adopting Jewish apocalyptic dualism, as well as its concept of Holy War, the enemy of God's people changed from Seleucid or Roman armies to Satan. There was no hope of ending persecution, and therefore the cause of their suffering

197. Of course this is not the 'escape from life' the Stoics sought. Through death, the Christians were, in their reality, rushing towards life.

198. For this reason, there was no substitutionary atonement before then in Jewish writings (Downing, 'Jesus', 280). Downing follows A. Büchler, *Studies in Sin and Atonement in the Rabbinic Literature of the First Century* (London: Oxford University Press, 1928).

199. Hengel (*The Zealots*, 282–7) casts the outbreak of the Jewish War in terms of an ancient Holy War. On the revolts and uprisings, see also, M.E. Smallwood, *The Jews under Roman Rule: From Pompey to Diocletian* (Leiden: E.J. Brill, 1981), 389–427; B. Isaac and A. Oppenheimer, 'Bar Kokhba', in *ABD*, I, 598–606. On the Diaspora revolt of 115–16 CE, see Barclay, *Jews*, 78–81.

200. Even though in Qumran the final battle is undoubtedly 'cosmic' (1QM), the community see themselves as participating in that battle through more or less traditional military means. So the ages of those able to participate (cols 5–7) as well as battle manoeuvres (col. 9) are noted. The War Scroll represents another possible trajectory that the potent mixture of suffering, apocalypticism and Holy War tradition could take. On the contrasting apocalypticism of Qumran and Christianity, see J.J. Collins, 'Qumran, apocalypticism, and the New Testament' in L.H. Schiffman, E. Tov and J.C. VanderKam, *The Dead Fifty Years after Their Discovery* (Proceedings of the Jerusalem Congress, July 20–25, 1997; Jerusalem: Israel Exploration Society, 2000), 133–8.

moved from God to Satan.[201] Death did not trigger an earthly military victory, but a future, cosmic, heavenly success. Therefore, as persecution was interpreted as a sign of the end,[202] enduring to death was a potent symbol of victory. Dying for God was imitating the model of Jesus, whose death marked the beginning of the decisive victory against Satan. The goal of each martyr's death was to bring closer the moment of eschatological salvation and judgement, when the Lamb would declare, and win, the final battle.

Conclusion

In conclusion, Jewish Holy War tradition has been a neglected factor as a source for Christian martyrology, and was adapted to the Christians' precarious and peculiar circumstances. Therefore, although both Judaism and Christianity combined this War tradition with apocalypticism, Jewish apocalyptic expectation maintained the hope that God would act decisively in the temporal arena, fighting synergistically with Israel's army, and restore the nation to pure worship. Christianity had no temporal outlet, however, and so Christian apocalyptic war was conceived in wholly cosmic terms, with a cosmic enemy, a cosmic outcome and a cosmic stage on which the martyrs lived and died: nothing less than cosmic conflict. This interpretation has the advantage of adequately explaining both Christian martyrological indebtedness to Judaism and its profound departure from it.

---

201. This was the Christians' solution to theodicy. For Judaism, the presence of martyrdom constituted a problem well into the Rabbinic period. See F. Avemarie, 'Aporien der Theodizee: zu einem Schlüsselthema früher Rabbinischer Märtyrererzählungen', *JSJ* 34 (2003), 119–215.
202. As it was in strands of Judaism. See Hengel, *The Zealots*, 245–9.

Chapter 5

RADICAL MARTYRDOM AND COSMIC CONFLICT IN THE NEW TESTAMENT

Introduction

We have seen that in early Christian martyrological literature several key features are present. In the first instance, participants saw themselves as being engaged in a cosmic conflict between the forces of Satan and those of God, in whose cause they interpreted their own deaths. The drama of death was not merely played out on the stage of Roman theatres, or in courtrooms, or before earthly governors and kings; for the early Christians who endured persecution and death, the stage was cosmic in its scope. In the eschatological battle between God and the legions of evil, disciples of Christ were principal players, foot-soldiers who could affect the outcome by their earthly actions.

The martyrdom of a Christian struck a mighty blow against the armies of Satan, even hastening the end. This belief was sustained by the inversion of the categories of present and future, and life and death. Radical dualism enabled Christians to view martyrdom in such a positive light that many actively sought death, the phenomenon I have termed *radical martyrdom*. However, this seeking after death was believed, in fact, to be the winning of life. By the late second century, some Christians interpreted their life of faith as engagement in the final apocalyptic battle in which victory was achieved, following the perceived pattern of their master, through the quest for death.

The question to which we now turn is to what extent are the component parts of this theological world-view – radical dualism, participation in cosmic conflict and the deconstruction of the categories of life and death, and present and future – found in the New Testament. Most importantly, to what extent does suffering and death play a role in the bringing about of cosmic victory, especially where there is a specific call to seek or embrace death? If I am correct that Christian martyrdom has its roots in Jewish Holy War tradition, yet departed from it dramatically by wholly spiritualizing the cosmic battle, then the New Testament straddles precisely this period of transition from Jewish martyrology to the developed Christian form found in the second century.

It will not be possible to offer a comprehensive survey of New Testament theologies of suffering, or even of martyrdom. I am concerned here only with that material which contributed to the development of radical martyrdom as outlined above. Having focused on these suppressed theologies of radical martyrdom in the second and third Christian centuries, I will examine to what extent radical martyrology may be instructive in reading some important New Testament texts on death.

We therefore begin with Paul, both his own writings and that of his heirs, before turning to a more detailed reading of Jesus' call to take up the cross, particularly in Mark (8.34). Finally, we will examine death in the book of Revelation, where the theology of radical martyrdom finds its fullest expression within the New Testament, with the near-total transformation of reality presented in the Apocalypse.

Paul

In his letters, the Apostle frequently refers to his own afflictions for the sake of both Christ and the Church. Imprisoned,[1] beaten, lashed and stoned,[2] Paul could claim to bear the στίγματα of Christ on his body.[3] These experiences shaped his own conception of what it meant to be a faithful follower of Christ.[4] Paul expected his followers to suffer affliction in the same way in which he already had. This suffering was inexorably linked with preaching[5] and receiving the gospel.[6]

Suffering in Paul

Initially, in Paul's thought, suffering was to be endured, though the Christians were to pray for deliverance from it.[7] In his first extant epistle, 1 Thessalonians,[8] suffering must be endured by the Church. Suffering is not a good in itself, but because Christians are suffering for the sake of Christ they can suffer with joy.[9] From this joyful suffering develops the idea that suffering can actually be

1.   For example, 2 Cor. 11.23; Phil. 1.7; Philm. 1.
2.   2 Cor. 11.23–5. See Paul's catalogues of hardships Rom. 8.35; 1 Cor. 4. 9–13; 2 Cor. 4.8–9; 6.4–5; 11.23–9; 12.10.
3.   Gal. 6.17. J.L. Martyn (*Galatians* [AB33A; New York: Doubleday, 1997], 568) takes Τὰ στίγματα τοῦ 'Ιυσοῦ to refer to physical scars which 'reflect the wounds of a soldier sent into the front trenches of God's redemptive and liberating war'.
4.   How a particularly harsh experience refashioned Paul's theology is explored in A.E. Harvey, *Renewal through Suffering: A Study of 2 Corinthians* (Edinburgh: T&T Clark, 1996). For discussion, see S. J., Hafemann, 'The role of suffering in the mission of Paul', in J. Ådna and H. Kvalbein (eds), *The Mission of the Early Church to Jews and Gentiles* (Tübingen: Mohr Siebeck, 2000), 165–84; J.D.G. Dunn, *The Theology of Paul the Apostle* (Grand Rapids/Cambridge: Eerdmans, 1998), 482–7.
5.   1 Thess. 1.6; 2.14–15; Phil. 1.29.
6.   1 Cor. 4.9–13; 2 Cor. 6.4–10.
7.   Gal. 1.4; 2 Thess. 3.1–2.
8.   However, the priority of 2 Thessalonians has been advanced, most recently by C.A. Wanamaker, *The Epistles to the Thessalonians: A Commentary on the Greek Text* (NIGTC; Grand Rapids: Eerdmans, 1990), 37–45.
9.   So present suffering is as nothing compared to the glory which will be revealed (Rom. 8.18).

beneficial, so that it makes one worthy,[10] produces endurance, character and hope,[11] and also can bring others to repentance,[12] as well as inspire boldness.[13]

In 2 Cor. 1.8–11, the apostle Paul recounts what appears to have been a near-death experience:

> For we do not want you to be ignorant, brethren, of the affliction we experienced in Asia; for we were so utterly, unbearably crushed that we despaired of life itself. Why, we felt that we had received the sentence of death; but that was to make us rely not on ourselves but on God who raises the dead; he delivered us from so deadly a peril, and he will deliver us; on him we have set our hope that he will deliver us again. You also must help us by prayer, so that many will give thanks on our behalf for the blessing granted us in answer to many prayers.

Harvey argues that Paul pioneered a new way of looking at suffering, until then unknown in the Graeco-Roman world.[14] For the first time, suffering was not seen as an evil thing, or something to be avoided, or even a problem for theology, rather, it brought the sufferer close to Christ. Moreover, suffering could also be interpreted as bringing benefit to others, and this thought became a prominent concept for Paul's self understanding for his own suffering. In some way, he actually suffers for the benefit of the church.[15]

Furthermore, part of Paul's important theological conviction, that believers somehow participate in Christ, also informed his positive reassessment of suffering. It would be no exaggeration to claim that the single most important factor that drove Christian theology in the direction it took, especially in its divergence from Judaism, was Jesus/Christ. The life and death of Jesus provided a potent example for those who were to follow their master, while the cosmic dying and rising of the Christ opened up a new theological framework in which Christians could place their own lives and struggles.[16] Therefore, in the paradigmatic Philippian Christ hymn (2.5–11), Paul presents Jesus as the supreme model of suffering, servanthood and humility to which all Christians should align themselves.[17]

---

10. 2 Thess. 1.5.

11. Rom. 5.3–5.

12. 2 Cor. 7.9.

13. Phil. 1.14.

14. Harvey, *Renewal*, 129.

15. 2 Cor. 1.6; Phil. 2.17; Col. 1.24; cf. Eph. 3.13; 2 Tim. 2.8–10. G.W.H. Lampe ('Inspiration and martyrdom', in W. Horbury and B. McNeil [eds], *Suffering and Martyrdom in the New Testament* [Cambridge: Cambridge University Press, 1981], 118–35, at 121) stops short of the idea that Paul saw his own suffering as somehow atoning, although he concedes that Phil. 2.17 (cf. 1 Tim. 4.6), where Paul speaks of his life as a libation on the sacrificial offering of the Philippians' faith, comes very close. Compare, Droge ('MORI LUCRUM', 263), who sees Paul being presented as a 'second Christ' in Col. 1.24. For discussion of this text, see below, 136–7. E. Lohse (*Colossians and Philemon* [trans. W.R. Poehlmann and R.J. Karris; Hermeneia; Philadelphia: Fortress Press, 1971], 70) goes so far as to suggest that Paul provided a 'vicarious service' for the Church.

16. Although the division has value for later Christian martyrology, Paul makes no distinction between Jesus and Christ. As Dunn (*Paul*, 183) correctly notes, 'the gospel for Paul was pre-eminently the gospel of Christ'. For discussion of Paul's knowledge of the life and ministry of Jesus, see Dunn, *Paul*, 182–206.

17. Phil. 2.5–11.

Moreover, not only did Christ provide a model of service, Christians actually shared in his suffering.[18] For Barrett, it was as though the sufferings of Christ overflowed and reached his followers.[19] Sharing in Christ's suffering was so important for Paul, that becoming an heir of Christ was *dependent* on suffering with him.[20] Therefore, believers were crucified with Christ[21] and baptized into his death.[22] Consequently, they shared in his resurrection and his glory.[23] Suffering and death were necessary prerequisites to share in Christ's glory to be revealed at the *parousia*.[24] It followed that in order for believers to share in Christ's exaltation and glory, they also had to share in his humiliation[25] and, because suffering was demanded of the believer, becoming the measure of faithfulness of a disciple,[26] Paul could boast in his sufferings[27] and even believe that it was God who led him into suffering.[28]

Thus suffering became a vital component in Paul's theology. For Paul, it was not only beneficial, but necessary.[29] Suffering marked out true followers,[30] and became a sign of the Church's legitimacy.[31] For Paul, suffering was the destiny of the Christian,[32] and so he prepared his churches for inevitable suffering,[33] calling it their glory and boast.[34] Suffering was not optional for the Christian; it

18. 2 Cor. 1.5; Phil. 3.10–11.

19. C.K. Barrett, *The Second Epistle to the Corinthians* (BTNC; London: A. & C. Black, 1973), 62.

20. Rom. 8.16–17.

21. Gal. 2.19. For an important discussion of this theme, see especially R.C. Tannehill, *Dying and Rising with Christ: A Study in Pauline Theology* (Berlin: Alfred Töpelmann, 1967), 32–43.

22. Rom. 6.3.

23. For classic treatments of ἐν χριστῷ theology, see A. Deissmann, *Paul: A Study in Social and Religious History* (trans. W.E. Wilson; London: Hodder and Stoughton, 1926), 135–57, where he speaks of Paul's 'Christ intimacy' or 'Christ mysticism'; and W. Bousset, *Kyrios Christos: A History of Belief in Christ from the Beginning to Irenaeus* (trans. J.E. Steely; Nashville: Abingdon Press, 1970), 153–60. A modern proponent of Participationism over and against Justification as the centre of Paul's theology is E.P. Sanders, *Paul and Palestinian Judaism: A Comparison of Patterns of Religion* (London: SCM Press, 1977), especially 453–72 and 501–8.

24. Dunn, *Paul*, 485.

25. M.D. Hooker, 'Interchange and suffering', in W. Horbury and B. McNeil (eds), *Suffering and Martyrdom in the New Testament* (Cambridge: Cambridge University Press, 1981), 70–83 (75). See Rom. 8.35; 2 Cor. 4.14; 2 Thess. 1.3–5.

26. So suffering is a characteristic mark of a Paul's discipleship: Gal. 6.17; 1 Cor. 2.1–5; 2 Cor. 11.23–9; Phil. 1.30.

27. 2 Cor. 11.21–30; 12.10; Phil. 1.19–26.

28. 1 Cor. 4.9; 2 Cor. 1.9; 2.14; 4.11. See also Barrett, *Second Corinthians*, 63.

29. See also 1 Peter, where suffering is judged to be necessary from the outset (1.6; and *passim*, but especially 5.9). On this theme of the necessity of suffering in 1 Peter, see especially, M. Dubis, *Messianic Woes in First Peter: Suffering and Eschatology in 1 Peter 4.12–19* (New York: Peter Lang, 2002).

30. See especially 2 Tim. 3.12: 'All who live a godly life will be persecuted'.

31. Gal. 4.12–15; Phil. 1.3–7; 4.14–15; 1 Thess. 1.1–6; 3.15.

32. 1 Thess. 3.14; Phil. 1.29–30. See J.S. Pobee, *Persecution and Martyrdom in the Theology of Paul* (Sheffield: JSOT Press, 1985), 108; and Baumeister, *Anfänge*, 156–7.

33. 1 Thess. 3.2–4.

34. Rom. 5.3; 1 Cor. 15.31; 2 Cor. 1.12; 11.30; 12.9.

came upon all who sought a godly life.[35] Through suffering, one attained the Kingdom of God.[36] If the Church was not suffering, it was not being faithful, and therefore, when suffering came, the appropriate response for the Christian was to rejoice.[37]

Therefore, for Paul, suffering was not so much an evil to be avoided as an opportunity to be grasped. This positive spin on suffering was crucial for the development of martyrology. Furthermore, Paul's theology of participation in Christ's death and life also provided an important foundation for the development of radical martyrdom, for a crucial pillar on which radical martyrdom rested was the belief that the martyrs were participating in cosmic conflict. We turn now to Paul's development of this theme.

Cosmic Conflict

Suffering, in much Christian interpretation, was seen firmly within the context of the last days.[38] Indeed, suffering was itself the sign that the persecuted communities were living at the cusp of the new cosmos.[39] For the early Church, the apocalyptic countdown had begun and, importantly, Christian communities, through participating in Christ's suffering, saw themselves as living through a period of eschatological distress.[40] These twin themes of participation and cosmic distress come together in a much-discussed Pauline text: Col. 1.24. 'Now I rejoice in my sufferings for your sake, and in my flesh I complete what is lacking in Christ's afflictions for the sake of the body, that is, the Church.'

Moule outlines two main strands of interpretation on this verse. First, οἱ ἐν Χριστῷ share in Christ's suffering, and so 'what is lacking' refers to what is still to be shared by the community of faith.[41] Alternatively, that which is lacking points to the set period of Messianic woes to be undergone by those faithful to God before the End.[42] Although Moule combines both of these ideas, he

35. See 2 Tim. 3.12.

36. See Acts 14.22.

37. Mt. 5.11–12//Lk. 6.22–3; Acts 5.41; Rom. 12.12; 2 Cor. 6.10; 8.2; 13.9; Phil. 2.17; 4.4–6; Col. 1.11, 24; Jas 1.2; 1 Pet. 1.6; 4.13.

38. D.C. Allison, *The End of the Ages Has Come: An Early Interpretation of the Passion and Resurrection of Jesus* (Edinburgh: T&T Clark, 1987).

39. This is of course an idea that comes from Judaism: Dan. 12.1; *Jub.* 23.13–14, 18–19, 22; *2 Bar.* 70.2–3, 5, 8–10; *4 Ezra* 5.1–12; 13.30–1; 14.16–17. See especially W.A. Meeks, 'Social functions'; E.S. Fiorenza, 'The phenomenon of early Christian apocalyptic' (in D. Hellholm [ed.], *Apocalypticism in the Mediterranean and the Near East* (Proceedings of the International Colloquium on Apocalypticism, Upsala, 1979, Tubingen: J.C.B. Mohr [Paul Siebeck], 1983), 295–316) especially 300–2.

40. See especially Allison, *End of the Ages*, 5–25.

41. See also 2 Cor. 1.5, 6–7; 4.12; 11.29; 13.4; Phil. 1.29–30; 3.10; 1 Pet. 4.13; 5.9; Rev. 1.9. Compare Lohse, *Colossians*, 68–73. However, a vigorous advocacy of this interpretation is advanced by W.F. Flemington, 'On the interpretation of Colossians 1.24', in W. Horbury and B. McNeil (eds), *Suffering and Martyrdom in the New Testament* (Cambridge: Cambridge University Press, 1981), 84–90.

42. See also Mk 13.8//Mt. 24.6//Lk. 21.9 and especially Lk. 21.24. 2 Thessalonians 2 speaks of a period of tribulation, and in Heb. 11.40 the witness of the heroes must be supplemented by the

considers the second to be more likely, and therefore paraphrases the passage: 'I am proud ... to undergo physical suffering in the work of evangelism. It is my contribution to the quota of sufferings which the whole Church must undergo in the working out of God's designs'.[43]

Both elements of participation and messianic woes are evident in the writings of Paul, and therefore it seems unwise to privilege one over the other, especially as both combine to form a potent contribution to Pauline understanding of cosmic conflict. Under the influence of these twin themes, suffering and death, in time, could easily be interpreted within the apocalyptic schema of God's decisive military triumph over Satanic powers. Pauline Christians believed 'they were engaged in a final struggle, that they were suffering the last great persecution, that never before had evil been so evil, and never again could it raise its head, for its final destruction was nigh'.[44]

However, not only were Christians engaged in that struggle, but through Paul's writings they were also provided with the means whereby they might begin to reflect on their contribution to God's cosmic war. Suffering was not simply a consequence of participation in this cosmic conflict, it became a contribution to it. 'Accordingly, the more the apostle suffers for the cause of Christ and in the cause of his ministry, the greater his contribution to the coming End. He is thereby hastening "the Day" '.[45] And if that was true for Paul, it was also true of his followers. Paul is therefore found to develop this critical component in radical martyrology: not only participation in but also contribution to God's cosmic war.

If, for those who came after Paul, the fight was not against flesh and blood, but principalities and powers,[46] Paul similarly believed himself and his communities to be living in the final eschatological era dominated by cosmic forces.[47] The Christian life was a battle between those of the day and those of the night,[48] requiring the armour of faith, hope and love.[49] Paul conceived the world in

Church before the end. Revelation 6.11 is a crucial text in this regard and will be discussed in some detail below. Advocates of this interpretation include Lohse, *Colossians*, 68–73; J.A. Baker, *The Foolishness of God* (London: Darton, Longman & Todd, 1970), 239; J.C. Beker, *Paul the Apostle: The Triumph of God in Life and Thought* (Philadelphia: Fortress Press, 1980), 145–6; and Allison, *End of the Ages*, 62–9.

43. C.F.D. Moule, *The Epistles of Paul the Apostle to the Colossians and to Philemon* (Cambridge: Cambridge University Press, 1962), 74.

44. H.H. Rowley, *The Relevance of Apocalyptic: A Study of Jewish and Christian Apocalypses from Daniel to the Revelation* (London: Lutterworth Press, 1963), 172.

45. Moule, *Colossians*, 76–7.

46. Eph. 6.12. On the various terms for the cosmic powers, see Dunn, *Paul*, 105 n. 14; and W. Wink's trilogy: *Naming the Powers: The Language of Power in the New Testament* (Philadelphia: Fortress Press, 1984); *Unmasking the Powers: The Invisible Forces That Determine Human Existence* (Philadelphia: Fortress Press, 1986); *Engaging the Powers: Discernment and Resistance in a World of Domination* (Minneapolis: Fortress Press, 1992).

47. On Pauline eschatological expectations see, Dunn, *Paul*, 461–98; O. Cullmann, *Christ and Time: The Primitive Conception of Time and History* (trans. F.V. Filson; London: SCM Press, 1962), 81–93.

48. 1 Thess. 5.1–11.

49. 1 Thess. 5.9; greatly expanded in Eph. 6.14–17.

dualistic terms, expressed starkly in 1 Thessalonians, where people are divided between those who have hope and those who have no hope (4.13), those destined for salvation and those for destruction and wrath (5.3–4; cf. 1.10), people of the light and day against people of darkness and night (5.5), those who are awake and those who sleep (5.6),[50] those who are sober and those who are drunk (5.6–7).

Second Thessalonians maintains this sharp divide between those destined for salvation and those who will face destruction (1.7–10; 2.10–12). Importantly, this letter places the conflict between believers and outsiders on the scale of a cosmic conflict between Jesus and the man of lawlessness. Inevitably, Jesus will triumph: 'And the lawless one will be revealed, and the Lord Jesus will slay him with the breath of his mouth and destroy him by his appearing and disappearing' (2.8). If Jesus will destroy the cosmic opponents of the Church, then the Church undergoing human opposition is also given hope. For example, the human opponents (ἀντικείμενοι) resident in Philippi will be destroyed, and so, Paul's church is urged to stand firm and not to be afraid of them, for what they are experiencing 'is a clear omen of their destruction and the salvation of the faithful' (1.27–8).[51] Even human conflict is given a cosmic, apocalyptic twist.

Paul, therefore, saw the Christian life as a struggle, a battle or a contest. The prominence of the ἀγών motif in Paul reflects this struggle.[52] In describing the Christian experience, Paul employs both military and athletic imagery. So, for example, he can utilize the image of the warrior to describe the Christian's struggle.[53] Athletic imagery is more prominent: Christian life is a struggle, the goal of which is to win the eternal crown. To that end, Paul was prepared to endure suffering, pummelling his body in order to win the prize.[54] It is in 1 Corinthians where the athletic imagery as a metaphor for Christian life is most developed (9.24–7), drawing from both running and boxing.[55] Earlier in that letter, Paul had employed the image of the arena when describing the suffering he endures for his calling: 'God has exhibited us apostles as last of all, like men sentenced to death; because we have become a spectacle to the world, to angels and to men.'[56] Paul here alludes to those criminals who would be paraded before being killed, suggesting that the Christian struggle could very well end in death. Significantly, the contest takes place before both men and angels, making it a cosmic contest. The image reaches its zenith in the Pauline corpus with the author of 2 Timothy summing up Paul's life in terms of an athletic contest:

---

50. Compare Eph. 5.14, where sleeping is equated with death, whereas those who are awake are with Christ.

51. Suffering is also a sign that wrath will come upon opponents in 1 Thess. 2.14–16 and 2 Thess. 1.6–9.

52. Phil. 2.16; 3.12–14; Col. 1.29; 1 Thess. 2.2; cf. 1 Tim. 6.12; 2 Tim. 4.7–8.

53. Rom. 6.13; 8.37; 13.12; 2 Cor. 6.7; 10.3–5; Phil. 2.25; Philm. 2; 1 Thess. 5.8.

54. 1 Cor. 9.27.

55. G.D. Fee, *The First Epistle to the Corinthians* (NICNT; Grand Rapids: Eerdmans, 1987), 433–41; V.C. Pfitzner, *Paul and the Agon Motif* (NovTSup, 4; Leiden: E.J. Brill, 1961), 87–93.

56. 1 Cor. 4.9.

> For I am already on the point of being sacrificed; the time of my departure has come. I have fought the good fight and finished the race,[57] I have kept the faith. Henceforth there is laid up for me the crown of righteousness, which the Lord, the righteous judge will award to me on that Day, and not only to me but also to all who have loved his appearing.[58]

The image of the Lord as judge of the games is one which will appear in our martyr texts of the second century, but the image of God's judgement also puts Paul's struggle, and indeed the struggle of all Christians,[59] in an apocalyptic context. Again, this is a cosmic struggle, and warfare imagery is not far from the surface.[60]

Nonetheless, Paul does not appear to attribute the suffering which Christians endure as coming directly from a cosmic satanic figure.[61] To be sure, Paul does attribute to Satan his difficulties in getting back to Thessalonica,[62] though nowhere else is Satan directly involved in bringing hardship to the Christians of his own volition.[63] Ultimately, the powers of evil will be destroyed by God,[64] and

57. Notice the same sports alluded to in 1 Cor. 9.24–7, though Pfitzner (*Agon Motif*, 183) judges the metaphor to be less specifically athletic. Compare C.K. Barrett, *The Pastoral Epistles* (Oxford: Oxford University Press, 1963), 118; J.N.D. Kelly, *A Commentary on the Pastoral Epistles* (BNTC; London: A. & C. Black, 1963), 208: I.H. Marshall, *A Critical and Exegetical Commentary on the Pastoral Epistles* (ICC; Edinburgh: T&T Clark, 1999), 807.

58. 2 Tim. 4.6–8, perhaps based on Phil. 2.16–17. Endurance is also associated with crowns, or at least reigning in 2 Tim. 2.11.

59. The image of fighting the good fight appears as a command in 1 Tim. 6.12 (ἀγωνίζου τὸν καλὸν ἀγῶνα). See also 4.7–10.

60. R.F. Collins (*1 & 2 Timothy and Titus: A Commentary* [NIGTC; Louisville, KY/London: Westminster John Knox Press, 2002], 273) suggests that the image of τὸν καλὸν ἀγῶνα comes from a military idea typified in an inscription from 267 BCE of a battle against the Athenians: πολλοὺς καὶ καλοὺς ἀγῶνας ἠγωνίσαντο μετ᾽ ἀλλήλων. He also observes a link with the way in which the philosophic moralists used the metaphors (Epictetus, *Discourses* 1.24.1–10; Seneca, *Letters* 34.2; 109.6).

61. With the exception of 2 Cor. 12.7, where a messenger from Satan sends Paul's thorn in the flesh.

62. 1 Thess. 2.18. Pobee (*Persecution*, 97) understands Paul to mean that certain people acted to prevent his travelling to Thessalonica, by the agency of Satan. This is, of course, an important theme in our second-century martyr texts. Nonetheless, whilst Pobee's suggestion is possible, given that Paul does attribute the actions of individuals, especially those hostile to him, as satanic (2 Cor. 11.14), it is difficult to be certain. Some have seen a Job typology in these attacks from Satan: S.R. Garrett, 'The God of this world and the affliction of Paul' (in D.L. Balch, E. Ferguson and W.A. Meeks [eds], *Greeks, Romans, and Christians: Essays in Honor of Abraham J. Malherbe* [Minneapolis: Fortress Press, 1990], 99–117), 104–6, and 111–15; P.T. O'Brien, *The Epistle to the Philippians: A Commentary on the Greek Text* (NIGTC; Grand Rapids: Eerdmans, 1991), 108–9. For other references to Satan in Pauline writings, see Rom. 16.20; 1 Cor. 5.5 (where Satan appears to be the means of the Corinthian offender's salvation; cf. 1 Tim. 1.20); 7.5; 2 Cor. 2.11; 11.14; 2 Thess. 2.9. See also 'the god of this age', 2 Cor. 4.4; 'Beliar', 2 Cor. 6.15; 'the evil one', 2 Thess. 3.3; Eph. 6.16; 'the ruler of the air', Eph. 2.2; and 'the devil', Eph. 4.27; 6.11; 1 Tim. 3.6–7; 2 Tim. 2.26. On Satan in Paul, see Dunn, *Paul*, 102–10; and especially Garrett, 'God of this World, 99–117.

63. Satan is involved in some way in what looks like a disciplinary act in 1 Cor. 5.5, which seems to imply some form of suffering, or even death for the Corinthian offender. However, in this case, the church is involved in Satan's act. See D.R. Smith, '"Hand the man over to Satan": curse, exclusion, and salvation in 1 Corinthains 5' (PhD dissertation, University of Durham, 2005).

the Christian need not fear any human or cosmic power, for as famously Paul asserts:

> Who shall separate us from the love of Christ? Shall tribulation, or distress, or persecu-
> tion, or famine, or nakedness, or peril, or sword? ... No, in all these things we are
> more than conquerors through him who loved us. For I am sure that neither death nor
> life, nor angels, nor principalities, nor things present, nor things to come, nor powers,
> nor height, nor depth, nor anything else in all creation, will be able to separate us from
> the love of God in Christ Jesus our Lord. (Rom. 8.35, 37–8)

Therefore, in Paul we have some, though by no means all, of the important elements developing, around which later Christian martyrological reflection would be constructed: eschatological dualism; placing of a high value of suffering, which can be (albeit ambiguously) salvific; imitation of Jesus; and participation in Christ's death and resurrection. We turn now to the presentation of death in Paul's thought, and discern if the embryonic form of radical martyrdom can be found.

Life and Death in Paul

The question of martyrdom in Paul's thought is hampered somewhat by the absence of martyrs in Paul's writing. Nowhere does Paul unambiguously refer to anyone martyred for the faith. However, F.F. Bruce believes the deaths that have occurred in the Thessalonian community (1 Thess. 4.13) are a result of θλίψις. He claims that the use of κοιμάω warrants this conclusion, as it is the same verb used at the climax of the martyrdom of Stephen (Acts 7.60) as a euphemism for his death.[65] Donfried agrees, contending that 'κοιμάω refers explicitly to one who has suffered death through persecution'.[66] He also points to parallels with 1 Thess. 2.14–16, Phil. 1.20, and Rom. 8.35, where there are possible allusions to Christian martyrdom. However, as Barclay rightly notes, Paul would certainly have made capital out of martyrdom in the Church.[67] Nonetheless, although martyrdom is difficult to detect, both life and death are important Pauline concerns, and he frequently utilizes verbs for both living and dying.[68]

If 2 Corinthians is Paul's letter of suffering par excellence,[69] death perhaps pervades no other in the same way as the epistle to the Philippians. For Lohmeyer, the letter is in fact a martyrological treatise, dealing, in turn, with Paul's impending martyrdom (1.12–26), the martyrdom of the church community (1.27–2.16), the help that will come their way through martyrdom (2.17–30), the dangers they will face (3.1–21), and last instructions about martyrdom (4. 1–9).[70]

---

64. Rom. 16.20.

65. F.F. Bruce, *The Acts of the Apostles* (Grand Rapids: Eerdmans, 1990), 327–8. Interestingly, he does not repeat this suggestion in his commentary on 1 Thess. (*1 & 2 Thessalonians* [WBC, 45; Waco, TX: Word Books, 1982).

66. Donfried, 'Cults of Thessalonica', 349.

67. Barclay, 'Conflict in Thessalonica', 514 n. 6. There is no eulogy such as the honours which Paul gives those who have risked their lives for the gospel (cf. Rom. 16.4; Phil. 2.25–30).

68. 'To die' 40 times and 'to live' 51 times, according to Collins, *I & II Timothy*, 226 n. 30.

69. So Harvey, *Renewal*.

70. E. Lohmeyer, *Die Brief an die Philipper* (Göttingen: Vandenhoeck & Ruprecht, 1961), 5–6.

Written from prison (1.7), Paul sees his current state of incarceration as being for Christ (1.13), and advancing the gospel (1.12). He speaks of his own θλίψις (1.17; 4.14) and how he shares in Christ's παθήματα, experiencing grief (2.27), humiliation, deprivation and hunger (4. 11–12). Furthermore, he considers himself to be poured out as a libation (2.17), and death appears to be a very real possibility (1.20). Yet through all this, Paul is able to rejoice (1.18). Instructive is Paul's discussion of the merits of death and life.

> For me to live is Christ and to die is gain. If it is to be life in the flesh, that means fruitful labour for me. *Yet which I will choose* I cannot tell. I am hard pressed between the two. *My desire is to depart and be with Christ, for that is far better.* But to remain in the flesh is more necessary on your account. Convinced of this, I know that I shall remain and continue with you all … (Phil. 1.21–5; emphasis added)

This turbulent internal debate, reflected in 'wild grammar'[71] demonstrates that Paul is genuinely torn between a decision that is in his power to make. Paul's decision to live or die is in his own hands. Some have seen in Paul's dilemma an echo of the Cynic choice between life and death, where both life and death are ἀδιάφορα, that is, something which makes no difference to the good life.[72] Instead what is important is honouring Christ,[73] or usefulness to the Church.[74]

> Paul would have killed himself if: he believed his mission work was finished; the necessity to minister was removed; he was convinced he's fought the good fight, finished the race and it was time to depart; failing ill health prevented him from carrying out the divine commission.[75]

Some play down Paul's own choice and say that Paul was choosing whether to allow himself to be killed by persecutors,[76] especially over the choice whether or

---

Lohmeyer's position is taken to be exaggerated by R. Jewett, 'The epistolary thanksgiving and the integrity of Philippians', *NovT* 12 (1970), 40–53 (51). For a rhetorical approach to suffering in Philippians, see L.G. Bloomquist, *The Function of Suffering in Philippians* (JSNTSup, 76; Sheffield: JSOT Press, 1993).

71. J.B. Lightfoot, *St Paul's Epistle to the Philippians* (London: Macmillan, 1891), 92.

72. J.L. Jaquette, 'Life and death, *Adiaphora* and Paul's rhetorical strategies', *NovT* 38 (1996), 30–54. On the relationship of Paul's catalogues of suffering to contemporary philosophical movements, see J.T. Fitzgerald, *Cracks in an Earthen Vessel: An Examination of the Catalogues of Hardships in the Corinthian Correspondence* (SBL Dissertation Series, 99; Atlanta: Scholars Press, 1988).

73. Jaquette, 'Life and death', 33.

74. W. Michaelis, *Der Brief des Paulus an die Philipper* (THKNT, 11; Leipzig: Deichert, 1935), 24; O'Brien, *Philippians*, 118.

75. A.J. Droge, 'Did Paul commit suicide?', *Bible Review* 5 (1989), 14–21, 42 (20). See also J.T. Clemms (*What Does the Bible Say about Suicide?* [Minneapolis: Fortress Press 1990], 70), who suggests that 'Paul had no immediate sense of wrong-doing in contemplating his self-chosen death'. In constrast, T.F. Dailey ('To live or die: Paul's eschatological dilemma in Philippians 1.19–26', *Interpretation* 44 [1990], 18–28); and D.W. Palmer (' "To die is gain": Philippians i 21', *NovT* 17 [1975], 203–18) both deny that Paul was contemplating suicide. For discussion of Paul and suicide tradition, see J.N. Sevenster, *Paul and Seneca* (SNT, 4; Leiden: E.J. Brill, 1961).

76. D.P. O'Mathúna, 'Did Paul condone suicide?: implications for assisted suicide and active euthanasia', *Ethics and Medicine* 12 (1996), 55–60; T. Engberg-Peterson, *Paul and the Stoics* (Edinburgh:

not to reveal that he is a Roman citizen.[77] Droge, however, argues that it should be taken to mean what it says, namely, that 'the question of life and death was a matter for Paul's *own* volition and not a fate imposed on him by others'.[78]

Though Droge perhaps overstates his case, it is important to note that for Paul the desire to be with Christ is strong and ultimately outweighed on balance only by the desire to stay and serve the Philippian church. In reaching this decision, Paul's internal discussion appears to chime with Stoic discussions of suicide, where self-killing is only justified where it is a necessity. Since Paul could still be of use to the Philippian community, staying with the Church was, for Paul, 'much better' (πολλῷ μᾶλλον κρεῖσσον),[79] a decision with which the Stoics would have concurred. 'One who by living is of more use to many has not the right to chose to die, unless by dying he may be of more use'.[80]

Nonetheless, the Philippian dilemma could only have been a dilemma if the desire for death was stronger than the desire to remain alive, and only ultimately overcome by the desire to be useful. We saw that in the martyrological convictions of the second-century Christians, a lust for death was facilitated by the remarkable conviction that remaining alive was death, and death was really life. If death was gain for Paul, it was doubly so for the radical martyrs.

In 2 Corinthians, Paul seems to have given up on the hope of remaining alive at the *parousia*,[81] as is clearly envisaged in 1 Thess. 4.15. Crucially, in Philippians, life and death does not affect the believer's communion with Christ, for although 'to die is to be with Christ, to live is also Christ' (1.21). A similar, though less developed thought is found in 1 Thessalonians 5, where whether one is living or dying, each will eventually live with the Lord (5.10). However, in 2 Corinthians, not only is the sense of communion heightened at death, but, while one is alive, Paul can say that the Christian is actually in some sense *away from* Christ. To be alive is almost to be in a state of impaired communion with Christ:

> We are always of good courage; we know that while we are at home we are away from the Lord ... [and therefore], we would rather be away from the body and at home with the Lord.[82]

T&T Clark, 2000), 88. For a full discussion and critique of interpretations of these verses, see Wansink, *Chained in Christ*, 96–125.

77. For a full discussion and critique of interpretations of these verses, see Wansink, *Chained in Christ*, 96–125. Although Wansink entertains the possibility that Paul was contemplating self-killing, he judges 'plausible' (124) the suggestion that Paul was deciding whether to be silent before his accusers (in imitation of Jesus), or to give defence. In any case, the important factor is that Paul makes his decision *for others* (125).

78. Droge and Tabor, *Noble Death*, 120 (their emphasis).

79. Elsewhere, for Paul, preaching is ἀνάγκη (1 Cor. 9.16).

80. Musonius Rufus (Fragments XXIX), who was almost an exact contemporary of Paul. See C.E. Lutz, 'Musonius Rufus: the Roman Socrates', *Yale Classical Studies* 10 (1947), 3–147 (132).

81. J. Lambrecht, *Second Corinthians* (Sacra Pagina; Minnesota: The Liturgical Press, 1999), 85.

82. 2 Cor. 5.6–8. See also 2 Cor. 6.3–10, where Paul recounts his catalogue of sufferings, concluding, 'Dying, we live'. However, Lohmeyer (*Philipper*) suggests that he can only say this because Paul is a potential martyr, and therefore at the point of martyrdom he will go straight to Christ, whereas everyone else will have to wait for the general resurrection. However, as Palmer ('To die is

Paul clearly here favours death over life.[83] This, as we have seen, is a crucial element in the later radical martyrdom movement. Paul reinterprets suffering in such a positive manner, he can proclaim, 'dying ... we live;'[84] a statement the radical martyrs would take quite literally. Therefore, Paul's contribution to radical martyrology is considerable.

Nonetheless, it is important not to overemphasize these words, or take them out of context. Paul is not a radical martyr, nor does he advocate radical martyrdom, though he does develop many of the theological concepts that enabled radical martyrology to develop. Three important aspects of radical martyrdom are crucially developed by Paul. First, the idea that suffering was the only way to demonstrate one was an authentic believer. Secondly, Paul advances the example of Jesus as the model of suffering to be imitated by Christians. Thirdly, not only did the believer imitate Jesus but also the participation theology pioneered by Paul could readily be transformed into the means by which the martyr could contribute to the cosmic war effort in later Christian martyrology. This development takes another dramatic turn in the Gospel of Mark.

Taking up the Cross: A Call to Martyrdom

We have seen that in the second century many Christians felt called to bring an end to their lives because of their devotion to Jesus. This could be achieved either at their own hand or by conspiring to provoke the Romans or the local populace into martyring them. This action was maintained by a particular theological world-view which saw the Christians being involved in cosmic conflict in a heavily dualistic world. To die was to live, and to live was to court eschatological death. We have already seen that many of the components of this theological construction of the world exist in Paul. We turn now in some detail to two places where I will argue that radical martyrdom can be found within the New Testament. Before we turn to the Apocalypse, we first examine the cross sayings, especially within the context of Mark's Gospel.

The Cross and Radical Martyrdom

'And Jesus called to him the multitude, with his disciples and said to them, "If anyone would come after me, let him deny himself and take up his cross and follow me"' (Mark 8.34). In this saying addressed to the community, Jesus appears to make seeking execution a condition of being a disciple, a suggestion from which Derrett recoils.

---

gain', 204) points out, Paul considers himself to be the model for other Christians, and therefore his fate should not be separated from those members of his churches. In any case, there is no evidence that a special resurrection for martyrs in Christian thought had developed by Paul's time.

83. Barrett denies this interpretation 'on the basis of the other letters' (*Second Corinthians*, 158) though does not say which letters. However, as we have seen, this interpretation is most likely in the context of Paul's thought.

84. 2 Cor. 6.10.

> Take up one's cross, meaning one's peculiar cross, found in different forms (Mark 8.34
> par.; Matthew 10.38; Ev. Thomas 55; Luke 14.27), can hardly be an injunction to seek
> crucifixion. This prospect can recruit none but the neurotic. It calls no one to surrender
> to death in some cabbalistic ecstasy.[85]

Derrett instead understands the saying as a call to discipline, as a 'peculiar com-
mendation of asceticism', with no contemplation of martyrdom.[86] Of course, this
interpretation has a long history, no doubt influenced by Luke's version of the
instruction (9.23), where the insertion of καθ' ἡμέραν de-emphasizes the literal
sense of the saying.[87] Luke's focus is less on martyrdom than daily loyalty to
Jesus.[88]

Derrett's emphatic assertion that Jesus' call to take up the cross cannot be
taken seriously rests upon the notion that such an interpretation would demand
the early Christians to be 'neurotic'. We have already been alerted to the danger
of limiting our interpretations by what we understand to be the 'normal' Christian attitude to martyrdom and the consequent suppression of the stories of many
authentic Christian radical martyrs from scholarly 'orthodox' martyrological
discussion.

Although Davies and Allison consider a martyrological interpretation 'possible' for the logion,[89] their understanding of the saying as a call to suppress the
self sounds suspiciously modern:

> It is only through loss of life – that is, displacement of the ego from the centre of its
> universe with the accompanying willingness to give up personal ambition and even to
> suffer and, if need be, die for God's cause – that life … is gained.[90]

85. J.D.M. Derrett, 'Taking up cross and turning the other cheek (Mk 8.34; Mt 5.38–42; 10.38;
Lk 14.27; Gosp. Thom. 55)', in A. Harvey (ed.), *Alternative Approaches to New Testament Study*
(London: SPCK, 1985), 61–78 (61).
86. Derrett, 'Taking up Cross', 64. It is more an issue for Derrett of crucifying the body in order
to save the soul. M.D. Hooker (*The Gospel according to Saint Mark* [BNTC; London: A. & C. Black,
1992], 209), and R.H. Gundry (*Mark: A Commentary on His Apology for the Cross* [Grand Rapids:
Eerdmans, 1993], 435) also shy away from understanding the saying as a call to literal death. See also
D. Juel, *Master of Surprise* (Minneapolis: Fortress Press, 1992).
87. See R.N. Longenecker, 'Taking up the cross daily: discipleship in Luke–Acts', in R.N.
Longenecker (ed.), *Patterns of Discipleship in the New Testament* (Grand Rapids: Eerdmans, 1996),
50–76.
88. I.H. Marshall, *The Gospel of Luke: A Commentary on the Greek Text* (NIGTC; Grand Rapids:
Eerdmans, 1978), 373. See also J.A. Fitzmyer, *The Gospel according to St Luke* (2 vols; AB, 28,
28A; New York: Doubleday, 1981, 1985), 787–88. There does appear to be a move in Luke to
remove much of the references to suffering from the life of the Church, so that the persecution of Mk
4.17 is replaced by temptation at Lk. 8.13. Similarly persecution is omitted at 6.22–3; cf. Mt 5.10–12;
and *Gos. Thom.* 69a, 68. Disciples are also told that nothing will harm them at Lk. 17.19, and even in
the apocalyptic discourse, they are promised that not a hair on their heads perish (21.18), though this
has been taken as spiritual safety rather than physical safety by A. Plummer, *A Critical and
Exegetical Commentary on the Gospel according to St Luke* (ICC; Edinburgh: T&T Clark, 1922),
480; J.M. Creed, *The Gospel according to St Luke* (London: Macmillan, 1930), 256; and Marshall,
Luke, 769. For the opposite view, see L.T. Johnson, *The Gospel of Luke* (Sacra Pagina; Minnesota:
Liturgical Press, 1991), 323; and Fitzmyer, *Luke*, 1341.
89. W.D. Davies and D.C. Allison, *A Critical and Exegetical Commentary on the Gospel according to Saint Matthew* (ICC; 3 vols; Edinburgh: T&T Clark, 1988, 1991, 1997), 2.224.
90. Davies and Allison, *Matthew*, 2.671.

The question then is this: did Mark intend this saying in particular, and Jesus' call to discipleship in general, to be read as a call to martyrdom or a call to a particular kind of asceticism, or some form of middle road where discipleship might lead to the possibility of death? By examining the cross saying in its immediate context, and in the context of discipleship in the Gospel, I will demonstrate that Mark does in fact understand Jesus' followers to be participating in a cosmic conflict at the end of the eschatological age, and that death will be an inevitable result of following Jesus. So, for Mark, the call to discipleship, the call to follow after Jesus, is in effect a call to martyrdom.

Discipleship and Death

Mark 8.34–8 records a collection of five sayings outlining the conditions of discipleship.[91] Each statement builds a picture of what it means to be a disciple, as well as betraying some of the experiences of the Markan community,[92] culminating in the warning to remain faithful, despite the pressures around them (8.38). In the midst of suffering and persecution, a true disciple is called to renounce oneself (ἀπαρνησάσθω ἑαυτόν), and take up one's cross. Indeed, this is not an optional choice for would-be followers of Jesus. If anyone wishes to follow after Jesus (ὀπίσω … ἀκολουθεῖν), that is, to respond to the call that Jesus issues (cf. 1.17), then there are three conditions.

First, there is the renunciation of self. Secondly, disciples must take up their own cross (ἀράτω τὸν σταυρὸν αὐτοῦ) and finally, follow (ἀκολουθείτω) Jesus (8.34). Though this second call to follow appears tautological, it is not merely emphasis;[93] those who 'follow' without bearing their cross are not following at all. Importantly then, bearing a cross is not simply a *consequence* of being a disciple of Jesus – it is a *condition*.[94]

This interpretation is reinforced by the Q version of the saying (14.27):[95] 'The one who does not take one's cross and follow after me cannot be my disciple.'[96]

---

91. It seems likely that the sayings were originally independent, since they are now pasted together by the introductory word γάρ. This may be the work of Mark himself or of his source. See D.B. Taylor, *Mark's Gospel as Literature and History* (London: SCM Press, 1992), 203.

92. Bauckham's recent attack on the community hypotheses (R. Bauckham [ed.], *The Gospels for All Christians: Rethinking the Gospel Audiences* [Grand Rapids: Eerdmans, 1998]) has been convincingly refuted, in the case of Mark, by J. Marcus (*Mark 1–8*, AB, 27; New York: Doubleday, 2000), 25–8; and D.C. Sim, 'The gospels for all Christians?: a response to Richard Bauckham', *JSNT* 24.84 (2001), 3–27.

93. Hooker, *Mark*, 209.

94. The voluntary nature of embracing the road of suffering is highlighted by E. Best's observation (*Mark: The Gospel as Story* [Edinburgh: T&T Clark, 1983], 86) that people do not normally take up a cross, rather they are laid upon a victim.

95. J.M. Robinson, P. Hoffman and J.S. Kloppenborg (eds), *The Critical Edition of Q* (Hermeneia; Minneapolis: Fortress Press; Leuven: Peeters Publishers, 2000), 454–5.

96. Robinson, Hoffman and Kloppenborg (eds), *Q*, 454. Or '… is not worthy of me', following Mt. 10.37.

Those who fail to take up their cross simply *cannot* be disciples of Jesus.[97] The Q saying is linked with the notice that disciples must also hate (μισεῖ) family members in order to be worthy of Jesus (14.26).[98] The author of the *Gospel of Thomas*, either influenced by the canonical gospels,[99] or independently,[100] also demands hatred of family (*Gos. Thom.* 55 and 110).[101]

Therefore, in order to follow after Jesus, not only must the disciples leave everything – career, family and possessions (Mk 10.28; cf. 1.18, 20; 10.22) – Jesus also demands that they take up their crosses and follow him. The extent to which the call to death should be taken literally is somewhat muddied by the fact that the method of death, the cross, could be literal or figurative.[102] Put simply, do we find in this logion a call to follow Jesus to his death, and imitate him through martyrdom?

Significantly, there is no evidence that 'taking up the cross' was a meta-phorical phrase in currency with the meaning of self-denial in the first century.[103] Luke appears to be the first writer to use it in this way (9.23).[104] Therefore, we ought to understand the phrase, as it stands in Mark, as a call to literal death unless good reason can be found to read it otherwise. With this question in mind, we examine Mark's development of the theme of cosmic conflict.

Cosmic Conflict

In the Gospel of Mark, there are three passion predictions, each following a similar pattern. After each prediction of Jesus' death, the disciples respond with some form of misunderstanding. Jesus, in turn, responds with teaching about discipleship. Significantly, the third as well as the first block of teaching relates specifically to the deaths of followers of Jesus.[105] The first of these passion predictions takes place firmly within the context of a cosmic war that has been brewing since the opening of the Gospel. After skirmishes with Satan's forces in the form of exorcism,[106] Jesus confronts Satan directly over the issue of suffering and death.

97. Presumably, because Luke has already interpreted 'taking up the cross' proverbially (9.23), this later occurrence, in the context of his Gospel, can also be read figuratively.

98. Matthew has redacted the Q version for the less harsh, 'the one who loves father or mother more than me' (10.37). See Robinson, Hoffman and Kloppenborg (eds), *Q*, 452; Davies and Allison, *Matthew*, 2.221.

99. Davies and Allison, *Matthew*, 2.221.

100. S.J. Patterson, *The Gospel of Thomas and Jesus* (Sonoma: Polebridge Press, 1993), 44–5.

101. Thomas also preserves the link between hating family and taking up the cross (*Gos. Thom.* 55).

102. It is of course entirely possible that the original context of this well-preserved and almost certainly dominical saying was in an expectation of Jesus that his own disciples would be crucified alongside him. This important question cannot be explored here, though, if this were the case, the original setting of the saying would constitute a literal call to death and also the means of achieving it.

103. See O'Neill, 'Did Jesus teach?', 12.

104. Although Paul's use of καθ' ἡμέραν in 1 Cor. 15.31 incorporates both physical and meta-phorical suffering.

105. Mk 10.39 signals the martyrdoms of James and John.

106. The role of exorcism (especially 3.27) and Satan's conflict with the Church is explored by J.K. Riches, *Conflicting Mythologies: Identity Formations in the Gospels of Mark and Matthew* (Edinburgh: T&T Clark, 2001), 148–57.

Having correctly declared Jesus to be the Messiah, Peter baulks at what Jesus understands messiahship to entail: 'the Son of Man must undergo great suffering, and be rejected by the elders, the chief priests, and the scribes, and be killed, and after three days rise again' (8.31). Peter rebukes him, but is in turn rebuked by Jesus and declared to be from Satan (8.33). In this rebuke and counter-rebuke, Mark introduces a theme to be developed through the second half of the Gospel. Those who deny the road of suffering are not only unworthy to follow Jesus, they are in fact on the side of Satan and his legions.

Interestingly, not only does Jesus rebuke (ἐπιτίμησεν) Peter/Satan (8.33), but Satan/Peter attempts to rebuke (ἤρξατο ἐπιτιμᾶν) Jesus (8.32).[107] So far in the Gospel, the verb ἐπιτιμάω has been used by Jesus to silence demonic activity. Jesus' first healing involved the rebuke (ἐπιτίμησεν) of an unclean spirit (1.25) who knew who Jesus was. Similarly, many demons are rebuked (ἐπιτίμα) in a Markan summary, again to prevent them from disclosing his identity (3.12).

The next time we find the verb, Jesus is rebuking (ἐπιτίμησεν) the elements of the storm (4.39), a miracle rich in demonic imagery[108] that leaves his disciples wondering about his identity (4.41). Therefore, the verb appears to be used in the context of supernatural conflict,[109] and at this crucial juncture in the Gospel – the point where Jesus declares his hand, embracing the way of suffering and death – Satan, through Peter, launches an assault against Jesus by attempting to 'exorcize' him.[110] However, Satan, who was last seen tempting Jesus in the desert after another divine disclosure of his identity (1.14–15),[111] is thwarted by Jesus'

107. Demons claiming to know who Jesus was (such as 1.24) may also be part of a demonic counter-attack strategy (see Marcus, *Mark*, 187–8). However, in this confrontation, Satan through Peter attacks first through the powerful rebuke.

108. Although some commentators have variously interpreted the stilling of the storm as evidence of a Hellenistic divine man typology (C.E.B. Cranfield, *The Gospel according to St. Mark* [Cambridge: Cambridge University Press, 1959], 174), a Psalmic motif of divine control of the sea (D.E. Nineham, *The Gospel of St. Mark* [Middlesex: Penguin Books, 1963], 146; B.F. Batto, 'The sleeping god: an ancient Near Eastern motif of divine sovereignty', *Biblion* 68 [1987], 153–77), or evidence of an Exodus of Jonah typology (Hooker, *Mark*, 138), the facts that the rebuke is accompanied by the verb φιμόω, which itself occurs only in demonic encounter (1.25); that the sea was a traditional location of monsters and a place associated with evil (Dan. 7.2–3; Rev. 13.1; cf. Rev. 21.1); and that this pericope is followed by the healing of the Gerasene demoniac (5.1–20), where the demons, in the bodies of pigs, return to the sea, where they belong, suggests that the stilling of the storm should be interpreted within the 'Jewish apocalyptic world of exorcisms and demons' (W.R. Stegner, 'Jesus' walking on the water: Mark 6.45–52', in C.A. Evans and R. Stegner [eds], *The Gospels and the Scriptures of Israel* [Sheffield: Sheffield Academic Press, 1994], 212–34 [231]).

109. Of the three other occurrences of ἐπιτιμάω, only one is further rebuke of a demon by Jesus (9.25). The other two are rebukes on the mouths of humans. First, the disciples rebuke (ἐπιτίμησαν) those who brought their children to Jesus (10.13), a rebuke which Jesus opposes. The final occurrence is also interesting; it is the crowd who rebuke (ἐπιτίμων), and tell blind Bartimaeus to be silent, who, ironically, recognizes Jesus as the 'Son of David' despite his disability (10.48–9).

110. The full force of the exorcistic verb should be retained here. What we witness in this instance is a clash of cosmic powers with Satan striking first.

111. Unlike Mark, Matthew makes explicit his understanding of Peter's confession as coming from God (16.17): 'Blessed are you, Simon son of Jonah. For flesh and blood has not revealed this to you, but my Father in heaven'. Compare God's revelation of Jesus at the transfiguration, echoing the

counter-rebuke. Jesus' power again proves to be stronger than Satan and his legions. The nearness of the Kingdom has been felt on earth through the skirmishes between Jesus and Satan, but Jesus always proves the more effective, for he is the powerful one who has already bound the strong man (3.27). Crucially, the reappearance of Satan at this point in the narrative emphasizes Mark's critical point: opposition to Jesus' mission to embrace the cross is, literally, Satanic.

In Mark's eschatological crisis, therefore, there is a distinct choice to be made: to be on the side of God/Jesus, or on the side of Satan, determined by the acceptance or rejection of the way of the cross. Significantly, when Peter rejected the way of suffering, he was associated with Satan – an antagonist against God. Jesus explicitly paralleled the thoughts of Satan and 'men' when he told Peter that his satanic outburst against God placed him on the side of men (8.33). It is clear that for Mark, the realm of Satan and the realm of humanity are on the same side against God.

It is in the satanic world of men that the eschatological decision of whether one is an insider or an outsider is to be made; the backdrop to this drama is 'this adulterous and sinful generation' (τῇ γενεᾷ ταύτῃ τῇ μοιχαλίδι καὶ ἁμαρτωλῷ; 8.38). Therefore, the world is divided into two distinct camps: those on the side of Jesus and the gospel (8.35), who are prepared to lose their lives for the sake of Jesus, through taking up their cross, embracing suffering and death,[112] and those who belong to Satan, the ones who cling to their lives and renounce the way of suffering and death. The realms of Satan and men form an alliance against Jesus and comprise 'this sinful generation'. By the last verse of ch. 8, the eschatological battle lines have been drawn; Jesus sets out on the way to the cross, and Mark's readers have to decide whether they are with Satan or with Jesus in the ensuing cosmic conflict.

Following Jesus

Central to the Gospel of Mark is the section where Jesus journeys on the way to Jerusalem (8.22–10.52).[113] It is significant that at the outset of this journey, on the way towards death, Jesus' identity is made known through Peter's confession (8.29). It is as the Christ that Jesus makes this journey; it is in fulfilment of his messianic office that he will go to his death.[114] In emphasizing this point, Jesus

words from the baptismal scene, 'This is my Beloved Son' (Mk. 9.7; 1.11). This time the disciples also hear the words. Although they are commanded to silence, there are three important differences from the injunction at Cesarea. First, they are commanded not to say of what they have seen, rather than heard. In the second instance, the time of silence is limited; they may speak after the resurrection and, thirdly, they are instructed (διεστείλατο, 9.9) rather than rebuked.

112. The 'Elect' of 13.30.

113. For an exploration of the significance of this section in the Gospel, see, among others, J. Marcus, *The Way of the Lord: Christological Exegesis of the Old Testament in the Gospel of Mark* (Edinburgh: T&T Clark, 1993).

114. It is significant that the divine recognition of Jesus as God's Son, found at the baptism (1.11) and transfiguration (9.7), is finally revealed to a human being at the crucifixion, where the centurion utters, 'Truly, this man was the Son of God' (15.39). Although the mocking by the Roman soldiers (15.16–20) could be seen as demonic recognition, in that they correctly, though unknowingly,

not only predicts his own suffering and death, but also outlines the path for those who follow after him. Disciples will follow after him on the road of suffering and death by taking up their crosses and following on (8.34). The fate of Jesus prefigures the fate of true disciples.[115] As Jesus will head to Jerusalem and carry his cross, so too disciples, if they are to follow on behind, will need to take up their own cross.

The passion of Jesus, described in chs 14–15, culminating in the crucifixion, is described as an apocalyptic event. For Mark, 'Jesus' passion is an eschatological battle.'[116] Discipleship in the gospel of Mark is given an apocalyptic orientation and related to the coming eschatological age. This point is emphasized by the positioning of the apocalyptic discourse immediately prior to the passion, where the themes of the *eschaton*, insiders and outsiders, discipleship and death form a potent matrix.

That the disciples also face the same fate as their master is emphasized by a series of interesting parallels to be found between the passion narrative and the apocalyptic discourse of ch. 13;[117] these may be outlined thus:

Παραδίδωμι signals the fate of the followers of Jesus 13.9, 11–12.	Παραδίδωμι is also used in connection with Jesus on ten occasions.[118]
13.2: Before the end comes the temple will be destroyed.	15.38: The veil of the temple is rent, signifying the destruction of the temple.[119]

proclaim Jesus to be the 'King of Israel', there is no compelling reason to follow Juel's (*Master of Surprise*, 74 n. 7) assertion that the affirmation ought to be taken as a taunt, 'Sure, this was God's Son'. He believes 'the centurion plays a role assigned to all Jesus' enemies: they speak the truth in mockery, thus providing for the reader ironic testimony to the truth'. Granted, irony is a prominent theme in the Gospel of Mark. Nonetheless, for Mark, the crucifixion is precisely the moment where Jesus has fulfilled his Messianic potential. He has carried his cross and not attempted to save his life. Furthermore, the centurion's response immediately follows notice of the Temple curtain being torn in two, symbolizing that God has left the Temple and can now be recognized by Gentiles. It is precisely at this moment, with this eschatological rending, coupled with apocalyptic darkness, that we are ready to hear an affirmation of Jesus' divine Sonship.

115. See R. Tannehill, 'The disciples in Mark: the function of a narrative role', *JR* 57 (1977), 386–405; and 'The Gospel of Mark as narrative Christology', *Semeia* 16 (1979), 57–95. Interestingly *Gos. Thom.* 55 presents taking up the cross as following Jesus' example: '[Whoever] will not take up one's cross as I do, will not be worthy of me'. However, R. Valantasis (*The Gospel of Thomas* [New Testament Readings; London/New York: Routledge, 1997], 132–3) notes that in the context of Thomas's theology, the 'cross' is not likely to refer to physical death, but rather 'the world', which, following Jesus' example, disciples would have to suffer before removing it like a garment.

116. Marcus, *Way*, 156.

117. It was R.H. Lightfoot who first made the observation in *The Gospel Message of St Mark* (Cambridge: Cambridge University Press, 1950), 48–59. See also Allison, *End of the Ages*, 36–9; and T.J. Geddert, *Watchwords: Mark 13 in Markan Eschatology* (Sheffield: Sheffield Academic Press, 1989), 89–92. Both Allison and Geddert demonstrate the parallels with the apocalyptic discourse found in Zechariah 9–14, as does Marcus (*Way*, 154–6), who postulates that early Christians read Zechariah 9–14 as a unit, because the New Testament has many references to these chapters of the prophet, but little from the first eight chapters.

118. These are: 14.10, 11, 18, 21, 41, 42, 44; 15.1, 10, 15.

119. The tearing of the Temple veil surely signifies in some sense the destruction or, at the very least, the passing away of the Temple as the locus of God's activity. See Allison, *End of the Ages*, 37.

13.12–13: 'Brother will betray brother to death' (παραδώσει ἀδελφὸς ἀδελφὸν εἰς θάνατον) and even close family ties will be broken by betrayal.

13.14–16: The end will be a time of flight (φεύγω) when the desecrating sacrilege is set up.

13.24: After the time of tribulation 'the sun will be darkened (ὁ ἥλιος σκοτισθήσεται), and the moon will not give its light, and the stars will be falling from the heaven'. It will be a time of cosmic darkness.

13.26: 'And then they will see the Son of Man coming in the clouds with great power and glory' (καὶ τότε ὄψονται τὸν υἱὸν τοῦ ἀνθρώπου ἐρχόμενον ἐν νεφέλαις μετὰ δυνάμεως πολλῆς καὶ δόξης).

13.32: No-one knows the day or the hour (τῆς ὥρας).

13.33: Disciples are urged to keep awake (ἀγρυπνεῖτε) and watch (βλέπετε).[122]

13.35: 'You do not know when the master will come ... in the evening (ὀψέ), at midnight (μεσονύκτιον), or at cockcrow (ἀλεκτοροφωνίας) or in the morning (πρωΐ)'.

13.36: True servants should be on their guard, lest, at the end, their master come (ἐλθών) and find (εὕρῃ) them sleeping (καθεύδοντας).

14.10, 20, 43: Mark stresses that Judas is 'one of the Twelve' (ὁ εἷς τῶν δώδεκα).

14.50: Jesus' disciples run away (φεύγω).
14.52: The young man fled (φεύγω) away naked at the arrest of Jesus.

15.33: At the crucifixion 'there was darkness (σκότος ἐγένετο) over all the land'. This should certainly be interpreted as a cosmic and apocalyptic darkness.[120]

14.62: 'You will see the Son of Man seated at the right hand of Power and coming with the clouds of heaven' (καὶ ὄψεσθε τὸν υἱὸν τοῦ ἀνθρώπου ἐκ δεξιῶν καθήμενον τῆς δυνάμεως καὶ ἐρχόμενον μετὰ τῶν νεφελῶν τοῦ οὐρανοῦ).

14.35: In the Gethsemane scene, Jesus prays that the hour (ἡ ὥρα) might pass.[121]

14.34, 37–8: The disciples are told to watch (γρηγορεῖτε)[123] and pray that they might not enter into temptation, but they fall asleep. Mark arranges the structure of the passion around these time periods; see 14.17 (καὶ ὀψίας γενομένης); 14.72 (ἀλέκτωρ ἐφώνησεν); and 15.1 (καὶ εὐθὺς πρωΐ).[124]

14.37: Jesus comes (ἔρχεται) and finds (εὑρίσκει) his disciples sleeping (καθεύδοντας); 14.40 has the same ἐλθών–εὗρεν–καθεύδοντας pattern.

---

120. Hooker (*Mark*, 375–6) is correct when she insists that attempts to explain the darkness by some natural phenomenon miss the point; the darkness, rather, symbolizes 'the terrible nature of what is taking place'. She understands the verse in the light of a prophecy such as Amos 8.9, 'On that day ... I will make the sun go down at noon and darken the earth in broad daylight'. She further observes, 'the darkness at midday symbolises the judgement that comes upon the land of Israel with the rejection of Israel's king'.

121. Lightfoot (*St Mark*, 53) observes, 'Clearly the hour has not yet arrived in all its fullness; and there is a possibility that it may pass'.

122. That many manuscripts read ἀγρυπνεῖτε καὶ προσεύχεσθε at 13.33 (for example, ℵ A C L W Δ Ψ 0223) demonstrate an early awareness of the parallels between the Passion and the apocalyptic discourse.

123. T.J. Geddert (*Watchwords*, 90) has noted that the verb 'to watch' has been served exclusively by βλέπω throughout the Gospel up until 13.33. After this point, including three times in the remainder of the apocalyptic discourse, γρηγορέω is used exclusively. A further parallel between these two sections is that the imperative γρηγορεῖτε is used twice at the conclusion of the discourse (13.35, 36) and in Gethsemane (14.34, 38).

124. 'The Four Watch Schema of the passion night' is explored at some length by Geddert, *Watchwords*, 94–111.

Therefore, many aspects of the passion are anticipated in the apocalyptic discourse. However, if the fate of Jesus is anticipated in the apocalyptic discourse, the discourse itself concerns what will happen to disciples of Jesus. And so, as we have already observed, the fate of Jesus and that of his followers are closely entwined. Within ch. 13, one block of teaching in particular focuses on what will happen to followers of Jesus:

> But take heed for yourselves; for they will deliver you up to councils; and you will be beaten in synagogues; and you will stand before governors and kings for my sake, to bear testimony before them. And the gospel must first be preached to all nations. And when they bring you to trial and deliver you up, do not be anxious beforehand what you are to say; but say whatever is given to you in that hour, for it is not you who speaks but the Holy Spirit. And brother will deliver up his brother to death, and the father his child, and children will rise against parents and have them put to death; and you will be hated by all for my name's sake. But the one enduring to the end will be saved. (13.9–13)

Like Jesus, his followers will stand before authorities[125] and be called to bear witness (13.9). It is through the testimony of disciples that the good news will be preached (13.10), and it is on account of that gospel that followers of Jesus will be brought to trial (13.11). In Mark's Gospel, family ties will mean nothing, and followers will endure betrayal, hatred and death. This is what it means for disciples to take up their cross and follow after Jesus. They will walk the road of Jesus' suffering, and share in his experience of rejection, betrayal, trial and death.[126]

Earlier in Mark, Jesus had promised that those who lose their lives for his sake and for the gospel (ἕνεκεν ἐμοῦ καὶ τοῦ εὐαγγελίου) will save it (8.35), and here, in ch. 13, we find the setting in which lives will be lost for the gospel (εὐαγγέλιον, 13.10) and for the sake of Jesus (ἕνεκεν ἐμοῦ, 13.9; διὰ τὸ ὄνομά μου, 13.13). The calling to discipleship reaches its climax in the eschatological hour (ὥρᾳ, 13.11), when those who follow after Jesus stand trial for the sake of the gospel and their master. It is for this time that the call to renounce self and let go of one's life is made. These are the experiences Mark expects his readers to face and conquer. Mark's call to discipleship does indeed contain a call to embrace martyrdom.

Like other occasions where persecution appears to lie behind the text, Jesus issues a call to be free from worry, anxiety and fear (13.11). Even in the throws of persecution and trial, even before governors and kings, Mark assures his readers that they need not worry about what testimony to give, for the Holy Spirit will give them the words to speak (13.11). It is precisely for this situation that the stern warning contained in 8.38 is given. And just as that warning is offset by an antithetical eschatological promise (9.1), so too at this juncture is found another

---

125. That it is both Jewish and Gentile authorities probably owes more to the parallelism between the discourse and the Passion narrative, than the actual situation in which Mark's readers find themselves.

126. Compare the experiences of the Church in Acts, where followers are threatened (4.21, 29), conspired against (9.23, 29; 14.5), mocked and vilified (13.5; 17.32; 18.6; 19.23–41; 21.27–36), arrested (4.3; 6.12; 8.3; 16.24; 26.29; 28.20), brought before councils (5.27; 22.30–23.10; 24.1; 25.23), flogged (5.40; 16.23; 22.19, 24), and killed (7.54–60; 12.1–2; 14.19).

such promise: the one who endures hatred for the name (διὰ τὸ ὄνομά μου) to the end (εἰς τέλος)[127] will be saved (13.13).

The conditions of discipleship have been set out. Mark has shown that true disciples must follow Jesus on the road to suffering. They must endure persecution, trials before governors, condemnation and abuse, betrayal and, ultimately, death, just as their master had before them; Jesus is the model par excellence of discipleship.

Death and Life

One motivation for following Jesus to death is eschatological reward (13.13), or at least the avoidance of eschatological punishment (8.38). However, just as we witnessed the dramatic and startling deconstruction of the categories of life and death in our second-century martyrological texts, enabling the Christians to interpret death as life and life as death, so too we find precisely this idea in the cross sayings.

The conclusion that literal death (even if the cross part is itself metaphorical) is called for in the cross saying (8.34) is strengthened by the next logion concerning saving and losing life (8.35),[128] coupled with the realistic trial accounts of 13.9–13 discussed above. The two sayings are linked by death – literal death, and that this is the traditional interpretation of 8.34 is made more likely by the fact that the link between carrying the cross and saving and losing life is found in Q, preserved by Matthew (10.38–9).[129]

However early this connection was made, in both of these traditions as they now stand, the second saying illuminates how the first is to be understood.[130] Taking up a cross in 8.34 is equated with losing life in 8.35. The choice is plain, if someone wants to follow Jesus, he or she must take up the cross and follow after Jesus on the road of suffering and death. This means losing one's life for Jesus' sake and for the sake of the gospel (8.36), resulting in life. Conversely, one may choose not to take up the cross, and fail to follow Jesus on the way to death. Such a person may save their own earthly life, but the ultimate consequence of doing so will be to forfeit their eschatological existence.

Verses 36–8 expand on the consequences of rejecting the road of suffering, perhaps indicating that Mark was concerned that members of his community were contemplating following the Way of Satan (the rejection of the road of suffering), rather than the Way of Jesus.[131] Those who manage to save their lives,

127. Both the end of one's life and the End of the Age are possible.

128. See also Q 12.4–5, where there is the distinction between the one able to kill the body and God who can destroy the soul. Compare *T. Job* 20.3, where the Devil has permission to harm Job's σῶμα but not his ψυχή.

129. Q 17.33 follows Q 14.26–7 in Robinson, Hoffman and Kloppenborg (eds), *Q. Luke*, who has already spiritualized the cross saying, separates the sayings (14.27; 17.33).

130. That the logia were connected at a very early stage is advanced by F. Bovon, *A Commentary on the Gospel of Luke 1.1–9.50* (trans. C.M. Thomson; Hermeneia; Minneapolis: Fortress Press, 2002), 365 n. 2. Davies and Allison (*Matthew*, 2.223) suggest the link may go back to Jesus.

131. B.M.F. van Iersel, 'Failed followers in Mark: Mark 13.12 as a key for the identification of the intended readers', *CBQ* 58 (1996), 244–63, advances the thesis that the Gospel was written to

even if they should manage to gain the whole world, will find that it is, in the end, a poor transaction, for they will lose their salvation (8.36).

Secondly, even if they gain the world, they will not be able to buy back their lives (8.37). The decision one makes appears to have permanent consequences. Life is won by laying it down for the sake of Jesus and the gospel, through carrying the cross and following after the Christ, and not through wealth or riches.[132] To those who would want to save their lives in this world, refusing to take up their cross, a dire warning is given. Those who are ashamed of Jesus' words, rejecting the call to take up their cross, and denying Jesus in time of trial, will in turn be rejected in the age to come, when the Son of Man comes in glory with all the holy angels (8.38). The call to discipleship, as we have seen, has been placed in the context of eschatological crisis. The decision whether or not to take up the cross is set in the context of eschatological judgement.

Losing one's life, interpreted as gaining life, is a crucial component in the theology of radical martyrdom. The only mechanism for saving one's life is to deny under pressure, and so escape execution. In martyrological discourse, this saving of one's life is interpreted as death, and conversely losing life is interpreted as gaining life. This exact formulation found in Mark 8.35–6, suggests that the cross saying in 8.34 should be read as calling for disciples to embrace death. The only true disciples of Jesus are those who follow with a cross. Those who refuse to embrace the way of suffering and death are not worthy of Jesus. Moreover, 8.38 suggests such a *Sitz im Leben* where followers will be called upon either to confess or deny Jesus. Under questioning, those who do not deny themselves, and instead deny Jesus, will save their earthly life, but become dead, and Jesus will in turn deny them at the climax of the eschatological age.

Confessing and Denying in the New Testament

Similar trial situations with the choice between confession and denial are suggested by other New Testament texts. Just as Mk 8.38 and 13.9–13 point to a

reinstate Christians who had denied under the Neronic persecutions, using the disciples as models of reinstated failures. However, aside from it being difficult to locate the Gospel as precisely as Rome (Hooker [*Mark*, 7–8] locates the Gospel 'somewhere in the Roman Empire; Marcus [*Mark*, 30–7] advances Syria as the locale), Mark's strong warnings against denial seem to point away from this interpretation. Admittedly, there is great tension in the Gospel with Mark issuing such strong irrevocable penalties for denying, and then not only having all the disciples desert, but the chief disciple clearly fail the challenge laid down by 8.34–8. He does not deny self, but denies Jesus. He saves his life, and therefore should lose it. If indeed it was Mark's intention to restore Peter and the others, leaving aside the question of whether this mirrors a real response to Christian desertion during the Neronic persecution, then it is strange that he does it so ambiguously with the women leaving the tomb, saying nothing (16.7–8), thereby apparently thwarting the restoration promised in 14.28. How to resolve this tension is beyond the scope of this project.

132. Cf. Mk 10.17–22, where a rich young man is invited to follow Jesus, but is impeded by his wealth. He could not even begin to follow on the road of suffering after Jesus, and so forfeited his life, which his wealth will not be able to buy back. To begin the journey on the Way of Jesus, followers must, as Peter protests (10.28), be prepared to give up everything, for that road leads to persecutions (10.30) and death.

situation where followers of Christ must renounce themselves rather than Christ, this would appear to be the most satisfactory background to the traditional saying[133] quoted at 2 Tim. 2.11–13: 'The saying is sure: If we have died with him, we shall also live with him; if we endure, we shall also reign with him; *if we deny him, he will also deny us* …' (emphasis added). Interestingly, this saying is preceded by the Pastor telling of Paul's endurance of sufferings for the gospel, and for the sake of the elect (2.8–10). Therefore, the unit is put in the context of suffering for the gospel. As with Mk 8.34–8, potential for denying Jesus or self is put alongside material about death and life, in the case of the Pastor, the Pauline theological concept of dying and living with Christ. Therefore in 2 Timothy, there gathers a cluster of concepts important for our study: a persecution and trial *Sitz im Leben*, with the opportunity to deny self or Jesus; participation in Christ; suffering; and the juxtaposition of life and death.

Denying and confessing Jesus also occurs in 1 Jn 2.22–4, where the relationship with the Father depends on whether one confesses or denies Jesus. In a strongly dualistic epistle,[134] set in the shadow of the last days (2.18), those who deny are in league with the anti-Christ. Those who confess Jesus have life (2.25), and, in an echo of Mk 8.38, there will be a contrast between those who will face the last day with confidence and those who will 'shrink with shame' (1 Jn 2.28). Believers may be called to lay down their lives for the brothers (3.16), which Brown takes as a possible allusion to martyrdom.[135] Edwards has taken the intriguing 'sin leading to death' (5.16) in conjunction with the exhortation to keep away from idols (5.21) as reference to a possible martyrological setting, where confessing Jesus would win eternal life, but denying by sacrificing to idols would constitute the sin leading to death.[136]

Hebrews 6.4–6 is another possible place where a trial setting may be indicated:

> For it is impossible to restore again to repentance those who have once been enlightened, who have tasted the heavenly gift, and have become partakers of the Holy Spirit, and have tasted the goodness of the word of God and the powers of the age to come, if they then commit apostasy, since they crucify the Son of God on their own account and hold him up to contempt.

Although the recipients of the epistle have not yet resisted to the point of shedding blood (12.4), suffering lies behind most of the letter. The harsh saying about the impossibility of redemption after apostasy has caused difficulties for interpreters, but should be allowed to stand,[137] since the threat is repeated at 10.26–31;

---

133. The introductory formula, 'the saying is sure', normally introduces and endorses traditional material (Collins, *1 & 2 Timothy*, 223–4). However, Marshall (*Pastoral Epistles*, 739) claims that phrase simply highlights an authoritative saying, not necessarily unoriginal.

134. Those outside of the community are reckoned to be τὰ τέκνα τοῦ διαβόλου (3.10).

135. R.E. Brown, *The Epistles of John* (AB, 30; New York: Doubleday, 1982), 449.

136. M.J. Edwards, 'Martyrdom in the First Epistle of John', *NovT* 31 (1989), 164–71. For other possibilities, see Brown, *Epistles of John*, 615–19.

137. H.W. Attridge, *A Commentary on the Epistle to the Hebrews* (Hermeneia; Philadelphia: Fortress Press, 1989), 167. Attridge devotes an excursus to the impossibility of repentance for apostates. See also C.R. Koester, *Hebrews* (AB, 38; New York: Doubleday, 2001), 318–23.

and again at 12.15–17. It may also find an echo in the unpardonable sin in the gospels.[138]

Interestingly, after the second of these threats, the author asks his recipients to remember former days when they 'endured a hard struggle with sufferings, sometimes being publicly exposed to abuse and afflictions' (10.32–3). The author asks them not to throw away their confidence, and indicates they will need continued endurance (11.35–6). Moreover, as well as the model of faith offered by those who have been martyred (11.35–40), the writer exhorts his readers to go and suffer in the way Jesus did: 'So Jesus also suffered outside the city in order to sanctify the people through his own blood. Therefore let us go forth to him outside the camp, and *bear the abuse he endured*' (13.12–13; emphasis added). Coming at the end of the letter, this exhortation implies movement for the readers.[139] The command is to go out and suffer, following the example of Jesus and the heroes of faith, especially the martyrs, who come at the climax of the list of faithful heroes. Now is the time for Church members who have not yet endured to the point of spilling their blood to do so, and in this context, the triple warning against apostasy becomes explicable.[140] Indeed, as Attridge observes, the call to go out of the camp is like Jesus' call to take up the cross.[141] Though he does not develop this point, the themes of following Jesus' example on the road of suffering, the possibility of death and the warning against denial are shared with Mk 8.34–8.

Furthermore, the author of Hebrews then goes on to contrast the two kinds of lives available to Christians: life in the earthly city, in which they do not belong, compared to the life in the city of God to come after death (13.14), constituting his own version of the life and death deconstruction found in our radical martyrological literature. Therefore, we find in various places echoes of the call to take up the cross, deny self and follow Jesus on the road to death.

Mark's version issues to his readers a radical challenge to martyrdom as a condition of discipleship. Though this call is spiritualized in Luke, we find in the first Gospel practically all of the theological raw materials for the construction of the world-view that made radical martyrdom possible in the second century. Only one aspect is missing. Whereas suffering and death helps the individual to gain an eschatological reward and a personal victory in the cosmic conflict, we do not find development of the Pauline theme that the martyrs actually contribute to the war effort. However, we do not have to look outside the New Testament for this pillar to find mature form. We will find this final piece of the puzzle in the Apocalypse.

The Apocalypse: A Martyr Charter

We have seen in our New Testament survey the development of important theological ideas from which the world-view of the radical martyrs would be

138. Mk 3.29//Mt. 12.32//Lk. 12.10. However, for problems with this interpretation, see Koester, *Hebrews*, 319 n. 181.

139. Attridge, *Hebrews*, 398.

140. Koester in his discussion of the possible meanings of 6.4–6 (*Hebrews*, 318–23) makes no mention of this possibility.

141. Attridge, *Hebrews*, 399.

constructed. We turn now to the Apocalypse, where, as I shall show, radical martyrdom is found in a developed form. First, we examine the expectation and achievement of martyrdom, before exploring the familiar martyrological themes of cosmic conflict, life as death, following the example of Jesus, and participation in Christ's victory.

Despite a lack of State persecution, John expected that his people would suffer persecution at the hands of 'Babylon'. In fact, he anticipates that there would be loss of life.[142] But these would be deaths with a purpose. John reinterprets death in such a way that not only did he offer Christians a reason to undergo martyrdom when the opportunity presented itself, he offered his Christian readers/ hearers a radical new way of understanding Christian death, so that *seeking* opportunities for martyrdom would seem desirable.

The Apocalypse sets up an alternative symbolic universe that encourages the Christian communities to which it was written to take control of their own deaths. Furthermore, martyrdom, according to John, is the most effective method of not only participating in but also contributing to the final victory of the Lamb. Crucial to John's understanding of martyrdom is the tableau of the souls under the altar, presented at the opening of the fifth seal (6.9).

> When he [the Lamb] opened the fifth seal, I saw under the altar the souls (ψυχάς) of those who had been slain for the word of God and for the witness they had borne (τὴν μαρτυρίαν ἣν εἶχον); they cried out with a loud voice, 'O sovereign Lord, holy and true, how long before you will judge and avenge our blood on those who dwell on the earth?'[143] They were each given a white robe and told to rest a little longer, until the number of their fellow servants and their brethren should be complete, who had been killed as they themselves had been. (Rev. 6.9–11)

In this vision, several elements of John's understanding of Christian martyrdom become clear. Most importantly, John knows that there will be more martyrs. The answer to the souls' question – how long it will be until Christ will come in judgement – is crucially and inextricably linked to the number of future martyrs. There is a set number that must be completed; judgement cannot be executed upon the inhabitants of the earth until the full number of martyrs is slain.

Moreover, this number is to be completed soon, for the souls under the altar are told to rest only a little while longer (ἔτι χρόνον μικρόν). The length of delay is dependent on how quickly the number of martyrs can be completed, for the full number of martyrs must be completed before final judgement can be initiated.[144] The cry for justice from those souls under the altar can be answered

---

142. So, see for example, γίνου πιστὸς ἄχρι θανάτου (2.10). Antipas, who was martyred was also called faithful (πιστός) to death (2.13). See also 12.10; 13.7; and 14.13 for hints that John expects more deaths.

143. Here the Markan idea that Satan controls the realm of men is found in the phrase τῶν κατοικούντων τῶν ἐπὶ τῆς γῆς, which occurs nine times in the Apocalypse, always negatively (Aune, *Revelation*, 410). P. Minear (*I Saw a New Earth: An Introduction to the Visions of the Apocalypse* [Washington: Corpus, 1968], 261–9) observes it is synonymous with Beast worshippers. In Qumran, the dwellers on the earth are opposed to the army of the holy ones (1QH 8.19–36).

144. *Pace* J.M. Ford (*Revelation* [AB, 38; New York: Doubleday, 1975], 111), who writes, 'In Christian apocalypses it is not the completion of the martyrs' role, but the coming of Christ which

only so long as other Christians present themselves for martyrdom. And so, this interesting tableau becomes a critical evangelical call to John's community. Martyrs are needed in order to bring about God's judgement, and from where will these martyrs come if not from the communities that hear John's words? *They* must fill up the number of martyrs if they are to be faithful witnesses. This is their task, their responsibility and their calling.

Faithfulness to Death

Martyrdom, for John, is the result of faithful witnessing. Those who had been slain were killed for the word of God and the witness they held. Christians are called to be witnesses, but faithful witness will result in death, just as in the case of Antipas, described by the risen Christ as ὁ μάρτυς μου ὁ πιστός μου (2.13). The content of this witness is 'the word of God and the testimony of Jesus Christ' (τὸν λόγον τοῦ θεοῦ καὶ τὴν μαρτυρίαν Ἰησοῦ Χριστοῦ); the word and testimony that John is witnessing to in the writing of his vision (1.2). It is his witnessing to the same word and testimony (τὸν λόγον τοῦ θεοῦ καὶ τὴν μαρτυρίαν Ἰησοῦ) that has led to his exile on the island of Patmos (1.9). Similarly, it was holding to this word and testimony (τὸν λόγον τοῦ θεοῦ καὶ ... τὴν μαρτυρίαν ἣν εἶχον) that led to the deaths of the souls under the altar (6.9),[145] just as holding onto the word and testimony (τὴν μαρτυρίαν Ἰησοῦ καὶ...τὸν λόγον τοῦ θεοῦ) will result in those souls being joined by others, including those who will be beheaded for the witness and the word (20.4).

The Apocalypse is addressed to seven churches, and rather than satisfy the future reader's curiosity of what will unfold in the future, the Apocalypse was written to specific groups of people in order to effect a certain reaction.[146] The opening letters, with their praise and criticism, enable the reader right at the outset of the book of Revelation to ascertain the kinds of action John expects of Christians. Central to John's message is that his followers be faithful witnesses.

Antipas is singled out among the seven churches (2.13) as one whose faithful witness led to his death at the hands of Satan (Σατανᾶς). Confessing and denying are also linked to Antipas' death, for he died when the church was holding fast to Jesus' name (κρατεῖς τὸ ὄνομά μου), and the fact that they did not deny

brings the righteous their full reward'. For this idea in the *Martyr Acts* and in other apocalypses, see above, 86–7.

145. That the testimony for which the souls under the altar have been slain is not specified as Ἰησοῦ has led A. Feuillet ('Les martyrs de l'humanitié et l'agneau égorgé: une interprétation nouvelle de la prière des égorgés en Ap 6,9–11', *NTR* 99 [1977], 189–207) among others, to conclude that the martyrs here are pre-Christian, slain for religious truth in the traditions contained in Mt. 23.31–5; and Heb. 11.4; 12.24. However, in Rev. 12.11, although the object of their testimony is not mentioned, clearly they are Christians. Though not precluding the possibility that the martyrs include the pre-Christian dead, they should be understood to refer to Christian martyrs, fellow servants of those Christian communities on earth, not yet having undergone martyrdom to join them. F.J. Murphy (*Fallen Is Babylon: The Revelation to John* [Pennsylvania: Trinity Press International, 1998], 289) identifies them as the Christians slain under Nero.

146. Garrow, *Revelation*, 110.

faith in Jesus is singled out for praise (οὐκ ἠρνήσω τὴν πίστιν μου, 2.13). Similarly, holding fast to what they have in the face of Satan and others' unfaithfulness, as well as confession rather than denial, are crucial elements in the messages to the churches of Thyatira (ὃ ἔχετε κρατήσατε, 2.25) and Philadelphia (κράτει ὃ ἔχεις, 3.11). The church in Philadelphia has little power, yet has remained faithful to their testimony by keeping Jesus' word and not denying his name (ἐτήρησάς μου τὸν λόγον καὶ οὐκ ἠρνήσω τὸ ὄνομά μου, 3.8). Further rich martyrological language occurs in their patient endurance (ὑπομονῆς); if they hold onto what they have until Christ comes, no one will seize their crown (στέφανος, 3.11).

Crowns, as we have seen, are an eschatological reward given especially to those who undergo martyrdom,[147] and this is also the case in the Apocalypse. When John writes to the church in Smyrna (2.10), he tells them that they are about to suffer and be thrown into prison by the devil (ὁ διάβολος), and that they may be tested (πειρασθῆτε).[148] On this occasion, the call to faithfulness is made explicit; it is a call to be faithful to death (γίνου πιστὸς ἄχρι θανάτου, 2.10), with the reward of the crown of life (τὸν στέφανον τῆς ζωῆς). Being faithful to death is, therefore, equated with conquering (2.11), and the one who conquers will not be harmed by the second death. Remaining faithful to Jesus, and being a faithful witness is to keep his words, and his faith, as well as not denying his name in a public context. They are called to gain a crown, which inevitably means losing their lives. This call to death is the call to conquer, a crucial concept in the Apocalypse. It is a call to which the souls under the altar had already responded. However impractical in practice, John was indeed calling all Christians to win martyrdom.[149]

The Call to Conquer
It is my contention that, in the Apocalypse, the call for Christians 'to conquer' *always* denotes a call to achieve death through martyrdom. Moreover, that call to conquer is made to *all* Christians. The latter of these two propositions is the easier to demonstrate. Conquering is a crucial component in the linguistic and theological matrix of the Apocalypse. The verb νικάω is found some 26 times in the New Testament, with well over half of the occurrences in Revelation.[150]

147. *TNDT*, VII.615–36.
148. The persecution at Lyons, including the throwing of Christians into prison, is put down to the fact that the 'Adversary swooped down with full force ... anticipating his final coming which is sure to come' (*Mart. Lyons* 1.5).
149. Compare, Hurtado, *Lord Jesus Christ*, 620: 'The only good Christian will likely be a dead Christian'.
150. Rev. 2.7, 11, 17, 26; 3.5, 12, 21, all relating to the seven churches. The remaining instances are found at 5.5; 6.2; 11.7; 12.11; 13.7; 15.2; 17.14; and 21.7. Elsewhere in the New Testament, νικάω occurs once in Luke (11.22, parable of the strong man); once in John (16.33; ἐν τῷ κόσμῳ θλῖψιν ἔχετε ἀλλὰ θαρσεῖτε, ἐγὼ νενίκηκα τὸν κόσμον); three times in Romans (3.4; twice in 12.21; see also ὑπερνικάω, at 8.37, where conquering is closely related to, though not identified with, death); six times in 1 John (2.13, 14; 4.4; twice in 5.4; 5.5; also νίκη at 4.4). It may be significant that more than half of the occurrences of νικάω in LXX appear in *4 Maccabees*, a book concerned with martyrdom.

Within the New Testament canon, conquering is a particular concern of the Seer. Seven of the incidences of νικάω arise in relation to the messages to the seven churches. Each letter ends with a call to hear what the Spirit says to the churches and notice of the rewards for the one who conquers (ὁ νικῶν). By comparing the rewards for those who conquer with rewards given to those explicitly slain for their testimony, we will find further evidence that conquering is in effect a technical term for martyrdom.

Rewards listed for ὁ νικῶν in the seven letters are as follows: they will eat of the tree of life (in the paradise of God; 2.7); they will not be hurt by second death (2.11); they will receive hidden manna, a white stone and a new secret name (2.17); they will receive power over the nations (2.26); they will rule with a rod of iron (2.27); and receive the morning star (2.28); the conquerors will be clad in white garments (3.5);[151] and their names will not be blotted out of the book of life, but rather confessed before Father and holy angels (3.5); they will become a pillar in the temple (3.12); and the name of God and Christ's own new name will be written on them (3.12); and as Christ has conquered and sat down with the Father, so those who conquer will sit on Christ's throne (3.22).

Many of these rewards are found to be the preserve of those who have been slain for their witness. In the first instance, the souls under the altar, slain for the Word of God and their testimony, were given a white robe (στολὴ λευκή, 6.11). Conquerors are to be dressed in white clothes (ἐν ἱματίοις λευκοῖς, 3.5), and are contrasted with the unfaithful, the 'dead' (νεκρός, 3.1) at Sardis, who have soiled their garments.[152] They are dead because their works are not perfect in the sight of God (3.3), and specifically because they are not keeping what they received and heard (3.3),[153] the Word of God and testimony of Jesus. Yet the few faithful who are holding to John's teaching will walk with Jesus in white (περιπατήσουσιν ... ἐν λευκοῖς, 3.4), for they are worthy (ἄξιοι). Their names will be found in the book of life (13.8; 17.8; 20.15; 21.27)[154] and confessed before the Father and the angels (3.6).[155] Crucially, in order to gain white clothing, Christians must publicly confess Christ's name which will result in death.

White robes appear again in ch. 7, after the sixth seal has been opened, and are again associated with death through witness. John sees a great multitude clothed in white robes (στολὰς λευκάς, 7.9). This clothing is emphasised when John is asked who those in white robes are (7.13). They are identified as those who have come out of the great tribulation, who have washed their robes (ἔπλυναν τὰς στολὰς αὐτῶν), and made them white (ἐλεύκαναν) in the blood of the lamb (ἐν τῷ αἵματι τοῦ ἀρνίου, 7.14).

---

151. Perhaps the white robes are heavenly attire (cf. *Asc. Isa.* 4.16; 9.9).

152. Inferred from the fact that they are contrasted with those who have not soiled their garments (3.4).

153. They are urged to remember what they had received and heard, and then keep it (τήρει).

154. On the names of the righteous being written in the book of life, see Ps. 69.28; Dan. 12.1; Phil. 4.3; *Apoc.Pet.* 17.7 (cf. Lk. 10.20; Heb. 12.23 for their names being written in heaven). Conversely, the wicked are blotted out of the book (Exod. 32.33; *Jub.* 20.22; *1 Enoch* 108.3).

155. An important connection with Mt. 10.32//Lk.12.8; and the negative form in Mk 8.38.

The great multitude has experienced great tribulation. Like John and his fellow sufferers (1.9), they have washed their robes so that they are white through the blood of the Lamb. As those who possess white garments, they are also conquerors. There are further rewards for those who wash their robes: first, they have the right to the tree of life (22.14), a reward for those who conquer (2.7). This tree of life is located in the new city, the holy city, new Jerusalem that has come down out of heaven from God (21.2), the city which will be given as a heritage to those who conquer (21.7), and, again, the same reward is given to those who wash their robes (22.14). Washing one's robes and conquering should be seen as identical concepts – that is, achieving death through martyrdom. In the Apocalypse, the possession of white robes is the preserve of the martyrs. This identification is confirmed by the only other place in Revelation that the phrase τὸ αἷμα τοῦ ἀρνίου occurs (12.11), where the themes of martyrdom and white robes are interpreted within the concept of cosmic conflict.

Cosmic Conflict [156]

After war in heaven (ch. 12), the dragon is cast out. Though he is the accuser of the brothers (12:10), they have conquered him (ἐνίκησαν, 12:11) by the blood of the lamb (διὰ τὸ αἷμα τοῦ ἀρνίου), and crucially, they have also conquered by the word of their testimony (διὰ τὸν λόγον τῆς μαρτυρίας αὐτῶν).[157] Therefore, a matrix of concepts linked to martyrdom emerges: testimony, robe washing, white robes and war, decisively so when it is said that the crowd have conquered, because, like the faithful witness Antipas (2.13), they loved not their own lives even to death (ἄχρι θανάτου, 12.11).[158] This crowd, clothed in the white garments of martyrdom is made up of people from every nation, from all tribes, peoples and tongues (7.9). John's call to martyrdom is universal. All Christians are to confess the name of Jesus and be faithful to death. Only when they are faithful and win martyrdom will Christians conquer and receive the rewards of a conqueror.

Before John sees the great multitude which no one could count (7.9), he hears an angel hold off judgement on the earth until the servants of God have been sealed (7.3). The number of those sealed was 144,000. A number of factors

---

156. I continue to use the term 'Cosmic Conflict' for consistency and so as not to confuse the Christian conception with the Jewish Holy War tradition from which it emerged. In the Apocalypse, however, a case could certainly be made that Jewish Holy War imagery is found in abundance. See especially, A. Yarbro Collins, *The Combat Myth in the Book of Revelation* (HDR, 9; Missoula, MT: Scholars Press, 1976); and R. Bauckham, *The Climax of Prophecy: Studies on the Book of Revelation* (Edinburgh: T&T Clark, 1993).

157. Linking τὸ αἷμα τοῦ ἀρνίου with ideas of atonement is probably misplaced in the Apocalypse. Whereas in ch. 7, the souls' robes are cleansed by the blood of the Lamb, the atonement idea is absent from this second reference. Washing robes in blood is primarily a reference to martyrdom and spilling ones own blood. The robes are washed because faithful Christians follow Christ through death into life and victory. For the other New Testament references to το αἷμα τοῦ ἀρνίου, see Aune, *Revelation*, 475.

158. Compare Dan. 11.35, where those who are wise will fall, to refine and to cleanse them and make them white, for the time at the end.

suggests that this counted group of which John hears should be identified with the innumerable number that John later sees. In the first instance, the great crowd are conquerors, those who have washed their robes. One of the rewards for the conquerors is citizenship of the new Jerusalem and to have Jesus' name on their foreheads (22.4).

This Christian army[159] is identified as men (παρθένοι) who have not defiled themselves with women (14.4). The fact that they are virgins may be explained by the requirement of purity for soldiers engaged in a Holy War,[160] or indeed it may be, as suggested by Yabro Collins, that John puts forward an ideal of celibacy for Christians.[161] After all, in an age of eschatological crisis, where the end is near and martyrdom is required, it would make sense not to marry.

> Christians are involved in a conflict that will determine their ultimate destinies. Life as it has been known is passing away. The world is corrupt and must be destroyed. Continence and voluntary death are intelligible responses of the individual Christian in such a framework.[162]

Therefore, though we need not see the two groups as identical, they undoubtedly correspond to one another. Bauckham draws attention to the hearing/seeing construction, found first in ch. 5,[163] where John hears a lion, but sees a lamb. Just as the two images are closely related, the second being a Christian reinterpretation of Jewish eschatological expectation concerning the Lion of Judah, so the great multitude of martyrs reinterpret the Jewish apocalyptic army drawn from the twelve tribes.[164] They are but the first fruits of those redeemed from the earth (14.4). They are as yet an 'uncompleted army',[165] and will draw their remaining number from those yet to be martyred. Crucially, in order to become a Holy Warrior, one must be martyred. In time, more will join them from John's communities in order to fill up the number of martyrs.

---

159. R. Bauckham, 'The list of tribes in Revelation 7 again', *JSNT* 42 (1991), 99–115 (104). This image is determined by the census of 7.4–5, following the Old Testament pattern of a census of the fighting men before battle. He observes (105) that the list may be modelled on the divinely commanded census of the tribes of Israel in the wilderness (Numbers 1), which in turn influenced the Qumran War Rule (1QM).

160. R. Bauckham, 'Revelation as a Christian war scroll', *Neotestamentica* 22 (1988), 17–40 (29).

161. Yarbro Collins, *Crisis and Catharsis*, 129. This verse has caused problems for many exegetes who simply cannot bear to see celibacy exalted in such a way. Swete (*Apocalypse*, 222) has gone as far as to call the verse 'one of the most misunderstood in the Bible', desperately suggesting that παρθένοι may refer to married men. G.R. Beasley-Murray (*Revelation*, 223) stresses its metaphorical significance and usefully observes that they are all male because they are *soldiers* of Christ. G.B. Caird (*A Commentary on the Revelation of St. John the Divine* [BNTC; London: A. & C. Black, 1966], 179–81); and Bauckham (*Theology of Revelation*, 78) draw on texts such as Deut. 20; 23.9–10; 1 Sam. 21.5; and 2 Sam. 11.11 to bring out the purity practice before a Holy War. However, given the Apocalypse's setting at the end as Christians are being urged to give up their lives, it is probably better to take the virginal aspect, in line with 1 Cor. 7.1, 32–5; and Mt. 19.10–12, of the vision quite seriously.

162. Yarbro Collins, *Crisis*, 131.

163. Seven times altogether: 5.9; 7.9; 10.11; 11.9; 13.7; 14.6; 17.15.

164. Bauckham, 'List', 103.

165. Garrow, *Revelation*, 92.

This call for faithfulness unto death is made explicit in three central chapters (12–14) of the Apocalypse, with two calls for the endurance of the saints (13.10; 14.12).[166] Chapter 11 ends with the completion of the cycles of seven seals and seven trumpets. The two witnesses have been slain and vindicated (11.3–13), and the seventh angel blows his trumpet. At that point, final judgement is anticipated: 'the kingdom of the world has become the kingdom of our Lord and of his Christ, and he shall reign for ever and ever' (11.15). The time for the vindication of the saints is at hand: 'The nations rage, but your wrath came, and the time for the dead to be judged, for rewarding your servants, the prophets and saints … and for destroying the destroyers of the earth' (11.18). The final battle is announced, and the following chapters prepare for that war.

First, ch. 12 narrates the war that took place in heaven, anticipating war on earth, dramatized with the dragon, cast out of heaven, pursuing the male child. Those who have already died have won the victory through their testimony and deaths (12.11). The dragon then sets out to make war on the remainder of those who keep the commandments of God and bear testimony to Jesus (12.17). This is the battle in which John's readers are involved. The following two chapters contrast the opposing armies: the followers of the Beast and the followers of the Lamb. The call for the endurance of the saints is a call to remain followers of the Lamb, despite the great power of the Beast, and against the fact that the Beast *will* conquer them (13.7)!

In ch. 13, the Beast rises from the sea. It is a symbol of both great evil and great power. All people are amazed at the Beast and worship it, 'Who is like the Beast and who can fight against it' (13.4)? The Beast is permitted to make war on the saints and will conquer them. Its power on the earth is total, for all the inhabitants of the earth, that is everyone except those who are in the Lamb's book of life, will worship the Beast (13.8). Therefore, those who *are* in the Lamb's book of life will be slain (13.15). This fearful time is also a time for the endurance of the saints: 'If anyone is to be taken captive, to captivity he goes; if anyone is to be slain with the sword, by the sword he must be slain' (13.10). The choice is plain. To be a follower of Jesus, to have one's name in the book of life will mean certain death. This is the call for endurance. It is a call for faithful witness. It is a call which will lead to martyrdom.

The followers of the Lamb are then presented (14.1–5). These are the symbolic 144,000 who, rather than take the mark of the Beast, were sealed by Christ. Again, there are two groups in humanity: the inhabitants of the world, those who have received the mark of the Beast and, in contrast, the redeemed, those who have received the mark of Christ.

---

166. M. Lee ('A call to martyrdom: function as method and message in Revelation' [*NovT* 40 (1998), 164–94], 174) locates the centre of the Apocalypse at this point by means of a complex chiasmic structure. Her two central sections, 13.1–18 and 14.1–20, revolve around a 'moment of decision' through the calls for endurance. Though there are many attempts at imposing a chiastic structure on Revelation, it seems to me that it is best understood as a series of contrasts between the elect and the inhabitants of the world. The message remains the same throughout the book; judgement will fall on the enemies of God and blessings for the martyrs. Christians must ensure that they stay on God's side and prove it with their testimony and, ideally, with their deaths.

A second call for endurance is made (14.12). This time in relation to the punishment that will befall those who receive the mark of the Beast. And so, two calls for endurance are made: one details the consequences of being a follower of the Lamb – death; the second, more negatively, outlines the consequences of failing to be faithful unto death – sharing in the punishment of the Beast-worshippers. For John, there can be no compromise. This is a time for endurance. John issues a call to keep the commandments of God and the faith of Jesus. In the face of temptation to worship the Beast and receive its mark, the Christians are reminded of the eventual fate of those who soil their garments. They are called to remain as pure as the 144,000, that they may also be slain as they had been. The call for endurance is the call to death, but critically a voice from heaven affirms, 'Blessed are the dead who die in the Lord'. The Spirit answers, 'Blessed indeed, that they might rest from their labours' (14.13).[167]

If there is any temptation to compromise the testimony of Jesus, then John's message is clear. Christians are to disassociate themselves from the world and maintain their testimony. This brings them into conflict with the world. Faithful Christians in this time will willingly give themselves to be martyred, for it is in martyrdom that they truly conquer. Most importantly, martyrdom actually contributes to the coming of the Kingdom.

Another reward for the conquerors is exemption from the second death (2.11). When the first resurrection is narrated (20.4–6), we find it is precisely those who have been beheaded for the testimony of Jesus and the word of God (20.4), over whom the second death will have no power (20.6). They who offer themselves to death and bring about Christ's judgement are those who did not receive the mark of the Beast or worship him (20.4). In other words, those whose names have been written in the book of life, for only they, we are told, did not worship the Beast (13.8).

It should now be clear that the call to conquer, issued to each of the seven churches, is a call to *all* Christians. The rewards promised to those who conquer are found throughout the Apocalypse as the rewards given to those who held to their witness to death. The book of Revelation is a call for Christians to prepare themselves for martyrdom – martyrdom for the sake of the Kingdom.

The Apocalypse displays 'near total dualism'.[168] It presents the cosmos engaged in all-out war.[169] It demands that the reader take sides. Death and blood dominates the Apocalypse; the Christ is the one who died (1.5, 18; 2.8), and appears in heaven as the lamb who was slain (5.6; also 1.5; 5.9, 12; 7.14; 12.11; 19.13). Christians are to be faithful to death (2.10, 11); the prophets' blood was shed (11.7–8), as was that of the saints (18.24) and also God's servants (16.6; 17.6; 18.24; 19.2). The blood of God's enemies is spilled too.[170] However, in the

---

167. E.S. Fiorenza ('The followers of the Lamb: visionary rhetoric and social-political situation', *Semeia* 36 [1986], 123–46 [124]) suggests that 14.13 was a traditional Christian expression.

168. D.L. Barr, 'The Apocalypse as a symbolic transformation of a world: a literary analysis', *Interpretation* 38 (1986), 39–50 (40).

169. See A. Yarbro Collins, *Combat Myth*.

170. See L.L. Thompson, 'Lamentation for Christ as hero: Revelation 1.7', *JBL* 119 (2000), 683–

bloodbath that will ensue, the result is not in doubt. In fact, the battle is narrated so swiftly, it is easy to miss it: 'they will make war on the Lamb, and the Lamb will conquer them' (17.14).

This is the result that has been promised from the beginning – not only that Christ would come to reign, but that his enemies will be judged (1.7). It is impressed that the action which is to unfold will take place soon (1.1). This is reinforced by the employing of the Danielic[171] vision of the son of man coming on the clouds. The throne room scene of chs 4 and 5 firmly establishes the alternative power base for John's world. Rome is the earthly seat of great power, but in heaven the Almighty reigns. The remainder of the Apocalypse is concerned with the fate of the world, and the rewards for faithful Christians.

We have already seen that the deaths of Christians affect the timing of judgement in filling up the necessary number of martyrs before Christ comes as judge, but they are also involved in the specific judgements on the earth. The censer that the angel throws upon the earth to such devastating effect (8.5) is filled by smoke and the prayers of the saints (8.3–4). In fact, the altar that is censed may be the same altar under which the souls have prayed for judgement (6.9–11). The answer to their prayers is narrated immediately.

Having endured to death and conquered, the saints, who have participated in the judgement of the earth, become heavenly observers, chorusing the Lamb's mighty power. Ultimately, what Rome has done to the Christians plays a large part in its judgement. Those who will undergo martyrdom know that their deaths will be avenged. Babylon[172] the great, mother of harlots and of earth's abominations, is intoxicated by the blood of the saints and the blood of the martyrs/witnesses of Jesus (μεθύουσαν ἐκ τοῦ αἵματος τῶν ἁγίον καὶ ἐκ τοῦ αἵματος τῶν μαρτύρων Ἰησοῦ, 17.6).

Similarly, after her destruction, a post-mortem examination reveals that in her was the blood of the prophets and the saints (18.24). Rome's destruction is as total as it is inevitable. 'Fallen, fallen is Babylon!' (14.8). The announcement is made between the two calls for the endurance of the saints (13.10, 14.12). These specific calls for endurance and death frame the announcement of Babylon's destruction. The Christians know that their deaths are to be viewed in terms of God's impending victory. As Rome has spilled their blood, so God, in turn, will make them drink blood (16.6). At this, the altar cries (recalling the cries for justice of the souls; 6.10), 'Yea, Lord God the Almighty, true and just are your judgements' (16.7). Rome is the harlot, the mother of all abomination, causing some of those who might otherwise constitute the Bride of Christ to play the whore; Rome is under the cosmic power of the Beast.

703, for the contemporary pagan charge that Christianity was a cult obsessed with death (and above, 36–8).

171. Dan. 7.13 conflated with Zech. 12.12–14.

172. John, in depicting the powers of Rome as a whore, probably has the goddess Roma in his sights. See DeSilva, 'Honor discourse and the rhetorical strategy of the Apocalypse of John', *JSNT* 71 (1998), 79–110 (99).

Death and Life

As Christians conquer the beast by their blood, they also conquer death itself, for paradoxically the call to death is in reality the call to life. The Christians at Smyrna are promised the conquerors' reward of the crown of life (τòν στέφανον τῆς ζωῆς) if they are faithful to death (πιστòς ἄχρι θανάτου, 2.10). As conquerors (i.e. those who achieve death), they are permitted to eat of the tree of life (τοῦ ξύλου τῆς ζωῆς, 2.7) and their names will be found in the book of life (ἐκ τῆς βίβλου τὴν ζωῆς, 3.5). The call to conquer, that is, the call to death is, therefore, strongly linked to themes of life. Those who die in the Lord are blessed (14.13), and those who die for their witness will reign with Christ, and not be harmed by the second death (20.4). It is through weakness and death that Christians win life and victory. 'In reality it is those who maintain their integrity, even at the price of their lives who will be vindicated whereas those who have the mark of the Beast drink the wine of God's wrath'.[173]

The hope and warning of Christ's coming dominates the book (1.7; 2.5, 16; 3.3, 11; 16.15; 22.7, 12, 20)[174] and on that day the 'wrath of the Lamb' will be revealed, so that even the kings of the earth will cry out and wail (6.15–17), and those who have not been sealed by God will be visited by a multitude of plagues (9.3–6; ch. 16). When the souls under the altar ask for vindication of their blood (6.10), they are effectively asking for the end to come. For it is at the *eschaton* that the nations will be judged. When Christ comes, he will come as judge (1.7), an event that will be catastrophic for all the nations (or tribes) of the earth, but an event that will bring vindication for the suffering Christians. Whereas faithful Christians will rest from their labours (14.12), the worshippers of the Beast will have no rest (14.11). Similarly, just as the smoke of the prayers of the saints raised heavenward (8.4), the smoke signalling the torment and punishment of Beast-worshippers will rise for ever (14.11). People are, therefore, divided in their post-mortem fate.

The world will be judged, and judged horribly, and that judgement will be brought about by Christian deaths. They will fill up the number of martyrs, triggering the end-time events, resulting in their vindication and the world's judgement and destruction. The call to death is the call to conquer, and a call to truly live.

The language of conquering and witness is crucial in the apocalypse. The message to each church ends with a call to conquer, but the way in which Christians conquer evil is *to be* conquered and win for themselves a white robe – the eschatological sign of salvation. Yet, even as the Beast is given permission to conquer the saints (13.7), we are then told that those who had conquered the Beast and its image are standing in heaven (15.2). In the Apocalypse, as with the theology of the radical martyrs, to die is to gain life and, conversely, to hold onto earthly life, through compromise with the world, is judgement, destruction and death.

---

173. Yarbro Collins, *Crisis and Catharsis*, 149.

174. Bauckham, *Theology of Revelation*, 64. Seven times Jesus says ἔρχομαι (2.5, 16; 3.11; 16.15; 22.6, 12, 20).

Chapter 11 provides a 'parable'[175] of how this may work in practice; the two witnesses become a 'paradigm for martyrs'.[176] When the witnesses are finished giving their testimony,[177] the Beast conquers and kills them (11.7). The witnesses have then fulfilled their task and, like all Christians who endure to the end, they are vindicated. They are taken up to heaven, and the earth is judged. Indeed, because of their role, the seventh angel can blow his trumpet and loud voices in heaven sing, 'The kingdom of the world has become the kingdom of our Lord and of his Christ' (11.15). In other words, ch. 11 contains the whole story of the saints who follow Christ's example: they witness, are killed, yet vindicated when the wicked are judged, and God's Kingdom is fulfilled.

The Lamb

The central figure in the book of Revelation is the Lamb. The call to Christians is to follow the Lamb wherever he goes, thereby making the Lamb a paradigm for all faithful Christian action. Through his death, resurrection and vindication, the Lamb becomes the prototype for Christian discipleship, which involves martyrdom, leading to subsequent victory. 'Christ's death and resurrection provide the model whereby the saints understand their own deaths as the prerequisite to eternal life.'[178]

At the opening of the Apocalypse (1.5), three things are immediately said of Jesus Christ: he is the faithful witness (ὁ μάρτυς ὁ πιστός); he is the first-born from the dead (ὁ πρωτότοκος τῶν νεκρῶν); and he is the ruler of the kings of the earth (ὁ ἄρχων τῶν βασιλέων τῆς γῆς).[179] Like the Lamb, martyrs are faithful witnesses (ὁ μάρτυς ὁ πιστός, 2:13), the redeemed are the first-fruits for God (14.4), and they reign with Christ (1.6).

The theme of Christ's dying and rising is employed when the Son of Man figure addresses John first with the command not to fear (1.17), and then makes himself known as the living one (ὁ ζῶν), who died (ἐγενόμην νεκρός), but is alive forever (ζῶν εἰμι εἰς τοὺς αἰῶνας τῶν αἰώνων). Because of his death and new life, he holds the keys of Death and Hades. Through his death and entering into Hades, Christ has conquered Death and it is now he, and not Death, who controls the destiny of humankind. Hence, Christians need not fear death. This underpins the conversion of apparent death to life in the theological universe of the Seer. For significantly, reference to Christ's dying and coming back to life is

175. Bauckham, *Theology of Revelation*, 90. Aune (*Revelation*, 588–93) clearly demonstrates the parallels between Rev. 11.3–13, *Apoc. Elijah* 4.7–19 and Lactantius' *Divine Institutes*, the date of which is uncertain. This makes interpretation difficult as John's hand may have been forced somewhat by his source.

176. Yarbro Collins, *Crisis and Catharsis*, 69. For the identity of the two witnesses, see Aune, *Revelation*, 598–603; D.K.K. Wong, 'The two witnesses in Revelation 11', *Bibliotheca Sacra* 154 (1997), 344–54.

177. See A.A. Trites, *The New Testament Concept of Witness* (Cambridge: Cambridge University Press, 1977), 165.

178. Lee, 'Call to martyrdom', 164.

179. Thomson ('Lamentation', 695 n. 48) points out the force of these last two statements to be saying that Christ is pre-eminent over both the dead and the living.

made at the head of the epistle to the church in Smyrna, where an explicit prophecy is made that the church will suffer, and that Christians will die. Satan is in control of the synagogue which is exerting some influence over them (2.9). The Christians are about to suffer, but are to have no fear (μηδὲν φοβοῦ, 2.10). For although they will be thrown into prison by the devil (ὁ διάβαλος), and experience tribulation (θλῖψις), they are called to be faithful to death (πιστὸς ἄχρι θανάτου). In following the example of Christ in faithfulness and death, he will give to them the crown of life (στέφανον τῆς ζωῆς). It is through his own dying, rising and conquering of Death and Hades that Christ can now confer the crown of life upon the martyrs.

The authority that Christ now has is further highlighted in the throne room scene in ch. 5. No one is found in heaven or on earth who is worthy to open the scroll and break its seals (5.3). Crucially, the opening of the seals is the catalyst for the events of the Apocalypse to unfold. Without someone being found to open the seals, there is no revelation. This significance is not lost on the seer, who weeps because no one can read from it. However, he is told that the Lion of the Tribe of Judah, the Root of David, has conquered, and he is able to open the seven seals (5.5). This conquering Lion turns out to be a slain Lamb (ἀρνίον ἑστηκὸς ὡς ἐσφαγμένον, 5.6). The incongruity of this image is typical of the way in which categories of conquering and conquered, life and death, weakness and strength are deconstructed and interchanged in the Apocalypse. The Lamb has conquered precisely by being slain. 'The Lamb is the Lion – Jesus is the Messiah, but he has performed his Messianic office in an extraordinary way, his death.'[180]

The sight of the conquering Lamb opening the scroll, and bringing about the events that will usher in God's final triumph, sends heaven into an orgy of praise. He is ascribed power and wealth and wisdom and might and honour and glory and blessing (5.12–13). Through his death and blood, the Lamb enables all those who are faithful to death to conquer. Furthermore, the new song sung by the elders (5.9–10) echoes that of 1.5–6, but now, as well as being ransomed by his blood and made a kingdom and priests to God, the Christians share in his rulership; they shall reign on earth (5.10), for just like the Lamb, they too are made worthy by their deaths (3.4 etc.). Those who are slain will be the ones whose names are in the book of life, for the book of life belongs precisely to the Lamb *that was slain* (13.8). Again, the experience of the Christians is mirrored by the Lamb. The Beast will conquer them and slay them, but being slain by the Beast results in finding one's name in the Book of Life of the slain Lamb. The familiar theme recurs again: death equals life.

At this critical juncture, those who will be slain for maintaining the testimony of Jesus are reminded that they will gain life, precisely by following the Lamb through death. They then stand with the Lamb with his name on their foreheads (14.1), for the martyrs are his holy army in the cosmic conflict against the forces of the Beast. They follow the Lamb wherever he goes (14.4), through death, vindication and inevitable victory.

180. Barr, 'Symbolic transformation', 41.

Conclusion

Therefore, the New Testament stands as a crucial transition between the theology of martyrdom found in Judaism and that of the Christian radical martyrs, among whom John and the readers of the Apocalypse are to be counted.[181] By reinterpreting the conception of Holy War in late Judaism, the early Christians built a world for themselves into which they could interpret not only their own sufferings and death but also the death and resurrection of the Christ.

The twin development of following Jesus as a model of discipleship and obeying his call to take up the cross and follow him, combined with the Pauline innovation of the believer sharing in Christ's death and victory, created a potent and explosive matrix which in turn enabled not only a positive interpretation of suffering and hardship but even resulted in suffering being a marker of true Christian discipleship. This interpretation of suffering led in turn to suffering and death being interpreted within the context of an apocalyptic battle waged by Christ against the forces of Satan.

Although the New Testament contains only one example – the book of Revelation – of the symbolic world wherein radical martyrdom could flourish, most authors contributed something to the development of that world. Through the valorization of suffering and death; the deconstruction of life and death; the death of Jesus being exalted as a mimetic model of discipleship; the social environment interpreted through an explosive apocalyptic matrix; and discipleship being played out amid a cosmic war between God and Satan, where Christians were called to follow the Lamb wherever he went, the Christians began to develop a semiotic world where they could interpret their deaths, not only as the result of participation in cosmic conflict but also as a contribution to God's final eschatological victory.

---

181. On the comparison between Jewish and Christian martyrology, see the discussion below, pp. 106–16 and 127–34.

CONCLUSION

If martyrdom is discourse, then I have sought to extend the Christian martyrological narrative to include radical martyrs, Christians who saw martyrdom as the greatest form of Christ-devotion, even to the point of handing themselves over to arrest in order to effect that martyrdom. Radical martyrdom was a prevalent and, indeed, idealized form of Christian attitude to death from the late first to early third centuries. It was only with Clement of Alexandria's assault on volitional death that the enterprise of 'unmaking' the radical martyrs began. The scholarly tendency to follow Clement and dismiss these martyrs as irrational, deviant or even heretical has little justification, and has resulted in a serious omission in the constructions of the theology and origins of Christian martyrdom.

I have sought to 'normalize' the radical martyrs by placing them within an early Christian apocalyptic world-view, where Christians saw themselves as being engaged in cosmic conflict against Satan and his legions. The martyrs were God's frontline troops in this cosmic war. Living at the end of time, Christians began to understand their suffering and deaths as taking place within the limited period of eschatological woes. Even as immediate eschatological expectation waned within the Church, the radical martyrs kept the apocalyptic edge of Christianity alive. This apocalypticism interpreted the world as comprising two opposing forces. Those who inflicted suffering upon the fragile communities were literally Satanic. An apocalyptic milieu also enabled a radical deconstruction of the world, so that as well as the boundaries between present and future beginning to crumble, the categories of life and death dissolved. Death *was* life and life *was* death. Taking up the cross and following Jesus to death won life for the faithful witness.

Crucially, the cosmos literally turned on their decision whether to confess or deny Jesus before earthly and cosmic archons. The apocalyptic battle depended on their contribution; therefore, actively seeking death became explicable, indeed necessary. Importantly, this development occurred not in the minds of fringe 'heretics' late in the second century; rather, we find the critical theological developments in the pages of the New Testament. Therefore, since their deaths contributed to the coming victory of Jesus Christ, death could be sought as a means of devotion to God.

The final battle which the early Christians believed they were fighting demanded total commitment to the God who called the Christians into a battle against principalities and powers. The radical martyr-warriors fought alongside Christ, their warrior-in-chief, sharing in his suffering, humiliation, exaltation and, through martyrdom, the inevitable victory over Satan and his legions. Through radical martyrdom and cosmic conflict, Christians won for themselves the ultimate eschatological reward, the right to join the noble army of the martyrs.

BIBLIOGRAPHY

Abel, F.M., *Les Livres des Maccabees* (Paris: Editions du Cerf, 1961).

Akbar, M.J., *The Shade of Swords: Jihad and the Conflict between Christianity and Islam* (London: Routledge, 2002).

Alexander, P.S., ' "The parting of the ways" from the perspective of Rabbinic Judaism', in J.D.G. Dunn (ed.), *Jews and Christians: The Parting of the Ways A.D. 70 to 135* (The Second Durham-Tübingen Research Symposium on Earliest Christianity and Judaism, Durham, September 1989; Tübingen: J.C.B. Mohr [Paul Siebeck], 1991), 1–25.

Allison, D.C., *The End of the Ages Has Come: An Early Interpretation of the Passion and Resurrection of Jesus* (Edinburgh: T&T Clark, 1987).

Anderson, D.W., 'Did early Christians lust after death?', *Christian Research Journal* 18 (1996), 11–21.

Ateek, N.S., 'What is theologically and morally wrong with suicide bombings? A Palestinian Christian perspective', *Studies in World Christianity* 8 (2002), 5–30.

Attridge, H.W., *A Commentary on the Epistle to the Hebrews* (Hermeneia; Philadelphia: Fortress Press, 1989).

Aune, D.E., *Revelation* (WBC, 52; 3 vols; Waco, TX: Word Books, 1997–8).

Avemarie, F., 'Aporien der Theodizee: zu einem Schlüsselthema früher Rabbinischer Märtyrererzählungen', *JSJ* 34 (2003), 119–215.

Baker, J.A., *The Foolishness of God* (London: Darton, Longman & Todd, 1970).

Balling, J., 'Martyrdom as apocalypse', in K. Jeppesen, K. Neilsen and B. Rosendal (eds), *In the Last Days: On Jewish and Christian Apocalyptic and Its Period* (Aarhus: Aarhus University Press, 1994), 41–8.

Barclay, J.M.G., 'Conflict in Thessalonica', *CBQ* 55 (1993), 512–30.

—*Jews in the Mediterranean Diaspora: From Alexander to Trajan (323 BCE–117 CE)* (Edinburgh: T&T Clark, 1996).

Barclay, J.M.G., and J. Sweet (eds), *Early Christian Thought in Its Jewish Context* (Cambridge: Cambridge University Press, 1996).

Barnes, T.D., 'Legislation against the Christians', *JRS* 58 (1968), 32–50.

—*Tertullian* (Oxford: Oxford University Press, 1987).

Barr, D.L., 'The Apocalypse as a symbolic transformation of a world: a literary analysis', *Interpretation* 38 (1986), 39–50.

Barrett, C.K., *The Pastoral Epistles* (Oxford: Oxford University Press, 1963).

—*The Second Epistle to the Corinthians* (BNTC; London: A. & C. Black, 1973).

Barton, C.A., 'Savage miracles: the redemption of lost honor in Roman society and the sacrament of the gladiator and the martyr', *Representations* 45 (1994), 41–71.

—'The scandal of the arena', *Representations* 27 (1989), 1–36.

Batto, B.F., 'The sleeping God: an ancient near eastern motif of divine sovereignty', *Biblion* 68 (1987), 153–77.

Bauckham, R., *The Climax of Prophecy: Studies on the Book of Revelation* (Edinburgh: T&T Clark, 1993).

—*The Theology of the Book of Revelation* (Cambridge: Cambridge University Press, 1993).

—'The list of tribes in Revelation 7 again', *JSNT* 42 (1991), 99–115.

—'Revelation as a Christian war scroll', *Neotestamentica* 22 (1988), 17–40.

Bauckham, R. (ed.), *The Gospels for all Christians: Rethinking the Gospel Audiences* (Grand Rapids: Eerdmans, 1998).

Bauer, W., *Orthodoxy and Heresy in Earliest Christianity* (trans. R.A. Kraft and G. Krodel; Philadelphia: Fortress Press, 1971).

Baumeister, T., *Die Anfänge der Theologie des Martyriums* (MBT, 45; Münster: Aschendorff, 1979).

—*Genèse et evolution de la théologie du martyre dans l'Eglise ancienne* (trans. R. Tolck; Berne: Peter Lang, 1991).

Beale, G.K., *The Book of Revelation: A Commentary on the Greek Text* (NIGTC; Grand Rapids: Eerdmans/Carlisle: Paternoster Press, 1999).

Beasley-Murray, G.R., *The Book of Revelation* (London: Marshall, Morgan & Scott, 1974).

Beker, J.C., *Paul the Apostle: The Triumph of God in Life and Thought* (Philadelphia: Fortress Press, 1980).

Bell, A.A., 'The date of John's apocalypse: the evidence of some Roman historians reconsidered', *NTS* 25 (1979), 93–102.

Benko, S., 'Pagan criticism of Christianity during the first two centuries A.D.', *ANRW*, II.23.2 (1980), 1055–118.

—*Pagan Rome and the Early Christians* (Bloomington: Indiana University Press, 1984).

Benner, M., *The Emperor Says: Studies in the Rhetorical Style in Edicts of the Early Empire* (Gothenburg: Acta Universitatis Gothoburgensis, 1975).

Bergman, S. (ed.), *A Cloud of Witnesses: 20th Century Martyrs* (London: HarperCollins, 1997).

Best, E., *A Commentary on the First and Second Epistles to the Thessalonians* (BNTC; London: A. & C. Black, 1972).

—*A Critical and Exegetical Commentary on Ephesians* (ICC; Edinburgh: T&T Clark, 1998).

—*Mark: The Gospel as Story* (Edinburgh: T&T Clark, 1983).

Betz, H.D., 'Orthodoxy and heresy in primitive Christianity', *Interpretation* 19 (1965), 299–311.

—'2 Cor 6:14–7:1: an antiPauline fragment?', *JBL* 92 (1973), 88–108.

Biguzzi, G., 'Revelation and the Flavian Temple in Ephesus', *NovT* 40 (1998), 276–90.

Bisbee, G.A., *Pre-Decian Acts of Martyrs and Commentarii* (HDR; Philadelphia: Fortress Press, 1988).

Bishop, J., *Nero, the Man and the Legend* (London: R. Hale, 1964).

Bloomquist, L.G., *The Function of Suffering in Philippians* (JSNTSup, 76; Sheffield: JSOT Press, 1993).

Borgen, P., *Early Christianity and Hellenistic Judaism* (Edinburgh: T&T Clark, 1996).

Boulluec, A. le, *La Notion d'hérésie dans la literature grecque (IIe–IIIe siècles)* (2 vols.; Paris: Études Agustiniennes, 1985).

Bousset, W., *Kyrios Christis: A History of Belief in Christ from the Beginning to Irenaeus* (trans. J.E. Steely; Nashville: Abingdon Press, 1970).

Bovon, F., *A Commentary on the Gospel of Luke 1:1–9:50* (trans. C.M. Thomson; Hermeneia; Minneapolis: Fortress Press, 2002).

Bower, R.A., 'The meaning of ἐπὶ τυγχάνω in the epistles of St Ignatius of Antioch', *VC* 28 (1974), 1–7.

Bowersock, G.W., 'Greek intellectuals and the Imperial cult in the second century A.D.', in W. den Boer (ed.), *Le Culte des souverains dans L'Empire Romain* (Vandoeuvres-Genève: Oliver Reverdin, 1972), 177–206.

—'The Imperial cult: perceptions and persistence', in B.F. Meyer and E.P. Sanders (eds), *Self-Definition in the Greco-Roman World*, vol. 3 of *Jewish and Christian Self-Definition* (Philadelphia: Fortress Press, 1983), 171–82.

—*Martyrdom and Rome* (Cambridge: Cambridge University Press, 1995).

Boyarin, D., *Dying for God: Martyrdom and the Making of Christianity and Judaism* (Stanford: Stanford University Press, 1999).

—'Martyrdom and the making of Christianity and Judaism', *JECS* 6 (1998), 577–627.

—*A Radical Jew: Paul and the Politics of Identity* (Berkeley: University of California Press, 1994).

Bremmer, J.N., 'The Passion of Perpetua and the development of early Christian afterlife', *Nederlands Theologisch Tijdschrift* 54 (2000), 97–111.

—'Scapegoat rituals in ancient Greece', *Harvard Studies in Classical Philology* 87 (1983), 299–320.

Brown, P., *The Cult of the Saints: Its Rise and Function in Latin Christianity* (London: SCM Press, 1981).

Brown, R.E., *The Epistles of John* (AB, 30; New York: Doubleday, 1982).

—'Not Jewish Christianity and Gentile Christianity but types of Jewish/Gentile Christianity', *CBQ* 45 (1983), 74–9.

Brown, R.E., and J.P. Meier, *Antioch and Rome: New Testament Cradles of Catholic Christianity* (London: Chapman, 1982).

Bruce, F.F., *The Acts of the Apostles* (Grand Rapids: Eerdmans, 1990).

—*1 & 2 Thessalonians* (WBC, 45; Waco, TX: Word Books, 1982).

Büchler, A., *Studies in Sin and Atonement in the Rabbinic Literature of the First Century* (London: Oxford University Press, 1928).

Burkert, W., *Structure and History in Greek Mythology and Ritual* (Berkeley: University of California Press, 1979).

Burrus, V., 'Reading Agnes: the rhetoric of gender in Ambrose and Prudentius', *JECS* 3 (1995), 25–46.

Buschmann, G., *Das Martyrium des Polykarp übersetz und erklärt* (Kommentar zu den Apostolischen Vätern, 6; Göttingen: Vandenhoeck & Ruprecht, 1998).

Butterweck, C., *'Martyriumssucht' in der alten Kirche?: Studien zur Darstellung und Deutung frühchristlicher Martyrien* (Tübingen: J.C.B. Mohr [Paul Siebeck], 1995).

Caird, G.B., *A Commentary on the Revelation of St. John the Divine* (BNTC; London: A. & C. Black, 1966).

Campenhausen, H. von, 'Beareitung und Interpolationen des Polykarpmartyriums', in *Aus der Frühzeit des Christentums: Studien zur Kirchengeschichte des ersten und zweiten Jahrhunderts* (Tübingen: J.C.B. Mohr [Paul Siebeck], 1963), 253–301.

—*Die Idee des Martyriums in der alten Kirche* (Göttingen: Vandenhoeck & Ruprecht, 1964).

Castelli, E.A., '"I will make Mary male": pieties of the body and gender transformation of Christian women in late antiquity', in J. Epstein and K. Straub (eds), *Body Guards: The Cultural Politics of Gender Ambiguity* (New York/London: Routledge, 1991), 24–49.

—'Imperial reimaginings of Christian origins: epic in Prudentius's poem for the martyr Eulalia', in E.A. Castelli and H. Taussig (eds), *Reimagining Christian Origins: A Colloquium Honoring Burton L. Mack* (Vally Forge, PA: Trinity Press International, 1996), 173–84.

Champlin, E., *Fronto and Antonine Rome* (Cambridge: Harvard University Press, 1980).

Chandler, A. (ed.), *The Terrible Alternative: Christian Martyrdom in the Twentieth Century* (London/New York: Cassell, 1998).

Charlesworth, M. P., 'Deus noster Caesar', *The Classical Review* 39 (1925), 113–15.

Chenu, B., C. Prud'homme, F. Quéré and J. Thomas, *The Book of Christian Martyrs* (trans. J. Bowden; London: SCM Press, 1990).

Clemms, J.T., *What Does the Bible Say about Suicide?* (Minneapolis: Fortress Press, 1990).

Cohen, N.F.C., *The Pursuit of the Millenium: Revolutionary Millenarians and Mystical Anarchists of the Middle Ages* (London: Maurice Temple Smith, 1970).

Coleman, K.M., 'Fatal charades: Roman executions staged as mythological enactments', *JRS* 80 (1990), 44–73.

Collins, J.J., 'Apocalyptic eschatology and the transcendence of death', *CBQ* 36 (1974), 21–43.

—'The court tales of Daniel and the development of apocalyptic', *JBL* 94 (1975), 218–34.

—'Qumran, apocalypticism, and the New Testament', in L.H. Schiffman, E. Tov and J.C. VanderKam, *The Dead Fifty Years after Their Discovery* (Proceedings of the Jerusalem Congress, July 20–25, 1997; Jerusalem: Israel Exploration Society, 2000), 133–8.

—'The root of immortality: death in the context of Jewish wisdom', *HTR* 71 (1978), 177–92.

Collins, R.F., 'Apropos the integrity of 1 Thess', in R.F. Collins, *Studies on the First Letter to the Thessalonians* (Leuven: Leuven University Press, 1984), 96–135.

—*The Birth of the New Testament: The Origin and Development of the First Christian Generation* (New York: Crossroad, 1993).

—*1 & 2 Timothy and Titus: A Commentary* (Louisville, KY/London: Westminster/John Knox Press, 2002).

Colwell, E., 'Popular reactions against Christianity in the Roman Empire', in J.T. McNeill, M. Spinka and H.R. Willoughby (eds), *Environmental Factors in Christian History* (Chicago: University of Chicago Press, 1939), 53–71.

Cranfield, C.E.B., *The Gospel according to St. Mark* (Cambridge: Cambridge University Press, 1959).

Creed, J.M., *The Gospel according to St Luke* (London: Macmillan, 1930).

Crossan, J.D., *The Birth of Christianity: Discovering What Happened in the Years Immediately after the Crucifixion of Jesus* (Edinburgh: T&T Clark, 1999).

—*Who Killed Jesus: Exposing the Roots of Anti-Semitism in the Gospel Story of the Death of Jesus* (New York: HarperSanFrancisco, 1996).

Cullmann, O., *Christ and Time: The Primitive Conception of Time and History* (trans. F.V. Filson; London: SCM Press, 1962).

Cuss, D., *Imperial Cult and Honorary Terms in the New Testament* (Paradosis, Contributions to the History of Early Christian Literature and Theology, 23; Fribourg: University Press, 1974).

Dailey T.F., 'To live or die: Paul's eschatological dilemma in Philippians 1.19–26', *Interpretation* 44 (1990), 18–28.

Daniel, J.L., 'Anti-Semitism in the Hellenistic-Roman period', *JBL* 98 (1979), 45–65.

Daube, D., *Civil Disobedience in Antiquity* (Edinburgh: Edinburgh University Press, 1972).

Davies, J., *Death, Burial and Rebirth in the Religions of Antiquity* (Religion in the First Christian Centuries; London: Routledge, 1999).

Davies, W.D., *Christian Engagements with Judaism* (Pennsylvania: Trinity Press International, 1999).

Davies, W.D., and D.C. Allison, *A Critical and Exegetical Commentary on the Gospel according to Saint Matthew* (ICC; 3 vols; Edinburgh: T&T Clark, 1988, 1991, 1997).

Dehandschutter, B.A.G.M., 'Example and discipleship: some comments on the biblical background of the early Christian theology of martyrdom', in J. den Boeff and M.L. van Pollvan de Lisdonk (eds), *The Impact of Scripture in Early Christianity* (Leiden: E.J. Brill, 1999), 20–7.

—'Le Martyre de Polycarp et le development de la conception du martyre au deuxième siècle', in E.A. Livingstone (ed.), *Studia Patristica XVII* (Oxford: Pergamon Press, 1982), 659–68.

—'The Martyrium Polycarpi: a century of research', *ANRW* II.27.1 (1993), 485–522.

Dehandschutter, B.A.G.M., and J.W. van Henten, 'Einleitung', in B.A.G.M. Dehandschutter, J.W. van Henten and H.J.W. van der Klaauw (eds), *Die Entstehung der jüdischen Martyrologie* (Leiden: E.J. Brill, 1989), 1–19.

—'Le Martyre de Polycarp et le développement de la conception du martyre au deuxième siècle', in E.A. Livingstone (ed.), *Studia Patristica XVII* (Oxford: Pergamon Press, 1982), 659–68.

Deissmann, A., *Light from the Ancient East: The New Testament Illustrated by Recently Discovered Texts of the Graeco-Roman World* (trans. L.R.M. Strachan; Massachusetts: Hendrickson Publishers, 1995).

—*Paul: A Study in Social and Religious History* (trans. W.E. Wilson; London: Hodder and Stoughton, 1926).

Delehaye, H., *The Legends of the Saints* (North Bend: University of Notre Dame, 1961).

—*Les Origines du culte des martyrs* (Brussels: Société des Bollandistes, 1933).

Derrett, J.D.M., 'Taking up cross and turning the other cheek (Mk 8.34; Mt. 5.38–42; 10:38; Lk. 14:27; Gosp. Thom. 55)', in A. Harvey (ed.), *Alternative Approaches to New Testament Study* (London: SPCK, 1985), 61–78.

DeSilva, D. A., 'Honor discourse and the rhetorical strategy of the Apocalypse of John', *JSNT* 71 (1998), 79–110.

—'The "Image of the Beast" and the Christians in Asia Minor: escalation of sectarian tension in Revelation 13', *Trinity Journal* 12 (1991), 185–208.

—*Introducing the Apocrypha* (Grand Rapids: Baker Academic, 2002).

Dodds, E.R., *Pagans and Christians in an Age of Anxiety: Some Aspects of Religious Experience from Marcus Aurelius to Constantine* (Cambridge: Cambridge University Press, 1965).

Donfried, K.P., 'The cults of Thessalonica and the Thessalonian correspondence', *NTS* 31 (1985), 336–56.

—'Paul and Judaism: 1 Thessalonians 2.13–16 as a test case', *Interpretation* 38 (1994), 242–53.

Doran, R., *Birth of a Worldview: Early Christianity in Its Jewish and Pagan Content* (Lanham: Rowman & Littlefield Publishers, Inc., 1999).

—'The martyr: a synoptic view of the mother and her seven sons', in G.W.E. Nickelsburg and J.J. Collins (eds), *Ideal Figures in Ancient Judaism: Profiles and Paradigms* (Septuagint and Cognate Studies, 12; Chicago: Scholars Press, 1980), 189–221.

Downing, J., 'Jesus and martyrdom', *JTS* (n.s.) 14 (1963), 279–93.

Droge, A.J., 'The crown of immortality: towards a redescription of Christian martyrdom', in J.J. Collins and M. Fishbane (eds), *Death, Ecstasy, and Other Wordly Journeys* (New York: State of New York Press, 1995), 155–69.

—'Did Paul commit suicide?', *Bible Review* 5 (1989), 14–21, 42.

—'*MORI LUCRUM*: Paul and ancient theories of suicide', *NovT* 30 (1998), 263–86.

Droge, A.J., and J.D. Tabor, *A Noble Death: Suicide and Martyrdom among Christians and Jews in Antiquity* (San Francisco: HarperSanFrancisco, 1992).

Dronke, P., *Women Writers of the Middle Ages: A Critical Study of Texts from Perpetua to Marguerite Porete* (Cambridge: Cambridge University Press, 1984).

Dubis, M., *Messianic Woes in First Peter: Suffering and Eschatology in 1 Peter 4,12–19* (New York: Peter Lang, 2002).

Duncan-Jones, R., *The Economy of the Roman Empire* (Cambridge: Cambridge University Press, 1982).

Dunn, J.D.G., *The Parting of the Ways: Between Christianity and Judaism and Their Significance for the Character of Christianity* (London: SCM Press, 1991).

—*The Theology of Paul the Apostle* (Grand Rapids/Cambridge: Eerdmans, 1998).

—*Unity and Diversity in the New Testament: An Inquiry into the Character of Earliest Christianity* (London: SCM Press, 1977).

Dunn, J.D.G. (ed.), *Jews and Christians: The Parting of the Ways, A.D. 70 to 135* (Tübingen: J.C.B. Mohr [Paul Siebeck], 1992).

Dupont-Summer, A., *Le Quatrième Livre des Macchabés* (Paris: H. Champion, 1939).

Durkheim, E., *Suicide: A Study in Sociology* (trans. J.A. Spaulding and G. Simpson; London: Routledge, 2002).

Edwards, M.J., 'Martyrdom in the First Epistle of John', *NovT* 31 (1989), 164–71.

Ehrhardt, A., 'Christianity before the Apostles' Creed', *HTR* 55 (1962), 73–112.

Ehrman, B.D., *Lost Christianities: The Battle for Scripture and the Faiths We Never Knew* (Oxford: Oxford University Press, 2003).

—*The Orthodox Corruption of Scripture: The Effect of Early Christological Controversies on the Text of the New Testament* (Oxford: Oxford University Press, 1993).

Elliot, J. H., *A Home for the Homeless: A Sociological Exegesis of 1 Peter, Its Situation and Strategy* (London: SCM Press, 1982).

Engberg-Peterson, T., *Paul and the Stoics* (Edinburgh: T&T Clark, 2000).

Fee, G.D., *The First Epistle to the Corinthians* (NICNT; Grand Rapids: Eerdmans, 1987).

Feldman, L.H., *Jew and Gentile in the Ancient World: Attitudes and Interactions from Alexander to Justinian* (Princeton, NJ: Princeton University Press, 1993).

Ferguson, E., *Demonology of the Early Christian World* (New York: Edwin Mellen Press, 1984).

—'Early Christian martyrdom and civil disobedience', *JECS* 1 (1993), 73–83.

Feuillet, M., 'Les Martyrs de l'humanitié et l'agneau égorgé: une interprêtation nouvelle de la prière des égorgés en Ap 6,9–11', *NRT* 99 (1977), 189–207.

Fiorenza, E.S., 'The followers of the Lamb: visionary rhetoric and social-political situation', *Semeia* 36 (1986), 123–46.

—'The phenomenon of early Christian apocalyptic', in D. Hellholm (ed.), *Apocalypticism in the Mediterranean and the Near East* (Proceedings of the International Colloquium on Apocalypticism, Upsala, 1979; Tübingen: J.C.B. Mohr [Paul Siebeck], 1983), 295–316.

Firestone, R., 'Conceptions on holy war in biblical and Qur'ānic tradition', *JRE* 24 (1996), 99–123.

Fischel, H.A., 'Prophet and martyr', *JQR* 37 (1946–7), 265–80, 363–86.

Fishwick, D., 'The development of provincial ruler worship in the western Empire', *ANRW* II.16.2 (1978), 1201–53.

Fitzgerald, J.T., *Cracks in an Earthen Vessel: An Examination of the Catalogues of Hardships in the Corinthian Correspondence* (SBL Dissertation Series, 99; Atlanta: Scholars Press, 1988).

Fitzmeyer, J.A., *The Gospel according to St Luke* (AB, 28, 28A; 2 vols; New York: Doubleday, 1981, 1985).

Flemington, W.F., 'On the interpretation of Colossians 1.24', in W. Horbury and B. McNeil (eds), *Suffering and Martyrdom in the New Testament* (Cambridge: Cambridge University Press, 1981), 84–90.

Ford, J.M., *Revelation* (AB, 38; New York: Doubleday, 1975).

Forsyth, N., *The Old Enemy: Satan and the Combat Myth* (Princeton, NJ: Princeton University Press, 1987).

Fox, R.L., *Pagans and Christians* (London: Viking, 1986).

Frend, W.H.C., 'Blandina and Perpetua: two early Christian heroines', reprinted in D.M. Scholer (ed.), *Women in Early Christianity* (Studies in Early Christianity, 14; New York and London: Garland Publishing Inc., 1993), 87–97.

—*Martyrdom and Persecution: A Study of a Conflict from the Maccabees to Donatus* (Oxford: Basil Blackwell, 1965).

Friesen, S.J., *Imperial Cults and the Apocalypse of John: Reading Revelation in the Ruins* (Oxford: Oxford University Press, 2001).

Fuller, R.H., *The Foundation of New Testament Christology* (London: Lutterworth Press, 1965).

Gagé, J., *Les Classes sociales dans l'Empire romain* (Paris: Payot, 1971).

Gardner, E. (ed.), *Visions of Heaven and Hell before Dante* (New York: Italica Press, 1989).

Garrett, S.R., 'The God of this world and the affliction of Paul', in D.L. Balch, E. Ferguson and W.A. Meeks (eds), *Greeks, Romans, and Christians: Essays in Honor of Abraham J. Malherbe* (Minneapolis: Fortress Press, 1990), 99–117.

Garrow, A.J.P., *Revelation* (NTR; New York/London: Routledge, 1997).

Geddert, T.J., *Watchwords: Mark 13 in Markan Eschatology* (Sheffield: Sheffield Academic Press, 1989).

George, L., *The Encyclopedia of Heresies and Heretics* (London: Robson Books, 1995).

Gibbon, E., *The Decline and Fall of the Roman Empire* (London: J.M. Dent, 1910).

Gillman, N., 'Death and the afterlife', in J. Neusner, A.J. Avery-Peck and W.S. Green (eds), *The Encyclopaedia of Judaism* (Leiden: E.J. Brill, 2000), 196–212.

Glasson, T.F., *The Revelation of St John* (Cambridge: Cambridge University Press, 1965).

Goldstein, J.A., *I Maccabees* (AB, 41; Garden City, NY: Doubleday, 1976).

—*II Maccabees* (AB, 41A; Garden City, NY: Doubleday, 1983).

Goodblatt, D., 'Suicide in the sanctuary: traditions on priestly martyrdom', *JJS* 46 (1995), 10–29.

Gordon, R., 'The veil of power', in R.A. Horsley (ed.), *Paul and Empire: Religion and Power in Roman Imperial Society* (Harrisburg, PA: Trinity Press International, 1997), 126–37.

Grant, R.M., *Augustus to Constantine: The Thrust of the Christian Movement into the Roman World* (London: Collins, 1971).

Gray, A.M., 'A contribution to the study of martyrdom and identity in the Palestinian Talmud', *JJS* 54 (2003), 242–72.

Grayston, K., 'Atonement and martyrdom', in J.M.G. Barclay and J. Sweet (eds), *Early Christian Thought in Its Jewish Context* (Cambridge: Cambridge University Press, 1996), 250–63.

Gregory, B.S., *Salvation at Stake: Christian Martyrdom in Early Modern Europe* (HHS, 134; Massachusetts: Harvard University Press, 1999).

Grisé, Y., *Le Suicide dans la Rome antique* (Montreal: Bellamin, 1982).

Gruenwald, I., 'Intolerance and martyrdom: from Socrates to Rabbi 'Aquiva', in G.N. Stanton and G.G. Stroumsa (eds), *Tolerance and Intolerance in Early Judaism and Christianity* (Cambridge: Cambridge University Press, 1998), 7–29.

Gundry, R.H., *Mark: A Commentary on His Apology for the Cross* (Grand Rapids: Eerdmans, 1993).

Hadas, M., *The Third and Fourth Book of Maccabees* (New York: Ktav, 1976).

Hafemann, S.J., 'The role of suffering in the mission of Paul', in J. Ådna and H. Kvalbein (eds), *The Mission of the Early Church to Jews and Gentiles* (Tübingen: Mohr Siebeck, 2000), 165–84.

Hall, J.R., P.D. Schuyler and S. Trinh, *Apocalypse Observed: Religious Movements and Violence in North America, Europe and Japan* (London/New York: Routledge, 2000).

Harrison, J.R., 'Paul and the imperial gospel at Thessaloniki', *JSNT* 25 (2002), 71–96.

Harvey, A.E., *Renewal through Suffering: A Study of 2 Corinthians* (Edinburgh: T&T Clark, 1996).

Haynes, S.R., *The Bonhoeffer Phenomenon: Portraits of a Protestant Saint* (London: SCM Press, 2004).

Heffernan, T.J., 'Philology and authorship in the *Passio Sanctarum Perpetuae et Felicitatis*', *Traditio* 50 (1995), 315–25.

Hengel, M., *The Atonement: The Origins of the Doctrine in the New Testament* (Philadelphia: Fortress Press, 1981).

—*Crucifixion in the Ancient World and the Folly of the Message of the Cross* (London: SCM Press, 1977).

—*Judaism and Hellenism: Studies in Their Encounter in Palestine during the Early Hellenistic Period* (trans. J. Bowden; 2 vols; London: SCM Press, 1974).

—*The Zealots: Investigations into the Jewish Freedom Movement in the Period from Herod I until 70 A.D.* (trans. D. Smith; Edinburgh: T&T Clark, 1989).

Henry, P., *New Directions in New Testament Study* (London: SCM Press, 1980).

—'Why is contemporary scholarship so enamoured of ancient heretics?', in E.A. Livingstone (ed.), *Studia Patristica XVII* (Oxford: Pergamon Press, 1982), 123–26.

Henten, J.W. van, 'Daniel 3 and 6 in early Christian literature', in J.J. Collins and P.W. Flint (eds), *The Book of Daniel: Composition and Reception* (2 vols; Leiden: E.J. Brill, 2001), I, 149–69.

—'Datierung und Herkunft des vierten Makkabäerbuches', in J.W. van Henten, H.J. de Jonge, P.T. van Rooden and J.W. Wesselius (eds), *Tradition and Reinterpretation in Jewish and Early Christian Literature: Essays in Honour of Jürgen C.H. Lebram* (Leiden: E.J. Brill, 1986), 136–49.

—*The Maccabean Martyrs as the Saviours of the Jewish People: A Study of 2 and 4 Maccabees* (Leiden: E.J. Brill, 1997).

—'Martyrion and martyrdom: some remarks about noble death in Josephus', in J.U. Kalms and F. Siegert (eds), *Internationales Josephus-Kolloquium Brüssels 1998* (Münster: Lit, 1999), 124–41.

—'Zum Einfluβ jüdischer Martyrien auf die Literatur des frühen Christentums II. Die Apostolischen Väter', *ANRW* II.27.1 (1993), 700–23.

Henten, J.W. van, and F. Avemarie, *Martyrdom and Noble Death: Selected Texts from Graeco-Roman, Jewish and Christian Antiquity* (London/New York: Routledge, 2002).

Himmelfarb, M., 'Judaism and Hellenism in 2 Maccabees', *Poetics Today* 10 (1998), 19–40.

—'The practice of ascent in the ancient Mediterranean world', in J.J. Collins and M. Fischbane (eds), *Death, Ecstasy, and Other Worldly Journeys* (New York: State of New York Press, 1995), 123–37.

Hoek, A. van den, 'Clement of Alexandria on martyrdom', in E.A. Livingstone (ed.), *Studia Patristica XXVI* (Oxford: Pergamon Press, 1993), 324–41.

Hooff, A.J.L. van, *From Autothanasia to Suicide: Self-Killing in Classical Antiquity* (London/New York: Routledge, 1990).

Hooker, M. D., *The Gospel according to Saint Mark* (BNTC; London: A. & C. Black, 1992).

—'Interchange and suffering', in W. Horbury and B. McNeil (eds), *Suffering and Martyrdom in the New Testament* (Cambridge: Cambridge University Press, 1981), 70–83.

Hopkins, K., 'Christian number and its implications', *JECS* 6 (1998), 185–226.

—*Conquerors and Slaves* (Cambridge: Cambridge University Press, 1978).

—*Death and Renewal* (Cambridge: Cambridge University Press, 1983).

Horbury W., *Jews and Christians: In Contact and Controversy* (Edinburgh: T&T Clark, 1998).

Horsley, G.H.R. (ed.), *New Documents Illustrating Early Christianity: A Review of Greek Inscriptions and Papyri Published in 1979*, IV (New South Wales: Macquarie University, 1987).

Horsley, R.A., 'Introduction', in R.A. Horsley (ed.), *Paul and Empire: Religion and Power in Roman Imperial Society* (Harrisburg, PA: Trinity Press International, 1997, 1–24.

Hummel, E.L., *The Concept of Martyrdom according to St Cyprian of Carthage* (Washington: Catholic University of America Press, 1946).

Hurtado, L.W., 'First-century Jewish monotheism', *JSNT* 71 (1998), 3–26.

—'Jesus' death as paradigmatic in the New Testament', *SJT* 57 (2004), 413–33.

—*Lord Jesus Christ: Devotion to Jesus in Earliest Christianity* (Grand Rapids: Eerdmans, 2003).

—*One Lord, One God: Early Christian Devotion and Ancient Jewish Monotheism* (Edinburgh: T&T Clark, 1998).

Iersel, B.M.F. van, 'Failed followers in Mark: Mark 13.12 as a key for the identification of the intended readers', *CBQ* 58 (1996), 244–63.

Isaac, B., and A. Oppenheimer, 'Bar Kokhba', in *ABD*, I, 598–606.

James, M.R., *The Apocryphal New Testament* (Oxford: Clarendon Press, 1924).

Jamison, K.R., *Night Falls Fast: Understanding Suicide* (London: Picador, 2000).

Janowitz, N., *Magic in the Roman World: Pagans, Jews and Christians* (Religion in the First Christian Centuries; London/New York: Routledge, 2001).

Janssen, L.F., 'Some unexplored aspects of the *Devotio Deciana*', *Mnemosyne* 4 (1981), 357–81.

Jaquette, J.L., 'Life and death, *Adiaphora* and Paul's rhetorical strategies', *NovT* 38 (1996), 30–54.

Jensen, A., *God's Self-confident Daughters: Early Christianity and the Liberation of Women* (trans. O.C. Dean; Louisville, KY: John Knox Press, 1996).

Jewett, R., 'The epistolary thanksgiving and the integrity of Philippians', *NovT* 12 (1970), 40–53.

Johnson, L.T., *The Gospel of Luke* (Sacra Pagina; Minnesota: Liturgical Press, 1991).

Johnston, J.T., *The Holy War Idea in Western and Islamic Tradition* (Pennsylvania: Pennsylvania State University Press, 1997).

Jones, B.W., *The Emperor Domitian* (London/New York: Routledge, 1992).

Jones, C.P., 'Stigma: tattooing and branding in Graeco-Roman antiquity', *JRS* 77 (1987), 139–55.

Jones, D.L., 'Christianity and the Roman Imperial cult', *ANRW* II.23.2 (1980), 1023–54.

—'Roman Imperial cult', *ABD*, V, 806–9

Jones, G.H., ' "Holy war" or Yahweh war', *VT* 25 (1975), 642–58.

Jonge, M. de, 'Jesus' death for others and the death of the Maccabean martyrs', in G.P. Luttikhuizen and A.S. van der Woude (eds), *Texts and Testimony: Essays in Honour of A.F.J. Klinj* (Kampen: Uitgeversmaatschappij J.H. Kok, 1988), 142–51.

Juel, D., *Master of Surprise* (Minneapolis: Fortress Press, 1992).

Jungmann, J.A., *The Early Liturgy to the Time of Gregory the Great* (trans. F.A. Brunner; London: Darton, Longman & Todd, 1959).

Kamm, A., *The Romans: An Introduction* (London/New York: Routledge, 1995).

Kelly, J.N.D., *A Commentary on the Pastoral Epistles* (BNTC; London: A. & C. Black, 1963).

Keresztes, P., *Imperial Rome and the Christians: From Herod the Great to around 200 A.D.* (London: United Press of America, 1990).

Khaduri, M., *War and Peace in the Law of Islam* (Baltimore: The Johns Hopkins University Press, 1955).

Khiok-Khng, Y., 'A political reading of Paul's eschatology in I & II Thessalonians', *Asia Journal of Theology* 12 (1998), 77–88.

Kiddle, M., *The Revelation of St John* (London: Hodder & Stoughton, 1940).

Kim, T.H., 'The anarthrous υἰὸς θεοῦ in Mark 15:39 and the Roman Imperial cult', *Biblia* 79 (1998), 221–41.

Klawiter, F.C., 'The role of martyrdom and persecution in developing the priestly authority of women in early Christianity: a case study of Montanism', *Church History* 49 (1980), 251–61.

Klijn, A.F.J., and G.F. Reinink, *Patristic Evidence for Jewish-Christian Sects* (NovTSup, 36; Leiden: E.J. Brill, 1973).

Koester, C.R., 'From Paul's eschatology to the apocalyptic schemata in 2 Thessalonians', in R.F. Collins (ed.), *The Thessalonian Correspondence* (Louvain: Louvain University Press, 1990), 441–58.

—ΓΝΩΜΑΙ ΔΙΑΦΟΡΟΙ: the origin and nature of diversification in the history of early Christianity', *HTR* 58 (1965), 279–318.

—*Hebrews* (AB, 38; New York: Doubleday, 2001).

Krodel, G., 'Persecution and toleration of Christianity until Hadrian', in S. Benko and J.J. O'Rourke (eds), *Early Church History: the Roman Empire as the Setting of Primitive Christianity* (London: Oliphants, 1971), 255–67.

Kümmel, W.G., *Introduction to the New Testament* (London: SCM Press, 1975).

Ladd, G.E., *A Commentary on the Revelation of John* (Grand Rapids: Eerdmans, 1972).

Ladouceur, D.J., 'Josephus and Masada', in L.H. Feldman and G. Hata (eds), *Josephus, Judaism and Christianity* (Leiden: E.J. Brill, 1987), 95–113.

Lambrecht, J., *Second Corinthians* (Sacra Pagina; Minnesota: The Liturgical Press, 1999).

Lampe, G.W.H., 'Inspiration and martyrdom', in W. Horbury and B. McNeil (eds), *Suffering and Martyrdom in the New Testament* (Cambridge: Cambridge University Press, 1981), 118–35.

—*A Patristic Greek Lexicon* (Oxford: Clarendon Press, 1961).

Lampe, P., *Die Stadrömischen Christen in der ersten beiden Jahrhunderten: untersuchen zur Sozialgeschichte* (Tübingen: Mohr Siebeck, 1987).

Lawrence, B.B., *Shattering the Myth: Islam beyond Violence* (Princeton, NJ: Princeton University Press, 2000).

Lebram, J.C.H., 'Jüdische Martyrologie und Weisheitsüberlieferung', in J.W. van Henten, B.A.G.M. Dehandschutter and H.J.W. van der Klaauw (eds), *Die Entstehung der jüdischen Martyrologie* (Leiden: E.J. Brill, 1989), 88–126.

Lee, M., 'A call to martyrdom: function as method and message in Revelation', *NovT* 40 (1998), 164–94.

Lewis, B., *The Crisis of Islam: Holy War and Unholy Terror* (London: Weidenfeld and Nicholson, 2003).

Liebeschuetz, J.H.W.G., *Continuity and Change in Roman Religion* (Oxford: Clarendon Press, 1979).

Lietzmann H., *Geschichte der Alten Kirche* (Berlin/Leipzig: W. de Gruyter, 1932).

Lieu, J. M., ' "I am a Christian": martyrdom and the beginning of "Christian Identity" ', in J.M. Lieu, *Neither Jew nor Greek?*, 211–31

—*Image and Reality: The Jews in the World of the Christians in the Second Century* (Edinburgh: T&T Clark, 1996).

—' "The parting of the ways": theological construct or historical reality?', in J.M. Lieu, *Neither Jew nor Greek?: Constructing Early Christianity* (London/New York: T&T Clark, 2002), 11–30.

Lieu, J.M., J. North and T. Rajak, *The Jews among Pagans and Christian in the Roman Empire* (London: Routledge, 1992).

Lightfoot, R.H., *The Gospel Message of St Mark* (Cambridge: Cambridge University Press, 1950).

—*St Paul's Epistle to the Philippians* (London: Macmillan, 1891).

Lind, M.C., *Yahweh Is a Warrior: The Theology of Warfare in Ancient Israel* (Scottsdale: Herald Press, 1980).

Loftus, F., 'The martyrdom of the Galilean troglodytes (*B.J.* i.312–3; *A.* xiv.429–430): a suggested Tradition-geschichte', *JQR* 66 (1976), 213–33.

Lohmeyer, E., *Die Brief an die Philipper* (Göttingen: Vandenhoeck & Ruprecht, 1961).

Lohse, E., *Colossians and Philemon* (trans. W.R. Poehlmann and R.J. Karris; Hermeneia; Philadelphia: Fortress Press, 1971).

Longenecker, R.N., 'Taking up the cross daily: discipleship in Luke–Acts', in R.N. Longenecker (ed.), *Patterns of Discipleship in the New Testament* (Grand Rapids: Eerdmans, 1996), 50–76.

Lüdemann, G., *Early Christianity according to the Tradition of Acts: A Commentary* (Minneaoplis: Fortress Press, 1989).

—*Heretics: The Other Side of Christianity* (trans. J. Bowden; London: SCM Press, 1996).

Luter, A.B., 'Martyrdom', in R.P. Martin and P.H. Davids (eds), *Dictionary of the Later New Testament and Its Development* (Downer Grove, IL: InterVarsity Press, 1996), 717–22.

Lutz, C.E., 'Musonius Rufus: the Roman Socrates', *Yale Classical Studies* 10 (1947), 3–147.

McDannell, C., and B. Lang, *Heaven: A History* (New Haven/London: Yale University Press, 1988).

MacDonald, M. Y., *Early Christian Women and Pagan Opinion: The Power of the Hysterical Woman* (Cambridge: Cambridge University Press, 1996).

MacMullen, R., 'What difference did Christianity make?', *Historia* 35 (1986), 322–43.

Maitland, S., 'Passionate prayer: masochistic images in women's experience', in L. Hurcombe (ed.), *Sex and God: Some Varieties of Women's Religious Experience* (New York/London: Routledge and Kegan Paul, 1987), 125–40.

Malone, E.E., *The Monk and the Martyr: The Monk as the Successor of the Martyr* (Washington, DC: The Catholic University of America Press, 1950).

Marcus, J., *Mark 1–8* (AB, 27; New York: Doubleday, 2000).

—*The Way of the Lord: Christological Exegesis of the Old Testament in the Gospel of Mark* (Edinburgh: T&T Clark, 1993).

Markus, R.A., *The End of Christianity* (Cambridge: Cambridge University Press, 1990).

Marshall, I.H., *A Critical and Exegetical Commentary on the Pastoral Epistles* (ICC; Edinburgh: T&T Clark, 1999).

—*1 & 2 Thessalonians* (New Century Bible Commentary; Grand Rapids: Eerdmans, 1983).

—*The Gospel of Luke: A Commentary on the Greek Text* (NIGTC; Grand Rapids: Eerdmans, 1978).

—'Orthodoxy and heresy in earlier Christianity', *Themelios* 2 (1976), 5–14.

Martyn, J.L., *Galatians* (AB, 33A; New York: Doubleday, 1997).

Meeks, W.A., 'Social functions of apocalyptic language in Pauline Christianity', in D. Hellholm (ed.), *Apocalypticism in the Mediterranean and the Near East* (Proceedings of the International Colloquium on Apocalypticism, Uppsala, 1979; Tübingen: J.C.B. Mohr [Paul Siebeck], 1983), 687–705.

Meyer, P.M., *Griechishe Texte aus Ägypten* (Berlin: Weidmannsche Buchhandlung, 1916).

Michaelis, W., *Der Brief des Paulus an die Philipper* (THKNT, 11; Leipzig: Deichert, 1935).

Miller, P.C., 'The Devil's gateway: an eros of difference in the dreams of Perpetua', *Dreaming* 2 (1992), 45–53.

Miller, P.D., *The Divine Warrior in Early Israel* (Cambridge: Harvard University Press, 1973).

Minear, P., *I Saw a New Earth: An Introduction to the Visions of the Apocalypse* (Washington: Corpus, 1968).

Mitchell, S., 'Festivals, games and civic life in Roman Asia Minor', *JRS* 80 (1990), 183–93.

Moberly, R.B., 'When was Revelation conceived?', *Biblica* 73 (1992), 376–93.

Moore, A.L., *Parousia in the New Testament* (Leiden: E.J. Brill, 1966).

Moore, S.D., and J.C. Anderson, 'Taking it like a man: masculinity in 4 Maccabees', *JBL* 117 (1998), 249–73.

Morris, K.R., ' "Pure wheat of God" or neurotic deathwish?: a historical and theological analysis of Ignatius of Antioch's zeal for martyrdom', *Fides et Historia* 26 (1994), 24–41.

Moule, C.F.D., *The Epistles of Paul the Apostle to the Colossians and to Philemon* (Cambridge: Cambridge University Press, 1962).

Mounce, R.H., *The Book of Revelation* (Grand Rapids: Eerdmans, 1977).

Mühlenberg, E., 'The martyr's death and its literary presentation', in E.A. Livingstone (ed.), *Studia Patristica XXIX* (Oxford: Pergamon Press, 1997), 85–93.

Munck, J., 'Jewish Christianity in post-apostolic times', *NTS* 6 (1960), 103–16.

Munoa, P.B., 'Jesus, the Merkavah, and martyrdom in early Christian tradition', *JBL* 121 (2002), 303–25.

Murphy, F.J., *Fallen Is Babylon: The Revelation to John* (Pennsylvania: Trinity Press International, 1998).

Musurillo, H., *The Acts of the Christian Martyrs* (Oxford: Clarendon Press, 1972).

Nickelsburg, W.E., *Resurrection, Immortality, and Eternal Life in Intertestamental Judaism* (Harvard Theological Studies, 26; Cambridge: Harvard University Press, 1972).

Niditch S., and R. Doran, 'The success story of the wise courtier: a formal approach', *JBL* 96 (1979), 189–93.

Nineham, D.E., *The Gospel of St. Mark* (Middlesex: Penguin Books, 1963).

Nock, A.D., 'The Roman army and the Roman religious year', *HTR* 45 (1952), 187–252.

Norris, F.W., 'Ignatius, Polycarp, and I Clement: Walter Bauer reconsidered', *VC* 30 (1976), 23–44.

O'Brien, P.T., *The Epistle to the Philippians: A Commentary on the Greek Text* (NIGTC; Grand Rapids: Eerdmans, 1991).

O'Mathúna, D.P., 'Did Paul condone suicide?: implications for assisted suicide and active euthanasia', *Ethics and Medicine* 12 (1996), 55–60.

O'Neill, J.C., 'Did Jesus teach that his death would be vicarious as well as typical?', in W. Horbury and B. McNeil (eds), *Suffering and Martyrdom in the New Testament: Studies Presented to G.M. Styler* (London: Cambridge University Press, 1981), 9–27.

Oberholzer, F., 'Interpreting the dreams of Perpetua: psychology in the service of theology', in M.H. Barnes (ed.), *Theology and the Social Sciences* (Maryknoll, NY: Orbis Books, 2001), 293–312.

Ollenburger, B.C., 'Introduction: Gerhard von Rad's theory of holy war', in G. von Rad, *Holy War in Ancient Israel* (Grand Rapids: Eerdmans, 1991).

Pagels, E., 'Gnostic and orthodox views of Christ's passion: paradigms for the Christian's response to persecution?', in B. Layton (ed.), *The Rediscovery of Gnosticism* (2 vols; Leiden: E.J. Brill, 1980), I, 262–83.

—*The Gnostic Gospels* (New York: Random House, 1979).

—'The social history of Satan, the "intimate enemy": a preliminary sketch', *HTR* 84 (1991), 105–28

Palmer, D.W., ' "To die is gain": Philippians i 21', *NovT* 17 (1975), 203–18.

Parker, R., 'Greek religion', in J. Boardman, J. Griffin and O. Murray (eds), *The Oxford History of the Classical World* (Oxford and New York: Oxford University Press, 1995), 254–74.

Partner, P., *God of Battles: Holy Wars of Christianity and Islam* (Princeton, NJ: Princeton University Press, 1998).

Patterson, S.J., *The Gospel of Thomas and Jesus* (Sonoma: Polebridge Press, 1993).

Pearson, B.A., '1 Thessalonians 2.13–16: a deutero-Pauline interpolation', *HTR* 64 (1971), 79–91.

—*Gnosticism, Judaism, and Egyptian Christianity* (Minneapolis: Augsburg Fortress, 1990).

—'The Testimony of Truth', *NHL*, 449.

Perham, M., *The Communion of Saints: An Examination of the Place of the Christian Dead in the Belief, Worship, and Calendars of the Church* (London: SPCK, 1980).

Perkins, J., *The Suffering Self: Pain and Narrative Representation in Early Christianity* (London: Routledge, 1995).

Perler, O., 'Das vierte Makkabäerbuch, Ignatius von Antiochien und die ältesten Martyrerberichte', *Rivista di Archeologia Christiana* 25 (1949), 47–72.

Petterson, A.L., 'Perpetua – prisoner of conscience', *VC* 41 (1987), 139–53.

Pfitzner, V.C., *Paul and the Agon Motif* (NovTSup, 4; Leiden: E.J. Brill, 1961).

Plass, P., *The Game of Death in Ancient Rome* (Madison: University of Michigan Press, 1995).

Pleket, H.W., 'Domitian, the Senate and the provinces', *Mnemosyne* 14 (1961), 296–315.

Plummer, A., *A Critical and Exegetical Commentary on the Gospel according to St Luke* (ICC; Edinburgh: T&T Clark, 1922).

Pobee, J.S., *Persecution and Martyrdom in the Theology of Paul* (Sheffield: JSOT Press, 1985).

Potter, D.S., 'Entertainment in the Roman Empire', in D.S. Potter and D.J. Mattingly (eds), *Life, Death, and Entertainment in the Roman Empire* (Ann Arbor: University of Michigan Press, 1999), 256–325.

—'Martyrdom as spectacle', in R. Scodel (ed.), *Theatre and Society in the Classical World* (Ann Arbor: University of Michigan Press, 1993), 53–88.

—'Persecution of the early Church', *ABD*, V, 231–5.

Price, S.F.R., 'Between man and God: sacrifice in the Roman Imperial cult', *JRS* 70 (1980), 28–43.

—'Gods and emperors: the Greek language of the Roman Imperial cult', *JHS* 54 (1984), 19–95.

—'Latin Christian apologetics: Minucius Felix, Tertullian, and Cyprian', in M. Edwards, M. Goodman and S. Price, *Apologetics in the Roman Empire: Pagans, Jews, and Christians* (Oxford: Oxford University Press, 1999), 105–29.

—'Rituals and power', in R.A. Horsley (ed.), *Paul and Empire: Religion and Power in Roman Imperial Society* (Harrisburg, PA: Trinity Press International, 1997), 45–71.

—*Rituals and Power: The Roman Imperial Cult in Asia Minor* (Cambridge: Cambridge University Press, 1984).

Rad, G. von, *Holy War in Ancient Israel* (trans. M.J. Dawn; Grand Rapids: Eerdmans, 1991).

Rajak, T., 'Dying for the Law: the martyr's portrait in Jewish-Greek literature', in M.J. Edwards and S. Swain (eds), *Portraits: Biographical Representation in the Greek and Latin Literature of the Roman Empire* (Oxford: Clarendon Press, 1997), 39–67.

Reasoner, M., 'Persecution', in R.P. Martin and P.H. Davids (eds), *Dictionary of the Later New Testament and Its Developments* (Downers Grove, IL: InterVarsity Press, 1997), 907–14.

Richard, E., *First and Second Thessalonians* (Sacra Pagina; Minnesota: The Liturgical Press, 1995).

Riches, J.K., *Conflicting Mythologies: Identity Formations in the Gospels of Mark and Matthew* (Edinburgh: T&T Clark, 2001).

Ricoeur, P., *Essays on Biblical Interpretation* (ed. L.S. Mudge; London: SPCK, 1981).

Rist, J.M., *Stoic Philosophy* (Cambridge: Cambridge University Press, 1969).

Ritter, A.M., 'Creeds', in I. Hazlett (ed.), *Early Christianity: Origins and Evolution to AD 600, in Honour of W.H.C. Frend* (London: SPCK, 1991), 92–100.

Robeck, C.M., *Prophecy in Carthage: Perpetua, Tertullian, and Cyprian* (Ohio: The Pilgrim Press, 1992).

Robert, L., *Les Gladiateurs dans l'Orient grec* (Paris: E. Champion, 1940).

Robinson, J.A.T., *Redating the New Testament* (London: SCM Press, 1976).

Robinson, J.M., P. Hoffman and J.S. Kloppenborg (eds), *The Critical Edition of Q* (Hermeneia; Minneapolis: Fortress Press; Leuven: Peeters, 2000).

Robinson, J.M. (ed.), *The Nag Hammadi Library in English* (Leiden: E.J. Brill, 1996).

Robinson, T.A., *The Bauer Thesis Re-examined: The Geography of Heresy in the Early Christian Church* (New York: The Edwin Mellen Press, 1988).

Rordorf, W., 'Wie steht es um den jüdischen Einfluss auf den christlichen Märtyrerkult', in *Lex Orandi Lex Credendi* (Université de Neuchâtel Publications de la Faculté de Théologie, XI; Freiburg: Universitätsverlag, 1993), 166–76.

Rowland, C., 'The Apocalypse: hope, resistance and the revelation of reality', *Ex Auditu* 6 (1990), 129–44.

—'The book of Daniel and the radical critique of empire: an essay in apocalyptic hermeneutics', in J.J. Collins and P.W. Flint (eds), *The Book of Daniel: Composition and Reception* (2 vols; Leiden: E.J. Brill, 2001), II, 447–67.

—*Christian Origins: An Account of the Setting and Character of the Most Important Messianic Sect of Judaism* (London: SPCK, 1985).

—*The Open Heaven: A Study of Apocalyptic in Judaism and Early Christianity* (London: SPCK, 1982).

Rowley, H.H., *The Relevance of Apocalyptic: A Study of Jewish and Christian Apocalypses from Daniel to the Revelation* (London: Lutterworth Press, 1963).

Russell, D.S., *The Method and Message of Jewish Apocalyptic* (Philadelphia: Westminster Press, 1964).

Salisbury, J.E., *Perpetua's Passion: The Death and Memory of a Young Roman Woman* (New York/London: Routledge, 1997).

Sanders, E.P., *Paul and Palestinian Judaism: A Comparison of Patterns of Religion* (London: SCM Press, 1977).

Sanders, J.T., *Schismatics, Sectarians, Dissidents and Deviants: The First One Hundred Years of Jewish-Christian Relations* (London: SCM Press, 1993).

Schmidt, D., '1 Thess 2:13–16: linguistic evidence for an interpolation', *JBL* 102 (1983), 269–79.

Schneemelcher, W., *New Testament Apocrypha* (trans. R. McL. Wilson; 2 vols;Cambridge: James Clarke & Co., 1991).

Schürer, E., *The History of the Jews in the Age of Jesus Christ* (3 vols; Edinburgh: T&T Clark, 1973).

Scott, J.C., *Domination and the Arts of Resistance* (New Haven: Yale University Press, 1990).

Seely, D., *The Noble Death: Graeco-Roman Martyrology and Paul's Concept of Salvation* (JSNTSup, 28; Sheffield: JSOT Press, 1990).

Segal, A.F., 'Jewish Christianity', in H.W. Hala and G. Hala (eds), *Eusebius, Christianity and Judaism* (Leiden: E.J. Brill, 1992), 326–51.

—*The Other Judaisms of Late Antiquity* (Atlanta: Scholars Press, 1987).

Self, W., *Revelation* (Pocket Canon Series; Edinburgh: Canongate, 1998).

Selinger, R., *The Mid-Third Century Persecutions of Decius and Valerian* (Frankfurt: Peter Lang, 2002).

Sevenster, J.N., 'Education or conversion: Eptictetus and the gospels', *NovT* 8 (1966), 247–62.

—*Paul and Seneca* (SNT, 4; Leiden: E.J. Brill, 1961).

Shaw, B.D., 'Body/power/identity: passions of the martyrs', *JECS* 4 (1996), 269–312.

Shaw, G.B., *Saint Joan: A Chronicle Play in Six Scenes and an Epilogue* (London: Chronicle, 1924).

Sherrer, S.J., 'Signs and wonders in the Imperial cult', *JBL* 103 (1984), 599–610.

Sherwin-White, A.N., 'Early persecution and Roman law again', *JTS* (n.s.) 3 (1952), 199–213.

—*The Letters of Pliny: A Social and Historical Commentary* (Oxford: Clarendon Press, 1966).

Sim, D.C., 'The gospels for all Christians?: a response to Richard Bauckham', *JSNT* 24.84 (2001), 3–27.

Slater, T.B., 'On the social setting of the Revelation to John', *NTS* 44 (1998), 232–56.

Smallwood, M.E., *The Jews under Roman Rule: From Pompey to Diocletian* (Leiden: E.J. Brill, 1981).

Smend, R.S., *Yahweh War and Tribal Confederation* (trans. M.G. Rogers; Nashville: Abingdon Press, 1970).

Smith, D.R., ' "Hand the man over to Satan": curse, exclusion, and salvation in 1 Corinthians 5' (PhD dissertation; University of Durham, 2005).

Smith, M., 'Ascent to heaven and the beginning of Christianity', *Eranus-Jahrbuch* 50 (1981), 403–29.

—*Jesus the Magician: Charlatan or Son of God?* (California: Seastone, 1998).

Stambaugh, J.E., and D.L. Balch, *The New Testament in Its Social Environment* (Philadelphia: Westminster Press, 1986).

Stark, R., 'The class basis of early Christians from a sociological model', *Sociological Analysis* 47 (1986), 216–25.

Ste Croix, B.A.G. de, 'Aspects of the Great Persecution', *HTR* 47 (1954), 75–109.
—'Why were the early Christians persecuted?', *Past and Present* 26 (1963), 6–38.
Stegner, W.R., 'Jesus' walking on the water: Mark 6.45–52', in C.A. Evans and R. Stegner (eds), *The Gospels and the Scriptures of Israel* (Sheffield: Sheffield Academic Press, 1994), 212–34.
Steinhauser, K.B., 'Augustine's reading of the *Passio sanctarum Perpetuae et Felicitatis*', in E.A. Livingstone (ed.), *Sudia Patristica XXXIII* (Leuven: Peeters, 1997), 244–9.
Stewart, Z., 'Greek crowns and Christian martyrs', in E. Lucchesi and H.D. Saffrey (eds), *Antiquité païenne et chrétienne: mémorial André-Jean Festugière* (Geneva: Cramer, 1984), 119–24.
Straw, C., 'Martyrdom and Christian identity: Gregory the Great, Augustine, and tradition', in W.E. Klingshirn and M. Vessey, *The Limits of Ancient Christianity: Essays on Late Antique Thought and Culture in Honor of R.A. Markus* (Ann Arbor: University of Michigan Press, 1999), 250–66.
Streete, G.C., 'Women as sources of redemption and knowledge in early Christian traditions', in R. Shepard Kraemer and R. D'Angelo (eds), *Women and Christian Origins* (New York/Oxford: Oxford University Press, 1999), 330–54.
Surkau, H.W., *Martyrien in jüdischer und früchristlicher Zeit* (Göttingen: Vandenhoeck & Ruprecht, 1938).
Swete, H.B., *The Apocalypse of St John* (London: Macmillan, 1922).
Tabor, J.D., 'Patterns of the end: textual weaving from Qumran to Waco', in P. Schäfer and M.R. Cohen (eds), *Toward the Millennium: Messianic Expectations from the Bible to Waco* (Leiden: E.J. Brill, 1998), 409–30.
Tannehill, R.C., 'The disciples in Mark: the function of a narrative role', *JR* 57 (1977), 386–405.
—*Dying and Rising with Christ: A Study in Pauline Theology* (Berlin: Alfred Töpelmann, 1967).
—'The gospel of Mark as narrative Christology', *Semeia* 16 (1979), 57–95.
Taylor, D.B., *Mark's Gospel as Literature and History* (London: SCM Press, 1992).
Taylor, L.R., *The Divinity of the Roman Emperor* (Connecticut: American Philological Association, 1931).
Theissen, G., *A Theory of Primitive Christianity* (trans. J. Bowden; London: SCM Press, 1999).
Thompson, L.L., *The Book of Revelation: Apocalypse and Empire* (New York/Oxford: Oxford University Press, 1990).
—'Lamentation for Christ as hero: Revelation 1:7', *JBL* 119 (2000), 683–703.
—'The martyrdom of Polycarp: death in the Roman games', *JR* 82 (2002), 27–52.
Trites, A.A., *The New Testament Concept of Witness* (Cambridge: Cambridge University Press, 1977).
Trumbower, J.A., '*Apocalypse of Peter* 14, 1–4 in relation to confessors' intercession for the non-Christian dead', in M.F. Wiles, E.J. Yarnold and P.M. Parvis (eds), *Studia Patristica XXXVI* (Leuven: Peeters, 2001), 307–12.
Turner, H.E.W., *The Pattern of Truth: A Study of the Relations between Orthodoxy and Heresy in the Early Church* (London: A.R. Mowbray & Co., 1954).
Tyan, E., 'Djihād', in H.A.R. Gibb (ed.), *Encyclopaedia of Islam* (Leiden: E.J. Brill, 1965), II, 538–9.
Valantasis, R., *The Gospel of Thomas* (New Testament Readings; London/New York: Routledge, 1997).
Vermes, G., *The Complete Dead Sea Scrolls in English* (London: Penguin, 1997).
Versnel, H.S., 'Two types of Roman de*votio*', *Mnemosyne* 29 (1976), 365–410.
Viscusi, P., 'Studies on Domitian' (PhD Dissertation; Ann Arbor University, 1973).

Walaskay, P.W., *'And so we came to Rome': The Political Perspective of St Luke* (Cambridge: Cambridge University Press, 1983).

Walzer, M., 'The idea of holy war in Ancient Israel', *JRE* 22 (1992), 215–27.

Wanamaker, C.A., *The Epistles to the Thessalonians: A Commentary on the Greek Text* (NIGTC; Grand Rapids: Eerdmans, 1990).

Wansink, C.S., *Chained in Christ: The Experience and Rhetoric of Paul's Imprisonments* (JSNTSup, 130; Sheffield: Sheffield Academic Press, 1996).

Warden, D., 'Imperial persecution and the dating of 1 Peter and Revelation', *JETS* 34 (1991), 203–12.

Weidmann, F.W., ' "Rushing judgment?": willfulness and martyrdom in early Christianity', *Union Seminary Quarterly Review* 53 (1999), 61–9.

Weiner, E., and A. Weiner, *The Martyr's Conviction: A Sociological Analysis* (Brown Judaic Studies, 203; Atlanta: Scholars Press, 1990).

Weinfeld, M., *Deuteronomy and the Deuteronomic School* (Oxford: Clarendon Press, 1972).

Wengst, K., *Christologische Formeln und Lieder des Urchristentums* (Gütersloh: Mohn, 1972).

—*Pax Romana and the Peace of Jesus Christ* (London: SCM Press, 1987).

Wiedemann, T., *Emperors and Gladiators* (London: Routledge, 1998).

Wilken, R. L., *The Christians as the Romans Saw Them* (New Haven/London: Yale University Press, 1984).

—'Diversity and unity in early Christianity', *The Second Century* 1 (1981), 101–10.

Williams, G., *The Sanctity of Life and the Criminal Law* (New York: Knopf, 2nd edn, 1970).

Williams, S.K., *Jesus' Death as Saving Event: The Background and Origin of a Concept* (Missoula, MT: Scholars Press, 1975).

Wilson, J.C., 'The problem of the Domitian date of Revelation', *NTS* 39 (1993), 587–605.

Wilson S., 'Introduction', in S. Wilson (ed.), *Saints and Their Cults: Studies in Religious Sociology, Folklore and History* (Cambridge: Cambridge University Press, 1983), 1–53.

Wilson, S.G., *Related Strangers: Jews and Christians 70–170 C.E.* (Minneapolis: Fortress Press, 1995).

Wink, W., *Engaging the Powers: Discernment and Resistance in a World of Domination* (Minneapolis: Fortress Press, 1992).

—*Naming the Powers: The Language of Power in the New Testament* (Philadelphia: Fortress Press, 1984).

—*Unmasking the Powers: The Invisible Forces That Determine Human Existence* (Philadelphia: Fortress Press, 1986).

Wong, D.K.K., 'The two witnesses in Revelation 11', *Bibliotheca Sacra* 154 (1997), 344–54.

Yarbro Collins, A.,

—*The Combat Myth in the Book of Revelation* (HDR, 9; Missoula, MT: Scholars Press, 1976).

—*Cosmology and Eschatology in Jewish and Christian Apocalypticism* (Leiden: E.J. Brill, 1996).

—*Crisis and Catharsis: The Power of the Apocalypse* (Philadelphia: Westminster Press, 1984).

—'Dating the Apocalypse of John', *BR* 26 (1981), 33–45.

—'From noble death to crucified Messiah', *NTS* 40 (1994), 481–503.

Zanker, P., 'The power of images', in R.A. Horsley (ed.), *Paul and Empire: Religion and Power in Roman Imperial Society* (Pennsylvania: Trinity Press International, 1997), 72–86.

—*The Power of Images in the Age of Augustus* (Ann Arbor: University of Michigan Press, 1988).

Zeev, M.P. ben, 'Did the Jews enjoy a privileged position in the Roman world?', *Revue des études juives* 154 (1995), 23–42.

INDEX OF REFERENCES

OLD TESTAMENT

NEW TESTAMENT

Index of References

OTHER EARLY CHRISTIAN WRITINGS

Rom
1.2	91
2.1	91
4.1–5.3	19
4.1	91
5	85
5.3	91
7	19
9.2	91
10.2	19

Smyr
4	19
11.1	91

Trall
4.1	74
12.2	91
13.3	91

Irenaeus
A.H.
3.18.5	23, 92
4.33.9	23, 85

John Chrysostom
de Droiside martyre
2	88

Homily IV on
1 Cor 1.18–20
	121

Justin
Apol. I
7	67
8	22, 87
12	22, 87
13	123
26	20, 68
57	81, 94

Apol. II
1	81
2	21, 22, 87
4	37
10	121
12	21, 79

Trypho
11	87
14	87
16	87
35	89
46	94
110	89

Lactantius
Divine Institutes
	169

Mart. Agapê
5.2	80

Mart. Apoll.
27–30	87
27	77
47	77, 81, 88

Mart. Carpus
	33–4, 80
1	83
3	84
5	81, 84
6–7	82
7–8	92
8	95
17	80, 81
23	84
34	84
35	73, 75, 77
36	35
37	35
38–9	77
39	92, 94
40	21, 78
41	35, 92
42–7	79
42–4	10, 33
47	33, 35

(Latin recension)
4.2	81, 82
4.4–5	95
4.4	87
6.3	34

Mart. Conon
3–4	80

5.7	95
6–7	85

Mart. Fruct.
1.4	78, 81, 90
4.1	78, 88, 90
6.1	73
6.3	21, 78

(Alternative ending)
	91

Mart. Ignatius
1	95
2	95
4	89
5	73, 78, 90
7	95

Mart. Justin
(Recension A)
2.1	95
2.2	85
3.4	84
4.1	84
4.3–4	87
4.3	84

(Recension B)
5.7	84

(Recension C)
2.1	94
3.5	84
4.1–4	93
4.6	93, 94
3.5	84

Mart. Lyons
	80, 109, 114
1.1	73
1.3–6	79, 81
1.3	76
1.4–5	81
1.5	79, 80, 82, 97, 161
1.6	74, 77, 87

1.7	74, 76
1.9	31, 95
1.10	31, 32, 88, 97
1.11–12	21
1.11	74, 77, 95
1.12	88
1.13	88, 97
1.14	82
1.15	76
1.16	81, 82
1.17	73, 74, 76
1.18	74
1.19	74, 76, 77, 86
1.20	84, 86
1.22	86
1.23	81, 86, 89
1.24–5	21
1.25–6	89–90
1.25	81, 82
1.26	97
1.27	80, 81, 82
1.29	6, 38, 89
1.30	76, 82
1.31	76, 81
1.32–5	87
1.33–5	22
1.35	81, 82
1.36	78, 88, 90
1.38	78, 90
1.39	76
1.40	85
1.41	83
1.42	73, 88, 89
1.43	76
1.44	76
1.45–6	95
1.45	95
1.48	97
1.50	76
1.51–2	85
1.51	77
1.52	67, 76
1.53–6	84
1.53	76
1.55	95, 110
1.56	77

1.57	76
1.60	75, 76, 81
2.6–8	73, 88, 91

Mart. Marian
2.2	81
2.5	81
6.1	78

Mart. Marinus
6.1	21

Mart. Perpetua
	32–3, 79
1.3	82
1.6	85
3.2	84
3.4	80
4.3–9	97–101
4.4	32
4.5	32, 33
4.6–7	81
4.10	100
5.5	94
6	80
6.4	85
7.9	72
10	73
10.1–14	99
10.11	81, 99
10.14	80, 81, 82, 100
11.4	94
15.6	84
17	92
17.2	95
18.1	95, 101
18.2	76
18.3	91
18.4	96
18.7	90, 96
18.9	76, 83
19.2	90
19.3	78
20.1	80, 81, 82
21.1–2	91
21.8–10	35
21.8	77
21.10	81

Mart. Pionius
4–5	80
12	80
20	80
20.5	95
21.4	95
22.2	88

Mart. Ptol.
	31–2
16	31
17–20	31
17–18	95

Mart. Pol.
	125, 126
1	85, 86
1.1	10
1.2	82
1.3	95
2	74
2.2–3	83
2.2	21, 77, 78
2.3	91
2.4–3.1	80, 88
3	35, 94
3.1	81
3.2	26, 76
4	25–7
4.2	83
5.1	26
6	86
6.1–2	85
6.2	83
7.1	83
7.3–8.1	83
7.3	77
8	35
8.2	57, 83
8.3	76
9–12	80
9	85
9.1	83
9.2	46, 75
9.3	57, 85
11.2	92, 95
12.1	76
12.2	76, 81
12.3	76

OTHER ANCIENT WRITINGS

Seneca
On Mercy
1.18	51

Epistles
7.2	76
34.2	142
78.15–19	76, 78
109.6	142

Tranq.
11.4	77

Silius Italicus
Punica
3.607	44

Statius
Silvae
3.3.171	44
4.1.34–9	44
4.3.159	44

Suetonius
Caligula
27.2	120

Claudius
5.25	66
25.4	56

Domitian
1.1	44
1.3	44
4.1	44
4.4	44
5	44
12.1	44
14.1	44
22	44

Nero
16.2	66
38	63

Tacitus
Annals
12.5	68
15.44	46, 63–4
15.60–3	123

Agricola
2–3	44
39	44
43	44
44–5	44

Chronicles
II.29	63

Germania
37	44

Histories
1.41	51
4.2	44
4.68	44
5.5	69, 106

Dailey T.F. 144
Daniel, J.L. 55
D'Angelo, R. 89
Daube, D. 93
Davids, P.H. 25
Davies, J. 85, 107, 126
Davies, W.D. 105, 147, 149
Dean, O.C. 89
Dehandschutter, B.A.G.M. 4, 10, 27, 73, 82, 106, 108, 123, 126
Deissmann, A. 40–1, 60, 138
Delehaye, H. 92, 112
Derrett, J.D.M. 146–7
DeSilva, D.A. 47, 131, 167
Dodds, E.R. 116
Donfried, K.P. 60, 105, 143
Doran, R. 112, 127
Downing, J. 111, 119, 133
Droge, A.J. 3, 4, 27, 28, 31, 33, 36, 75, 91, 106, 107, 108, 116, 117, 121, 123, 137, 144, 145
Dronke, P. 89
Dubis, M. 138
Duncan-Jones, R. 72
Dunn, J.D.G. 17, 104, 136, 137, 138, 140, 142
Dupont-Summer, A. 111
Durkheim, É. 35–6

Edwards, M. 4, 37
Edwards, M.J. 157
Ehrman, B.D. 16, 18, 34
Elliot, J.H. 57, 69
Engberg-Peterson, T. 144–5
Epstein, J. 89
Evans, C.A. 150

Fee, G.D. 141
Feldman, L.H. 108. 118
Ferguson, E. 5, 25, 80, 81, 93, 142
Feuillet, M. 160
Fiorenza, E.S. 139, 166
Firestone, R. 128, 129
Fischel, H.A. 104
Fischbane, M. 75, 98
Fishwick, D. 48
Fitzgerald, J.T. 144
Fitzmeyer, J.A. 147
Flemington, W.F. 139

Flint, P.W. 131
Ford, J.M. 159–60
Forsyth, N. 132
Frend, W.H.C. 3, 4, 27, 37, 66, 73, 81, 85, 87, 91, 98, 104, 106–10, 111, 115, 123, 124–5, 131
Friesen, S.J. 42
Fox, R.L. 82
Fuller, R.H. 41

Gagé, J. 65–6
Gardner, E. 100
Garrett, S.R. 142
Garrow, A.J.P. 45, 160, 164
Geddert, T.J. 152, 153
George, L. 16
Gibb, H.A.R. 7
Gibbon, E. 68
Gillman, N. 129
Glasson, T.F. 42
Goldenberg, S. 7 8
Goldstein, J.A. 108, 113, 115, 130
Goodblatt, D. 108, 118
Goodman, M. 37
Gordon, R. 53
Grant, R.M. 65
Gray, A.M. 107
Grayston, K. 129
Green, W.S. 129
Gregory, B.S. 9
Gressman, H. 106
Grisé, Y. 116
Gruenwald, I. 117
Gundry, R.H. 147

Hadas, M. 111
Hafemann, S.J. 136
Hala G. 18
Hala H.W. 18
Hall, J.R. 7
Harrison, J.R. 58, 60, 61
Harvey, A.E. 136, 137, 143, 147
Hata, G. 108
Haynes, S.R. 11
Heffernan, T.J. 98
Hellholm D. 45, 139
Hengel, M. 111, 117, 119, 123, 129, 130, 133, 134